# Object-Oriented Analysis and Design

## Understanding System Development with UML 2.0

**Mike O'Docherty**

John Wiley & Sons, Ltd

*Other Wiley Editorial Offices*

John Wiley & Sons Inc., 111 River Street, Hoboken, NJ 07030, USA

Jossey-Bass, 989 Market Street, San Francisco, CA 94103-1741, USA

Wiley-VCH Verlag GmbH, Boschstr. 12, D-69469 Weinheim, Germany

John Wiley & Sons Australia Ltd, 33 Park Road, Milton, Queensland 4064, Australia

John Wiley & Sons (Asia) Pte Ltd, 2 Clementi Loop #02-01, Jin Xing Distripark, Singapore 129809

John Wiley & Sons Canada Ltd, 22 Worcester Road, Etobicoke, Ontario, Canada M9W 1L1

Wiley also publishes its books in a variety of electronic formats. Some content that appears
in print may not be available in electronic books.

*Library of Congress Cataloging-in-Publication Data*

O'Docherty, Mike.
  Object-oriented analysis and design : understanding system development
with UML 2.0 / Mike O'Docherty.
    p. cm.
Includes bibliographical references and index.
ISBN-13 978-0-470-09240-8
ISBN-10 0-470-09240-8 (pbk. : alk. paper)
1. Object-oriented programming (Computer science) 2. Computer
software–Development. I. Title.
QA76.64.O35 2005
005.1'17 – dc22
 2005004182


*British Library Cataloguing in Publication Data*

A catalogue record for this book is available from the British Library

ISBN-13 978-0-470-09240-8
ISBN-10 0-470-09240-8

Typeset in 10/14 Berkeley-Medium by Laserwords Private Limited, Chennai, India
Printed and bound in Great Britain by Biddles Ltd, King's Lynn
This book is printed on acid-free paper responsibly manufactured from sustainable forestry
in which at least two trees are planted for each one used for paper production.

*For Alice and George*

# Contents

# 1

# Introduction

The aim of this book is to give you a broad understanding of the processes and techniques used in object-oriented software development, the production of computer programs using object-oriented techniques. The **Unified Modeling Language** (UML) comes into play as the standard notation used in industry for software documentation.

You may be a student at a university or on a commercial training course. Or you may be an experienced software developer, moving into object orientation for the sake of your career. In either case, this book is for you. Little prior knowledge is required on your part and there is no attempt to teach you everything there is to know. Instead, you will be guided through the essential parts of the process, so that you can do your job more effectively.

Although this book is broad, it only goes as deep as the point where you would normally start writing lines of code. Describing how to write code would mean choosing a particular programming language; the decision about the most appropriate language is for you to make. You should consider this book as a generic front-end that will work for any pure, object-oriented programming language.

The objectives of this first chapter are to describe the background to this book, to give you an idea of the content and to describe how to navigate your way around.

# Chapter Outline

**1**

# 1.1 BACKGROUND

These days, new software is usually **object-oriented**. That is, the software is written using an abstraction called an **object**. There is, naturally, much more to commercial software development than simply writing lines of code: there is investigation of the business requirements, analysis of the problem, design of the solution, and so on. Objects should be used at every stage of the development because they reduce the amount of information that has to be understood and improve the communication between members of the development team.

# 1.2 A BRIEF HISTORY OF PROGRAMMING

Commercial programming has had a number of generations, of which 'object-oriented' is just the latest:

- Machine code: Programming using binary numbers.
- Assembly language: Programming using alphanumeric symbols, or **mnemonics**, as shorthand for machine code. Assembly language is translated into machine code by a program called an **assembler**.
- High-level languages: Programming using languages (such as Fortran and COBOL) that have high-level constructs such as types, functions, loops and branches. High-level languages (and later generations of programming languages) are translated into machine code using a program called a **compiler**.
- Structured programming: Programming using cleaner high-level languages (such as Pascal, Modula and Ada) that are characterized by fewer pitfalls for the programmer and more discipline in the way a program is broken down into sub-tasks and sub-systems.
- Object-oriented programming: Programming using independent modules of data and functions that correspond to concepts in the problem domain, such as Customer or ScrollBar. This modularity leads to even fewer pitfalls for the programmer and encourages the reuse of code across separate programs. Good object-oriented programming languages include Java and Eiffel, because they're well designed, pure and portable (available on many platforms). Other examples include Smalltalk, C# and, in general, any language that started life as a structured language and grew up with object-oriented extensions (C++ and various dialects of Pascal, for example).

You may also have heard of **functional programming** and **logic programming**. So far they have had little commercial impact.

All the generations above survive today, to a greater or lesser extent. Which one we end up using depends on the situation we walk into; personal preference; and the constraints of the problem that we're trying to solve – for example, video games need every ounce of raw speed, so they're sometimes written in assembly language.

# 1.3 METHODOLOGIES

Around the time that structured programming was becoming popular, in the 1980s, experienced programmers began trying to describe how the entire software development process should be controlled, from **mission statement** through to maintenance of the finished product. This led to **structured methodologies** such as SSADM [Weaver *et al.* 02]. A **methodology** is a description of the steps a development team should go through in order to produce a high-quality system. A methodology also describes what should be produced (documents, diagrams, code, etc.) and what form the products should take (for example, content, icons, coding style).

When object-oriented programming was catching on, in the 1990s, developers invented **object-oriented methodologies**, better suited to an object-oriented programming style. Early object-oriented methodologies included the Booch method [Booch 93], Objectory [Jacobson *et al.* 92] and OMT [Rumbaugh *et al.* 91]. These days, one of the market leading methodologies is the **Rational Unified Process (RUP)** [Jacobson *et al.* 99], owned by IBM (www.rational.com). Roughly speaking, RUP is a convergence of Objectory, Booch and OMT. Another methodology that is gaining in popularity is **extreme programming (XP)** [Beck 99], a so-called 'agile' methodology – in the context of software development, agile means responsive to changes in software requirements or changes in our understanding of the problem.

The methodology used in this book, **Ripple** (summarized in Appendix 1), is a simplified one based on widely accepted theory and practice. As a result, you won't have to learn the complexities of a full industrial methodology. Nor will you be told exactly what to do at each stage, which will allow you to be more creative as you learn.

# 1.4 ABOUT THIS BOOK

In order to avoid confusion, there is no detailed comparison between structured and object-oriented methodologies in this book. Instead, you will be taken through object-oriented software development, as if traditional methods had never existed. You will encounter everything you need to know to start producing large amounts of good, object-oriented software (you just have to add the effort and the experience yourself).

If you're already familiar with structured techniques, you may find yourself having to un-learn things from time to time. But don't worry, the object-oriented approach really does work: it's been around in the research community since 1970, in the marketplace since 1990 and it's used every day by millions of developers.

As ever, the goal of software development is code, code and more code. Whatever your particular background, if you've got experience programming a computer, you'll be on safe ground. On the other hand, if you don't have much programming experience, you'll be pleased to learn that this book is straightforward – there's no attempt to make your head spin with obscure jargon and magic tricks. However, before you start, you should make sure that you're comfortable with basic computer concepts such as hardware, software and networks. At the very least, you should have written a few hundred lines of code in a high-level language.

## 1.4.1 Content Overview

Although the writing of code won't be covered in any detail, from time to time there will be a need to illustrate a point using code fragments. All the code fragments are written in **Java** [Joy *et al.* 00] because it is popular, pure, simple and free. The meaning of each code fragment is clearly explained in the text. If you're not a great fan of Java, rest assured that the code fragments can easily be translated into other languages such as C#, because the unique elements of Java have been avoided. Everything you see here in Java can be accomplished in any other language that you choose. Similarly, the discussion of system design is focussed on Java technologies rather than .Net technologies – since Java and .Net provide similar facilities, consider this simply a matter of personal preference. All the pieces of Java system design that are presented can be implemented in a similar way using .Net.

A few words of warning, however: for illustrative purposes, classes (such as **Iterator** and **List**) are described that don't match those in the Java library exactly. Although you can certainly use this book to see how Java works and get familiar with most of the syntax, it is no substitute for a pure Java language text [Campione *et al.* 00]. In any case, it is good practice always to have the library documentation to hand when writing in Java, since no-one could keep the details of thousands of classes in their head.

Another major omission is project management (issues such as planning and scheduling). Project management is omitted in order to focus on technical issues, rather than human factors.

The notation used for illustrations, wherever possible, is the **Unified Modeling Language (UML)** [OMG 03a]. This has become the accepted standard for software diagrams. UML presentation conventions mean that some lines are thicker than others and that some characters are in bold or italics. Some of these conventions are difficult to accomplish when drawing by hand (on a piece of paper or on a whiteboard, for example), however only the italicized text is really important, so the other conventions can be ignored when hand-drawing. For italicized text, alternatives will be identified at the appropriate time.

UML doesn't satisfy all documentation needs, so some of the documentation ideas in this book have been taken from RUP.

## 1.4.2 Case Studies

The case study used throughout is a rental and reservation system called **Coot**, developed for a fictitious company called **Nowhere Cars**. Thus, many of the examples in the text will use cars in one way or another. Using the same application area for most of the examples means that you don't have to keep adjusting to different areas from one page to the next. To keep things simple, most of the discussion involves those parts of Coot that provide Internet facilities to customers, a cut-down system called **iCoot**.

Because there are many concepts to illustrate, not all of which are relevant to the renting of cars, some of the examples in the text do not make it into iCoot itself (they would be more appropriate for car salespeople or car mechanics). However, every time you're presented with a major diagram, it will be one that has been taken from the finished system.

Because newcomers to object orientation often ask for full case study documentation, the finished documentation for iCoot has been included in Appendix B, for further study. The iCoot documents have been designed to be understandable, despite representing a realistic and useful piece of software.

If you want to try out the techniques described in this book with fellow students or colleagues, a set of group exercises is available at www.wiley.com/go/odocherty for the **Automated Quiz System (AQS)**. AQS is an on-line tool for taking multiple-choice quizzes. The exercises are organized according to the main chapters of this book, so that you can complete them while you read. For lecturers and instructors wishing to use this book as a course text at a University or commercial training organization, sample solutions are available for the AQS exercises, subject to registration.

## 1.4.3 Navigation

After reading Chapter 1, you can take the straightforward approach to navigation and work through all the chapters in order.

Alternatively, if you're already comfortable with object-oriented concepts and jargon, you could skip Chapters 2, 3 and 4 and jump straight to Chapter 5. If you're completely new to the field of object orientation, you should read Chapter 2, but you may like to leave Chapters 3 and 4 until a second reading.

If you're not interested in an overview of Ripple and methodologies in general but would prefer to get straight down to the details, you could skip Chapter 5 and go straight on to Chapter 6.

The remaining chapters follow a strict sequence, the progress of a typical software development, so jumping around is not recommended. It would be valuable to read

Chapter 11 as part of the main sequence; however, since many of the issues are advanced, you may wish to leave it until a later date.

You can use Appendix 1 as a reference whenever you need to check where you've got to or if you're attempting the case study for yourself.

Appendix B contains the finished artifacts for the iCoot case study, organized according to the progress of a typical development. Use these, along with the main development chapters, to see how the iCoot artifacts turned out. Appendix B also includes the iCoot project glossary, which was continually updated during iCoot development. Use this to see how a typical glossary might look and to look up the definition of any iCoot term.

Whenever you need to remind yourself how to draw part of a UML diagram, you should refer to Appendix 3.

Happy reading.

# I

# Setting the Scene

## Object Concepts

The concepts we'll look at in this chapter come out of **object-oriented programming**. Typically, programming languages are invented before the **methodologies** that help us to use them. You should find that object-oriented concepts make a lot of sense. This is because object-oriented development allows you to think in real-world terms, rather than bending your mind towards the needs of a computer.

# Learning Objectives

**Understand what we mean by a software object.**

**Understand how objects can communicate, using messages, to accomplish some task.**

**Understand what happens when an object is no longer needed (garbage collection).**

**Understand what we mean by a class.**

**Understand how to reuse code.**

# Chapter Outline

**2**

## 2.1 INTRODUCTION

The basic concepts of the **object-oriented paradigm** (way of doing things) are relatively easy to understand and to apply. Alan Kay, the inventor of Smalltalk, had been working on 'A Personal Computer for Children of all Ages' [Kay 72] as early as 1968: as his target was children, it isn't surprising that the basic concepts are simple.

So, why all the fuss about objects? Surely developers wouldn't change the fundamentals of software development without good reason? Some of the justifications for using objects might seem rather obscure at this early stage, especially if you haven't much experience with the techniques that came before (structured programming and structured methodologies). The object-oriented approach was invented (or, rather, it evolved) because of the difficulties people were having trying to get good quality systems produced on time and within budget, especially for large systems with many people involved.

Once you've worked your way through this book, the justifications given below should make sense and you should agree with most of them. Here then, for the record, are some of the justifications typically given for object orientation:

- Objects are easier for people to understand: This is because the objects are derived from the business that we're trying to automate, rather than being influenced too early by computer-based procedures or data storage requirements. For example, in a bank system, we program in terms of bank accounts, bank tellers and customers, instead of diving straight into account records, deposit and withdrawal procedures, and loan qualification algorithms.
- Specialists can communicate better: Over time, the software industry has constructed career ladders that newcomers are expected to climb gradually as their knowledge and experience increases. Typically, the first rung is **programmer**: fixing faults (bugs) in the code written by others. The second rung is **senior programmer**: writing the code itself. The third is **designer**: deciding what code needs to be written. Finally comes the role of **analyst**: talking to customers to discover what they need and then writing down a specification of what the finished system must be able to do.

  Such a career ladder may not be a bad idea in itself. The problem comes when you realize that each specialist is expected to learn a whole new set of concepts and techniques, depicting their conclusions using notations that are tailored to their specialty. This means that there's a big gap in understanding between the different roles, made worse by the fact that the documents are being passed down the career ladder rather than up, so we tend to have to read documents without understanding the techniques used to produce them. This can lead to 'throw it over the wall' syndrome: the analyst produces a large amount of documentation, throws it over the wall to the designer and walks away. The designer, after weeks of effort, produces even more documentation, using completely different techniques, and throws it over the wall to the programmers. The programmers then start all over again . . .

With the object-oriented approach, everyone is dealing with the same concepts and notations. Moreover, there are generally fewer concepts and fewer notations to deal with in the first place.

- Data and processes are not artificially separated: In traditional methods, the data that needs to be stored is separated early on from the algorithms that operate on that data and they are then developed independently. This can result in the data being in inconvenient formats or inconvenient locations, with respect to the processes that need access. With object-oriented development, data and processes are kept together in small, easy-to-manage packages; data is never separated from the algorithms. We also end up with less complex code that is less sensitive to changes in customer requirements.

- Code can be reused more easily: With the traditional approach, we start with the problem that needs to be solved and allow that problem to drive the entire development. We end up with a monolithic solution to today's problem. But tomorrow always brings a different problem to solve; no matter how close the new problem is to the last one we dealt with, we're unlikely to be able to break open our monolithic system and make it fit – we hamper ourselves by allowing a single problem to influence every part of the system.

  With object-oriented development, we're constantly looking for objects that would be useful in similar systems. Even when a new system has minor differences, we're much more likely to be able to change our existing code to fit, because objects are like the pieces in a jigsaw puzzle: if one piece is changed, it might affect a few pieces next to it, but the rest of the puzzle will remain intact.

  When we build an object-oriented system, we try to find existing objects (written by us, by our colleagues or by third parties), before we consider writing any code ourselves. As one sage put it, 'object-oriented programming is about *not* writing code'.

- Object orientation is mature and well proven: This is not a new fad. The programming concepts emerged in the late 1960s while the methodologies have been around for at least a decade. Applying objects in such areas as software, databases and networks is now well understood.

Once you've read the whole of this book, try reviewing this list to see if you fully understand, and agree with, the justifications.

## 2.2 WHAT IS AN OBJECT?

An **object** is a thing, an entity, a noun, something you can pick up or kick, anything you can imagine that has its own identity. Some objects are living, some aren't. Examples from the real world include a car, a person, a house, a table, a dog, a pot plant, a check book or a raincoat.

All objects have **attributes**: for example, a car has a manufacturer, a model number, a color and a price; a dog has a breed, an age, a color and a favorite toy. Objects also have **behavior**: a car can move from one place to another and a dog can bark.

In object-oriented software, real world objects migrate into the code. In programming terms, our objects become stand-alone modules with their own knowledge and behavior (or, if you prefer, their own data and processes). It's common to think of a software object as a robot, an animal, or a little person: each object has certain knowledge, in the form of attributes, and it knows how to perform certain **operations** for the benefit of the rest of the program. For example, a person object might know its title, first name, last name, date of birth and address; it would be able to change its name, move to a new address, tell us how old it is, and so on.

By concentrating on the characteristics of a person when we write the code for the Person object, we can put the rest of the system out of our mind – this makes our programming simpler than it would otherwise be (it also helps that we have a real-world concept to get us started). If we decide later that our Person needs to know its height, we can add that extra knowledge (and associated behavior) directly to the Person code. Only the code in the rest of the system that needs to use the height attribute has to be modified; all other code would remain unchanged. Simplicity and localization of change are important characteristics of object-oriented software.

It's easy enough to think of a living thing as some kind of robot. It is a little strange, though, when we try to think of a lifeless object as having behavior. We wouldn't normally consider a video capable of changing its price or giving itself a new advert. However, when it comes to object-oriented software, that's exactly what we need to do. The key is that if the video didn't do those jobs, some other part of the system would have to. This would lead to video characteristics leaking into other parts of the code, so we'd start to lose the simplicity and locality that we crave (we would be going back to 'the old way of doing things'). Don't be put off by the **anthropomorphism** (the assignment of human characteristics to inanimate objects or animals) that's common in object-oriented development, imagining software objects as little people.

Figure 2.1 shows some real-world objects that would make good software objects. Can you think of any others? Can you think of anything that *wouldn't* make a good object? Well, that's a trick question really: 'thing' at the end of 'anything' suggests that the answer has to be no. It turns out that almost anything would make a good object in some context or another. A bad object is one that merges several concepts, for example, a bank account object that has been polluted with the knowledge and behavior that belongs to a bank clerk. Always keep in mind that separate concepts in the real world suggest separate concepts in the program.

aPerson

aNumber

aBankAccount

aDate

aCat

**Figure 2.1: Objects in the real world**

Before we go any further, it's important to note that we're not trying to **simulate** the real world, that would be far too difficult. we're simply trying to make sure that our software is influenced by real-world concepts, so that it is easier to produce and easier to change. The needs of the system and the needs of computers are important influences too. Some developers are uncomfortable with the close proximity of the real world and software; however, an object-oriented system developed for a hospital that *didn't* include some kind of Patient object would be of little use.

You shouldn't think that it's possible to code the ideal Person object or any other kind of perfect object. There are simply too many characteristics and capabilities that can be applied to real-world objects – if we tried to capture them all, we'd never get as far as coding the second object in our system.

Most aspects of a real-world object are not needed for a typical program, especially since software systems tend to address a single problem area. For example, a bank system will be interested in the age and salary of a customer, but not their shoe size or favorite color. It's quite reasonable to code an object that is useful for *many* systems, especially for well understood areas of programming: for example, all systems with a user interface are likely to be able to make use of the same 'scrollable list' object. The trick is to start by considering the business you're dealing with, to ask yourself 'If I worked in this business area, what would a "person" mean to me: a customer, an employee, a patient, or what?' All good software developers start by modeling the business.

A **model** is a representation of a problem domain or a proposed solution that allows us to talk, or reason, about the real thing. This allows us to increase our understanding and avoid potential pitfalls. Think of an architect's model of a new concert hall: it allows the architects to say 'This is what the finished concert hall will look like' and it helps them to come up with new ideas, such as 'I think we're going to need a steeper roof'. A model allows us to learn a lot without actually building anything. Much of software development involves creating and refining models, rather than cutting lines of code.

---

**Implementation Point 1**

Let's consider how we can create a new object in an object-oriented programming language. Pure object-oriented languages typically provide a **creation expression**. Here's how one looks in Java:

```
new Person("Sue Smith")
```

The effect of this expression is to create space for a new `Person` object and pass it the string "Sue Smith", so that it can initialize itself (presumably, in this case, the object would record its name).

Once we've created an object, we can put it somewhere where we can find it later, by **assigning a name** to it, as in:

```
aPerson = new Person("Sue Smith");
```

Now, whenever we write down `aPerson`, we will be referring to the object that we just created.

---

# 2.3 IDENTICAL OR EQUAL?

Objects have their own independent existence. Consider holding a blue pen in your left hand and a blue pen in your right hand. You're holding separate pens: they exist independently and each one has its own identity. But the pens can have similar attributes: blue ink, half full, same manufacturer, same model, etc. In terms of their attributes, the pens are interchangeable – if you wrote something down on a piece of paper, no-one would be able to tell which pen you'd used (unless they saw you do it). The pens are **equal** but not **identical**. This is an important distinction in software, as well as in real life.

To take another example, consider the situation illustrated in Figure 2.2. In Acacia Avenue there are two families, the Smiths and the Joneses: the Smiths live at number 4 and the Joneses live at number 7. The families have similar tastes in lawn mowers; so similar, in fact, that they both own a GrassMaster 75, purchased on the first day the new model became available. The lawn mowers are so similar that if someone switched them round overnight, the Smiths and the Joneses wouldn't notice.

As well as a lawn mower, the Smiths have a cat called Tom. Tom is a round friendly cat, three years old, whose favorite pastime is chasing mice around the local gardens. The Joneses also have a cat, called Tiddles. Tiddles is a round, friendly cat, three years old, whose

**Figure 2.2: Identical or equal?**

favorite pastime is chasing balls of wool. Anyone visiting the Smiths and the Joneses would notice a remarkable similarity between Tom and Tiddles, not surprising when you realize that Tom and Tiddles are the same cat, round on account of being fed so often.

In this situation, we have two lawn mowers and one cat. Although the lawn mowers have a separate identity, recorded on the serial-number plates riveted to their bodies, they are equal, because they have the same attributes. The cat also has an identity, it may even have a name for itself ('Me' or 'Hfrrr', perhaps). The difference between the cat and the lawn mowers is that the cat is shared and the lawn mowers aren't. It's rarely necessary for any person, thing or animal to be concerned with its own identity: the cat doesn't think about whether it's separate from other cats; a lawn mower doesn't need to know which lawn mower it is in order to mow the lawn. The families don't need to know that Hfrrr is fed twice as much as other cats, as long as he purrs in their laps from time to time; nor do the families need to know that the lawn mower in their shed is the one they actually purchased, as long as it's there when they need it.

Generally speaking, in an object-oriented system, if we use one software object to represent each real world object, we won't go far wrong. So, in the example that we've just seen, we would expect to find in our system two lawn mower objects and a single cat object.

We may sometimes share objects. We may sometimes swap equal objects. But we rarely need to worry about identity: we just tell an object what to do and it uses its knowledge and capabilities to carry out the request.

---

**Implementation Point 2**

Object-oriented programming languages allow us to test whether objects are identical or equal if necessary.

The following fragment of Java code does just that. There are two tests in it: if (tom == tiddles) is a test of identity that evaluates to true if tom and tiddles both point to the same object; tom.equals(tiddles) is an instruction that asks tom to perform the equals operation, with tiddles as a parameter – it evaluates to true if tom and tiddles are separate but equivalent to each other.

```
if (tom == tiddles) {
    result = "The Smiths and the Joneses share one cat";
}
else if (tom.equals(tiddles)) {
    result = "The Smiths and Joneses have equivalent cats";
}
else {
    result = "The Smiths and the Joneses have different cats";
}
```

# 2.4 DEPICTING OBJECTS

Once we've decided to work with objects, we need some way of showing them on a diagram so that we can describe them and think about them. Figure 2.3 shows how we can draw an object. The notation used here is a UML **object diagram** – you'll see more details of UML and its history as you go through this book; for now, the notation will be introduced by example.

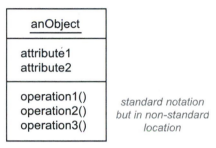

*standard notation but in non-standard location*

**Figure 2.3: An object**

The three parts of the box show the object's name (which is underlined), its attributes (its knowledge) and its operations (its behavior). (Showing operations on an object diagram is not actually legal UML, but it suits our purposes for now.) The parentheses next to the operation names indicate any parameters that are required: even though none of the operations shown here have parameters, it's a good idea to keep the parentheses so that operation names stand out from attribute names (this becomes even more important when we omit one or more parts of the box).

The attributes are hidden inside the object; the only way to access them is via the operations. This is reasonable from analogy with the real world: most of us are much more interested in the fact that a television has a 'change channel' operation than we are in the fancy electronics inside the box that actually perform the change.

Let's examine a coffee machine object. First, we should decide what operations a coffee machine needs:

- display drinks
- select drink
- accept money
- dispense drink

Next, we should think about what the coffee machine needs to know in order to perform these operations:

- available drinks
- drink prices
- drink recipes

Having designed our coffee machine object, we can record our findings on an object diagram, like the one shown in Figure 2.4.

**Figure 2.4: A coffee machine object**

# 2.5 ENCAPSULATION

**Encapsulation** refers to an object hiding its attributes behind its operations (it seals the attributes in a capsule, with operations on the edge). Hidden attributes are said to be **private**. Some programming languages (for example, Smalltalk) automatically make attributes private and some languages (for example, Java) leave it to the programmer.

Encapsulation is one of the ways that a programming language protects programmers from themselves: if programmers could bypass the operations, they would become dependent on the attributes that were being used to represent the object's knowledge. It would then be much harder to change the internal representation of the object in the future, because we'd have to find all the pieces of code that access the attributes directly and change those too. Without encapsulation we would lose simplicity and locality.

As an example of why encapsulation is a good idea, consider an object representing a circle. A circle would be likely to have operations allowing us to discover its radius, diameter, area and perimeter. What attributes would we need to store in order to support this behavior? Well, we could store the radius and calculate the other attributes on demand. Or, we could store the diameter and calculate the other attributes from that. In fact, we could store any one of the four attributes and calculate the other three on demand. (Our choice may depend on personal preference or it may depend on predicting how the circle will normally be used.)

Let's say we choose to store the diameter. Any programmer who was allowed to access the diameter might do so, rather than going via the 'get diameter' operation. If, for a later version of our software, we decided that we wanted to store the radius instead, we would have to find all the pieces of code in the system that used direct access to the diameter, so that we could correct them (and we might introduce faults along the way). With encapsulation, there's no problem.

Another way to think of encapsulation is to imagine that objects are courteous to one another. If you wanted to borrow some money from a colleague to buy food in the staff canteen, you wouldn't grab their wallet and look through it to see if they had enough cash. Instead, you would ask them whether they could lend you some money and they would look in their own wallet.

# 2.6 ASSOCIATION AND AGGREGATION

No object is an island. All objects are connected to other objects, directly or indirectly, strongly or loosely. By connecting objects, we make them more powerful. Connections allow us to navigate around to find extra information and behavior. For example, if we were processing a Customer object representing Freda Bloggs and we wanted to send Freda a letter, we would need to know that Freda lives at 42 Acer Road. We would expect the address information to be stored in some kind of Address object, so we would look for a connection from the Customer to the Address, to find out where to send the letter.

When we're modeling with objects, we can connect them in two principal ways: association or aggregation. It's sometimes hard to spot the difference between the two, but here are some ideas.

- Association is a weak form of connection: the objects may be part of a group, or family, of objects but they're not completely dependent on each other. For example, consider a car, a driver, a passenger and another passenger. When the driver and the two passengers are in the car, they're associated: they all go in the same direction, they occupy the same volume in space, and so on. But the association is loose: the driver can drop off one of the passengers to go their separate way, so that the passenger is no longer associated with the other objects. Figure 2.5 shows how we can draw an association on an object diagram – the attributes and operations have been omitted here in order to emphasize the structure.
- Aggregation means putting objects together to make a bigger object. Manufactured items usually form aggregations: for example, a microwave is made up of a cabinet, a door, an indicator panel, buttons, a motor, a glass plate, a magnetron, and so on. Aggregations usually form a **part–whole** hierarchy. Aggregation implies close dependency, at least of

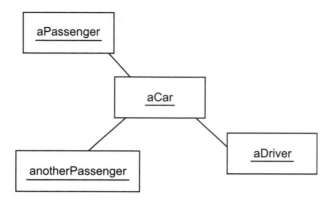

**Figure 2.5: Association**

the whole to the part; for example, a magnetron is still a magnetron if you take it out of its microwave, but the microwave would be useless without the magnetron, because it wouldn't be able to cook anything.

Figure 2.6 shows how we can draw a house as an aggregation: in order to emphasize the difference between this kind of connection and an association, we place a white diamond on the 'whole' end.

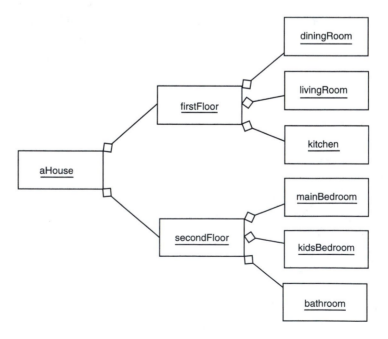

**Figure 2.6: Aggregation**

As suggested, the distinction between association and aggregation can be subtle. The 'What happens if you remove one of the objects?' test can be helpful, but it doesn't always solve the problem: hard thinking and experience are often needed.

We often need to choose between aggregation and association, because the choice can affect the way we design our software. Here are some examples:

- Friends: We would expect friends to be an association: there is no sense in which we could put the friends together to make a larger friend; friends come and go over time.
- Components in a television set: This is one of the easier ones to reason about because it's the classic part–whole hierarchy: you put the buttons and the knobs together to make the control panel; you put the glass screen, the electron gun and the magnetic coils together to make the tube; once the small parts have been assembled, then assembled into bigger components, you put everything into the cabinet and screw the back on. The end users see a single television object: if one of the components fails, they probably don't think they have a television set anymore, just a useless heap of junk.
- Books on a bookshelf: A bookshelf doesn't need books to be a bookshelf, it's just a place to put the books that we own. Conversely, when a book is on a bookshelf, it is certainly associated with it (if you move the bookshelf, the book moves too; if the bookshelf collapses, the book falls). This is a classic association.
- Windows in an office block: The windows are part of the office block. Although we could remove a broken window, leaving the office one window short, we would expect a replacement to be provided soon afterwards. This is probably aggregation.

**ACTIVITY 1**

**Now it's your turn. Which of the following examples are association and which are aggregation?**
1. **Houses on a street.**
2. **Pages in a book.**
3. **Notes in a symphony.**
4. **Components in a home entertainment system (television, VCR, tape deck, amplifier, games console).**

# 2.7 GRAPHS AND TREES

As well as associations and aggregations, you may hear about **trees** or **graphs** of objects. A tree is another name for a hierarchy. If we redraw the object diagram from Figure 2.6, as we have in Figure 2.7, you can see why aggregation is often referred to as a tree (it doesn't have a trunk, but it's close enough). For reasons best known to themselves, programmers usually draw trees upside down, as shown in Figure 2.8.

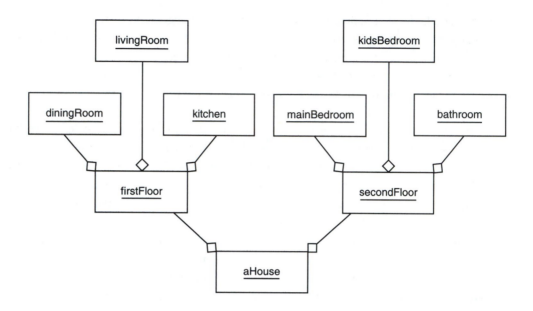

**Figure 2.7: Aggregation as a tree**

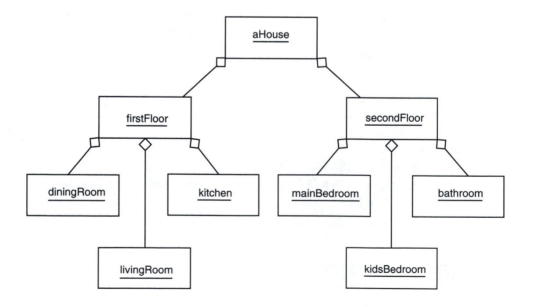

**Figure 2.8: An upside-down tree**

A graph is an arbitrary set of connections between a group of objects. Objects in an association often form a graph, as in the car example in Figure 2.5. Another example, with more interesting connections, is the underground train system in London. Figure 2.9 represents part of the London Underground system: in this case it's possible to get from any **node** (station) to any other node, usually via several routes.

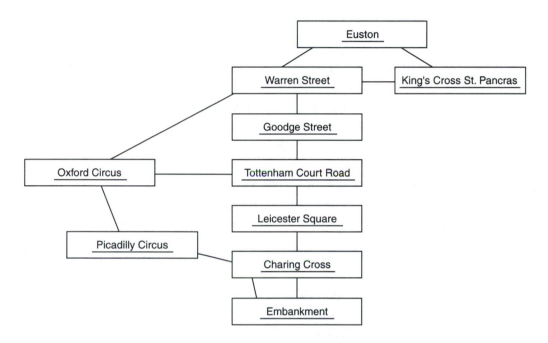

**Figure 2.9: An object graph showing connections between London Underground stations**

A tree is a special case of a graph: each node in a tree has only one **parent** node, but it can have any number of **children**. (A parent contains the children, in a part–whole sense.) This corresponds well to the difference between aggregation and association: any group of connected objects forms an association, but only associations which have the right inter-dependencies and the right structure qualify as trees.

## 2.8 LINKS AND NAVIGABILITY

The connections that you've seen on object diagrams until now are called **links**. If we want to show that one object knows where the other one is, we can add an arrowhead, as shown in Figure 2.10. This shows a Customer linked to an Address and a String. (A **string** is a staple value in programming that comprises a sequence of characters.)

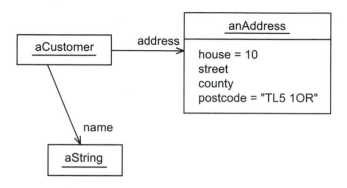

**Figure 2.10: Navigable links**

Each link can be thought of as an attribute: the label, or **role**, indicates the attribute's name. Thus, we might say that aCustomer has an attribute, called address, that links it to an Address object, and another attribute, called name, that links it to the String representing its name. The arrowhead indicates **navigability**, knowing where the other object is. Because there's no arrowhead on the customer end, the implication is that String doesn't know that it's associated with aCustomer. Navigable links often end up as **pointers** in object-oriented programs. (A pointer is the address of an object in memory, so that we can find it when we need to.)

The links in Figure 2.10 are more detailed than the connections you've seen until now (which didn't have any arrow-heads). One of the advantages of an object diagram is that it allows us to show what's going on in our model at an arbitrary level of detail – this can increase our understanding and make us more confident that we're on the right track. Simple values are shown as attributes; important objects are shown as linked boxes; intermediate values are shown as attributes or linked boxes, as the need arises.

Figure 2.10 shows other information too, information that you probably understood and accepted without too much trouble: names have been given to the linked objects and to the attributes; some literal values are also shown – the number 10 and the string TL5 1OR, for example. The naming convention used here for objects, attributes and roles is a common one: use one or two descriptive words and run them together, capitalizing each word after the first. As for the literal values, we all know how to write down numbers and putting characters inside double quotes shouldn't be any surprise either.

In some places, objects have been expanded while, in other places, they haven't. For example, the name attribute on aCustomer has been shown as a separate object whereas the street and county on anAddress haven't even been given a value.

The key in all diagrams is to show as much detail as needed to achieve our goal. Don't let anyone suggest that a diagram is wrong just because they would have drawn it differently. In general, as we go through development, we will have to deal with more and more information, but we rarely show everything in one place (if we did, things would get cluttered and tedious).

A final few words about values: although everything can be modeled as an object, for trivial values we may not bother. For example, the number 10 can be thought of as an object: it has internal data to represent its ten-ness and it has operations such as 'add another number' and 'multiply by another number'. However, in many object-oriented programming languages, simple values such as numbers are treated differently: you can only use them as attribute values; they have no identity; you can't decompose them.

## 2.9 MESSAGES

Every object is connected to at least one other object: an isolated object wouldn't be much use to anyone. Once objects are connected, they can **collaborate**, to perform more complex tasks than they could on their own. Objects collaborate by sending **messages** to each other, as shown in Figure 2.11. The message is shown next to a solid arrow indicating the direction in which the message is being sent; the reply is shown next to a 'tadpole' that indicates the movement of data.

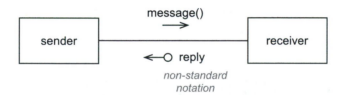

**Figure 2.11: Collaboration using messages**

Figure 2.11 is a UML **communication diagram**. Communication diagrams look rather like object diagrams, except that the links have no direction and the object names are not underlined. Officially, there is no way to show replies on a communication diagram, so a long-standing convention, the tadpole, has been used instead. Ideally, we would also show **sequence numbers**, but they've been omitted here, because the UML numbering scheme is rather involved.

Some example messages are: 'What's the time?', 'Start the engine' and 'What is your name?', as shown in Figure 2.12. As you can see, the receiving object may or may not need to provide a reply: we would expect replies to 'What's the time?' and 'What is your name?', but not to 'Start the engine'.

As mentioned earlier, objects are courteous: when an object receives a message, it carries out the request without question. This way, the sending object doesn't need to cope with

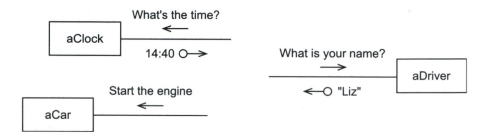

**Figure 2.12: Some example messages**

the possibility of a message being refused. In practice, some requests can't be carried out, despite the best intentions of the receiver. Consider the reasons why requests can fail, listed in Table 2.1.

Sometimes, we can't allow things to fail: we would be rather disappointed if a fly-by-wire plane crashed because of a software fault. Ensuring success under such circumstances is a specialist area, **software reliability**. Just to give you an idea, here's one strategy for reliability: install three computers on the plane and get them to vote on what to do next; if one computer says 'fly to the left' but the other two say 'fly to the right', the plane flies to the right.

Now that you've seen why messages can fail, you should put the problem out of your mind for the time being and assume that messages always succeed. (This is actually good practice, as explained in Chapter 12.)

# 2.10 INVOKING AN OPERATION

When a software object receives a message, it executes some code. As you've probably guessed, each piece of code is an operation. To put it another way, a message **invokes** an operation. In UML, we can show a message being sent from the sender to the receiver, or we can show the operation on the receiver, or we can do both.

As well as replies, messages can have **parameters** (also called **arguments**). A parameter is an object or a simple value that the receiver needs in order to fulfill the request. We might, for example, send a person object the message 'What is your height in meters' one minute and 'What is your height in feet and inches' the next: in this case, 'What is your height?' would be the message, while 'meters' and 'feet and inches' would be the parameters. Parameters are shown in parentheses, after the message, as in getHeight(meters) or getHeight(aUnit). If you have several parameters, you can separate them with commas.

We also need a way of specifying which object should receive a message – here's how to do it in Java, using a full stop to separate the receiver and the message:

```
aPerson.getHeight(aUnit)
```

**Table 2.1: Reasons for request failure**

| Problem | Example | Solution |
|---|---|---|
| The sender should not have been allowed to send the message. | Sending a fly message to a penguin. | The compiler should spot most of these mistakes and we expect to find the rest during testing or maintenance. |
| The sender makes a mistake. | Telling a microwave to start cooking when there's no food inside. | The compiler can help but mostly we rely on good design, good programming, testing and maintenance. |
| The receiver makes a mistake. | Assuming that $2 + 2 = 5$. | The compiler can help but mostly we rely on good design, good programming, testing and maintenance. |
| The receiver encounters a predictable but rare problem. | Telling a lift to 'go up' when there are too many people inside. | **Exception handling** uses the programming language's facilities to separate normal from abnormal activity. |
| The computer fails to do what it's supposed to do. | Knocking the computer off the desk; a cosmic ray blasting through the central processor; changing an internal bit from 1 to 0; an operating system fault; . . . | The software developer can't do much apart from **failing gracefully** by reporting the problem to a user interface or writing to a log file. |
| Human error. | Removing a diskette while an object is writing information to it. | **Exception handling** uses the programming language's facilities to separate normal from abnormal activity. |

Sometimes, you'll find yourself wondering whether a message that you're designing should get the object to do something, or retrieve some information from the object, or some combination of the two. A good guideline for message styles, one that helps us to avoid many difficulties, is 'A message should be a question or a command, but not both'.

A question message asks the object for some information, so it always has a reply. A question should not alter the attributes of the object (or of any object that it's connected to). Examples of question messages are 'What loaves do you have?' or 'What's the time'. We wouldn't expect more loaves to appear under the counter just because we'd asked the question; similarly, we would be surprised (ignoring Quantum theory) if the time inside a clock changed just because we had looked at it.

A command message tells an object to do something – this time the object doesn't need to provide a reply. Examples of commands include telling a bank account to 'Withdraw 100 Euros' and telling a microwave to 'Switch off'. If we've issued a reasonable command, we expect the object to go ahead and do it, so we don't need any information back. A command alters the receiving object or some object that it's connected to.

Messages that are both questions and commands can be useful, but they're an advanced technique, one that doesn't warrant an example.

## 2.11 AN EXAMPLE COLLABORATION

To solidify the concept of collaboration let's look at a bigger example, first from a human perspective, then from a software perspective. The example is 'Buying a loaf of bread from a baker's shop'. The human version is this:

> A customer walks into a baker's shop and asks the baker what kind of loaves she has for sale. The baker looks under the counter and tells the customer that she has two white loaves and one wholemeal loaf. The customer says that he would like to buy the wholemeal loaf. Now the business transaction takes place: the baker wraps the loaf and offers it up with a request for payment; the customer gives the baker some money; the baker gives the customer some change. The customer leaves, satisfied.

We can show this collaboration on a communication diagram such as the one in Figure 2.13. For simplicity, the bits about the customer entering and leaving the shop have been ignored; also, message directions have been shown alongside each message, to make things more compact.

We could code this kind of collaboration pretty much directly in a pure object-oriented language. However, most object-oriented designers wouldn't do it that way. If we consider the customer and the baker for a moment, the main problem is that we have a complicated two-way interaction – programming computers is hard enough without adding this kind of real-world complexity. Also, we have a customer that depends on the interface of the baker and a baker that depends on the interface of the customer – changing one object would mean changing the other object too, a maintenance nightmare.

Contrast the design problems of our baker and customer objects with the way the baker might interact with the counter: the baker would send a message to the counter and receive a reply, but the counter wouldn't send any messages to the baker – the counter is a passive object that sits there waiting to be used. The counter still does its job, and the baker still gets what she needs, but the interaction is one-way, making it less complex and easier to change. We call this style of interaction **client–supplier**: the baker is the client and the counter is supplying the services. A further advantage of supplier-style objects is that they're more

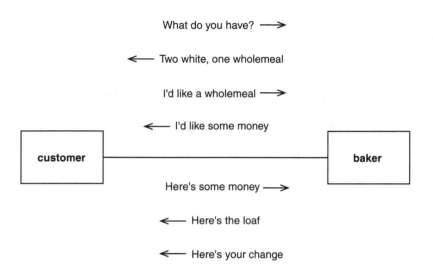

**Figure 2.13: Buying a loaf of bread**

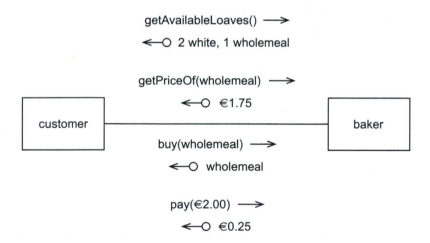

**Figure 2.14: Buying a loaf, client–supplier style**

likely to be useful in other contexts, because they're independent of the client – they're more **reusable**, one of the major goals of object-oriented development.

We can usually transform a two-way collaboration into a client and supplier interaction with a little thought and a little practice. To help us with this, there are two mechanisms that were not used in Figure 2.13: message replies and message parameters. Figure 2.14 shows the interactions between the customer and the baker as a pure client–supplier implementation.

Client–supplier is not the only way to go, but it is certainly the most common style, and it works well in most cases.

## 2.12 HOW AN OBJECT-ORIENTED PROGRAM WORKS

An object-oriented program works by creating objects, connecting them together and getting them to collaborate by sending messages to each other. But who gets the ball rolling? Who creates the first object and who sends the first message? To solve this problem, all object-oriented programs have an **entry point**. For example, Java expects to find an operation called main on an object that the user names when they launch the program. All the instructions in the main operation are executed, one after the other, and the program stops when main has finished.

Every instruction in main can create an object, connect objects together or send a message to an object. When an object sends a message, the object that receives the message executes an operation. This operation can also create an object, connect objects together or send a message to an object. Thus, you should appreciate that this mechanism allows us to do anything we might want to do.

Figure 2.15 shows an object-oriented program in action. Typically, there is not much code in a main operation – most of the behavior is inside operations on the other objects. As shown in Figure 2.15, it's quite valid for an object to send a message to itself: a human equivalent would be asking yourself a question such as 'What did I do yesterday?'

The idea of a main operation applies not just to programs executed from a console – it works equally well for more exotic programs such as graphical user interfaces (GUIs), Web servers and **servlets**. Here are some hints as to how these work:

- The main operation for a user interface creates the top-level window and tells it to show itself.
- A Web server's main operation has an infinite loop telling a socket object to listen for incoming requests on some port.
- A servlet is an object hosted by a Web server that receives requests passed in from Web browsers – again, the Web server has the main operation.

## 2.13 GARBAGE COLLECTION

Let's consider what happens when an object is no longer needed by the program that created it. This may seem like a trivial issue, but remember that objects in a program don't come

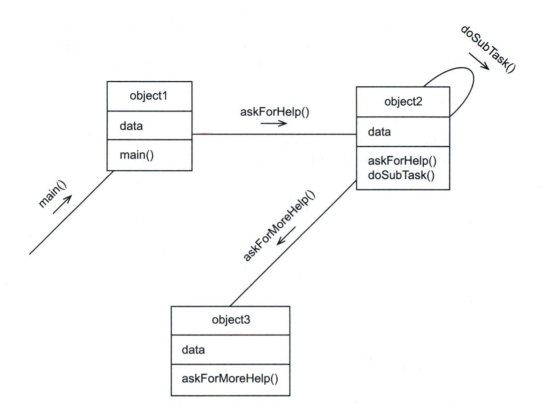

**Figure 2.15: An object-oriented program at run time**

for free: each new object occupies a small area of the computer's memory; as the program runs, it tends to create more and more objects, reducing the memory available to run other programs. If we didn't reclaim objects after we had finished with them, our computer might run out of memory unnecessarily. (The memory used by a program is usually returned to the computer when the program finishes, but we might have several programs running simultaneously: some of them might be running for days, weeks or years.)

It's bad programming practice to allow more and more objects to be created by our program without taking steps to clean them up at the end of their useful life. Traditionally, programmers have had to decide for themselves when the last connection to an object was about to be removed so that they could explicitly **delete** or **free** the object's memory. (Structured languages don't have objects, but they do have **records**, **structures** and **arrays** that might need to be freed.) Keeping track of object lifetimes is complicated. It's very easy for a programmer to forget about some of their unused objects, causing the program to keep growing – a fault called a **memory leak**.

Languages such as Java have popularized the idea of a program that reclaims its objects automatically, without the programmer having to do anything. The basic idea is that every program has an assistant called a **garbage collector**, wandering around, looking for unconnected objects and sweeping them away. Sounds like magic? Well, not really. It is common these days for every program to have a **run-time system** – a piece of software that's always present underneath the code that we write ourselves. It's the run-time system that performs housekeeping tasks, such as garbage collection.

Without going into any detail about how a garbage collector might work, it's enough to know that the garbage collector is prepared to delete any object that can't be reached, directly or indirectly, from any name that is active within the program. Any object that can't be reached can never be sent a message; if it can never be sent a message, it can never answer a question or execute a command; therefore, it must be garbage.

Pure object-oriented languages – such as Smalltalk, Java and Eiffel – tend to have garbage collectors. Hybrid object-oriented languages – such as Object Pascal – do sometimes have garbage collectors, although the fact that the languages themselves are over-complicated still means that they should be avoided if possible. C++ has no garbage collector; instead, programmers have to remember to use 'smart pointers', which delete an object when it appears that the last reference has gone.

# 2.14 CLASSES

A class encapsulates characteristics common to a group of objects. There are a number of ways you could think of a class – some of them are illustrated in Figure 2.16. Putting this picture into words:

- A factory manufactures objects according to some blueprint.
- A set specifies what features its member objects will have.
- A template allows us to produce any number of objects of a given shape.
- A dictionary definition describes an object as precisely as possible.

Figure 2.17 shows some example classes. In UML, classes are drawn as boxes on a **class diagram**. So that we can easily tell the difference between classes and objects, class names (on class diagrams) are not underlined, while object names (on object diagrams) are. Classes and objects are rarely mixed on the same diagram: it turns out that we can do most of our modeling in terms of classes, reserving object diagrams for illustration and verification purposes. Object-oriented programmers are often heard to say 'Every object is an instance of a class', hence the use of the term **instance** as a synonym for object.

By convention, class names start with a capital letter. On a class diagram, they're shown in bold, although, admittedly, that may be tricky when drawing by hand. In an object-oriented context, class names tend to be short and in the singular.

factory        category or set

template        description or definition

**Figure 2.16: Different ways of thinking about a class**

**Classification** – grouping things into classes – is something that humans are rather good at. We start doing it from the age of 12–18 months – 'toy', 'food', 'girl', 'boy', 'doggy' – so it's nice to see it in programming, which is not otherwise known for its accessibility or its closeness to nature. Object-oriented software development is meant to be natural: close to the real world and close to the way that we reason about it. Since, in the real world, classes are the next major step after objects, that should be justification enough for introducing them into our programs. Another justification for having classes, from a software point of view, is that they allow us to share the definition of elements between related objects, so that we don't have to repeat ourselves.

Looking at Figure 2.17 again, can you spot any similarity between the classes? You would probably conclude that they're all kinds of vehicle: some work on water, some on land and so on. By drawing lines to show how the classes are related, we come up with the picture shown in Figure 2.18.

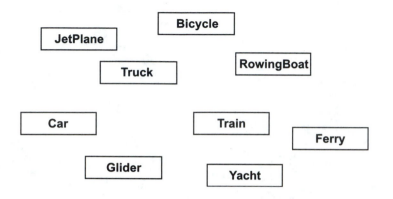

**Figure 2.17: Some example classes**

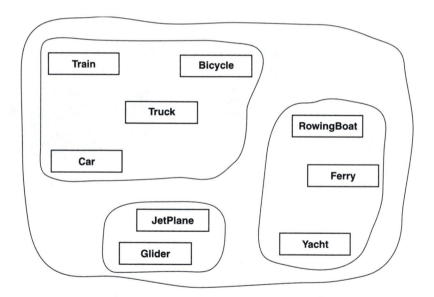

**Figure 2.18: Groups of classes**

This picture shows a hierarchy of classes, a point that should be obvious when the relationships are redrawn using the proper UML notation, as in Figure 2.19. Here, a white arrow-head is used to point from each detailed concept to the less detailed one on its left.

Just like the aggregation hierarchy we saw earlier, with its common name 'part–whole hierarchy', there are a few common names for this kind of hierarchy too:

- Inheritance: Trains **inherit** the characteristics of land vehicles.
- Generalization/specialization: A train is more **specialized** than a land vehicle; a land vehicle is more **generalized** than a train.

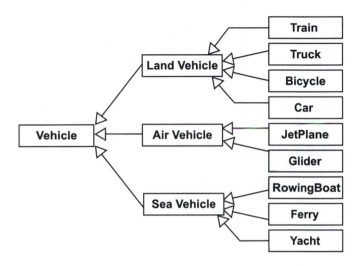

**Figure 2.19: A class hierarchy**

- Parent/child: LandVehicle is the **parent** of Train; Train is a **child** of LandVehicle.
- Superclass/subclass: LandVehicle is the **superclass** of Train; Train is a **subclass** of LandVehicle.
- Base/derived: LandVehicle is the **base** from which Train is **derived**.

In this book, the terms **base** and **derived** won't be used.

# 2.15 WHAT DOES A CLASS DEFINE?

Object-oriented developers use classes to describe the programming elements that particular kinds of object will have. Without classes, we would have to add these elements to every individual object.

For illustration, Figure 2.20 shows a complete class written in Java. Although this book is not about the details of Java as such, this example is simple enough for us to see in it the six essential elements of a class (see Table 2.2).

New objects are created by the Actor operation; this is a special operation called a **constructor** that is only used when an instance of the class is created. In Java, we create an object using an expression of the form:

```
new Actor("Charlie Chaplin");
```

In this case, the expression would result in a new instance of Actor with a stage name of "Charlie Chaplin" and a name of "<None>". Operations such as getName() and setName() are known as **getter** and **setter** operations, because they get and set pieces of information.

```
1   // An actor with "name" and "stage name" attributes
2   public class Actor {
3
4      // Fields
5      private String name, stageName;
6
7      // Create a new actor with the given stage name
8      public Actor(String sn) {
9          name = "<None>";
10         stageName = sn;
11     }
12
13     // Get the name
14     public String getName() {
15        return name;
16     }
17
18     // Set the name
19     public void setName(String n) {
20        name = n;
21     }
22
23     // Get the stage name
24     public String getStageName() {
25        return stageName;
26     }
27
28     // Set the stage name
29     public void setStageName(String sn) {
30        stageName = sn;
31     }
32
33     // Reply a summary of this actor's attributes, as a string
34     public String toString() {
35        return "I am known as " + getStageName() +
36                ", but my real name is " + getName();
37     }
38  }
```

**Figure 2.20: A simple Java class**

| | Table 2.2: Information defined by a class | |
|---|---|---|
| **Element** | **Purpose** | **Example in Figure 2.20** |
| Class name | Referring to the class elsewhere in our code. | Actor, line 2 |
| Fields | Describing the information stored by this kind of object. | name and stageName, line 5 |
| Constructors | Controlling initialization of the objects. | Actor(), line 8 |
| Messages | Providing other objects with a way to use the objects. | getName(), line 14; setName(), line 19; getStageName(), line 24; setStageName(), line 29; and toString(), line 34 |
| Operations | Telling the objects how to behave. | lines 15, 20, 25, 30, 35 and 36 |
| Comments | Telling programmers how to use or maintain the class (ignored by the compiler). | lines starting //, e.g. lines 1 and 4 |

In addition to the elements listed above, pure object-oriented programming languages allow the programmer to specify which parts of a system can access the elements: we can usually specify, at least, that elements are public (visible everywhere) or private (only available to the objects themselves) – hence the public and private keywords in Java. Some languages allow the programmer to add **assertions** – logical statements that must always be true, such as 'Objects of this class will always have a positive balance' or 'This message will always return a nonempty string'. Assertions are useful for reliability, debugging and maintenance.

# 2.16 SHARED DATA AND SHARED OPERATIONS

In an object-oriented program, all the information and services the program needs must be available somewhere. If the program has been designed properly, the information and services will be available in obvious places. Bearing this in mind, where would you place the information and services listed below?

1. The current interest rate for savings accounts.
2. The number of days in January.

3. The calculation of compound interest for a given number of years.

4. The calculation of whether the current year is a leap year.

You may have concluded that each of them should be associated with an object of some kind – a SavingsAccount for cases 1 and 3 and a GregorianCalendar for cases 2 and 4. However, none of these pieces of information or services are related to a particular SavingsAccount or GregorianCalendar. Rather, they're related to *all* savings accounts and *all* calendars. It would seem inappropriate to place these elements on particular objects. (If you prefer the practical argument, think of the waste of space if we had to place an interestRate on every instance of SavingsAccount, or the waste of time having to create a GregorianCalendar just so that we could find out whether the current year is a leap year.)

Because information and services such as those listed above don't seem to fit well with objects, object-oriented languages usually allow the programmer to put elements onto the class itself. So, as well as field, message and method, we have **class field**, **class message** and **class method**. Java programmers, for example, can use the keyword static to indicate that an element is associated with the whole class rather than any of its instances. Some languages go so far as to treat the class as an object in its own right.

Class elements are not as easy to use as they could be, because some languages don't treat a class as a pure object – inheritance between class elements doesn't work, for example. Even languages that do treat classes as pure objects run into messy complications with **metaclasses**. So you should expect to come across class fields, class messages and class methods in other people's designs and code and you may even find a reason to use them yourself, but always try the following alternatives first:

- Find, or introduce, another kind of object. For example, rather than making interestRate a class field, make it a field on a Bank object. (This would also help you to extend your software to deal with more than one bank.)
- Use a **Singleton**, a class that is guaranteed, by careful programming, to have only one instance: the **singleton object** (see Chapter 11 for more information). This is a good match for the 'Is it a leap year?' case, because there is only one Gregorian calendar.

## 2.17 TYPES

In the pure object-oriented universe, everything is an object. Or, to put it in programming terms, the type of every value is a class. Smalltalk and Eiffel are two languages that stick to this fundamental rule. However, most object-oriented languages also have nonobject types, called **primitives**. The reasons given for this impurity usually include brevity, performance and ancestry. A cynic would suggest that laziness (on the part of the language designers) might also be a factor. Whichever argument you prefer, primitives are everywhere. Therefore, you need to get used to them.

Taking Java as an example, we can declare that a field has a class type such as String – a sequence of characters – or a primitive type such as int – a simple number. In Figure 2.21, the age field of anActor is an integer primitive and the string object pointed to by name contains primitive characters.

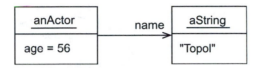

**Figure 2.21: Object-oriented types**

The main distinction between objects and primitives is that, although primitives can be used as values in the same way that objects can, you can't send a message to a primitive, or give it a field, or treat it as an object in any other way. (At a deeper level, most of the time objects are accessed via pointers while primitives aren't.)

You might expect that treating some things as objects and others as primitives would lead to all sorts of confusion, but it turns out not to be a major issue. Just remember that primitives are good for simple values like numbers and individual characters, but everything else should be an object. Most languages provide us with a handful of ready-made primitive types. For example, Java gives us byte, short, int, long, float, double, char and boolean. Even if your language does allow you to define your own primitives (for example, C++ and Eiffel), you should consider this to be an advanced technique.

Arrays, denoted in Java with the [] operator, sit somewhere between objects and primitives: they're special objects that are known to the compiler and the run-time system for efficiency reasons. However, if you wish to be pure, you can avoid arrays altogether and use classes such as List instead.

UML contains a mechanism for defining language-independent primitives with names such as Integer, Real and Boolean. However, Java primitives will be used in this book as all the code fragments are in Java. Using language-dependent types is sanctioned by the UML standard, as long as you're clear about what you're doing.

# 2.18 TERMINOLOGY

There are many terms available for the object concepts we've seen and different people use different terms to refer to the same thing. To make matters worse, some people use terms incorrectly. Figure 2.22 shows some of the terms, grouped to show how they can be used interchangeably (the underlined words are used in this book).

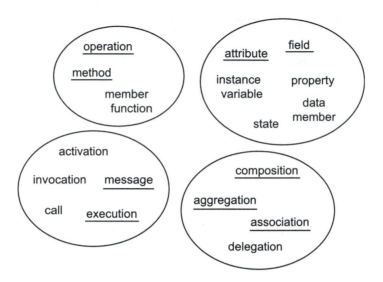

**Figure 2.22: Object-oriented terminology**

## Table 2.3: Terms used in this book

| Term | Definition |
| --- | --- |
| Attribute | A small piece of information – such as color, height or weight – that describes one characteristic of an object. |
| Field | A named value inside an object. |
| Operation | A piece of code belonging to an object. |
| Method | A synonym for 'operation'. |
| Message | A request sent from one object to another. |
| Invocation | The carrying out of an operation in response to a message. |
| Execution | A synonym for invocation. |
| Association | A direct or indirect connection between two objects. |
| Aggregation | A strong association implying some kind of part–whole hierarchy. |
| Composition | A strong aggregation, where the part is inside exactly one whole – the part may also be created and destroyed by the whole. |
| Interface | A set of messages understood by an object. |
| Protocol | An agreed way of passing messages over a network. |
| Behavior | A collective term for all of an object's operations. |

You may also come across collective terms such as **behavior** (a collection of operations), **interface** (a collection of messages), **object protocol** (a synonym for interface) and **data** (a collection of fields). In this book, only the terms listed in Table 2.3 will be used, in the manner described.

An attribute can be stored (encapsulated) by an object, but it doesn't have to be. For example, a circle has radius and diameter attributes, but we need only store the radius because the diameter can be calculated on demand. To avoid confusion, only stored attributes will be shown in this book – if necessary, derived attributes will be implied by the addition of one or more operations, such as getDiameter.

A field is not quite the same as an attribute. Firstly, a field represents a decision to store something; secondly, a field can be used to store a connection to another object, as shown by navigable links on our object diagrams. When we move into design, the attributes and associations end up as fields.

In the early stages of object-oriented software development, we tend to use the terms attribute and operation (because that's UML terminology). In the later stages, when dealing with low-level design and source code, we tend to refer to fields and methods (because that's programming terminology).

# 2.19 REUSING CODE

The term **reuse** has been mentioned several times now, so let's take a closer look at what it means and what its implications are. To put it simply, reuse refers to using code more than once, resulting in:

- Faster and simpler development.
- Easier maintenance (less code to harbor faults).
- More robust code (every time it is reused, it is retested and, over time, more and more faults are squeezed out).

There are historical and technical reasons why reuse has taken a long time to emerge. From a historical point of view, the software industry was initially preoccupied with the problem of how to program computers at all (starting with machine code), then with how to program them more efficiently and then with how to develop large systems in a reliable, systematic way.

The potential of reusing code in different contexts became apparent as more and more systems were constructed – millions upon millions of lines of code being written every year over many decades. Surely there couldn't be that many distinct systems that needed writing, could there? Since most software was written in software departments behind the closed doors of individual companies, using a variety of different programming languages, it's easy to see why reuse was rare. Even when packaged software started making it out through company doors, the source code, and even the binaries, were kept a closely guarded secret. Even so, protecting a company's commercial advantage and intellectual property doesn't justify failing to reuse code within the company itself.

From a technical point of view, reuse was difficult because of an attitude in development teams and central to the development methodology that 'We only need to solve today's problem'. This was exacerbated by the lack of facilities provided in programming languages and methodologies to promote reuse: there was a tendency to scatter the data and operations in small pieces throughout the system, making it difficult to collect related pieces into a larger chunk that would be worth reusing.

Because object orientation is driven by the modeling of general concepts from an entire domain, it's much more likely that reuse opportunities will emerge. For example, developing a payroll system would normally involve the development of an Employee class. Since the development should be driven by 'What does the employee concept mean to this company?' rather than 'What employee information does the payroll system need?', the end result is likely to be applicable to other systems developed by the same company. In addition, the modularity of objects reduces the tendency to spread attributes and operations around the system, making it easier to extract and refine the Employee code.

Gradually, the situation has improved, to the extent that, often, we will only need to write the parts of the system that are unique to our problem – the rest of the system can be implemented using prewritten code. This is especially true for common, well understood, application areas such as: user interfaces; database access; distributed programming; input/output; network access; e-commerce; access to legacy (pre-existing) systems; security (authentication, authorization, privacy, integrity checking, origin checking); text processing; mathematics; games; service look-up; sound synthesis and playback; 2D graphics; 3D graphics; e-mail; image processing; multimedia encoding and decoding; messaging; transaction processing; telephony; speech synthesis and recognition; and integration with digital TV broadcasts.

Reuse opportunities can be summarized into the categories listed below:

- Reusing functions within a system: The simplest form of reuse (used in traditional systems development) involves writing utility functions that are called from various places. For example, you may discover that various parts of your system need to search through a list of customer names, so you write a general search function that can be called from each context. Writing reusable functions is different from writing functions that break a complex process into simpler steps.
- Reusing methods within an object: Methods encapsulated within an object can be invoked from other methods. For example, a nonpublic drawFilledRectangle method inside a GUIComponent class can be used by any GUIComponent method that needs to fill an area of the screen with the current background color. You should aim to reuse methods within an object whenever possible. Nonpublic methods within an object are often used to break up a complicated process, in traditional fashion.

- Reusing classes within a system: Many of the classes that we define can be used in different parts of our system. For example, if you define a Customer class for use in a marketing system, you expect the same Customer object to appear in many different pieces of system code. This kind of reuse is fundamental to the object-oriented approach.

- Reusing functions across systems: General functions can be reused (in traditional systems development as well as in object-oriented development) in other systems that you and your colleagues produce. For example, you might write a function that extracts the year that an employee joined the company from the employee's payroll number. For such a function to be reused by your colleagues, you would have to make them aware of it, preferably by putting it in a **reuse repository**: a database of useful functions that developers are expected to peruse when they're writing new code.

- Reusing classes across systems: We can publish and reuse a whole class (with all its attributes and operations) rather than just a single function. An example would be an Employee object that encapsulates the employee attributes used throughout the company, along with a useful set of operations. Object-orientation enthusiasts were the ones who popularized the idea of a **reuse repository** containing classes rather than functions.

  In order to get developers to put in the extra effort required to make their classes reusable enough for a repository, it's a good idea to offer some kind of reward (a mug with a humorous logo on it is a common choice). Access to class repositories may be offered to third parties, perhaps for a fee. Reusing classes across your own systems is not difficult, once you have a little practice.

- Reusing classes across all systems: A software component is analogous to a hardware component. Software components are designed to be reusable in any context; are strongly encapsulated (clients can't see the inner workings); come with a standard style of interface; and are available from third parties, usually in return for payment. Every object-oriented programming language has its own form of software component, for example, Java has JavaBeans. There is no real equivalent of software components in the traditional arena, because a handful of related functions would not be of much use to third parties.

  Examples of software components include a spreadsheet that can be dropped into any office productivity suite and an income tax object that can be dropped into any home tax package. A software component is really just an object that obeys sensible rules about its style of interface (as in using naming conventions to identify getters and setters).

- Function libraries: Related, high quality functions can be grouped into a **library**, so that they're available all at once. An example would be the stdio function library, originating on Unix systems, that provides input/output facilities for C programmers. Function libraries are used in both traditional systems development and object-oriented development. Well-designed libraries sometimes become standardized by bodies such as ISO or ANSI. Function libraries may be internal to a company, free, or sold for profit.

- Class libraries: An improvement on function libraries, class libraries offer whole classes rather than mere functions. Writing a class library requires lots of experience. A good example is the **Java 2 Enterprise Edition (J2EE)** library [Bodoff *et al.* 02], which provides code for all of the well-understood reuse areas listed above. Just like function libraries, class libraries may be internal to a company, free, or sold for profit.

- Design patterns: A design pattern is a description of how to create part of an object-oriented system elegantly and effectively. Since their introduction, patterns have also been applied to other areas such as system architectures. Each pattern has a short description, a detailed description, advice on where to use it, and code samples (see Chapter 11). For example, the description of the Adapter pattern is 'An adapter translates the interface of one object into another interface that clients expect'. Designing patterns requires a lot of experience, but less than producing a class library.

- Frameworks: A framework, as its name suggests, is a pre-existing structure to which you attach your own code. In the object-oriented case, a framework consists of a number of prewritten classes, along with a document describing the construction rules that must be followed by the developer. A large example is the **Enterprise Java Beans** (**EJB**) framework [Bodoff *et al.* 02]: this consists of the J2EE library plus a document, hundreds of pages long, that specifies how programmers should write reusable enterprise components and how third parties should implement Java application servers. Most frameworks are designed by gurus (a guru is an expert's expert).

So, how should you design for reuse? We'll leave aside the issues of designing patterns and frameworks, since such techniques are beyond the scope of this book, and concentrate instead on writing reusable classes. Even a single reusable class will often have one or two closely collaborating classes – thus, we might produce a small family of reusable classes rather than just one. Here are some tips:

- Always follow style guidelines: Style guidelines are recommendations for how you should write your classes. If you write your classes in an exotic or personal style, potential reusers of your software will quickly move on to look at other code, rather than learn your personal idiosyncrasies. Style guidelines may originate from your company, or they be more widely accepted. For example, since Sun has control over the Java standard, whatever Sun says is good style is normally accepted by the Java community. As well as having a plethora of object-orientation gurus and experts of its own, Sun pays close attention to the opinions of external experts and gurus.

- Be thorough with your documentation: Few programmers will be able to understand how your classes should be reused just by reading the source code. At the very least, your class should have an explanatory name, a short comment (one or two sentences) summing up the class, a longer comment (maybe several paragraphs) describing how the class should be used and a short comment alongside each public message describing how the method should be used. Your comments should always describe the contract between the object and its clients, setting out the obligations on both sides. Documentation that is separate from the classes, such as design or tutorial information, should also be provided.

- Be prepared to write more code than you need: Often, when you're implementing a class for a particular system, you will find yourself thinking along the lines of 'I bet a foo method would come in handy here'. For example, even if you currently only need a getRadius message for your Circle class, it would be a good idea to add a getDiameter message too, making the class more useful in other systems.

- Use patterns and frameworks: Patterns and frameworks reduce your workload, but they're also understood by other developers, which means that the other developers will have less to learn before reusing your code.

- Design client–supplier objects: If you have two-way, or even cyclical, collaborations between your objects, you may end up with what is referred to in the trade as **code spaghetti**. Things will be a lot simpler if you design your objects as a client–supplier hierarchy. For example, a reusable Employee does not make any assumptions about its context; instead, it provides public messages that are generally useful. Taking this idea further, the Employee would be in control of its EmploymentHistory, but the EmploymentHistory would not know about the Employee. Imagine that your objects are servants that do what they're told, without caring about who asked them to do it. To compensate for their servile lives, the objects have servants of their own to control.

- Make each object single-purpose: This is referred to as **high cohesion**. Avoid coding objects that serve multiple purposes, such as maintaining an employee's personal information as well as their employment history.

- Separate the interface from the business behavior: A reusable object should be usable in any context. For example, the object might need to be used, directly or indirectly, in many different kinds of interface (workstation, mobile phone, or Web server). If you pollute the object with the details of a particular interface, you will run into problems. Therefore, write business objects that contain only business behavior. You can also provide interface objects to view your business objects, but that's optional. Such interface objects will become reusable in their own right.

- Design for questions and commands: Objects are simpler if their messages are either questions – 'What's the time?' – or commands – 'Set the time to . . .' Although messages that are questions and commands at the same time are occasionally useful, you should consider their use to be an advanced technique. Combined messages, such as 'Set the time to . . . and tell me what the time was before I set it', can be confusing.

## 2.20 SUMMARY

In this chapter, we have looked at:

* Software objects, which represent real-world things, are described by attributes and can carry out behavior (operations, usually called methods).

* Messages, which enable objects to communicate and collaborate to accomplish some task.

* Garbage collection, which reclaims the space used by objects when they are no longer needed by the program that created them.

* Classes, which enable us to group similar objects and share the definition of elements between related objects, so that we don't have to repeat ourselves.

* Reusing code, which results in faster and simpler development, more robust code and easier maintenance.

## FURTHER READING

One of the original books on object concepts, and why they're a good thing, is by David Taylor. [Taylor 97] is aimed at nontechnical readers, so it constitutes a gentle introduction for those who won't end up producing the actual code.

In order to promote the use of Java, there is a huge amount of free information on Sun's web site at http://java.sun.com, including tutorials. Because Java is continually being updated and improved, Sun's web site is an essential resource for Java developers. If you need help with the code fragments in this book, check out the on-line language tutorial, which is also available as [Campione *et al.* 00].

## REVIEW QUESTIONS

1. In a UML diagram, how are objects distinguished from classes? Choose only one option.

   (a) Object labels are shown in italics.
   (b) Class labels have a box drawn around them.
   (c) Object labels are underlined.

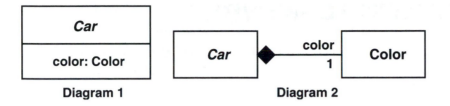

**Figure 2.23: For use with Review Question 2**

2. In Figure 2.23, what do Diagrams 1 and 2 illustrate? Choose only one option.

   (a) 1: An aggregation, 2: A composition.
   (b) 1: An attribute, 2: An aggregation.
   (c) 1: An aggregation, 2: An attribute.
   (d) 1: An attribute, 2: A composition.
   (e) 1: A composition, 2: An attribute.

3. What is meant by 'object identity'? Choose only one option.

   (a) Two objects are identical if their attributes have the same value.
   (b) Every object's class has a unique serial number.
   (c) All objects are the same as each other.
   (d) Every object has a unique identity that distinguishes it from all other objects.

4. Which of the following terms best describes an object that is made up of other objects? Choose only one option.

   (a) Generalization.
   (b) Inheritance.
   (c) Association.
   (d) Aggregation.
   (e) Specialization.

5. What is 'encapsulation'? Choose only one option.

   (a) Depicting objects using doughnut diagrams.
   (b) Ensuring that the data inside an object can only be accessed via operations.
   (c) Sealing the state of an object so that it cannot be changed.
   (d) Putting objects into a collection.

# ANSWERS TO ACTIVITY 1

1. A street exists independently of its houses. Although the street and the houses may be constructed at the same time, as time passes new houses will be added and old ones will be knocked down. Even if there are no houses at all, the street is still a street. This must be association.

2. If the book is a novel, we can't tear out a page and still have a useful novel, so this is probably aggregation. If, on the other hand, it is a reporter's notebook with pages that were designed to be torn out, it might be considered an association.

3. Notes in a symphony are similar to the pages in a novel, i.e. aggregation. If the symphony is being performed and the orchestra accidentally drops a note, people are going to notice – the orchestra members will be accused of not playing the whole symphony.

4. It may be tempting to think that components of the home entertainment system are put together to form a whole (this is implied by the use of the word 'components'). However, if we move the games console into the kids' bedroom, we're still left with a home entertainment system, albeit a less entertaining one. Also, we could add a DVD player: this wouldn't suddenly transform what we already have into a home entertainment system, it would just improve it. This looks like an association.

   Aggregation is still involved: the television is an aggregation, as is each of the other components. Therefore, we can have aggregations inside associations. We can also have associations inside aggregations (consider a DVD being played by a DVD player). Whether we view something as an aggregation or an association often depends on the scale we're looking at.

# ANSWERS TO REVIEW QUESTIONS

1. In a UML diagram, objects are distinguished from classes because c. Object labels are underlined.
2. In Figure 2.23, Diagrams 1 and 2 illustrate option d. 1: An attribute, 2: A composition.
3. 'Object identity' means that d. Every object has a unique identity that distinguishes it from all other objects.
4. An object that is made up of other objects is described as d. Aggregation.
5. 'Encapsulation' means b. Ensuring that the data inside an object can only be accessed via operations.

# 3

## Inheritance

**A**lthough inheritance is widely considered essential, it's rather more complicated than what we've seen so far, so this chapter can be skipped on a first reading. It is quite reasonable to develop software without the use of inheritance. However, if you do skip this chapter, you will have to accept a certain lack of understanding of some of the topics later in this book.

# Learning Objectives

**Understand what we mean by inheritance.**

**Understand the difference between abstract and concrete classes.**

•

**Know when to use inheritance.**

# Chapter Outline

# 3.1 **INTRODUCTION**

Inheritance allows us to specify that a class gets some of its characteristics from a **parent class** and then adds unique features of its own – this leads to the description of whole families of objects. Inheritance allows us to group classes into more and more general concepts, so that we can reason about larger chunks of the world that we live in.

From a programming point of view, we want inheritance because:

- It supports richer, more powerful, modeling. This benefits both the development team and other developers who might want to reuse code.
- It allows us to define information and behavior in one class and share the definitions in related subclasses. This means that we have less code to write.
- It's natural. This is one of the prime motivations for object orientation in the first place.

A subclass inherits all of the fields, messages, methods (and assertions) of its superclass. For example, if we wanted to model land vehicles, we might come up with the hierarchy shown in Figure 3.1.

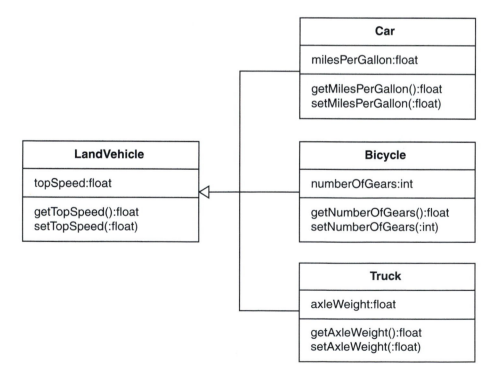

**Figure 3.1: What is inherited?**

In this diagram, the types of fields, message parameters and message replies have been shown. In UML, types are shown after a colon, for example, :String. For brevity, parameter names have been omitted from Figure 3.1: this is only reasonable because there are few parameters and their meaning is obvious. It does, however, show the type of parameter and we must still include the colon, otherwise the label is ambiguous; so :float indicates a field or parameter of *type* float, whereas float indicates a field or parameter with the *name* float. If parameter names had been included, they would have looked something like newTopSpeed:float.

Using this class hierarchy, if we were to create a Car, it would have one field inherited from LandVehicle – topSpeed – and another field introduced by the Car class itself – milesPerGallon. It would also have four methods (getTopSpeed, setTopSpeed, getMilesPerGallon and setMiles-PerGallon), two inherited and two introduced by Car. If we were to create a Bicycle, it would have the TopSpeed elements, just the same as a Car, but it would have the numberOfGears elements instead of the milesPerGallon elements.

So, the hierarchy shown, as well as allowing us to reason about general classes and specific classes, reduces our programming effort (because all the TopSpeed elements from LandVehicle, for example, appear automatically in its subclasses, without us having to repeat them).

# 3.2 DESIGNING A CLASS HIERARCHY

Let's look at a larger example. We want to model **collections**, objects that can hold on to other objects for later use. After some deliberation, we decide that we need four styles of collection:

- List: A collection that keeps all of its objects in the order in which they were inserted.
- Bag: A collection that doesn't keep its objects in order.
- LinkedList: A collection that keeps its objects in order using an implementation of a sequence of objects in which each object points to the next in the sequence. A linked list can be updated easily, but access is slow because we have to walk down the list.
- ArrayList: A collection that keeps its objects in order using an array, a sequence of adjacent memory locations. Arrays have fast access but updating is slow because we may have to shift elements around or create a new array on each update.

How could we place these four classes, along with Collection, into an inheritance hierarchy? The key is to look for major similarities between the concepts. Clearly, they're all collections in their own right, so Collection must go at the top. Next, we notice that most of the collections keep their objects in order, but Bag doesn't – this suggests that Bag should be placed directly under Collection, in a separate branch from the other classes. Next, we notice

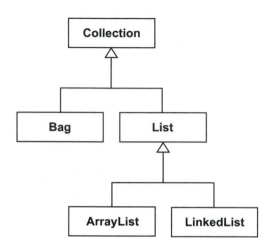

**Figure 3.2: A collection hierarchy**

that List has no commitment to internal implementation, whereas LinkedList and ArrayList do (the only difference between LinkedList and ArrayList is their time–space trade-off). So, we decide that List must be a superclass of ArrayList and LinkedList. This logical process leads to the hierarchy shown in Figure 3.2. The inheritance arrows have been drawn a little differently to those in the previous chapter; this form, also an official part of UML, is neater and more compact.

The process just described is somewhat artificial, because we had all the classes in the hierarchy to begin with, and then built the result from the top down. In reality, it tends to happen the other way round: first, we decide what classes we want at the bottom of the hierarchy – ArrayList, LinkedList and Bag – then we look for more general concepts, so that we can enrich our model and share element definitions. Thus, we might group ArrayList and LinkedList into List and then group Bag and List into Collection.

While we're developing a hierarchy, we look for messages that we can share – the higher up the hierarchy we can place the messages, the better. We tend to look for messages before we look for any other class elements because the messages represent the interface that our objects will present to the outside world, their most important feature.

Now consider the following three messages, which we've decided are good candidates for placement in our collection hierarchy:

- contains(:Object):boolean searches for an object in the collection and returns true if the receiver contains the parameter or false otherwise.

- elementAt(:int):Object retrieves the object at the position indicated by the parameter.
- numberOfElements():int replies with the number of objects in the collection.

Where can we place these messages on the classes that we already have? Well, contains is something that we should be able to ask any kind of collection, so we need to guarantee that by putting it on Collection. Now, elementAt takes a position as parameter, so it must be dealing with ordered objects (it wouldn't make sense for Bag). So, we can't put elementAt on Collection; we could put it on ArrayList and repeat it on LinkedList, because both of these classes keep their objects in order. However, we can avoid the repetition by putting it on List instead. Finally, numberOfElements is something we might want to ask of any collection, so the Collection class is the appropriate place to put it.

These deliberations lead us to the distribution of messages shown in Figure 3.3. Even though attributes have not been shown in this class diagram, the attribute box has been retained – this makes it easier to see that the list shows messages rather than fields. The message names are in italics to emphasize that we are not yet considering methods.

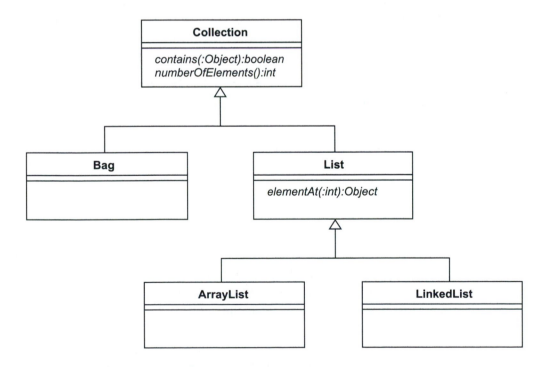

**Figure 3.3: Placing messages in a hierarchy**

We now have a complete set of classes that would be valuable to other developers. However, the classes don't yet do anything: they have no implementation.

# 3.3 ADDING IMPLEMENTATIONS TO A CLASS HIERARCHY

Okay, so we have our class hierarchy and we've decided where the messages should be introduced. Now the implementation elements (fields, constructors and methods) must be added. At this stage, let's not worry about the fields that our hierarchy would need, because that would be getting into detailed design. Similarly, let's ignore the issue of constructors for our classes – we can just assume that our finished classes will be furnished with a useful and complete set of initialization choices. Instead, we'll look at the issue of where to put the methods, because that will lead us on to two important concepts: **abstraction** and **redefinition**.

We conclude that it's impossible to write a contains method on the Collection class because the search algorithm is going to be different for ordered and unordered collections. So we must, at least, implement a contains method on Bag. But how about List and its subclasses? With a little thought, using the other messages that we've introduced, we can write a contains algorithm that works for any kind of List (see Implementation Point 3).

> **Implementation Point 3**
>
> ```
> 1   boolean contains(Object o) {
> 2     for (int i = 0; i < numberOfElements(); ++i) {
> 3       if (elementAt(i) == o) {
> 4         return true;
> 5       }
> 6     }
> 7     return false;
> 8   }
> ```
>
> Notice that parameters in Java have their type followed by their name (see line 1), unlike parameters in UML which are given as name:type. The for-loop (line 2) sets i to every value from 0 up to, but not including, the number of elements in the list. Inside the loop, the current object is retrieved and tested (line 3).
>
> Writing aMessage without specifying the object that is to receive the message means 'send aMessage to the current object' (some programmers prefer to write this.aMessage() instead). For example, elementAt(i) means 'find the value of the ith element of the current List object'.

Now we're really reaping the benefits of inheritance: we've written a single method that will work perfectly for any direct or indirect subclass of List, which could be many classes.

The elementAt message is going to have a different implementation for ArrayList and LinkedList. So, we must add two separate elementAt methods: one to ArrayList, which will access the elements directly; and one to LinkedList, which will walk down the list.

Last, but not least, we have to place numberOfElements. This implementation depends on whether we store the value as a field or calculate it when asked. Let's look at each alternative:

- Storing the number of elements as a field
  The field has to be incremented whenever we add an object and decremented whenever we remove an object. This approach allows us to report the number of objects quickly, at the cost of extra storage and slightly slower operations to add and remove objects.
- Calculating the number of elements on demand
  This is likely to be very slow for a LinkedList, involving walking down all the elements. For ArrayList and Bag, the internal objects would probably store the number of elements anyway, so the operation would be fast. Either way, with this approach, we don't waste storage and we don't slow down the adding and removing of objects.

There is a time–space trade-off that the designer needs to resolve. On this occasion, for example, we decide that neither option works well for all classes, nor even for all List objects. Therefore, we decide to put a separate numberOfElements method on each of the three **leaf** classes, Bag, ArrayList and LinkedList.

Having made our implementation decisions, we arrive at the hierarchy shown in Figure 3.4. So that you can distinguish between them, we've shown messages in italics and methods in roman text (which is also correct UML notation).

On our Collection classes, we now have two styles of message: those with an associated method and those without. A message without a method is unfinished – we know that the associated class has the message as part of its interface, but we have to look down the subclass chain to find the actual method.

An unfinished method is called an **abstract method** (or **abstract operation**), because it's not real, it's not solid, you can't kick it. The complement to an abstract method is a **concrete method** (or **concrete operation**). A concrete method has real lines of code, it's solid, you can kick it. In UML, abstract methods are shown in italics and concrete methods are not – where italics are impractical, you can put {abstract} to the right of the method instead.

# 3.4 ABSTRACT CLASSES

An **abstract class** is a class with at least one abstract method – the abstract method may be introduced on the class itself, or it may be inherited from a superclass. Figure 3.5 shows

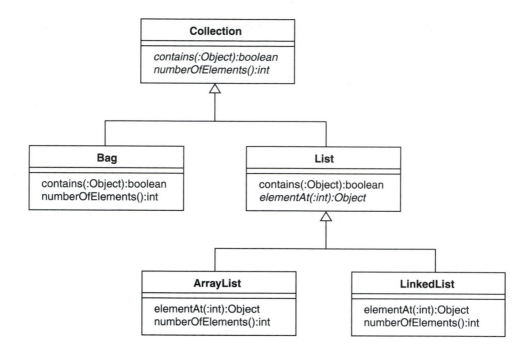

**Figure 3.4: Placing methods in a hierarchy**

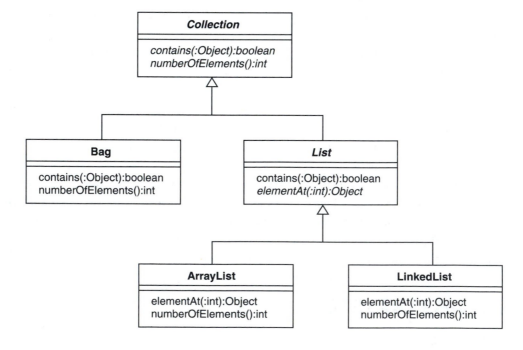

**Figure 3.5: Abstract class names in italics**

our collection hierarchy again, with the names of the abstract classes in italics (this is also correct UML). Again, if italics are impractical, you can write {abstract} above or to the left of the class name.

Abstract classes have the following advantages:

- They permit richer and more flexible modeling; for example, our List class has all three messages – contains, elementAt and numberOfElements – despite the fact that we can't provide concrete methods for all of them.
- They lead to more code sharing, because we can write concrete methods that use abstract methods; for example, the contains method for List invokes abstract methods.

Once again, abstraction is a natural thing to want to do, so object orientation provides the facility. Consider peeling a piece of fruit: we know that we can take the skin off any piece of fruit, but we can't describe how to do it in a way that will work well for every variety. Therefore, peeling fruit must be an abstract method and fruit itself must be an abstract concept.

With the abstraction facilities presented so far, we have a disaster waiting to happen: what do you think would happen if we created a Fruit and then sent it the peel message? How about if we created a Collection and sent it the contains message? We would be trying to invoke an abstract method – a thing that doesn't really exist – so the objects wouldn't know what to do.

Most object-oriented languages stop us creating instances of abstract classes. For example, a Java compiler won't compile any program containing the expression new List(). The compiler is being paranoid in this case, because we might never invoke an abstract method on the new object, but the compiler can't check that for us.

The rule that instances of abstract classes can't be created corresponds well to the real world: if I give you some money and ask you to go to the shop to buy a piece of fruit, you're likely to ask 'What kind of fruit would you like?', because you need a *concrete* request.

When designing a class hierarchy, you should bear in mind that most superclasses are abstract. This follows from the fact that inheritance hierarchies are naturally derived from the bottom up:

1. We look for the concrete concepts that exist in our problem domain and reason about their knowledge and behavior.
2. We look for commonalities between the concrete classes so that we can introduce more general superclasses.
3. We group superclasses into more superclasses, until we arrive at our most general root class (Fruit or Collection, for example).

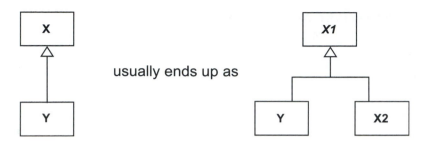

**Figure 3.6: Most superclasses are abstract**

When we identify generalizations (superclasses), we expect them to be abstract – otherwise it's likely that they would have been identified as concrete concepts in Step 1. Most of the time, the observation that most superclasses are abstract is borne out by the discovery, sooner or later, of abstract methods on the superclasses (possibly inherited). In order to help with this, Java and UML allow us to mark a class as abstract even if we haven't yet discovered any abstract methods for it.

So, what do you do if you find yourself with a concrete class inheriting from another concrete class? One thing you can try is the transformation shown in Figure 3.6. Here, we have a concrete class called Y inheriting from another concrete class X; we can transform this into an abstract superclass X1, with two concrete subclasses, X2 and Y.

If you try to work with the hierarchy on the left, you will tend to find that Y is not a true subclass of X – it doesn't quite work as **a kind of** X, leading you to change the meaning of some methods, or even to disable them. Imagine if X were Fruit and Y were Orange; we would expect an Orange to work exactly like a Fruit, with extra knowledge and behavior added on, so the disabling of methods would be unacceptable.

For the hierarchy on the right, every piece of knowledge and behavior that is truly common to X and Y has been put in X1; everything in X that is not common to Y has been moved into X2. (The old X has been split in two.) We now have a much cleaner picture: X1 is likely to be abstract; X2 and Y behave exactly as kinds of X1; X2 and Y have their own extra knowledge and behavior.

Sometimes, we're tempted to inherit from a concrete class, in order to tweak the elements of something that already exists: for example, we may already have an ArrayList class implemented by another developer, but it doesn't quite do what we want it to do, so we introduce a new subclass called MyArrayList and add minor modifications. Although this is sometimes reasonable, it has one fundamental drawback: any existing code that creates instances of ArrayList will still do so: there's no way that we can force the existing code to create instances of our improved class.

# 3.5 REDEFINING METHODS

Object orientation allows us to **redefine** elements that we inherit. In its simplest form, redefinition allows a subclass to change the implementation of an inherited method – the message stays the same but the lines of code are replaced. Another form of redefinition allows us to make a message more visible in a subclass: since we've only seen public and private visibilities up to this point, this means that a subclass can turn a private message into a public message. Yet another form of redefinition allows us to change the name or type of an attribute.

For the rest of this discussion, let's concentrate on redefining the content of methods, since that's the most important reason for redefinition. There are three good reasons why we would redefine a method:

- The inherited method was abstract and we want to make it concrete, by giving it some code – for example, contains is abstract on Collection but we need it to be concrete on Bag and List.
- The method needs to do some additional work in the subclass – for example, a toString method would have to summarize any new attributes that were introduced by the subclass.
- We can provide a better (more efficient or more accurate) implementation for the subclass – for example, if we add an index to our LinkedList class, we can redefine contains to be faster than the linear algorithm used by List.

When we are just doing additional work, we should make sure that the superclass definition still does everything it used to – this increases code sharing and simplifies maintenance (for example, if we modify the superclass definition, the subclass gets the new behavior automatically). Every object-oriented language allows a redefined method to invoke the one on its superclass (see Implementation Point 4).

---

**Implementation Point 4**

Here's a Java example:

```java
void initialize() {
   // Invoke the inherited initialize method
   super.initialize();
   // Now do the extra stuff
   ...
}
```

---

When you redefine an element, do not change its meaning. When implementing a subclass, you mustn't forget your contract with users of the superclass: anyone has the right to assume that your subclass works exactly like the superclass, with *additional* knowledge and behavior. For example, when redefining `contains` for `LinkedList`, it wouldn't be fair to make it return true when the parameter is *not* in the list.

# 3.6  IMPLEMENTING A STACK CLASS

Let's look more closely at the idea of reusing code by sharing. With a Stack (see Figure 3.7), we can push an object onto the top, peek at the top object, see if the stack is empty, and pop an object off the top.

So, what we need is a Stack class with the following four messages:

- `push()` to add an object to the top of the stack.
- `peek():Object` to return the object on the top of the stack.
- `isEmpty():boolean` to return true if there are no objects on the stack.
- `pop():Object` to remove an object from the top of the stack and return it.

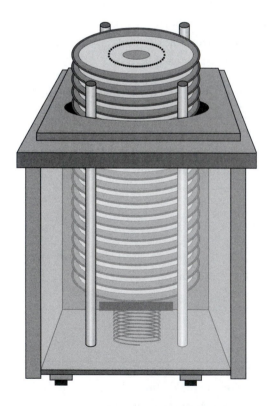

**Figure 3.7: A spring-loaded plate dispenser**

Now, object-oriented software development is supposed to be about *not* writing code, so the first thing we should do is to look around for a similar class that already exists. During our search, we come across the LinkedList class, part of which we developed earlier. We discover that it has four messages that we ought to be able to reuse:

- addElement() which adds an object to the end of the list.
- lastElement():Object which returns the object at the end of the list.
- numberOfElements():int which returns the number of objects in the list.
- removeLastElement() which removes the object at the end of the list.

If we view a stack as running from left to right, instead of bottom to top, it looks as though all the methods we need are already written, but with the wrong messages. We must decide how to incorporate the existing LinkedList behavior into our new Stack class. We could do it by inheritance (see Figure 3.8) or by **composition** (see Figure 3.9).

Composition is a strong aggregation where the composed object is inside a single composite; the composed object is usually created at the same time as the composite and can be deleted at the same time. In UML, in order to emphasize that composition is stronger than aggregation, we use a black diamond instead of a white one.

## 3.6.1 Implementing a Stack using Inheritance

Let's say that we choose to make our new class a subclass of LinkedList, as shown in Figure 3.8. Next, we define our stack messages in terms of the inherited messages. The following code shows four such definitions (in Java, **extends** means 'inherits from'):

```java
public class Stack extends LinkedList {

    public void push(Object o) {
        addElement(o);
    }
    public Object peek() {
        return lastElement();
    }
    public boolean isEmpty() {
        return numberOfElements() == 0;
    }
    public Object pop() {
        Object o = lastElement();
        removeLastElement();
        return o;
    }
}
```

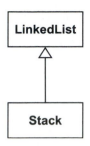

**Figure 3.8: Stack by inheritance**

We can now create a stack object and use it:

```
Person aPerson = new Person();
Stack aStack = new Stack();
aStack.push(new Plate("Wedgwood"));
aStack.push(new Plate("Royal Doulton"));
aStack.push(new Plate("Domestic green"));
aPerson.take(aStack.pop());
```

However, we have a potentially serious problem with this way of implementing Stack. Since Stack is a sublass of LinkedList, all other LinkedList messages are also available to stack objects. That should be no surprise, since a subclass is expected to offer at least the same services as its superclass. Our problem is that LinkedList has messages, such as firstElement, that are inappropriate for stacks, but a client programmer would still be able to use them, for example:

```
aPerson.take(aStack.firstElement());
```

This piece of code means that the client of aStack has just removed the element from the bottom of the stack – something that they're not supposed to be able to do.

## 3.6.2 Implementing a Stack using Composition

Figure 3.9 shows a Stack implemented with an internal reference to a LinkedList. The behavior of the encapsulated LinkedList is used by Stack, but none of the extra LinkedList behavior is exposed to Stack clients. Another way of describing this situation is to say that aStack **delegates** its behavior to aLinkedList. Since aLinkedList is encapsulated, the only reference to it is inside aStack. Therefore, if we're using a pure object-oriented language with a garbage collector, aLinkedList is deleted as soon as aStack is deleted.

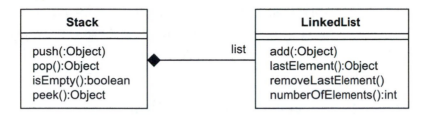

**Figure 3.9: Stack by composition**

Using composition, Stack can be implemented like this:

```
public class Stack {

    private LinkedList list;

    public Stack() {
        list = new LinkedList();
    }
    public void push(Object o) {
        list.addElement(o);
    }
    public Object peek() {
        return list.lastElement();
    }
    public boolean isEmpty() {
        return list.numberOfElements() == 0;
    }
    public Object pop() {
        Object o = list.lastElement();
        list.removeLastElement();
        return o;
    }
}
```

This class provides all the messages that a stack needs, but it does not work with:

```
aPerson.take(aStack.firstElement());
```

because there is no longer a firstElement message.

To achieve this improved behavior only meant that the Stack class had to declare and create a field and the methods had to reference that field. Although there may be a slight overhead in creating the delegated field and forwarding messages to it, it shouldn't be enough to concern us, especially considering the sophistication of today's compilers and run-time systems.

## 3.6.3 Inheritance versus Composition

Inheritance has some unique advantages:

- It's natural.
- It's elegant.
- It allows us to write generic code – for example, code written to work for Fruit will also work for Apple and Pear.

However, inheritance suffers from the following problems:

- It's difficult to do well.
- It's difficult to change when you discover deficiencies in your design.
- It's more difficult for client programmers to understand.
- The hierarchy 'leaks' into client code, making it more difficult to change too.

Composition achieves the same end result as inheritance (concrete classes, concrete messages and reuse of existing code). However, it has the following advantages:

- It's simpler to produce.
- It's easier to change.
- It's easier for clients to understand.
- It doesn't leak into client code.

On the whole, especially for beginners, composition wins over inheritance: it's reasonable to implement a sizeable application with no inheritance at all. Inheritance is best left to the experts, especially for when they're implementing large libraries of reusable code (even then, inheritance works best for well-understood domains such as graphical user interfaces, databases, networks and collections).

Some languages (such as Eiffel and C++) permit **private inheritance**, also called **implementation** inheritance. Private inheritance, as its name suggests, allows one class to inherit from another without the inherited elements becoming part of the new interface. For example, with such a facility, our Stack class could inherit privately from LinkedList: the Stack methods would have direct access to LinkedList methods, without having to introduce a delegate, so there would be no arguments about convenience or efficiency; but, because the inheritance would be private, we would not be allowing clients of Stack to use inappropriate LinkedList messages, such as removeFirstElement, so the purists would be happy too.

Private inheritance is not available in all languages, so it's another one of those features that you should avoid during analysis and design, if you don't want to tie yourself to a particular language. Private inheritance is usually provided as a side effect of **multiple inheritance**, which is also not supported by many languages.

# 3.7 MULTIPLE INHERITANCE

When we design an inheritance hierarchy, we generalize classes into higher-level abstractions (when moving up the hierarchy) and specialize them into lower-level abstractions or concrete classes (when moving down). As we move up or down, we often have to choose between alternative generalizations and specializations, even though they may all seem equally valid. For example, consider the two inheritance hierarchies in Figure 3.10.

In the first hierarchy, Vehicles have been classified as Powered or Unpowered; in the second, they've been classified as Land, Air or Sea. So, we have alternative hierarchies, but which do we choose? The answer may depend on what your problem domain is (engine maker, globe-trotter or luggage manufacturer). Or, you may not be able to come up with an answer at all until you've tried out one of the hierarchies and found whether or not it is adequate.

This kind of dilemma is a side effect of **single inheritance**. With single inheritance, a class is only allowed to have one parent. Single inheritance works well, which is why languages like Smalltalk and Java have nothing else. But **multiple inheritance**, where each class has any number of parents, is also possible. (Java does have a form of multiple inheritance, but only for **interfaces**, explained in Chapter 8.) With multiple inheritance, we might be tempted to combine the hierarchies in Figure 3.10 into the hierarchy shown in Figure 3.11, in the hope of getting the best of both worlds.

Looking at Figure 3.11, you might think that multiple inheritance is rather complicated and not worth the bother. But there are many points for and against.

Advantages of multiple inheritance are that:

- It is powerful.
- It permits private inheritance.
- It is closer to the real world.
- It allows **mix-in** inheritance.

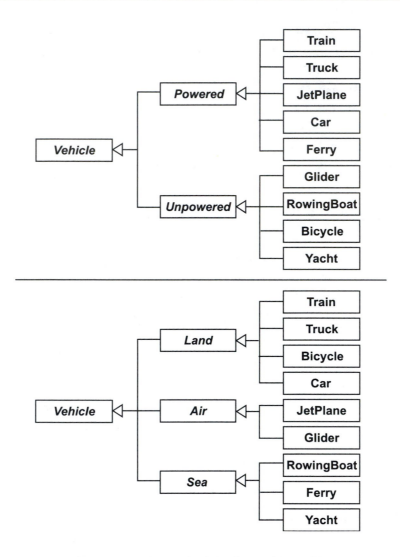

**Figure 3.10: Alternative inheritance hierarchies**

Mix-in inheritance is a design style in which we maintain a single inheritance backbone for our principal classes, while permitting individual classes to inherit from one or more decorating classes, each of which adds a few simple elements. For example, Lorry may get most of its important elements from LandVehicle but may inherit an engine attribute from a simple Powered class.

Disadvantages of multiple inheritance are that:

- It introduces complexity (for the designer and the client programmer).
- It causes **name clashes**.

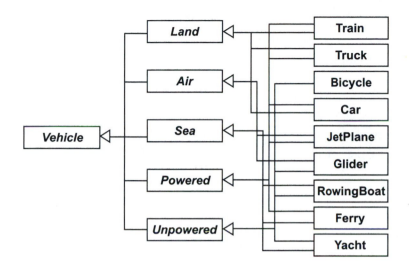

**Figure 3.11: Multiple inheritance – best of both worlds?**

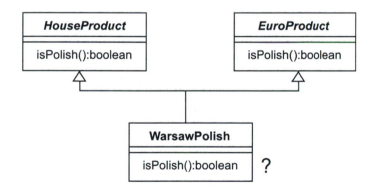

**Figure 3.12: Name clashes**

- It causes **repeated inheritance**.
- It makes compilers more difficult to write.
- It makes (fast) run-time systems more difficult to write.

**Name clashes** occur when elements with the same name, but different implementations, are inherited via different routes. For an example, consider the hierarchy in Figure 3.12. Here we have two superclasses: HouseProduct is something bought for the house; EuroProduct is something manufactured in Europe. On HouseProduct, we have a message isPolish that returns true if the associated product is used for polishing; in contrast, on EuroProduct, we have an isPolish message that returns true if the associated product is manufactured in Poland.

Once we introduce the mutual subclass WarsawPolish, denoting polish manufactured in Warsaw, we have a problem: we would like the new class to have two messages with different meanings; however, they can't both use the same name, because that would make aWarsawPolish.isPolish() ambiguous. If we rename the two messages, clients of WarsawPolish will be surprised to learn that it has no isPolish message at all, despite what it says on HouseProduct and EuroProduct.

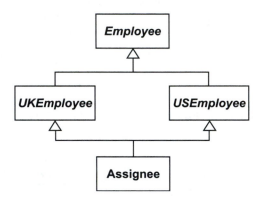

**Figure 3.13: Repeated inheritance**

**Repeated inheritance** means inheriting the same element from more than one route. For example, if a getName method is defined on the Employee class in Figure 3.13, Assignee inherits getName from both UKEmployee and USEmployee. In this simple case, it should be easy for a compiler to work out that Assignee should end up with one getName method. However, things get trickier if UKEmployee or USEmployee choose to redefine the getName method; Assignee could end up with two getName methods (in which case, how do we deal with the name clash?) or just one (in which case, how do we choose which one to have?).

The problems of writing efficient compilers and run-time systems to handle multiple inheritance are difficult to overcome. However, any programmer that yearns for the power of multiple inheritance is unlikely to be satisfied if these are the reasons given for dropping the facility altogether. In support of multiple inheritance, it should be noted that all the problems can be overcome with the help of clever designers and good programming style.

However, since it may not be available in your implementation language, you may well choose to avoid multiple inheritance altogether, especially for analysis purposes. If you do use multiple inheritance during design, restrict yourself to a single-inheritance backbone, with the addition of simple mix-in classes when appropriate.

For the record, here's a summary of the multiple inheritance facilities available in common languages:

- Eiffel provides straightforward multiple inheritance, plus private inheritance and mix-in inheritance. Eiffel has a rich set of facilities for dealing with name clashes and repeated inheritance.
- Smalltalk provides only single inheritance. Multiple inheritance facilities have been tried with Smalltalk, with limited success.
- C++ provides some multiple inheritance facilities. However, the facilities are incomplete, poorly designed and poorly implemented, so they should be avoided.
- Java provides single inheritance for classes but multiple inheritance for interfaces (abstract classes that have no methods). This is a good compromise that allows some degree of multiple inheritance modeling and mix-in inheritance (for messages only). Java has no special facilities to deal with name clashes or repeated inheritance, but a simple form of repeated inheritance is allowed.

## 3.8 GUIDELINES FOR USING INHERITANCE

- Don't overdo it: Don't think that you have to use inheritance a lot, or even at all. Remember that there are alternatives, such as composition and the use of attributes (for example, a Car class with a color attribute is probably better than three classes called Car, RedCar and BlueCar).
- A class should be 'a kind of' its superclass(es): Whenever you subclass X to produce Y, ask yourself 'Is Y a kind of X?' For example, Orange is a kind of Fruit and Truck is a kind of LandVehicle, so they are valid; conversely, Potato is not a kind of Fruit and Airplane is not a kind of LandVehicle, so these would not make good subclasses. (Some developers use the terms subtyping to mean 'I am following the guideline' and subclassing to mean 'I might not be'.)
- A class should be an extension of its superclass(es): In a subclass, make sure that you only add new features; don't be tempted to break the superclass contract by deleting, disabling or reinterpreting features.

## 3.9 SUMMARY

In this chapter, we examined inheritance, a tool for code sharing and higher-level modeling:

- Classes can be grouped into more general concepts and a class can get (inherit) some of its characteristics from a parent class.

- An abstract class has at least one method without code (an abstract method); in a concrete class, all the methods contain lines of code.

# FURTHER READING

One of the best-known books on object-oriented design and programming theory is [Meyer 97], covering everything you should and shouldn't do with objects. Meyer illustrates his ideas using his own language, Eiffel, but Eiffel's syntax is simple and based entirely on object-oriented concepts, so it makes a good complement to the main text. Apart, perhaps, from the choice of programming language, even the most stringent theoretician would find it difficult to disagree with anything Meyer has to say.

# REVIEW QUESTIONS

1. Why is the ability to redefine a method important in object-oriented programming? Choose all options that apply.

   (a) Because it allows us to add extra work to a method.
   (b) Because it allows us to introduce abstract methods that are redefined as concrete methods.
   (c) Because it allows us to provide a more accurate or faster definition in a subclass.
   (d) Because it allows us to disable a method in a subclass.
   (e) Because it allows us to change the meaning of a method.

2. Which of the following statements about multiple inheritance are true? Choose all options that apply.

   (a) It offers more modeling choices.
   (b) It makes it more difficult to write compilers and (fast) runtime systems.
   (c) It simplifies inheritance hierarchies.
   (d) It solves the problem of repeated inheritance.

3. Which of the following statements are true? Choose all options that apply.

   (a) Most superclasses are abstract.
   (b) Inheritance is preferable to composition.
   (c) Most superclasses are concrete.
   (d) Composition is preferable to inheritance.

4. In UML diagrams, how are abstract classes distinguished from concrete classes? Choose only one option.

(a) Concrete classes are shown as boxes with dashed outlines.

(b) Labels on abstract classes are shown in italics.

(c) Labels on concrete classes are shown in italics.

(d) Abstract classes are shown as boxes with dashed outlines.

5. What is an 'abstract' class? Choose only one option.

(a) An object.

(b) A class with no methods.

(c) A class with no concrete subclasses.

(d) A class with at least one undefined message.

(e) An interface.

6. Which of the following terms best describes the case where a Stack class is implemented using an internal instance of List? Choose only one option.

(a) Association.

(b) Specialization.

(c) Genericity.

(d) Composition.

(e) Singularity.

7. With reference to Figure 3.14, what is the difference between the two diagrams? Choose only one option.

(a) In Diagram 1, color is public but in Diagram 2 color is private.

(b) Diagram 2 indicates that the car's color can be removed and replaced.

(c) Diagram 1 shows an abstract class and Diagram 2 shows a concrete class.

(d) None, they mean the same thing.

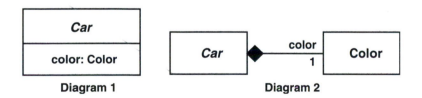

**Figure 3.14: For use with Review Question 7**

# ANSWERS TO REVIEW QUESTIONS

1. The ability to redefine a method is important in object-oriented programming:

(a) Because it allows us to add extra work to a method.

    (b) Because it allows us to introduce abstract methods that are redefined as concrete methods.

    (c) Because it allows us to provide a more accurate or faster definition in a subclass.

2. Multiple inheritance a. offers more modeling choices and b. makes it more difficult to write compilers and (fast) runtime systems.

3. The following statements are true a. Most superclasses are abstract b. Composition is preferable to inheritance.

4. In UML diagrams, abstract classes are distinguished from concrete classes because b. Labels on abstract classes are shown in italics.

5. An 'abstract' class is d. A class with at least one undefined message.

6. The term that best describes the case where a Stack class is implemented using an internal instance of List is d. Composition.

7. The difference between the two diagrams is d. None, they mean the same thing.

# Type Systems

**A**s with inheritance, type systems are widely considered essential but are rather complicated, so this chapter could be skipped on a first reading. You can get away without a detailed knowledge of type systems. However, if you do skip this chapter, you will have to accept a certain lack of understanding of some of the topics later in this book.

# Learning Objectives

**Understand what we mean by a type system.**

•

**Understand polymorphism.**

**Understand implicit and explicit casting.**

•

**Recognize that Java templates provide genericity.**

# Chapter Outline

# 4.1 INTRODUCTION

A type system is a simple concept: it's a set of rules that stop us misusing values (primitives and objects). Usually, this is done by forcing us to declare how we intend to use a value before we actually use it – this allows compilers and run-time systems to spot potential abuses before they happen.

A simple example of a type system in use is declaring that a variable will always hold a value of a particular type:

```
int i;
Employee fred;
```

But why would we misuse a value in the first place? The most common reasons are:

- Not understanding how the value is supposed to be used.
- Because we have spelled something incorrectly.

As well as preventing the misuse of values, a type system can have a couple of other benefits: it can ensure that we provide some documentation of the code ('fred is an Employee') and it can improve run-time performance, because the compiler and run-time system have more information about what the code intends to do (compiler) or what it actually is doing (run-time system).

# 4.2 DYNAMIC AND STATIC TYPE SYSTEMS

Type systems can either be **static** ('done by the compiler') or **dynamic** ('done by the run-time system'). Both varieties of type system ensure that values are not misused by the programmer: a static type system spots the abuse at compile time while a dynamic type system waits to see if the abuse actually happens and then stops it.

Smalltalk is the archetypal dynamically-typed language. In Smalltalk, a programmer often declares the expected type of a value using a naming convention. For example, to ensure that a parameter for the addEmployee method always pointed to an Employee object, the programmer might give it the name anEmployee. Anyone using addEmployee would assume from the parameter name that they were supposed to pass in an Employee. (Similar naming conventions can be applied to fields and local variables.)

But Smalltalk is dynamically typed, so the client programmer still has to make sure that they don't invoke addEmployee with, say, a Banana. Let's assume that, inside the addEmployee method, the getPayrollNumber message is sent to anEmployee. Therefore, if we pass in a Banana, getPayrollNumber will be sent to the Banana, which is clearly nonsense. Smalltalk's reaction to this misuse of a Banana would be to generate a run-time error with the message Banana doesn't understand payrollNumber.

Smalltalk's approach still constitutes a type system, albeit a rather simple one, because the run-time system has prevented the client programmer from abusing the Banana – the object hasn't been forced to answer a question that it doesn't understand. However, we have to wait until the code is run before we discover the error. Worse still, if our test code only sends messages to anEmployee that are also supported by Banana, we won't discover the error until we write more code or run the system in a live setting.

If we write the addEmployee method in Java, we are forced to declare a type for the parameter:

```
public void addEmployee(Employee anEmployee) {
    ...
    pay = anEmployee.getPayrollNumber()
    ...
}
```

Here, the programmer is telling the compiler that the parameter passed in by the client must be an Employee (and that the message doesn't return anything, using the void keyword). Therefore, the compiler will refuse to compile the following code fragment:

```
aPayroll.addEmployee(new Banana());
```

So, in Java, the abuse of Banana is stopped by the compiler, rather than by the run-time system.

A Smalltalk programmer would argue that dynamic typing is the better option, because:

- It makes compilation quick and simple.
- The programmer can work quickly – ideas flow easily from the programmer's head into the program, because they don't have to keep stopping to think what kind of object they must use in this context.
- The lack of a static compiler encourages thorough testing.
- Object-oriented code is continually being reused, so faults are always found eventually.

A Java programmer would argue that static typing is a good thing because:

- Compilation is still pretty quick and, anyway, programmers don't care how difficult it is to write a compiler.
- It can be used to improve run-time performance.
- It can be used to pick up spelling mistakes.
- It forces some documentation of the code.

In object-oriented terms, a static type system guarantees that it's impossible to send a message to an object unless that object has a corresponding method.

# 4.3 POLYMORPHISM

**Polymorphism** is derived from the Greek word stems **poly**, meaning many, and **morph**, meaning shape. Therefore, **polymorphic** means 'having many shapes'. We can apply the term separately to variables and to messages: a **polymorphic variable** refers to different types of value at different times; a **polymorphic message** has more than one method associated with it.

In a pure object-oriented language, all nonprimitive variables are polymorphic and all messages are polymorphic. We'll take a look at each in turn.

## 4.3.1 Polymorphic Variables

The following Java declaration states that t will always point at an object of type Truck:

```
Truck t;
```

Therefore, the following assignment would be valid and would lead to the situation shown in Figure 4.1:

```
t = new Truck();
```

**Figure 4.1: Attaching a Truck variable to a Truck object**

Now consider the class hierarchy shown in Figure 4.2, which tells us that a Truck is a kind of LandVehicle. Given this hierarchy, we would expect to be able to treat a Truck just like a LandVehicle. Therefore, the following statement would also be valid and would give us the situation shown in Figure 4.3:

```
LandVehicle lv = new Truck();
```

That may surprise you. But, consider this: we've just told the compiler that we will only ever use lv as a LandVehicle, i.e. we will only ever send it LandVehicle messages; since all the LandVehicle messages are on Truck too, everything will be fine.

In the same way that we can make lv refer to a Truck, we can make it refer to a Train (see Figure 4.4):

```
lv = new Train();
```

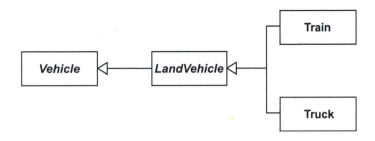

**Figure 4.2: Truck inheritance**

**Figure 4.3: Attaching a LandVehicle variable to a Truck object**

**Figure 4.4: Attaching a LandVehicle variable to a Train object**

Although lv was pointing at a Truck, it's now pointing at a Train, so it must be a polymorphic variable. This should be intuitive: lv is a LandVehicle, so it can point at any kind of LandVehicle.

The polymorphism of variables is controlled by inheritance. For example, because Orange is not a kind of LandVehicle, it wouldn't be sensible to write

```
lv = new Orange();
```

So, polymorphism allows us to attach a variable to a subclass object. But we can't go the other way round. For example, because a Vehicle is not a kind of LandVehicle, it wouldn't be reasonable to write:

```
lv = new Vehicle();
```

If this was allowed, we could send any LandVehicle message to the Vehicle, even though some of the LandVehicle messages won't be understood by Vehicle.

## 4.3.2 Polymorphic Messages

Any message, in a pure object-oriented language, can have more than one method associated with it. This happens either because the methods appear independently on more than one class or because a method is redefined by subclasses. Redefined methods normally have similar algorithms, but methods defined independently usually have completely different algorithms.

For example, consider the four classes in Figure 4.5, where any possible relationships between humans and birds have been ignored. All of these classes have a message flyTo, which means 'Use flight to get to the given location': the method is abstract on Bird and concrete on the other three classes. Since flyTo has three implementations, it is a polymorphic message.

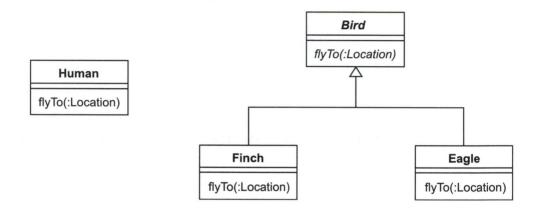

**Figure 4.5: Polymorphic animal messages**

Although flyTo on Human can be compared to flyTo on Bird, the meanings are really quite different: for birds, flying involves flapping and gliding; for humans, it involves getting on a plane.

Polymorphic messages are linked to inheritance, in the same way as polymorphic variables. For example, in the following code fragment, we would expect the run-time system to execute the flyTo method on Finch, not the one on Bird (which is abstract anyway, so there would be nothing to execute):

```
Bird b = new Finch();
b.flyTo(someLocation);
```

Here we see the full power of abstract methods: we've been able to state that 'All birds have a flyTo message', even though we can't define one at the level of Bird – the run-time system has the job of picking the correct implementation. If we added the following code fragment to the one above, we would be telling an Eagle to fly to someLocation, which presumably involves more of the gliding and less of the flapping.

```
b = new Eagle();
b.flyTo(someLocation);
```

A polymorphic variable is just a place holder – the business end is the object it happens to be pointing to. So, in the following code fragment, we have one Cat, but two references to it (each reference is a separate name for the cat):

```
Cat tiddles, tom;
tiddles = new Cat("Hfrrr");
tom = tiddles;
```

# 4.4 DYNAMIC BINDING

Dynamic binding means attaching a message to a method at run time. This is the way that object-oriented languages cope with polymorphic variables and redefined methods. Take a look at Figure 4.6. Here, we have two abstract classes – Shape and Quadrilateral – and one concrete class – Square. All three classes have a getPerimeter message: on Shape, it is abstract; on Quadrilateral, it sums the length of all four sides; on Square, it multiplies the length of a single side by four. The fact that aSquare is an instance of class Square has been shown as a UML **dependency**, a dashed, open-ended arrow.

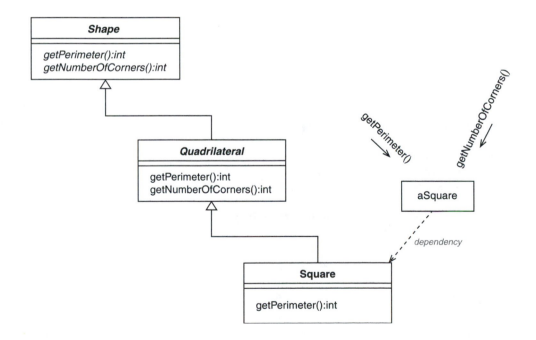

**Figure 4.6: Dynamic binding and redefinition**

In the following code fragment, how does the run-time system know which of the three methods to execute when the getPerimeter message is sent?

```
Shape sh = new Square();
int i = sh.getPerimeter();
```

Conceptually, what happens is this: the object that receives the message (a Square in this case), knows its own class, so it goes there to look for the method; since Square defines a getPerimeter method, it is executed.

Figure 4.6 also shows a getNumberOfCorners message, which is abstract on Shape and concrete on Quadrilateral. In the following code fragment, the Square will again look to its class for a getNumberOfCorners method.

```
int j = sh.getNumberOfCorners();
```

This time, there is no matching method, so the search continues with the Quadrilateral superclass. Quadrilateral does have a matching method, so that's the one that is executed. Although this dynamic binding algorithm looks a little slow, it is only a conceptual algorithm and can be implemented much more efficiently, especially with the help of a static type system.

With static typing, we can be sure that dynamic binding will find a concrete method somewhere in the superclass chain (because the type of every variable has to be declared and we can't create abstract objects). With a dynamic type system, we might encounter an abstract method or fall off the top of the hierarchy altogether – this would result in a run-time error message.

For multiple inheritance, dynamic binding is more complicated, but it is still feasible and is not appreciably slower than with single inheritance.

---

**Figure 4.7 shows our Shape hierarchy with an additional class Triangle. Consider the following code fragment:**     **ACTIVITY 2**

```
Shape sh;
Triangle tr = new Triangle();
Square sq = new Square();
```

**Which of the following assignments would be correct? (Remember to think 'Is it a kind of?')**

**1. sh = tr;**
**2. sh = sq;**
**3. sq = tr;**
**4. tr = sq;**
**5. tr = sh;**
**6. sq = sh;**

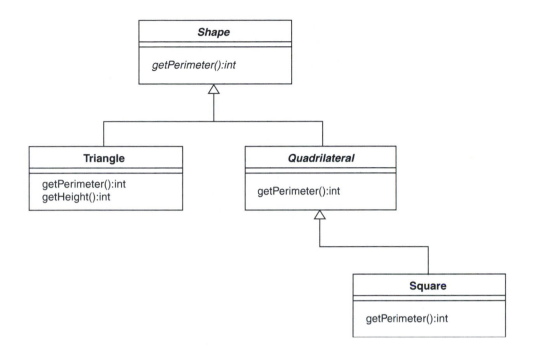

**Figure 4.7: Polymorphism and type systems**

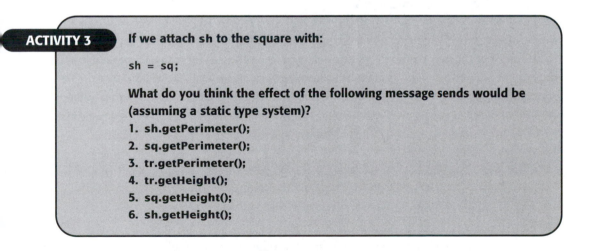

ACTIVITY 3

**If we attach sh to the square with:**

`sh = sq;`

**What do you think the effect of the following message sends would be (assuming a static type system)?**

1. **sh.getPerimeter();**
2. **sq.getPerimeter();**
3. **tr.getPerimeter();**
4. **tr.getHeight();**
5. **sq.getHeight();**
6. **sh.getHeight();**

# 4.5 POLYMORPHISM GUIDELINE

Before we leave the subject of polymorphism, consider the following style guideline: 'Always program using as high a level of abstraction as you can'. That is, always declare the type of your fields, local variables and method parameters to be the highest class possible in the inheritance hierarchy, then let polymorphism do the rest.

The reason for this guideline is that the higher the abstraction level you use, the more reusable your code will be. For example, any code written in terms of Shape will work for any kind of Shape – Square, Quadrilateral, Triangle, and any other subclasses that we might add later. But code written for Square will only work for Square objects, code written for Triangle will only work for Triangle objects, and so on.

Designers of class hierarchies have a complementary responsibility here: they should make sure, wherever possible, that the specifics of each class are hidden behind general messages that apply to all the related classes. For example, drawing a square on screen is significantly different to drawing a triangle. Rather than exposing the difference to the client programmer, we should design a message, or a group of messages, that can be placed on Shape.

For example, we might provide a draw message on Shape, so that the client programmer can tell a Shape to draw itself without knowing anything about how the drawing is done. Alternatively, we could add a message called getLines to the Shape class, so that a client programmer could retrieve the lines that make up the shape's perimeter and draw them on screen, without caring about how they were generated.

# 4.6 TYPE CASTING

In a statically typed language, when we pass a value from one context to another we need to be sure that the new context is compatible with the old one (for example, we don't want to pass a Banana to a context that expects an Employee). Even when we're sure that the new context is compatible with the old one, we may still need to convert the value to a different type (for example, passing an Employee object from an Employee context to a Person context).

There are three situations in which a value changes context:

- Expression evaluation: In the expression 2 + 2, the compiler is being asked to add two integers together to produce another integer. No problem, because the new context and the old context are both integer.

  On the other hand, if we code the expression 3.75 + 2, the compiler begins with a real number and an integer, but it must produce a real number. In this case the integer is compatible with the new context – because we can add any two types of number together to produce another type of number – so the expression is valid. However, computers represent integers and real numbers in different ways so, in order to perform the arithmetic above, the compiler must first convert the integer into a real number (because integers can be represented as real numbers, but not vice versa).

Some languages allow objects to take part in expressions, as in the Java expression "The date is " + aDate. These expressions must obey similar rules to the primitive examples above. In this case, the compiler will translate the Date into a String by sending it the toString message.

- Assignment: An assignment that doesn't require a conversion is Person p = new Person(), because the expression context and the variable context are both Person. However, the assignment Person p = new Employee() requires a conversion from Employee to Person. Person pointers are not represented differently from Employee pointers but the compiler must be sure that an Employee can be used as a Person. If Person is a direct or indirect superclass of Employee, the conversion will be safe, because the client programmer can only use elements of the Person class.

  An example of a primitive assignment that requires a conversion is float f = 2, in which the integer 2 must be converted to a floating point number.

- Parameter passing: This is the same as assignment. The value of the actual parameter is assigned to the declared parameter, for example, aUniversity.enrollPerson(new Employee()).

  A primitive example is aLiquid.setBoilingPoint(100), where the parameter is declared to be float.

Converting a value from one type to another is called **casting** (because we cast the value in a new light). The examples above are all **implicit casts** because the client programmer doesn't have to do anything special: the compiler can see that the conversions are valid and just does them. In general, an implicit cast is possible if the new context is **wider** than the old context. In terms of primitive values, wider means 'the new context can accommodate all possible values of the old context'; for object values, wider means 'the new context is a direct or indirect superclass of the old context'.

Dynamically-typed languages have a much easier time passing values between contexts. For example, when executing the Smalltalk method addEmployee with a Banana as a parameter, no compatibility testing or casting needs to be done: as long as addEmployee only uses elements that are common to Employee and Banana, the method will run without error. (We would still have a problem later if we attempted to transfer money to the Banana's bank account, but that would manifest itself as a run-time error.)

# 4.7 EXPLICIT CASTS

Implicit casts enrich statically-typed programming languages by allowing us to combine different types of values in expressions and by allowing us to assign different types of values to variables. But we can go one step further, by allowing the programmer to use an **explicit cast**, to move from one context to a compatible, but **narrower**, context.

It turns out that the explicit casting of a value can cause problems, but the explicit casting of a pointer is not nearly so bad. This is because, when we cast a value, we're modifying the way the value is stored – storing the value using a narrower representation may lose information. In contrast, if we cast a pointer, we're modifying the way we access the value, but the value itself remains unchanged.

In a pure object-oriented language, primitives are always accessed as values and objects are always accessed via pointers (efficiency versus polymorphism). In contrast, in a language like C++, primitives and objects can be accessed either as values or via pointers: the programmer has the choice. The upshot of this is that C++ programmers have to be much more careful. For the rest of this discussion, let's assume that we're using a pure object-oriented language. Let's also assume that explicit casts are used only when necessary: turning an implicit cast into an explicit one is allowed, but it has no effect.

Java allows a programmer to write

```
int i = (int) 3.75
```

(int) explicitly casts the real value 3.75 as an integer. The programmer, aware that an implicit cast from float to int is impossible, is telling the compiler to force a square peg into a round hole. In real life, forcing a square peg into a round hole tends to shear off the peg's corners. In programming, it's no different: the fractional part of the real number is sheared off.

The explicit cast above only works at all because int and float are compatible: boolean b = (boolean) 3.75 would never make sense. In general, if there exists an implicit cast in one direction, we can force an explicit cast in the other direction.

How about explicit casting for object pointers? Could the following example ever work?

```
Employee e = (Employee) new Person();
```

For pure object-oriented languages, the answer is no. Remember that casting a pointer doesn't change the representation of the value, it just changes the way we look at it. So, our example is asking the compiler to let us treat a Person as an Employee. If the compiler allowed this, we might try to use an Employee-only element which wasn't there (getPayrollNumber, for example).

How about the following pair of statements, could these ever work?

```
Person p = new Employee();
Employee e = (Employee) p;
```

In this case, the object we're trying to get e to point to really is an Employee, so the explicit cast ought to be safe – we can't abuse an Employee via an Employee pointer. But the compiler is stuck. In order to work out that those statements are valid, the compiler would have to analyze both statements. As already noted, compilers don't do this kind of analysis because it's difficult and often impossible.

However, occasionally this is a useful thing for the programmer to be able to do. Therefore, the compiler enlists the help of the run-time system in order to allow the explicit cast, but only because Employee is a subclass of Person. Subsequently, the run-time system needs to check that the object pointed to by p is an instance of Employee at the time of the assignment (or an instance of a direct or indirect subclass): if not, a run-time error will occur.

Because the explicit cast of an object pointer involves the run-time system, it is sometimes referred to as a **dynamic cast**. Some people also use the terms **upcast** and **downcast** to refer to implicit and explicit casting of object pointers, respectively, because an implicit cast moves the type *up* the hierarchy and an explicit casts moves the type *down*.

Downcasts aren't needed very often. You should only use them when retrieving an object using a **generic message** – a message whose return type must be compatible with all possible objects. For example, the Stack class we saw earlier has a generic message for popping an object: it always returns a pointer of type Object, regardless of what's actually on the top. (It also has a generic message for pushing an object: the parameter's type is Object, which might require an upcast.)

Generic messages allow the stack to work for all kinds of object – cars, strings or whatever. But they wouldn't allow a client programmer to do the following:

```
aStack.push(new Plate("Domestic blue"));
Plate aPlate = aStack.pop();
```

The first line works, because it's an implicit upcast, but the second line doesn't. However, with the help of a downcast, the client programmer can do this:

```
aStack.push(new Plate("Domestic blue"));
Plate aPlate = (Plate) aStack.pop();
```

# 4.8 GENERICITY WITH TEMPLATES

Some languages, such as Java, hardly need downcasts at all, because they have a facility called **genericity**, which is better than downcasts. A **generic class** uses one or more **class parameters** to refer to the types of objects that it expects to deal with. In Java, a generic class is called a **template**. For example, the Java programmer can define a Stack class like this:

```
public class Stack<X> {

   private List<X> list;

   public Stack<X>() {
      list = new LinkedList<X>();
   }
   public void push(X anX) {
```

```
        list.addElement(anX);
    }
    public X peek() {
        return list.lastElement();
    }
    public boolean isEmpty() {
        return list.numberOfElements() == 0;
    }
    public Object pop() {
        X anX = list.lastElement();
        list.removeLastElement();
        return anX;
    }
}
```

Despite the new syntax, you should be able to pick out the important parts of this class. The most important aspect is the class referred to throughout as X: this is a place-holder for the actual kind of Stack created by the client programmer. Notice also that the type of the field is more general than the implementation class (this is just good style for object-oriented code in general).

Now, the client programmer can manipulate a stack using the following lines of code:

```
Stack<Plate> s = new Stack<Plate>();
s.push(new Plate("Hospital white"));
Plate p = s.pop();
```

Because the programmer has declared that the Stack contains Plate objects, there's no need for an explicit cast before s.pop().

A programmer who wants a quick-trick-brick stack can write the following:

```
Stack<QuickTrickBrick> s = new Stack<QuickTrickBrick>();
```

The Stack class is a relatively simple generic type, because none of its methods needs to use the elements of the objects it contains. If we want to make assumptions about the class of the stacked objects, we need something more. For example, we might decide that Stack objects should only contain food – this would allow the Stack methods to treat the pushed objects as Food, counting calories, for example.

If we want to make assumptions about the class parameters, we have to use **constrained genericity**: adding constraints to the class parameters. Here's part of a modified Stack class written in Java, one that only works for different kinds of Food:

```
public class Stack<X extends Food> {
    ...
    private int caloriesConsumed;
    ...
```

```
public X pop() {
   X anX = list.lastElement();
   list.removeLastElement();
   // Now add anX's calories to the total,
   // only possible because X is always a Food
   caloriesConsumed = caloriesConsumed + anX.getCalories();
   return anX;
}
...
}
```

# 4.9 SUMMARY

In this chapter, we looked at:

- Type systems, which stop us misusing values by forcing us to declare how we intend to use a value. A static type system detects abuses at compile time while a dynamic type system waits until run time.

- Polymorphism, which enables a variable to hold different types of value and a message to be associated with more than one method. The specific type of value or method applicable in any case is determined at run time.

- Casting between object types: with implicit casting, the compiler can automatically convert between types of variable; with explicit casting, the programmer must specify that an object is to be considered as a different type.

- Templates in Java, in which a generic class uses parameters to refer to the types of objects that it expects to deal with.

# FURTHER READING

For more on Java templates, a relatively recent addition to the language, go to the Java web site at java.sun.com.

# REVIEW QUESTIONS

1. With reference to Figure 4.8, which methods correspond to the following message sends (in the order given)? Choose only one option.

```
tr.height();
sh.perimeter();
sq.height();
sq.perimeter();
sh.height();
tr.perimeter();
```

(a)  3, 1, none (error), 4, none (error), 5
(b)  3, 5, none (error), 4, 3, 5
(c)  3, 1, none (error), 4, 3, 5
(d)  3, 5, none (error), 4, none (error), 5

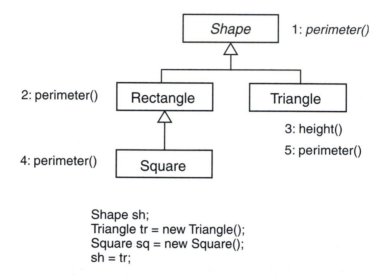

**Figure 4.8: For use with Review Question 1**

2. With reference to Figure 4.8, which of the following message sends would be allowed by a compiler? Choose all options that apply.

   (a)  sh.perimeter();
   (b)  tr.perimeter();
   (c)  sh.height();
   (d)  sq.height();
   (e)  sq.perimeter();
   (f)  tr.height();

3. With reference to Figure 4.8, which of the following assignments would be allowed by a compiler? Choose all options that apply.

   (a)  sq = sh;
   (b)  sh = tr;
   (c)  tr = sq;
   (d)  tr = sh;

(e)  sh = sq;

(f)  sq = tr;

4. What can an object-oriented type system be used for? Choose only one option.

   (a)  Improving runtime performance.
   (b)  Preventing misuse of a class.
   (c)  Avoiding spelling mistakes.
   (d)  Making sure that all messages invoke a concrete method.
   (e)  Documentation.
   (f)  All of the above.
   (g)  None of the above.

5. What does the term 'polymorphism' refer to? Choose all options that apply.

   (a)  The ability of a variable to point at different classes of object at different times.
   (b)  The fact that a message with the same signature can invoke different methods at different times.
   (c)  All object-oriented programming languages are different.
   (d)  All object-oriented methodologies use a different notation.

6. What is a generic class? Choose only one option.

   (a)  A class with no declared copyright.
   (b)  A class that represents all objects.
   (c)  A class that has other classes as parameters.

# ANSWERS TO ACTIVITY 2

1. This is fine: a Shape variable must be able to point at a Triangle, because a Triangle is a kind of Shape.
2. This is fine: a Square is a kind of Shape.
3. This is an attempt to point at a Triangle with a Square variable, so that must be wrong, because a Triangle is not a kind of Square.
4. Similarly, a Square is not a kind of Triangle.
5. A Shape is not a kind of Triangle.
6. A Shape is not a kind of Square.

# ANSWERS TO ACTIVITY 3

1. The getPerimeter message is introduced on Shape, so that is correct; since sh is pointing at a Square, it's the getPerimeter method on Square that is invoked.

2. The getPerimeter method on Square is invoked.

3. The getPerimeter method on Triangle is invoked.

4. The compiler is happy and the getHeight method on Triangle is executed.

5. This is an error, because there is no getHeight message on Square, nor on its super-classes – the compiler will reject this one.

6. We're trying to send getHeight to a Shape variable. If sh points at a Triangle, the message would not be a problem; but sh could point at a Square, in which case the message would be invalid. Compilers for static type systems tend to err on the side of caution: as the message might arrive at an object that doesn't know how to deal with it, the compiler would reject the statement.

# ANSWERS TO REVIEW QUESTIONS

1. In Figure 4.8, the methods correspond to the message sends d. 3, 5, none (error), 4, none (error), 5

2. In Figure 4.8, the following message sends would be allowed by a compiler:

   (a)  sh.perimeter();
   (b)  tr.perimeter();
   (e)  sq.perimeter();
   (f)  tr.height();

3. With reference to Figure 4.8, the following assignments would be allowed by a compiler:

   (b)  sh = tr;
   (e)  sh = sq;

4. An object-oriented type system can be used for f. All of the above:

   (a)  Improving runtime performance.
   (b)  Preventing misuse of a class.
   (c)  Avoiding spelling mistakes.
   (d)  Making sure that all messages invoke a concrete method.
   (e)  Documentation.

5. The term 'polymorphism' refers to a. The ability of a variable to point at different classes of object at different times and b. The fact that a message with the same signature can invoke different methods at different times.

6. A generic class is c. A class that has other classes as parameters.

# 5

## Software Development Methodologies

In this chapter, we're going to take a look at the software development process itself: the steps we go through to write good software and the things that we produce along the way. Collectively, the process, its steps and its products are referred to as a **methodology**.

# Learning Objectives

**Understand the classical phases of software production.**

•

**Compare static (structural) modeling with dynamic (time-based) modeling.**

**Understand the notation of Unified Modeling Language (UML).**

# Chapter Outline

# 5.1 INTRODUCTION

All software, especially large pieces of software produced by many people, should be produced using some kind of methodology. Even small pieces of software developed by one person can be improved by keeping a methodology in mind.

A methodology is a systematic way of doing things. It is a repeatable process that we can follow from the earliest stages of software development (the germ of an idea or a new business opportunity) through to the maintenance of an installed system. As well as the process, a methodology should specify what we're expected to produce as we follow the process (and what form the products should take). A methodology will also include advice or techniques for resource management, planning, scheduling and other management tasks.

Good, widely available methodologies are essential for a mature software industry – the alternatives are highly unsatisfactory. The worst alternative is downright chaos, where members of the development team run around in a panic, wondering how on earth they're going to come up with the latest system that they've been told to implement. Only slightly better is the situation where an *ad hoc* development process is designed by amateur methodologists within one organization – such in-house efforts need to be learnt by every newcomer to the organization and they're useless to anyone moving on.

Although most methodologies are designed to cope with teams of developers producing large amounts of software, understanding the basics of a good methodology is essential for those at the other end of the scale too (lone developers working on small problems) and at all points in between. This is because:

- A methodology can help to impose discipline on the coding effort.
- Going through even the basic steps of a methodology increases our understanding of the problem, improving the quality of our solution.
- Writing lines of code is only one of the many activities in software development: performing some of the other activities helps us to spot conceptual and practical mistakes before we commit them to source code.
- At every stage, a methodology specifies what we should do next, so we're not left scratching our heads, thinking 'Okay, what now?'
- A methodology helps us to produce code that is more extensible (easier to change), more reusable (applicable to other problems) and easier to debug (because it has more documentation).

Large development projects also benefit from:

- Documentation: All methodologies promote thorough documentation of every stage of the development effort, so that the finished system is not an impenetrable monolith.

- Reduced latency: Since the workflows, activities, roles and inter-dependencies are better understood, there is less opportunity for human (and other) resources to lie idle for want of something to do.
- Improved chances of delivery on time and within budget.
- Better communication between users, sales people, managers and developers: A good methodology is based on logic and common sense, so it will be easy for all participants to grasp the basics; thus, we have a more orderly development, with less scope for misunderstanding and wasted effort.
- Repeatability: Since we have well-defined activities, similar projects should be delivered to similar time-scales and with similar costs. If we produce similar systems over and over again for different customers (e-commerce shop fronts, for example) we can streamline the methodology in order to concentrate solely on the unique aspects of the latest development; eventually we might automate parts of the development and even sell the automations to third parties (think of a 'shop front in a box' product).
- More accurate costing: When asked 'How much will it cost?', there will be less temptation to reply 'How much have you got?'

A good methodology will address at least the following issues:

- Planning: Deciding what needs to be done.
- Scheduling: Mapping out when things will be done.
- Resourcing: Estimating and acquiring the human, software, hardware and other resources that are needed.
- Workflows: The subprocesses within the wider development effort (for example, designing the system architecture, modeling the problem domain and planning the development effort).
- Activities: Individual tasks within a workflow, such as testing a component, drawing a class diagram or detailing a use case, too small or indefinable to be a workflow in their own right.
- Roles: The parts played by personnel within the methodology (developer, tester or sales person).
- Artifacts: The products of the development effort: pieces of software, design documents, training plans and manuals.
- Education: Deciding how to train personnel, if necessary, to fulfill their required roles; deciding how end users (staff, customers, sales people) will learn how to use the new system.

For the purposes of this book, we won't be looking at the details of an industrial methodology – that would require a book in its own right. Instead, we'll use a special-purpose methodology, called **Ripple**, which is derived from but is rather simpler than the **Rational Unified Process**. Before we examine Ripple, we need to have an idea of the processes, activities and artifacts of software development in general.

# 5.2 CLASSICAL PHASES IN SOFTWARE PRODUCTION

So, what does software development involve? There are a number of phases common to every development, regardless of methodology, starting with requirements capture and ending with maintenance. With the traditional approach, you're expected to move forward gracefully from one phase to the other. With the modern approach, on the other hand, you're allowed to perform each phase more than once and in any order.

The list below describes the common phases in software development – you may have seen different names for some of these, but the essentials remain the same. At this stage, we're interested in the intent of the phases rather than details of how you might actually go about performing them. Be warned, though, that some methodologists combine requirements and analysis, while others combine analysis and design.

## 5.2.1 Requirements

Requirements capture is about discovering what we're going to achieve with our new piece of software and has two aspects. **Business modeling** involves understanding the context in which our software will operate – if we don't understand the context, we have little chance of producing something to enhance that context. The sort of question we ask during the business modeling phase is 'How does a customer purchase a television from this shop?'

**System requirements modeling** (or **functional specification**) means deciding what capabilities the new software will have and writing down those capabilities. We need to be clear about what our software will do and what it won't do, so that the development doesn't veer off into irrelevant areas and we know both when we've finished and whether we've been successful. The sort of question we ask during the system requirements modeling phase is 'How do we update the inventory system when a television has been purchased?'

## 5.2.2 Analysis

Analysis means understanding what we're dealing with. Before we can design a solution, we need to be clear about the relevant entities, their properties and their inter-relationships. We also need to be able to verify our understanding. This can involve customers and end users, since they're likely to be subject-matter experts. The sorts of question we ask during the analysis phase are 'What products do we sell in this shop? Where do they come from? How much do they cost?'

## 5.2.3 Design

In the design phase, we work out how to solve the problem. In other words, we make decisions, based on experience, estimation and intuition, about what software we will write and how we will deploy it. **System design** breaks the system down into logical subsystems (processes) and physical subsystems (computers and networks), decides how machines will communicate, chooses the right technologies for the job, and so on. The sort of decision we make during the system design phase is 'We're going to use an intranet and the Java Messaging Service for communicating sales results to head office.' In **subsystem design** we decide how to cut each logical subsystem into effective, efficient and feasible code. The sort of decision we make during the subsystem design phase is 'Line items in an inventory are implemented as a hash table, keyed by part number.'

## 5.2.4 Specification

Specification is an often-ignored, or at least often-neglected, phase. The term specification is used in different ways by different developers. For example, the output of the requirements phase is a specification of what the system must be able to do; the output of analysis is a specification of what we're dealing with; and so on. In this book, the term is used to mean 'describing the expected behavior of our programming components'. (Since the specification techniques described are performed on classes of objects, some of the confusion can be avoided by using the term **class specification**.) A class specification is a clear, unambiguous description of the way the components of our software should be used and how they will behave if used properly. The sort of statement we make during the specification phase is 'If the shop assistant object is logged on, it can ask the store object for today's special offers; in return, it receives a list of products, sorted in alphabetical order'.

This book gives special attention to specification, because of the crucial underlying principle of **Design by Contract**. The idea behind a contract is that whenever one piece of software calls upon the services of another, both the caller and the called have obligations to fulfill. Bearing software contracts in mind is useful at all stages of development.

Specification can be used in the following ways:

- As a basis for designing test software to exercise the system.
- To demonstrate that our software is correct (this is desirable for life-critical applications).
- To document our software components to the extent that they could be implemented by third parties.
- To describe how our code can be reused safely by other applications.

### 5.2.5 Implementation

This is where we do the donkey work, writing pieces of code that work together to form subsystems, which in turn collaborate to form the whole system. The sort of task we carry out during the implementation phase is 'Write the method bodies for the Inventory class, in such a way that they conform to their specification'. Although we would expect most of the difficult coding decisions to have been made before we reach this phase (during design), there is still plenty of scope for creativity: although the public interfaces of our software components will have been well designed, specified and documented, programmers have free rein to decide on the inner workings. As long as the end result is effective and correct, everyone will be happy.

### 5.2.6 Testing

When our software is complete, it must be tested against the system requirements to see if it fits the original goals. The sort of question we ask during the testing phase is 'Can a shop assistant use the till interface to sell a toaster, decreasing the product's inventory as a side-effect?' As well as this kind of conformance testing, it's a good idea to see if our software can be broken via its external interfaces – this helps to protect us against accidental or malicious abuse of the system when it's been deployed.

It is a good idea for programmers to perform small tests as they go along, to improve the quality of the code that they deliver. Generally speaking, however, major tests should not be designed, implemented or carried out by the developers who wrote the software. To understand why, consider buying a new house and spending vast amounts of time and money refurbishing it from top to bottom. It's unlikely that you would want to whack the structures and fixtures with a sledgehammer to see if they're durable, ask passing strangers whether they think that you have good taste or pretend to be a burglar to see if you can break in. These are exactly the kinds of things that we need to be doing during software testing. (It helps if members of the test team have a cruel streak.)

### 5.2.7 Deployment

In the deployment phase, we're concerned with getting the hardware and software to the end users, along with manuals and training materials. This may be a complex process, involving a gradual, planned transition from the old way of working to the new. The sort of task we carry out during the deployment phase is 'Run the program setup.exe on each server machine and follow the instructions that appear'.

### 5.2.8 Maintenance

When our system is deployed, it has only just been born. A long life stretches before it, during which it has to stand up to everyday use – this is where the real testing happens.

The sort of problem we discover during the maintenance phase is 'When the log-on window opens, it still contains the last password entered.'

As software developers, we're normally interested in maintenance because of the **faults** (bugs) that are found in our software. We must find the faults and remove them as quickly as possible, rolling out fixed versions of the software to keep the end users happy. As well as faults, our users may discover deficiencies (things that the system should do but doesn't) and extra requirements (things that would improve the system). From the business point of view, we would hope to fix and improve our software over time to maintain competitive advantage.

## 5.2.9 Key Questions

These key questions will help you to remember the purpose of each of the software development phases:

- Requirements phase:
  'What is our context?'
  'What are we trying to achieve?'
- Analysis phase:
  'What entities are we dealing with?'
  'How can we be sure we have the right ones?'
- System design phase:
  'How are we going to solve the problem?'
  'What hardware and software will we need in the finished system?'
- Subsystem design phase:
  'How are we going to implement the solution?'
  'What will the source code and supporting files look like?'
- Specification phase:
  'What rules govern the interfaces between the system components?'
  'Can we remove ambiguity and ensure correctness?'
- Implementation phase:
  'How can we code the components to meet the specification?'
  'How do we write stylish code?'
- Testing phase:
  'Does the finished system satisfy the requirements?'
  'Can we break the system?'
- Deployment phase:
  'What do the system administrators have to do?'
  'How can we educate the end users?'

- Maintenance phase:
  'Can we find and fix the faults?'
  'Can we improve the system?'

# 5.3 SOFTWARE ENGINEERING AND THE WATERFALL METHODOLOGY

During the 1970s, software gurus gave much thought to the problem of how best to write software. How could they replace *ad hoc*, proprietary mechanisms with scalable, portable methodologies? What the gurus came up with was **software engineering**. The idea was that software production could be like building a real-world structure, such as a road bridge. With the help of physics, engineering is systematic: if we follow the rules, we will deliver a working product, complete with safety margins to protect against abnormal conditions.

There are some obvious drawbacks to this analogy. Most programming is done with **imperative** programming languages that require the programmer to tell the computer exactly what to do – statement by statement, branch by branch, function by function. This is analogous to the bridge engineer having to tell a piece of steel exactly how to behave, rather than relying on the laws of physics. And that's not all: the programmer also has to assemble the data piece by piece. Can you imagine a bridge builder having to assemble the bridge's road surface, stone by stone, and then telling each stone exactly which other stones it was touching?

As well as requiring the programmer to be precise about behavior and structure, imperative languages don't cope well with imprecise data. Generally speaking, if a piece of data in the system is slightly inaccurate, the system might not behave as expected. In contrast, a bridge builder can happily connect girders using rivets that are all slightly different in size: the engineer can count on **tolerances** and **margins of error**, but the programmer can't.

These drawbacks did not prevent the growth in popularity of software engineering and methodologies grew up around the assumption that software production could be systematic and predictable. This led to the so-called **waterfall methodology** (see Figure 5.1).

Development flows smoothly over the classical phases (requirements, analysis, system design, etc.), with each phase being completed satisfactorily before the next phase is attempted. It's easy to plan (because the plan is similar every time) and it's easy to schedule (use the complexity of the problem and the number of developers to work out how long the development will take, then divide the result by the total number of phases...). The waterfall methodology allows us to have developers with different kinds of expertise at each stage (hence the classical roles of business analyst, systems analyst, designer, programmer, tester and system administrator). Each team of specialists slogs away during their own phase, until

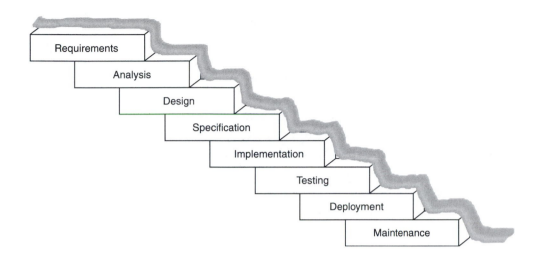

**Figure 5.1: Waterfall development**

they're sure that they have solved their part of the problem; then they document their work, using their own jargon and notation, and pass the baton to the next team of specialists.

The waterfall methodology is a nice idea, but unrealistic. Even if we're clever enough to work out how long the development might take, before we've looked in detail at the problem, we can't tell what difficulties we will encounter along the way (bad design decisions, pernicious faults, inadequate technology, or earthquakes). So, any individual phase may take longer than expected. Also, work tends to expand to fill the time available, so the phases that precede a problem are likely to have used up all the time available to them. The net effect is that the whole project is delivered late. In practice, this is exactly what happens in the majority of cases.

The waterfall methodology may fail for other reasons too, such as **analysis paralysis** – the analysts are reluctant to sign off their documentation because they can't decide whether they've understood and documented the system entities well enough to allow the designers to do their job. To be fair, this kind of problem is not restricted to analysts: the designers might be worried that their design is inadequate; the specifiers might worry that their specification is too ambiguous to be coded; and so on, leading to even more delays. In practice, it's not possible to complete each phase perfectly. Throughout the development, members of the team will discover problems with the work that's gone before. Whenever this happens, we have a tricky choice: we can return to the earlier documentation and fix it, but that would mean climbing back up the waterfall (which we're not supposed to do); or we could make a note of the problems, with the intention of repairing the documentation at the end of the project (which rarely happens, so the final documentation doesn't match the final system).

And what about the end users? Are they going to get what they want or need? The potential users of the system will be colleagues or third parties, probably paying us real money. These **customers** will presumably have been consulted during the requirements phase: we will have asked them how they currently work; we will have brainstormed the kind of system functions that could be delivered; we will have reached an understanding about what is going to be delivered and what isn't. But what if we find that we can't deliver some of the functions, because they're too difficult or we run out of time? The customers won't find out until testing or maybe even deployment – far too late to change anything. What if the project takes two years to complete? End users' requirements will normally change significantly in two years. Are we going to deliver a system that's no longer relevant? What we need is a way of involving users throughout the development, so that we don't deliver something that's a nasty surprise. We also need to reduce the time between the promised functionality and the point where we can demonstrate that functionality. But the waterfall model is too rigid to allow us to incorporate user feedback and take corrective action.

And these aren't the only problems. For example, the waterfall methodology will always suffer from being focussed on solving one particular problem – this makes it more difficult to produce reusable code. Eating an elephant is a daunting task (see Figure 5.2); if you were told to eat one, would you prefer to open wide and swallow the beast whole or to eat a manageable portion, have a rest, eat another portion, have a rest, and so on, until the whole elephant had been consumed? Waterfall development uses the first approach and attempts to produce a complete solution in one go. As we'll see, it's possible to use the second approach, delivering the solution piece by piece.

Given the large number of problems with the waterfall methodology, some of which should have been obvious at the outset, you may find it hard to believe that any software development was ever done this way. Well, it was and in some places it still is. Some corporations have been quite happy to base large developments on the waterfall methodology, integrate it into their software departments as **best practice** and base entire career ladders on it (start as programmer, get promoted to designer, then systems analyst, and so on). However, most object-oriented enthusiasts and, shall we say, enlightened corporations, prefer something rather more flexible.

Having debunked the waterfall methodology, it's only fair to point out that it is still useful in the following cases:

- When repeating a particular kind of development with only minor differences (for example, an e-commerce shop front for a particular company may only differ from the previous one in terms of product descriptions, prices, company name and logo).
- As a framework for learning the different techniques used in software development: although the waterfall methodology is too simplistic for real-world development, it does contain the classical phases in a logical order, so it's good for learning.
- As a single pass around a **spiral** methodology.

**Figure 5.2: Eating an elephant**

- As a framework to support an **iterative** methodology.
- For the quick development of small projects with small numbers of developers, as in **prototyping**, **production prototyping**, **proof-of-concept** or Rapid Application Development (RAD).

Four new styles of programming have been developed as a result of the simplicity and power of objects, the reuse of code in new applications, and the advent of **application builders**:

- A software **prototype**, just like an engineering prototype, is something that we build in order to try out some of the functions of the finished product. A prototype doesn't need to be elegant, or industrial strength, because it's just an experiment. We should set aside a prototype once it has served its purpose and start afresh.
- A **production prototype** is similar to a prototype, except that we retain some or all of the code through to completion of the project.
- A **proof-of-concept** is a project or a piece of software designed to demonstrate the feasibility of some technology, or group of technologies. For example, we might need to convince a

customer that we're qualified to take on a particular project or we might need to convince management to adopt a new approach to software production.

- The phrase **Rapid Application Development** (RAD) was coined by enthusiasts of object orientation to mean building a system more quickly than with traditional techniques. As object-oriented systems became practical in the 1980s, object enthusiasts were able to impress traditional developers (and managers) with how quickly they could assemble small systems.

An application builder is a tool that allows the programmer to assemble software in the same way that a computer manufacturer assembles hardware. As time has passed, application builders have employed larger and larger components so that systems can be constructed more quickly than before. In most cases, objects destined for an application builder need to have a particular kind of interface in order to work properly. This means that the programmer needs to follow predefined style guidelines rather than designing their objects any way they see fit. For example, Java application builders expect to work with objects that follow the **JavaBeans** guidelines [Campione *et al.* 98].

# 5.4 NEW METHODOLOGIES

Before we can replace the waterfall methodology with something better, we need to accept that it is impossible to develop a piece of software in one pass. However hard we try, the first time around our software will be incomplete or imperfect or both. Therefore, we need to perform the classical phases of software development several times, adding to and perfecting the system as we go.

## 5.4.1 Spiral Methodology

One way to look at this is as a **spiral methodology** (see Figure 5.3). We start, as ever, with requirements capture, which may be relatively complete or rather vague at this stage; next, we perform some exploratory analysis to increase our understanding of what it is that we're dealing with; then we sketch out a system design that we feel will fit the requirements and design part of the system; then, despite the fact that all the preceding phases are incomplete, we write some code. Once we've finished our initial coding effort we can try out what we have so far, perhaps by running some informal tests or by showing what we have to our **sponsors** (end users, managers and customers paying for the system).

By the time we've been through the cycle once, we've increased our understanding of the problem domain and our understanding of the proposed solution. We've also involved our sponsors, so that they can correct any misunderstanding of the business or the functionality that they expect to see in the final system. Armed with our new body of knowledge, we

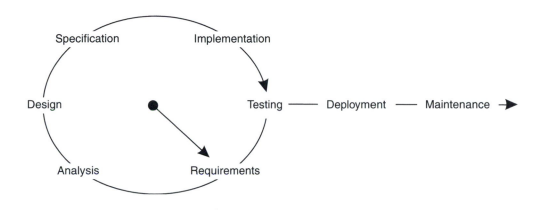

**Figure 5.3: Spiral development methodology**

can go around the spiral again: now we flesh out the requirements; we're more thorough (and correct) with our analysis; we reinforce the system design; we add detail to the subsystems; and then we write some more code, code that stands more chance of meeting the requirements.

Once our system is complete, perhaps after three or four spirals, we can perform rigorous testing and deploy the system. Compared to the waterfall methodology, we're now working more like a sculptor creating a statue: we put together a basic framework of chicken-wire, then we add clay, layer by layer, until we achieve the desired effect. As we work: it becomes clearer and clearer how long our project will take; all our sponsors can see that progress is being made; and our confidence that we can deliver a good result grows. We finish when everyone is happy.

It looks as though the spiral methodology has fewer problems than the waterfall methodology: it involves our sponsors throughout the life cycle; everyone can see that we're on track; it's less rigid (we can tune the number of revolutions and how long each one takes). Altogether, it's a better fit to the creative nature of software development, as opposed to the engineering nature of building a bridge.

The spiral methodology isn't perfect though. The trouble is that we've simply attacked the waterfall by doing everything three or four times, which means that, although the problems have got smaller, they haven't gone away altogether. We still have some inflexibility, because we're supposed to proceed in an orderly manner through the classical phases; if we find mistakes, we can't fix them until the next revolution. Therefore, the spiral methodology on its own is not much use – we need to combine it with something else.

## 5.4.2 Iterative Methodology

So how do we improve the spiral methodology? To extend our sculpture analogy, the spiral methodology forces us to complete each layer of clay before we go on to the next. For

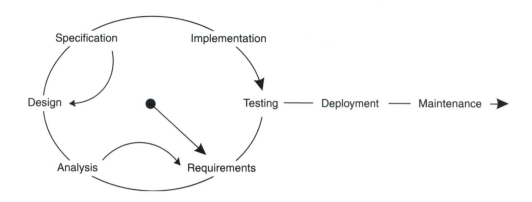

**Figure 5.4: Iterative development methodology**

example, let's say that our sculpture is going to be of a person. Having put the first layer of clay on the head, what if we decide that we want to work on the nose for a while before moving on to the rest of the body? What if, having added the torso, we decide that the forehead is now too narrow and warrants some immediate attention?

What we need is a methodology that allows us to iterate over the phases, moving backwards and forwards, or round and round, as the need arises. This leads to the **iterative methodology** depicted in Figure 5.4. (Here, iterations are shown taking place within a spiral, but they could also be applied to a waterfall.) Now, we have a much more natural way of massaging our software from its early stages into a well-formed, elegant whole that satisfies all the sponsors. But, you're probably wondering, how do we avoid chaos? We have at least three life-savers here:

- The classical phases remind us what we should be doing at each stage and in which general direction we should be moving.
- The artifacts (diagrams, descriptions, code, etc.) that we produce as we work within the classical phases do not get thrown away but are gradually improved as we move towards deployment.
- The software production tools that support our chosen methodology and the notations help us to ensure that the artifacts are consistent and kept in one place.

But we still have a problem. With the iterative and spiral methodologies, we're still trying to eat the elephant: we're still trying to deliver a complete system for deployment. So, we need to add a final element: increments.

## 5.4.3 Incremental Methodology

Let's return to our sculpture analogy one last time. If we're asked to produce a family of sculptures – the parents, the kids, the cat, the dog – it's a good idea to deliver one sculpture at a time, so that our sponsors can see our progress as each piece is delivered; we get to sign off each piece of work and concentrate on the next; we can ask for incremental payment. In software development, this is the **incremental methodology** (see Figure 5.5).

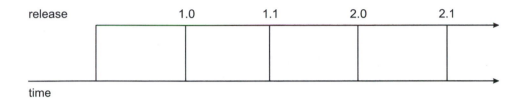

**Figure 5.5: Incremental development**

With the incremental methodology, we aim to deliver version 1.0 of our system with basic, critical functionality. Then, some time later, we deliver version 1.1 with additional functionality (as a replacement for version 1.0). Next, we might deliver version 2.0 with a whole raft of changes. And so on, throughout the lifetime of the system. Not only do we acknowledge from the start that we need several bites at the elephant, but we're keeping up with changing requirements and a shifting marketplace. As you probably know from your own experience as a software purchaser, incremental delivery is what tends to happen in practice anyway, whether or not we plan for it. In other words, if we try to swallow the elephant whole, we fail. By planning for incremental delivery, we turn the perception of failure into a perception of wisdom.

However, we must avoid at all costs the nightmare scenario of rewriting all our code for each new increment – this would be like an endless series of separate waterfalls. Thus, good analysis, good design, reusable code and extensibility become critical.

## 5.4.4 Combining the Methodologies

So, the waterfall methodology is inadequate in most cases – although it does have the phases in the correct logical order – and the alternative methodologies (spiral, iterative and incremental) all have desirable properties but none of them is good enough on its own. So, we must combine all four in some way, but how?

At the highest level, we know from the incremental methodology that we must plan a succession of increments. Within each increment, the spiral methodology suggests that we should have at least two attempts to produce each increment. Within each spiral, the waterfall methodology specifies the phases and the order in which they occur. Within each mini-waterfall, the iterative methodology allows us to repeat phases, or combinations of phases, as we see fit (for example, several cycles of requirements and analysis); the iterative methodology also allows us to fix a problem as soon as we discover it (for example, we might discover during subsystem design that the system design makes some piece of functionality impossible, so we fix the system design before we carry on). The combination of the methodologies is shown in Figure 5.6.

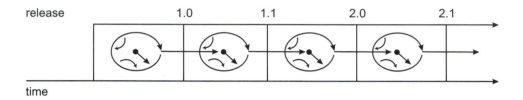

**Figure 5.6: Combining spiral, iterative and incremental development**

None of this discussion indicates how we should plan and schedule a particular project, which depends on the size of the project, the number of developers, the experience of the developers, the experience of the managers in planning and scheduling this kind of development, and so on. As far as this book is concerned, detailed planning and scheduling are management issues rather than software issues, so they're not covered. Suffice to say that, in object orientation, there should be no absolutes: it's quite reasonable for the managers, mentors and experienced developers to decide on the increments, spirals, iterations and artifacts that are appropriate for each new development. Then, the planning must be adapted in the light of increasing knowledge and changing requirements.

Although most theorists agree on the nature of the waterfall methodology, there is some disagreement about the terminology used for the others. In this book, you've seen particular definitions of the spiral, iterative and incremental methodologies but you should be aware that other people use these terms differently or even as synonyms. In particular, 'spiral' is sometimes referred to as 'iterative'. However, the ideas discussed here are equally valid whatever name you give them.

# 5.5 OBJECT-ORIENTED METHODOLOGIES

All object-orientation experts agree that a good methodology is essential for software development, especially when working in teams. Thus, quite a few methodologies have been invented over the last decade. Broadly speaking, all object-oriented methodologies are alike – they have similar phases and similar artifacts – but there are many small differences.

Object-oriented methodologies tend not to be too prescriptive: the developers are given some choice about whether they use a particular type of diagram, for example. Therefore, the development team must select a methodology and agree which artifacts are to be produced, before they do any detailed planning or scheduling.

In general, each methodology addresses:

- The philosophy behind each of the phases.
- The workflows and the individual activities within each phase.
- The artifacts that should be produced (diagrams, textual descriptions and code).
- Dependencies between the artifacts.
- Notations for the different kinds of artifact.
- The need to model static structure and dynamic behavior.

Static modeling involves deciding what the logical or physical parts of the system should be and how they should be connected together. Dynamic modeling is about deciding how the static parts should collaborate. Roughly speaking, static modeling describes how we construct and initialize the system, while dynamic modeling describes how the system should behave when it's running. Typically, we produce at least one static model and one dynamic model during each phase of the development.

Some methodologies, especially the more comprehensive ones, have alternative development paths, geared to different types and sizes of development. The methodology used in this book, **Ripple**, is geared towards learning what's involved in all software development, large or small, but it is applicable to the real world as well.

## 5.5.1 UML, RUP and XP

By the mid-1990s, the best-known methodologies were those invented by Ivar Jacobson [Jacobson *et al.* 92], James Rumbaugh [Rumbaugh *et al.* 91] and Grady Booch [Booch 93]. Each had his own consulting company using his own methodology and his own notation. By 1996, Jacobson and Rumbaugh had joined Rational Corporation (founded by Booch), and they had developed a set of notations which became known as the **Unified Modeling Language (UML)** [OMG 03a]. The 'three amigos', as they have become known, donated UML to the Object Management Group (OMG) for safekeeping and improvement. OMG (www.omg.org) is a not-for-profit industry consortium, founded in 1989 to promote open standards for enterprise-level object technology; their other well-known work is **CORBA** [OMG 04].

Some developers consider UML simply as a notation to be used for brainstorming and high-level documentation. Others consider UML to be a pictorial programming language, generating code from it or synthesizing it from existing code. UML was used as a notation during brainstorming of the case study for this book. At the end, the main diagrams were made to match the finished code exactly – thus, the end result looks the same as it would have done if UML had been used as a pictorial programming language.

Once UML was in safe hands, the three amigos set about designing a methodology that drew on the best aspects of their individual work. Within a couple of years, they had come up with their own spiral, iterative and incremental method called the **Rational Unified Process (RUP)** [Jacobson *et al.* 99]. As you might expect, RUP is not the only methodology available, nor even the only one that uses UML as the notation.

Another popular methodology is **extreme programming (XP)** [Beck 99]. XP is referred to as an **agile methodology** because it is responsive to change. XP is distinguished by two radical ideas: **pair programming** and **test-driven development**. With pair programming, all development is carried out by two people sitting in front of the screen rather than one – the idea is that, rather than improving the speed at which software is produced, pair programming improves the *quality* of the software (it also helps developers to accelerate their growth by the sharing of ideas). According to fans of test-driven development, continuous testing is so important that not only should it be done by the developers themselves, but the tests should be written before the code.

## 5.5.2 The Need for Development Tools

To be effective, any spiral, iterative and incremental methodology requires an end-to-end development tool. The need to amend project artifacts iteratively is a strong justification for the use of a software tool. Such a tool should allow members of the project team to produce the artifacts and then to store them. More specifically, it should support:

- Traceability: Recording the connections between an artifact and the artifacts derived from it, for example, recording which particular subsystem gave rise to a group of implemented classes. Most traceability information will be entered by developers rather than inferred by the tool.
- Change history: Recording the changes that were made to artifacts, who made the changes and when. Where feasible (that is, with textual artifacts) the tool should be able to provide a summary of the differences between one edition of the artifact and another.
- Multiuser access control: Making sure that simultaneous access to artifacts doesn't cause problems. There are three mechanisms relevant here: authorization (controlling who can read the artifacts and who can edit them); multiuser read–single-user edit (only allowing one developer at a time to edit an artifact or group of artifacts, but allowing all authorized users to see the unedited version); versioning (allowing any number of developers to edit an artifact, each producing a distinct **version** of the artifact – at any time, only one version will be the official one).
- Reduced redundancy: Ensuring that we never have to update anything in more than one place. Typically, information will appear in several artifacts at once. If we have a tool, it can treat the artifacts as alternative projections on a single model.

- Consistency checking: Ensuring that an artifact is consistent with related artifacts. It's not always possible to enforce consistency. For example, in an ideal world, a tool would be able to check that the code written for a method conforms to its specification, but modern computers simply can't do that (it's just too difficult, or even impossible). Even in cases where the tool can enforce consistency (or traceability for that matter), the developer must be allowed to disable the check. For example, one developer might want to carry analysis classes through to the design phase, while another might prefer to start design with a new set of classes altogether: any tool that requires every analysis class to appear in the design model would be a help to the first kind of developer and a hindrance to the second.
- Networked operation: Providing access to all artifacts from any machine on the project network. These days, the best foundation for networked operation is TCP/IP, the basis of all protocols that operate over the Internet and individual intranets.
- Testing the artifacts that we produce, as we go along. The most obvious case is where implementation code is tested for effectiveness and correctness, but the principle can be applied to other artifacts too (as in the case of recording the results of design review).

Rational Corporation developed a tool called Rose, based on RUP and UML. Rose became probably the best-known object-oriented development tool. In 2003, Rational was bought by IBM and the tool has been reworked as a set of modular products (and is now called Rational Application Developer). Of course, there are many development tools available – Rational products are only mentioned here because of the historical perspective.

# 5.6 RIPPLE OVERVIEW

In this book, you will find object-oriented versions of all the classical phases of software development and you will see how they fit into an object-oriented methodology. Because object orientation is so accessible, developers can be involved in all of the phases; customers can be involved in the early stages, which helps developers to do their job; and managers are not shut out of the developers' world, so communication is improved.

We have seen how the classical phases fit into the ideal object-oriented methodology – one that draws on the best aspects of the spiral, iterative and incremental approaches. In subsequent chapters, we'll look at each of the major phases that are carried out before the release of code: requirements, analysis, system design, subsystem design, specification and testing. Implementation won't be covered extensively, because that would require detailed knowledge of a particular programming language. Design patterns will be discussed, because they allow us to take implementation ideas off the shelf.

By the end of this book, you will find that you have traveled around one spiral of an initial increment (version 1.0, after an iterative spiral, if you like). Although this may look suspiciously like the waterfall methodology dressed up as something more elegant, it's simply the nature of a book: content laid out end to end with no repetition. It can't be emphasized enough that, when you come to try these techniques for yourself, you must be prepared to spiral, iterate and deliver incrementally.

The case study used from here on, **iCoot**, was certainly not developed in a waterfall fashion. The artifacts included in Appendix B resulted from two increments, each comprising a number of iterative spirals.

Since UML, the *de facto* standard notation, is used throughout this book, you can be sure that the diagrams that you see will be similar to the ones that you'll encounter in the real world. For Ripple, UML notation is employed whenever possible.

UML has 13 types of diagram. The UML specification doesn't say where these diagrams should be used in any particular methodology – we're free to use whichever we think is appropriate at any stage.

- Use case diagrams categorize the ways in which a system is used.
- Class diagrams show classes and how they can be fitted together (they can also show objects).
- Object diagrams show only objects and how they can be fitted together.
- Activity diagrams show activity by humans or objects in a similar way to a flow chart.
- State machine diagrams show the various states of any object with an interesting or complicated life cycle.
- Communication diagrams show the messages sent between objects in some scenario.
- Sequence diagrams show similar information to communication diagrams, but emphasizing sequences rather than connections.
- Package diagrams show how related classes are grouped together, for the benefit of developers.
- Deployment diagrams show machines, processes and deployed artifacts for a finished system.
- Component diagrams show reusable components (objects or subsystems) and their interfaces.
- Interaction overview diagrams show individual steps of an activity using sequence diagrams.
- Timing diagrams show precise timing constraints for messages and object states.
- Composite structure diagrams show how objects fit together in an aggregation or composition, showing interfaces and collaborating objects.

Table 5.1 summarizes the artifacts of Ripple, organized by phase. As you can see, some of these artifacts are found in UML and some are not. This is simply because UML doesn't cover everything; to a large extent, it just allows us to draw pictures of our code. For the Ripple artifacts that are not covered by UML, alternative notation is used. Despite the fact that this notation is nonstandard, its content is based on widely accepted theory and practice.

## Table 5.1: Ripple artifacts by phase

| Phase | | Artifacts | UML |
|---|---|---|---|
| Genesis | | Mission statement or informal requirements | No |
| | | Roles | No |
| | | Responsibilities | No |
| | | Project plan | No |
| | | Workbook | No |
| | | Glossary (update throughout) | No |
| | | Test plan | No |
| Requirements | Business | Actor list (with descriptions) | No |
| | | Use case list (with descriptions) | No |
| | | Use case details | No |
| | | Activity diagrams (optional) | Yes |
| | | Communication diagrams (optional) | Yes |
| | System | Actor list (with descriptions) | No |
| | | Use case list (with descriptions) | No |
| | | Use case details | No |
| | | Use case diagram | Yes |
| | | Use case survey | No |
| | | User interface sketches | No |
| Analysis | | Class diagram | Yes |
| | | Communication diagrams | Yes |
| Design | System | Deployment diagram | Yes |
| | | Layer diagram | No |
| | Subsystem | Class diagrams | Yes |
| | | Sequence diagrams | Yes |
| | | Database schema | No |
| Class Specification | | Comments | No |
| Implementation | | Source code | No |
| Testing | | Test reports | No |
| Deployment | | Shrink wrapped solution | No |
| | | Manuals | No |
| | | Training material | No |
| Maintenance | | Fault reports | No |
| | | Increment plans | No |

Ripple is described progressively as we go through the chapters, but if you would like to read a quick summary at any point, go to Appendix 1. Since this book has an emphasis on software-related artifacts, the focus is on requirements, analysis, design and specification. Glossaries, test plans and mission statements are also discussed. Other issues, such as management, implementation, deployment and maintenance won't be covered in any detail.

Although you will see an example of an activity diagram and a state machine diagram, they're not used widely here and are generally considered optional. Also, not all of the UML diagram types are used. Component diagrams, interaction overview diagrams, timing diagrams and composite structure diagrams are simply not necessary for the purposes of this book. Most of these types of diagram can be expressed using the other diagrams, apart from timing diagrams, which are more useful for the design of real-time software and hardware.

As well as the diagrams, UML has a class specification language called **Object Constraint Language (OCL)**. OCL won't be covered, because it would require an entire book in its own right; however, in Chapter 12, you will find a small example, to give you a taster. Most of the specification discussion is informal, relating to comments in code and design artifacts.

In the next few sections, you'll see examples of some of the UML diagrams that are used for Ripple. You should bear in mind, though, that UML, like most comprehensive standards, is rather large. Therefore, for practical reasons, you will be shown only the fundamentals of the notation, with some of the finer detail left out.

Whenever you look at one of the diagrams in this book, bear in mind that UML allows us to suppress information that is not relevant to the discussion. For example, just because you only see labeled boxes when a class is being discussed, don't assume that the class has no attributes or operations.

## 5.6.1 Use Case Diagram

A **use case** is a static description of some way in which a system or a business is used, by its customers, its users or by other systems. A **use case diagram** shows how system use cases are related to each other and how the users can get at them. Each bubble on a use case diagram represents a use case and each stick person represents a user. Use case diagrams (static artifacts) are described in Chapter 6.

Figure 5.7 depicts a car rental store accessible over the Internet. From this picture, we can extract a lot of information quite easily. For example, an Assistant can make a reservation; a Customer can look for car models; Members can log on; users must be logged on before they can make reservations; and so on.

Each use case is more than just a title such as U7:Make Reservation or U13:Look for Car Models; it must include the actual steps involved in using the system or business. Although

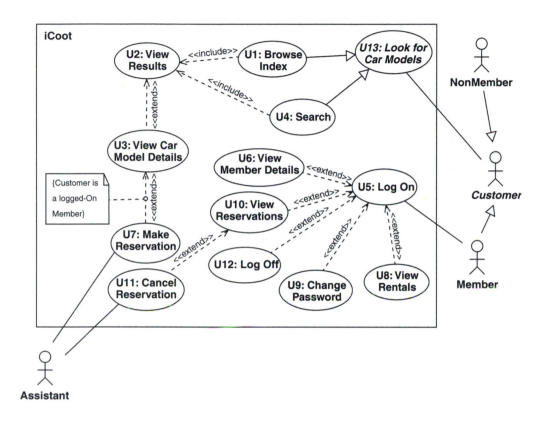

**Figure 5.7: A use case diagram**

UML specifies a notation for use case diagrams, it doesn't do so for the steps of the use case itself. RUP refers to the steps of a use case, and a few other bits and pieces, as **use case details**.

The details for U3:View Car Model Details are shown in Figure 5.8. It should be easy for you to appreciate that viewing car model details involves a customer selecting a car model, requesting its details, and then receiving specific information about the car model in return. Use case details (dynamic artifacts) are described in Chapter 6.

## 5.6.2 Class Diagram (Analysis Level)

A **class diagram** shows which classes exist in the business (during analysis) or in the system itself (during subsystem design). Figure 5.9 shows an example of an analysis-level class diagram, with each class represented as a labeled box. Class diagrams (static artifacts) are introduced in Chapter 7.

As well as the classes themselves, a class diagram shows how objects of these classes can be connected together. For example, Figure 5.9 shows that a CarModel has inside it a CarModelDetails, referred to as its details.

U3: View Car Model Details. (Extends U2, extended by U7.)
Preconditions: None.
1. Customer selects one of the matching Car Models.
2. Customer requests details of the selected Car Model.
3. iCoot displays details of the selected Car Model
   (make, engine size, price, description, advert and poster).
4. If Customer is a logged-on Member, extend with U7.
Postconditions: iCoot has displayed details of selected Car Models.
NonFunctional Requirements:
r1. Adverts should be displayed using a streaming protocol
   rather than requiring a download.

**Figure 5.8: Details of a system use case**

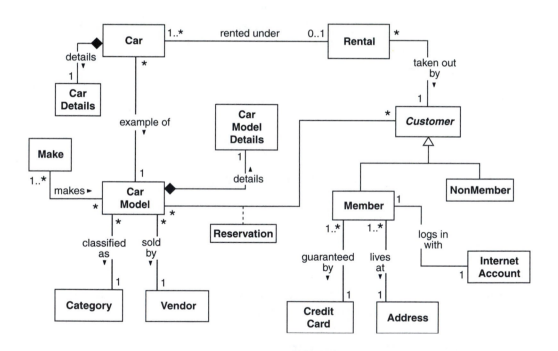

**Figure 5.9: A class diagram at the analysis level**

## 5.6.3 Communication Diagram

A **communication diagram**, as its name suggests, shows collaborations between objects. The one shown in Figure 5.10 describes the process of reserving a car model over the Internet: A Member tells the MemberUI to reserve a CarModel; the MemberUI tells the ReservationHome to

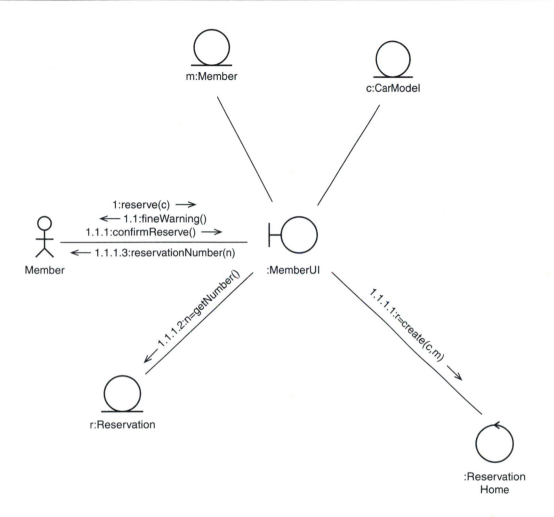

**Figure 5.10: A communication diagram**

create a Reservation for the given CarModel and the current Member; the MemberUI then asks the new Reservation for its number and returns this to the Member. Communication diagrams (dynamic artifacts) are described in Chapter 7.

## 5.6.4 Deployment Diagram

A **deployment diagram** (see Figure 5.11) shows how the finished system will be deployed on one or more machines. A deployment diagram can include all sorts of features such as machines, processes, files and dependencies.

Figure 5.11 shows that any number of HTMLClient nodes (each hosting a WebBrowser) and GUIClient nodes communicate with two server machines, each hosting a WebServer and

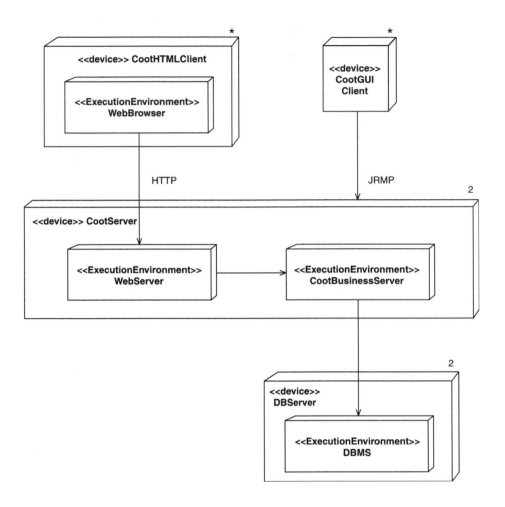

**Figure 5.11: A deployment diagram**

a CootBusinessServer; each WebServer communicates with a CootBusinessServer; and each CootBusinessServer communicates with a DBMS running on one of two DBServer nodes. Deployment diagrams (static artifacts) are described in Chapter 8.

## 5.6.5 Class Diagram (Design Level)

The class diagram shown in Figure 5.12 uses the same notation as the one introduced in Figure 5.9. The only difference is that design-level class diagrams tend to use more of the available notation, because they're more detailed. This one expands on part of the analysis class diagram to show methods, constructors and navigability. Design-level class diagrams (static artifacts) are described in Chapter 10.

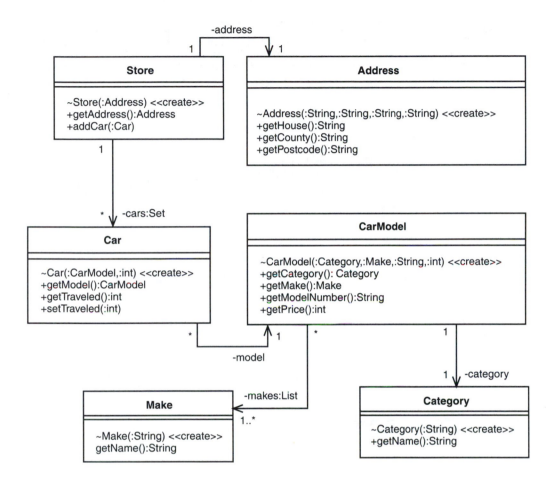

**Figure 5.12: A design-level class diagram**

## 5.6.6 Sequence Diagram

A **sequence diagram** shows interactions between objects. Communication diagrams also show interactions between objects, but in a way that emphasizes links rather than sequence. In this book, sequence diagrams are used during subsystem design, but they're equally applicable to dynamic modeling during analysis, system design and even requirements capture.

The diagram in Figure 5.13 specifies how a Member can log off from the system. Messages are shown as arrows flowing between vertical bars that represent objects (each object is named at the top of its bar).

Time flows down the page on a sequence diagram. So, Figure 5.13 specifies, in brief: a Member asks the AuthenticationServlet to logoff; the AuthenticationServlet passes the request on

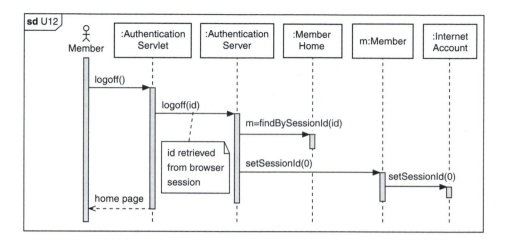

**Figure 5.13: A sequence diagram from the design phase**

to the AuthenticationServer, reading the id from the browser session; the AuthenticationServer finds the corresponding Member object and tells it to set its session id to 0; the Member passes this request on to its InternetAccount; finally, the Member is presented with the home page. Sequence diagrams (dynamic artifacts) are described in detail in Chapter 10.

# 5.7 SUMMARY

In this chapter, we looked at:

- The classical phases of software production – requirements, analysis, system design, subsystem design, specification, implementation, testing, deployment and maintenance – and how they can be used in a combination of spiral, iterative and incremental methodologies.

- Static modeling, which describes how we construct a system, and dynamic modeling, which describes how the system should behave when it's running.

- The UML notation and the Ripple methodology that is used in the rest of this book.

# FURTHER READING

Steve McConnell provides a good overview of managing a successful software project [McConnell 98], from planning through to testing. It is an easy read because of its high-level approach and conversational style.

The original book on Rational's Unified Process [Jacobson *et al.* 99] provides a good overview of the theory underlying RUP. For the current status of RUP, take a look at the Rational web site, www.rational.com.

For more information on XP, see [Beck 99] by one of its inventors or the following web sites: www.extremeprogramming.org and www.xprogramming.com. To find out more about agile development in general, see [Cockburn 01] and the Manifesto of Agile Software Development at www.agileManifesto.org.

The best-known introduction to UML is [Fowler 03]. Although Martin Fowler doesn't cover the whole of UML, his book is a good stepping-stone between the book you're currently reading and the UML Specification itself [OMG 03a]. For the serious UML user, the specification is still an essential tool for answering questions about obscure pieces of notation and the semantics of the language itself, so that you can ensure that your diagrams are correct. Specifications are hard to read at the best of times; with the UML Specification it can be a shock to find that UML is defined using UML, but it turns out to be a good idea: it means that the descriptions are precise; it is a good opportunity to see how UML can be used to document a large and complicated object-oriented model; and it allows you to see what is and is not legal according to the model.

# REVIEW QUESTIONS

1. Which of the following UML artifacts are used to show the distribution of processes, resources and objects in a system? Choose only one option.

    (a) Interaction diagrams.
    (b) Sequence diagrams.
    (c) Deployment diagrams.
    (d) Communication diagrams.
    (e) State machine diagrams.
    (f) Class diagrams.
    (g) Glossaries.

2. What are the traditional steps in software production? Choose all options that apply.

    (a) Maintenance.
    (b) Design.
    (c) Iteration.
    (d) Incrementation.
    (e) Deployment.
    (f) Analysis.
    (g) Requirements Capture.

(h) Testing.

(i) Reuse.

(j) Implementation.

(k) Specification.

# ANSWERS TO REVIEW QUESTIONS

1. The UML artifacts used to show the distribution of processes, resources and objects in a system are c. Deployment diagrams.

2. The traditional steps in software production are:

(a) Maintenance.

(b) Design.

(e) Deployment.

(f) Analysis.

(g) Requirements Capture.

(h) Testing.

(j) Implementation.

(k) Specification.

# II

## Understanding the Problem

# Gathering Requirements

In this chapter we'll look at the **requirements** phase of software development, detailing the starting points and introducing **use cases**. We also look at how to model the business into which our system will fit by identifying and validating business use cases.

# Learning Objectives

**Understand the purpose of the requirements phase.**

**Model the business context and system functionality.**

**Record the system requirements on a complete use case model.**

# Chapter Outline

**6**

# 6.1 INTRODUCTION

The aim of the requirements phase is twofold:

- Examine the business context: We need to clarify the reasons for wanting the software to be developed in the first place – if we can't come up with good reasons, we shouldn't write the software at all. When we've decided that we do want to produce a software system, we need to make sure that we understand the business and that our understanding matches that of our sponsors – this is also a good opportunity to clarify just who the sponsors are.
- Describe the system requirements: This involves not only deciding on the functionality of the system but also detecting any constraints – performance, development cost, resources and so on.

We would expect system requirements to form part of the requirements phase, but why do we model the business? Figure 6.1 shows the alternative to a well-defined requirements phase. These two developers start with some vague idea of the kind of system that *they* believe ought to be produced, while paying only grudging attention to their sponsors. This blinkered approach is common among novice programmers who don't yet know what they're doing, but we would hope that little of this attitude remains by the time we have become serious professionals.

**Figure 6.1: Self-taught developers**

The tendency to dive into coding is not only born of arrogance. It can come from fear: 'We're not sure we can produce what the sponsors need, but we know what we *can* produce: hopefully, once we've finished, we can persuade everyone that what we have is what they really needed in the first place'. Difficult as it may be to stay away from our keyboards, we must first make sure that we understand the business context for the new system, then work with our sponsors to agree what the system will do. The term 'sponsor' is used to mean anyone who has an interest in seeing the final system delivered: for example, the internal or external customer commissioning the system, the potential end users, the managers, and even the shareholders.

Before we even consider writing a piece of software, we must investigate the business in which the software will operate – without a thorough understanding of the business, we could hardly expect to produce something that would enhance that business. (We must be aiming to enhance what's already there, otherwise why would we go to the trouble of writing software in the first place?) The term business is used here in its loosest sense: although, admittedly, this book has a bias towards business systems in the sense of banking, administration, e-commerce and the like, most of what is presented applies equally well to scientific systems, home systems, or anything else that requires software. If you prefer, think of 'business' as 'problem domain'.

Once we have understood the business and documented our understanding as **business requirements**, we need to think about what our software will do for the users. Deciding what the system needs to be able to do and, just as importantly, what it should *not* do, will help us to focus on producing only the necessary code. Without a thorough understanding of the **system requirements**, we would risk wasting time on developing code that we're not being paid to produce. (Again, 'being paid' shouldn't be taken too literally – you may be writing a small system purely for your own benefit, in which case you'll be more concerned with not wasting your time.)

System requirements are commonly separated into two categories: functional and non-functional. Functional requirements are the things the system must be able to do, i.e. the services that it must provide in response to external stimuli, such as 'browsing the catalog' and 'reserving a car model'. Nonfunctional requirements are everything else that needs to be specified. Nonfunctional requirements might include the client Web browsers that must be supported, the use of streaming video (as opposed to downloadable files) for adverts, a user interface that can be used easily by novice Internet surfers, and so on.

# 6.2 THE BIRTH OF A SYSTEM

Every system starts somewhere. We may be lucky enough to get a detailed document from the customer, usually with proprietary layout and content. Or, we may simply be presented with something like a **mission statement**, a short statement of some new, desirable, business direction.

As developers, we must transform the customer's requirements document or mission statement into a complete, unambiguous description of the system to be developed, in a standard format that the customer can understand and ratify. Admittedly, 'complete' and 'unambiguous' are impossible to achieve in practice. We shouldn't expect to come close to these goals the first time round. However, it's still useful to know that eventually we will have a document that describes everything the system *will* do (and, by omission, everything that it *won't* do), with little room for misinterpretation.

---

**Case Study**

*Nowhere Cars mission statement*

Since we automated the tracking of cars at our stores – using bar codes, counter-top terminals and laser readers – we have seen many benefits: the productivity of our rental assistants has increased 20%, cars rarely go missing and our customer base has grown strongly (according to our market research, this is at least partly due to the improved perception of professionalism and efficiency).

The management feels that the Internet offers further exciting opportunities for increasing efficiency and reducing costs. For example, rather than printing catalogs of available cars, we could make the catalog available to every Internet surfer for browsing on-line. For privileged customers, we could provide extra services, such as reservations, at the click of a button. Our target saving in this area is a reduction of 15% in the cost of running each store.

Within two years, using the full power of e-commerce, we aim to offer all of our services via a Web browser, with delivery and pick-up at the customer's home, thus achieving our ultimate goal of the virtual rental company, with minimal running costs relative to walk-in stores.

Even this three-paragraph mission statement contains a lot of information: history of automation at the company; customer satisfaction to date; on-line catalogs and reservations; privileged and non-privileged customers; savings history and savings targets; company end-game (the 'virtual rental company'). Admittedly, some of the management's dreams are a long way off (it may be more than two years before customers are comfortable with virtual rental stores), but at least we have two good starting points for our investigation: What services do the company's stores currently offer? Which of those services are appropriate for Internet delivery?

**Case Study (cont'd)**

The mission statement above is the basis for the case study used in the rest of this book. The fictitious company's new system is referred to as **Coot**, with the Internet facilities available to customers referred to as **iCoot**.

The unique selling point of Nowhere Cars is that they rent specialist cars to wealthy enthusiasts for extended periods. Since the supply of each kind of car is limited, customers must turn up at a store when they actually want to rent. Cars are rented on a first-come, first-served basis and customers can take their pick from what is currently available. Alternatively, customers who are keen to rent a model of car which is not available can make a reservation. An assistant will contact the customer directly when a matching car becomes available; the customer must collect it within two days (or pay a levy for depriving other customers of the car). As yet, there are no home delivery or home pick-up services (partly for insurance reasons). For members, who must register, reservations can be made by telephone.

# 6.3 USE CASES

Ivar Jacobson invented **use cases** to define the way in which part of a business or a system is used [Jacobson *et al.* 92]. Although, at first sight, use cases appear more process-oriented than object-oriented, they're widely considered to be the most effective tool for describing a system's functional requirements. Most nonfunctional requirements can be recorded alongside a closely-related use case (any others can be listed separately).

The use cases in this book contain all the essential elements in a format which is convenient for learning. In this book, use cases are used to document our understanding of the way a business operates – **business requirements modeling** – and to specify what our new software system should be able to do – **system requirements modeling**. The business use cases in this book use an informal, *descriptive* style: they describe, for the benefit of nonexperts, something that already exists. The system use cases, on the other hand, will be more *prescriptive*: they specify, mainly for the benefit of software developers, exactly what functionality needs to be implemented.

A use case starts with a participant called an **actor**; it then descends into the business, or the system, and eventually returns to the actor. The effect of each use case should be of value to the actor (otherwise, why would they initiate it in the first place?). Of course, value can mean different things to different people: it could be some information that the actor wishes to retrieve, some effect that the actor wishes to have on the system, some money, a purchase, or pretty much anything else that might motivate them. Being driven by use cases, far from sending us down the traditional path, actually helps us to find objects, attributes and operations.

---

**Case Study**

*Nowhere Cars use cases*

- Member Reserves Car Model is a business use case that describes how, according to current practice, a member makes a reservation. It may be couched in terms that would apply to any car-rental business or it may bring in details specific to the way that Nowhere Cars operates. We look for business use cases during business modeling, the first step of requirements capture.

    A business use case may refer to existing software systems, or it may not involve computers at all – for example, the last time you telephoned a car-rental shop and asked them to reserve a particular car model, were you able to tell if the assistant at the other end of the line, in the course of performing the transaction, used a computer or a pad and paper? More to the point, did you care?

- Make Reservation is a system use case that describes how the system that we intend to produce will allow Nowhere Cars to conduct reservations over the Internet.

    A system use case describes a service that the new, or replacement, system will provide: in this example, the member definitely does use some software – a Web browser and a back end server. Part of our job is to specify exactly what input the user should provide and what they should expect to get in return.

---

For the sake of simplicity, use cases, especially system use cases, should not overlap. A use case is written in natural language, broken up into a sequence of steps. Diagrams can accompany the use case if more explanation is needed.

# 6.4 BUSINESS PERSPECTIVE

In this section, we'll see how to put together a model of the business, as a precursor to modeling the functionality of the proposed system. A business model can be as simple as a class diagram, showing the relationships between business entities – this is sometimes referred to as a **domain model**. A domain model may be sufficient for small projects, however, for most projects, we would want to produce an entire **business model** representing how the business operates, or at least that part of the business that surrounds the system we expect to develop.

Use cases are not the only way of modeling a business, but they're simple. More complex alternatives include **business process modeling** and **workflow analysis**. Use cases are simple because producing one doesn't require specialist knowledge, just common sense and a certain amount of logic. The **use case model** that we produce here will contain the use cases themselves plus some other bits and pieces:

- Actor list (with descriptions).
- Glossary.
- Use cases (with descriptions and details).
- (Optional) Communication diagrams.
- (Optional) Activity diagrams.

UML defines the notation and semantics for activity diagrams and communication diagrams. The other artifacts are recommended by Jacobson.

We'll look at the business model components one by one, in the order in which you would typically create them in real life. However, bear in mind at all times that this is not a rigid workflow: as with any aspect of object-oriented development, we can iterate forwards, backwards, or round and round, until we have a complete picture.

## 6.4.1 Identifying Business Actors

The first thing we need to do is to identify the business actors. An actor is either a person playing some role within the business (as you might expect from the name), a department, or a separate software system.

The reason for identifying departments and systems as actors is that, in logical terms, they interact as if they were people themselves: we're interested in who (or what) initiates inter-actions and the sequence of steps. We don't care whether a particular actor is 'implemented' as a person, a department or a piece of software. Identifying actors helps us to identify the ways in which the business is used, which will, in turn, indicate what the use cases are.

Just as in real life, an actor can play different business roles at different times. For example, Fred Bloggs might be an assistant within the Nowhere Cars store until he clocks off; if he decides to rent a car before going home, he becomes a customer. At this stage of the development, you will be working with the other sponsors (principally the customers) to find out how the business operates – the actors should fall out of your discussions easily.

---

**Case Study**

*Nowhere Cars business actor list*

- Assistant: An employee at one of our stores who helps Customers to rent Cars and reserve Car Models.
- Customer: A person who pays us money in return for one of our standard services.

---

**Case Study (cont'd)**

- Member: A Customer whose identity and credit-worthiness have been validated and who, therefore, has access to special services (such as making Reservations by phone or over the Internet).
- NonMember: A Customer whose identity and credit-worthiness have not been checked and who, therefore, must provide a deposit to make a Reservation or surrender a copy of their license to rent a Car.
- Auk: The pre-existing system that handles Customer details, Reservations, Rentals and the catalog of available Car Models.
- DebtDepartment: The department of Nowhere Cars that deals with unpaid fees.
- LegalDepartment: The department of Nowhere Cars that deals with accidents in which a rented Car has been involved.

---

## 6.4.2 Writing the Project Glossary

Even at this early stage, it's a good idea to start maintaining a **glossary** – the modern alternative to a **data dictionary**. The phrase 'data dictionary' includes the word 'data', the kind of thing that object-oriented theoreticians are uncomfortable with, because it implies that data is being modeled in isolation. Separating data from processes was the old way of doing things: it's much better to keep data and process together, hence the less emotive term 'glossary'.

A glossary de-mystifies the jargon for anyone examining our software development artifacts. It also allows us to file away groups of synonyms, leaving us free to use one of each throughout the rest of the documentation.

---

**Case Study**

*Nowhere Cars Glossary*

| Term | Definition |
|---|---|
| Car (Business object) | Instance of a CarModel kept by a Store for Rental purposes. |
| CarModel (Business object) | A model in our Catalog, available for Reservation. |
| Customer (Business actor, business object) | A person who pays us money in return for one of our standard services. |
| Member (Business object) | A Customer whose identity and credit-worthiness have been validated and who, therefore, has access to special services (such as making Reservations by phone, or over the Internet). |
| . . . | |

Each entry in the glossary defines a term – the definition can be short or long, as appropriate. The actor descriptions that we've seen so far are good starting points as glossary definitions, but the glossary definitions will often end up being more general, because most of the terms will apply in several contexts.

As you can see from the case study glossary, you can record the relationships that each term has to the development phases (business actor, system actor, and so on). Below is a list of relationships that you can use (each entry may qualify as more than one of these):

- Business actor: An actor appearing in the business requirements.
- Business object: An object appearing in the business requirements.
- System actor: An actor appearing in the system requirements.
- System object: An object appearing (inside the system) in the system requirements.
- Analysis object: An object appearing in the analysis model.
- Deployment artifact: Something deployed in the system, such as a file.
- Design object: An object appearing in the design model.
- Design node: A computer or process that forms part of the system architecture.
- Design layer: A vertical partition of a subsystem.
- Design package: A logical grouping of classes, used to organize the development.

In each of these cases, object means entity or 'encapsulated data and process', as usual. Each category of object – business, system, analysis or design – is subtly different, with some objects qualifying in more than one category. For example, when a Customer rents a Car, we're dealing with a business object that is external to the system – the physical vehicle in the display area – and a system object that is inside the system itself, instantiated from a class that we implement.

Glossary entries use the class naming style (words run together with initial capitals). As long as we use the same style in all our project documentation, it will be obvious to the reader that a definition exists in the glossary.

## 6.4.3 Identifying Business Use Cases

Once we have the actors, the next task is to identify the business use cases. Each use case is a snippet of the business. At this stage, use cases may involve two-way communication between a number of actors, especially if they're human actors. Later on, we'll see that *system* use cases are more structured, because people normally tell the system what to do, rather than the other way round.

There's no set rule for deciding how to break the business down into use cases – common sense, logic and experience will help, as usual. Working with the sponsors (which you should be doing anyway) will also help. While talking to an assistant on the shop floor, for example, try to identify the different tasks that they find themselves doing every day. Since assistants interact with customers, they should also be able to identify the ways in which customers use the business. Employee and management training manuals, mission statements, proprietary requirements documents, sales brochures and other kinds of document can also provide inspiration. At all times, when trying to find use cases, keep the following question at the back of your mind: 'What are the key activities that make this business work?'

---

**Case Study**

*iCoot Business use case list*

- B1:Customer Rents Car: Customer rents a Car that they have selected from those available.
- B2:Member Reserves CarModel: Member asks to be notified when a CarModel becomes available.
- B3:NonMember Reserves CarModel: NonMember pays a deposit to be notified when a CarModel becomes available
- B4:Customer Cancels Reservation: Customer cancels an unconcluded Reservation, by phone or in person.
- B5:Customer Returns Car: Customer returns a Car that they have rented.
- B6:Customer Told CarModel is Available: Customer is contacted by an Assistant when a Car becomes available.
- B7:Car Reported Missing: Customer or Assistant discovers that a Car is missing.
- B8:Customer Renews Reservation: Customer renews a Reservation that has been outstanding for more than a week.
- B9:Customer Accesses Catalog: Customers browse the catalog, in-store or at home.
- B10: Customer Fined for Uncollected Reservation: Customer fails to collect a Car that they have reserved.
- B11:Customer Collects Reserved Car: Customer collects a Car that they have reserved.
- B12:Customer Becomes a Member: Customer provides CreditCard details and proof of Address to become a Member.
- B13:Customer Notified Car is Overdue: Assistant contacts Customer to warn them that a Car they have rented is more than a week overdue.
- B14:Customer Loses Keys: Replacement Keys are provided for a Customer who has lost them.
- B15:MembershipCard is Renewed: Assistant contacts Member to renew membership when their CreditCard has expired.
- B16:Car is Unreturnable: A Car is wrecked or breaks down.

**Case Study (cont'd)**

We have now started to narrow down the business to the area we're particularly interested in. We know from the original mission statement that our customer is only hoping to make parts of the rental and reservation business available over the Internet so, for example, the sale of ex-rental cars has not been modeled.

```
B3: NonMember Reserves CarModel.
1. NonMember tells Assistant which CarModel to reserve.
2. Assistant finds CarModel on Auk.
3. Assistant asks for a deposit for the Reservation.
4. Assistant asks for NonMember's License and phone number.
5. Assistant checks License visually.
6. If License looks okay, assistant creates new Reservation and
   records License number, phone number and a scan of
   the License in Auk.
7. Assistant gives NonMember a ReservationSlip containing
   the unique reservation number.
```

**Figure 6.2: A business use case for Nowhere Cars**

Remember that, during business modeling, we're not interested in the way that our new system might operate. At this stage, we're simply trying to describe the way the business *currently* operates. This may, or may not, involve existing software.

The numbering scheme is arbitrary: UML does not specify a scheme and the list does not imply an order. Once we have a list of candidate use cases, we can list the steps involved in each one. UML specifies nothing about the contents of a use case (or about the numbering or the descriptions, for that matter). Thus, we're free to use natural language, step-by-step descriptions, structured language (natural language with if–then–else and loop structures), or whatever.

Using steps rather than natural language encourages us to restrict ourselves to the bare bones of a use case. If we were to use structured language, we would be in danger of making our descriptions too algorithmic (computer-oriented). To make the use cases clear and independent of the implementation, unstructured steps will be used for the use case details in this book (see Figure 6.2).

## 6.4.4 Illustrating Use Cases on a Communication Diagram

As well as writing down use case details, we can provide an illustration of use cases using **communication diagrams**. A communication diagram shows a series of interactions between

actors and objects. A **sequence diagram** focuses on the interactions themselves and the order
in which they take place. In order to discourage the use of too much technical detail early in
the development process, the communication diagram is preferred for business modeling.

Because UML is designed to apply to every possible situation, there is a lot of notation
available to the developer for use in each of the different kinds of diagram. In this book,
so as to avoid covering every possible detail, only the essential parts are used. Alternative
ways of illustrating the same piece of information and anything too complex will also be
ignored.

Figure 6.3 shows five communicating elements. The nature of each element is shown
by the icon used to represent it: a stick person represents an actor; a circle standing on a
line represents a business object or **entity**; a circle connected to a vertical bar represents a
**boundary** (something that manages the interaction between other elements – usually this is
a piece of software, but it could also be a person); a stick person inside a boundary icon
represents a human actor playing some kind of interface role (this shows that the boundary
is a person rather than a piece of software).

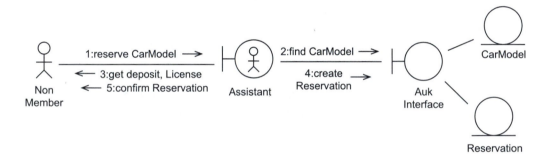

**Figure 6.3: A communication diagram for B3:NonMember Reserves CarModel**

Without too much knowledge of the notation, it's easy to appreciate from Figure 6.3 that
making a reservation involves a nonmember, an assistant acting as a business boundary,
a piece of software called Auk (acting as a boundary to some system) and two business
objects. Since, at this stage, we're modeling an *existing* way of doing things, we know that
the interface and the system that it accesses must already be implemented and deployed.
There is no mention of any software that we might eventually produce ourselves, because
we haven't got to that stage yet.

A line connecting two elements on a communication diagram indicates that the elements
can interact. So, we can see from Figure 6.3 that: the NonMember is requesting services from
the Assistant; the Assistant is requesting services from the AukInterface; the AukInterface is
requesting services from a CarModel and a Reservation. Since the CarModel and Reservation

are accessed by a software interface, the implication is that they're software objects inside the existing system, rather than physical objects outside (the distinction may or may not be important to us).

As well as icons and connections, Figure 6.3 depicts individual interactions as numbered labels with an associated arrow. You can think of these as messages being sent from one element to another: the number indicates the message's position in the sequence. So, we can interpret the entire collaboration as:

- The NonMember asks the Assistant to reserve a CarModel.
- The Assistant asks the AukInterface to find the CarModel (this involves the CarModel object in some unspecified way).
- The Assistant asks the NonMember for a deposit and a License.
- The Assistant asks the AukInterface to create a Reservation (this involves a Reservation object in some way).
- The Assistant confirms the Reservation to the NonMember.

You might think that this sequence of interactions should exactly match the sequence of steps in the use case details. However, because natural language is not a sequence of steps, a one-to-one match is unlikely. It's more likely that each interaction will represent a summary of one or more steps.

Despite the lack of an exact match with a use case, a communication diagram is still useful because it enhances the use case details and can help us to produce the details in the first place.

Since the interactions we deal with at this early stage are straightforward, it's reasonable for us to produce one communication diagram per use case, but no more. For brevity, any collaboration that we depict should be the **normal path** through the use case. When we deal with system use cases, we can be more specific about **abnormal paths**, but for now we should be able to imply their existence within the use case itself: for example, step 6 in our business use case (Figure 6.2) begins If License looks okay: this implies that sometimes the License is invalid, but what the Assistant should do in that case has not been specified.

## 6.4.5 Illustrating Use Cases on an Activity Diagram

UML includes another kind of diagram that can be useful during business modeling. An **activity diagram** shows dependencies between (parallel) activities as we move from an initial starting point to a desired goal. They are similar to **flow charts** or **Petri nets**, traditionally used to model program flow or human activity. Figure 6.4 shows an activity diagram being used to illustrate a business use case.

Each rounded box in an activity diagram represents an **action**; an open ended arrow (an edge) indicates that the source action must be completed before the destination action is

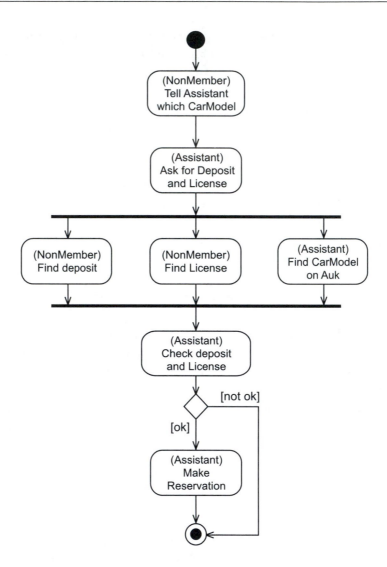

**Figure 6.4: An activity diagram for B3:NonMember Reserves CarModel**

started; a black dot indicates the starting point for the activity; a black dot inside a white circle indicates the end of the activity; a diamond represents a **decision** – a **guard** on a departing edge indicates the reason for following that edge; thick black lines, known as **forks** and **joins**, are used to indicate the beginning and end of a set of concurrent actions.

For each action, we can show who or what is responsible for the action by putting a name in parentheses, before the name of the action itself. The name identifies a **partition** within the activity, and can be used to identify actors, departments, systems or objects. Partitions can also be indicated by grouping actions into rows, columns or cells.

We can see quite easily from Figure 6.4 that, to reserve a CarModel:

1.  The NonMember tells the Assistant which CarModel to reserve.
2.  The Assistant asks for a deposit and License.
3.  While the NonMember is looking for the deposit and License, the Assistant looks for the CarModel on the Auk system.
4.  Once everything has been found, the Assistant checks the deposit and the License.
5.  If the deposit and License are valid, the Assistant makes the Reservation and the activity is finished.
6.  Otherwise, the activity is finished.

As with communication diagrams, we should not expect this interpretation to match the use case details step-for-step.

In common with many UML diagrams, activity diagrams can be used for more than one purpose. For example, an activity diagram can be used to construct an entire business model or to document the algorithm employed by some software object.

# 6.5 DEVELOPER PERSPECTIVE

The second part of requirements capture is modeling the software that we're going to develop in order to improve the business. Regardless of whether you choose to document the business using a simple domain model, a fully-fledged use case model, or something even more detailed such as a business process model or workflow analysis, it is widely accepted that the requirements of the software system should be captured using a use case model. This is because use cases are relatively easy to produce and easy for all sponsors to understand.

The use case model for a system is more detailed and more prescriptive than for a business. For Ripple, the system use case model comprises:

*   An actor list (with descriptions).
*   A use case list (with descriptions).
*   A use case diagram.
*   Use case details (including any related nonfunctional requirements).
*   A use case survey.
*   Supplementary requirements (system requirements that don't fit with any particular use case).
*   User interface sketches.
*   An enhanced glossary.
*   Use case priorities.

We'll look at how to produce each of these artifacts in turn.

The list above includes several artifacts that we haven't come across before. Even the ones that we've already seen during business modeling generally include more detail in system modeling. Communication diagrams have not been included; although there is nothing to stop you using them to illustrate your system use cases at this stage, for Ripple they have been deferred to a later phase in the development (dynamic analysis), where they're considered more important.

We should also spend some time evaluating existing systems. Such a system is referred to as a **legacy system**, because we inherited it as part of the existing business.

---

**Case Study**

*Nowhere Cars legacy system*

We need to decide whether Auk can reasonably be extended, or whether we should replace it altogether. This decision is not an easy one to make: on the one hand, we have a finished system that has been up and running for some time, one that assistants are familiar with; on the other hand, it may be too difficult to open up Auk in order to add new facilities, or to write new software that communicates with it process-to-process (which may be inefficient).

Let's assume that we have made the decision to replace Auk with a whole new system that will be compatible with Internet access and will support the 'virtual rental store' that our customer desires. Our new system will be called **Coot**. To alleviate the problems of staff training, the new interfaces (counter-top terminals and laser readers) will look and feel similar to the Auk ones.

For the purposes of this book, we don't need to examine all the facilities of Coot. Instead, we can concentrate on those parts of the system that provide the first round of Internet facilities to customers. This cut-down set of facilities is called **iCoot**.

---

## Identifying System Actors

The first thing we need to do is to identify and describe the system actors, with the help of our sponsors. The actors we identify at this stage should include only the people (and external systems) that interact directly with our proposed system, rather than actors from the wider business context.

---

**Case Study**

*iCoot system actor list*

- Customer: A person using a Web browser to access iCoot.

---

**Case Study (cont'd)**

- Member: A Customer who has presented their name, address and CreditCard details at one of our Stores; each Member is given an Internet password to accompany their membership number.
- Assistant: An employee at a Store who contacts Members to tell them about the progress of their Reservations.

## Identifying System Use Cases

Once we have actors, we can look for use cases, again asking our sponsors for help. Each use case must have a short description.

**Case Study**

*iCoot system use case list*

- U1:Browse Index: A Customer browses the index of CarModels.
- U2:View Results: A Customer is shown the subset of CarModels that was retrieved.
- U3:View CarModel Details: A Customer is shown the details of a retrieved CarModel, such as description and advert.
- U4:Search: A Customer searches for CarModels by specifying Categories, Makes and engine sizes.
- U5:Log On: A Member logs on to iCoot using their membership number and current password.
- U6:View Member Details: A Member views a subset of their details stored by iCoot, such as name, address and CreditCard details.
- U7:Make Reservation: A Member reserves a CarModel when viewing its details.
- U8:View Rentals: A Member views a summary of the Cars they're currently renting.
- U9:Change Password: A Member changes the password that they use to log on.
- U10: View Reservations: A Member views a summary of Reservations that are not yet concluded, such as date, time and CarModel.
- U11:Cancel Reservation: A Member cancels a Reservation that is not yet concluded.
- U12:Log Off: A Member logs off from iCoot.

System use cases can be depicted on a **use case diagram** showing the actors and their associations with particular use cases – this helps us to see at a glance how the system will be used. A use case diagram for iCoot is shown in Figure 6.5.

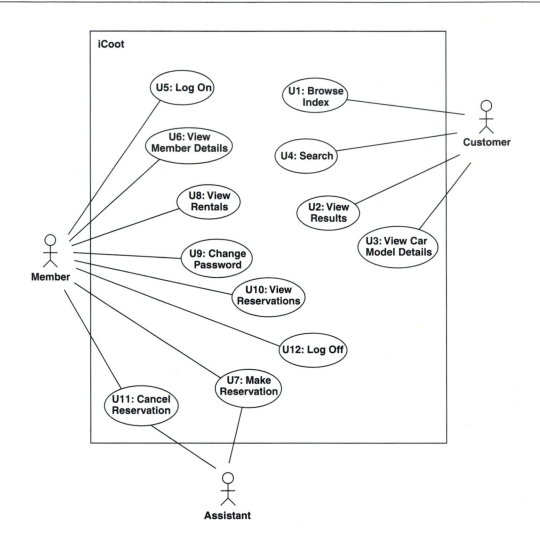

**Figure 6.5: A simple use case diagram for iCoot**

On a use case diagram, each use case is shown as a number and a title, inside a bubble. The box around all the use cases represents the boundary of the system – we can put the system name just inside the box. Outside the system boundary, we show the actors, adding associations between the use cases and the actors that use them.

A **use case survey** (Jacobson's terminology for one of our non-UML artifacts) is an informal description of how a group of use cases fit together: the kind of narrative that a developer might produce when walking sponsors through a use case diagram. A use case survey allows sponsors to get a greater understanding of the use cases without any of the developers present.

---

**Case Study**

*iCoot use case survey*

Any Customer can look for CarModels in the catalog, either by browsing the CarModel index (U1) or by searching (U4). In the latter case, the Customer specifies the Categories, Makes and engine sizes that they're interested in. Either way, after each retrieval, the Customer is shown the results as a collection of matching CarModels (U2), along with basic information such as CarModel name. The Customer can then choose to view extra information about particular CarModels such as a description and an advert (U3).

Customers who have become Members can log on (U5) and gain access to extra services. The extra services are: making a Reservation (U7), canceling a Reservation (U11), checking membership details (U6), viewing outstanding Reservations (U10), changing their log-on password (U9), viewing their outstanding Rentals (U8) and logging off (U12).

Assistants are involved in the life cycle of Reservations, moving Cars to and from the reserved area, for example.

---

## 6.5.1 Specializing Actors

Any actor can **specialize** (inherit behavior from) another actor. This adds more expressive power to the system use case model. For example, we may decide that Customer is an abstract concept that should be specialized by Member; once we have introduced this specialization, it makes sense to introduce the concept of NonMember too.

It's up to you whether to introduce inheritance between actors early, or late, or not at all. You (and your colleagues) need to be happy that each particular use of inheritance is beneficial rather than confusing. Remember that all your sponsors must be able to understand the artifacts that you produce, from business modeling right the way through to static analysis, at least. This will help to ensure that you have understood the problem domain correctly and that you will deliver what the sponsors actually want. Will nonprogrammers be happy with NonMember is a kind of Customer? It's up to you to decide.

> **Case Study**
>
> *iCoot system actor list with inheritance*
>
> Having decided to introduce inheritance for the iCoot actors, the finished system actor list looks like this (with one extra actor and the inheritance relationships in parentheses):
>
> - Customer: A person using a Web browser to access iCoot.
> - Member: A Customer who has presented their name, address and CreditCard details at one of our Stores; each Member is given an Internet password to accompany their membership number. (Specializes Customer.)
> - NonMember: A Customer who is not a Member. (Specializes Customer.)
> - Assistant: An employee at a Store who contacts Members to tell them about the progress of their Reservations.

We can modify our use case diagram to show inheritance relationships between actors in the same way as we would show them between classes, see Figure 6.6. The Customer class has been shown as abstract – its name is italicized – because no-one is literally a Customer; everyone is either a Member or a NonMember. (If you don't have italics to hand, you can add the keyword {abstract} to the left or above the actor name.)

Even though Customer is abstract, we can still associate it with a use case, to indicate that every kind of Customer is involved in that use case. As a side effect, some actors, such as NonMember, will have only indirect associations.

Our diagram now shows specializations explicitly, but it's useful to have the annotations in the actor list as well, in case the list is viewed separately.

## 6.5.2 Use Case Relationships

As well as specialization between actors and associations between actors and use cases, there are three kinds of relationship between use cases themselves: **specializes**, **includes** and **extends**. These allow us to group related use cases; to decompose large use cases; to reuse behavior; and to specify optional behavior:

- Specializes: Just like actors, use cases can inherit from each other. In order to avoid all sorts of complexity relating to the redefinition of steps and the addition of extra ones, we can restrict ourselves to specializing **abstract use cases**. A (pure) abstract use case has no steps at all: its sole purpose is to group other use cases. For example, we might decide that U1:Browse Index and U4:Search are both varieties of the abstract use case U13:Look for CarModels.

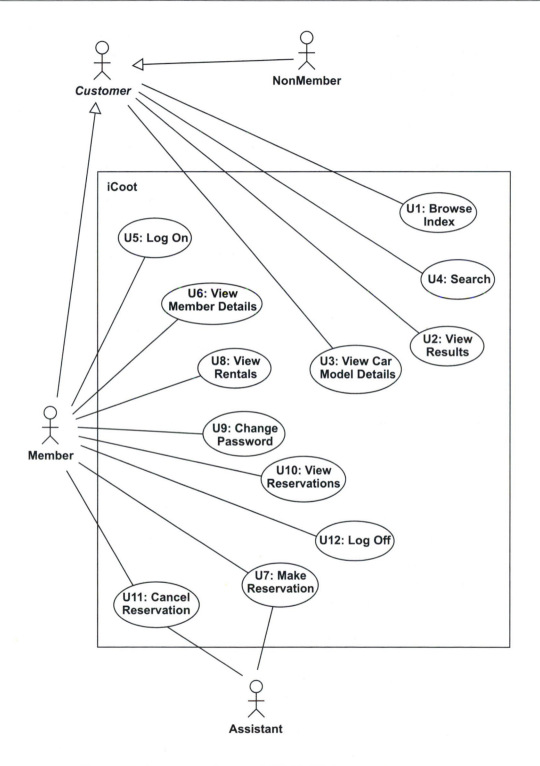

**Figure 6.6: A use case diagram showing inheritance between actors**

- Includes: A use case that has some of its steps provided by another use case is said to **include** that use case. For example, U1:Browse Index includes, at some point in its behavior, all the steps of U2:View Results. Inclusion can be used to extract steps common to a number of use cases, or just to break a large use case down into more manageable chunks.
- Extends: A use case that adds value to another use case is said to **extend** that use case. For example, when viewing results (U2), a Customer can choose to view details (U3). Extension allows us to add optional extras – often, these extras will appear at the end of the use case (hence the name), but they can also occur at the beginning, or somewhere in the middle.

There is a fundamental difference between inclusion and extension: with inclusion, the source use case won't work without the target, whereas, with extension, the source works perfectly well without the target. Going in the other direction, use cases that are included in other use cases may have independent existence – they may be executable directly via other routes. A use case that extends another use case, in contrast, will usually only exist as an extension.

You're unlikely to identify use case relationships on your first pass through system requirements modeling. Beyond that, it is up to you to decide whether they're really needed, and whether your sponsors will be able to appreciate them. If you do use relationships, as with other areas of object orientation, there will be many ways of decomposing use cases into inclusions, extensions and inheritance. No one way is correct – just try to develop a model that makes sense to you and your customers.

---

**Case Study**

*iCoot use case relationships*

Our use case descriptions now look like those below. Abstract use cases and both ends of relationships have been identified – the rationale is that, seeing the annotation, the reader knows that they will have to look at other use cases to get a complete picture.

- U1:Browse Index: A Customer browses the index of CarModels. (Specializes U13, includes U2.)
- U2:View Results: A Customer is shown the subset of CarModels that were retrieved. (Included by U1 and U4, extended by U3.)
- U3:View CarModel Details: A Customer is shown the details of a retrieved CarModel, such as description and advert. (Extends U2, extended by U7.)
- U4:Search: A Customer searches for CarModels by specifying Categories, Makes and engine sizes. (Specializes U13, includes U2.)
- U5:Log On: A Member logs on to iCoot using their membership number and current password. (Extended by U6, U8, U9, U10 and U12.)

**Case Study (cont'd)**

- U6:View Member Details: A Member views their (censored) details stored by iCoot, such as name, address and CreditCard details. (Extends U5.)
- U7:Make Reservation: A Member reserves a CarModel when viewing its details. (Extends U3.)
- U8:View Rentals: A Member views a summary of the Cars they're currently renting. (Extends U5.)
- U9:Change Password: A Member changes the password that they use to log on. (Extends U5.)
- U10: View Reservations: A Member views summaries of their unconcluded Reservations, such as date, time and CarModel. (Extends U5, extended by U11.)
- U11:Cancel Reservation: A Member cancels an unconcluded Reservation. (Extends U10.)
- U12:Log Off: A Member logs off from iCoot. (Extends U5.)
- U13:Look for CarModels: A Customer retrieves a subset of CarModels from the Catalog. (Abstract, generalized by U1 and U4.)

Use case relationships can be shown on a use case diagram (see Figure 6.7). Inheritance between use cases is shown in the normal way, using a line with a white arrowhead. An inclusion is shown as a dashed, open-ended arrow from the including use case to the included one, labeled with the keyword <<include>> (a word in guillemets in UML indicates a well-known concept). Therefore, U4:Search includes, at some point in its behavior, all the steps of U2:View Results. An extension is shown with a similar arrow from the extending use case to the extended one, labeled with <<extend>> – thus, U3:View CarModel Details is an optional extra for U2:View Results.

Although we could reduce the two inclusions shown to a single inclusion, from U13 to U2, that would arguably be less clear. It would also mean that the abstract use case would have steps, something that we try to avoid. Finally, it would mean that U1 and U4 would not be able to control where the inclusion took place.

In some cases, an extension is only allowed under certain conditions. We can show this by adding a UML **comment** (which looks like a piece of paper) detailing the conditions. A comment, which may contain any text, can be connected to the relevant point in the diagram with a dashed line, optionally terminated with a small circle that makes the join clearer. Conditions in UML are expressed as **constraints** (text in braces) and may be stated in natural language, in pseudocode or in UML's formal **Object Constraint Language** (OCL). In Figure 6.7, natural language has been used, to reflect the fact that we're at a relatively informal stage of development. As you can see, U7:Make Reservation is only allowed for Member objects who have logged on.

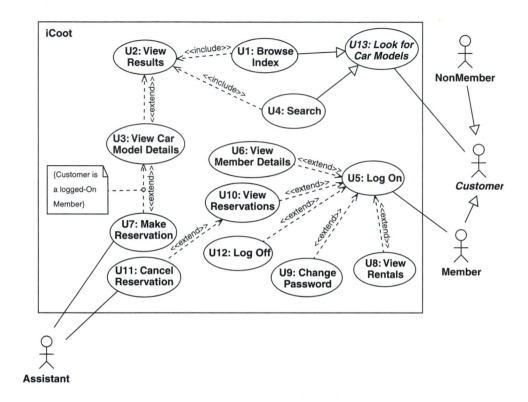

**Figure 6.7: The final use case diagram for iCoot**

Normally, a dashed line with an open-ended arrow in UML indicates a **dependency** – the source relies on the target in some way. The implication is that, if the target changes, the source is affected. For use cases, the use of dependency notation is historical and not strictly correct. For example, an extending use case doesn't necessarily depend on the extended use case. Hence, with a use case diagram, we talk about **use case relationships** rather than dependencies. One last point about the notation: for inclusion, the subordinate use case is the target whereas, with extension, the subordinate is the source – this can cause confusion.

**Case Study**

*iCoot use case survey (complete)*

Any Customer can look for CarModels in the catalog, by browsing the CarModel index (U1) or by searching (U4). In the latter case, the Customer specifies the Categories, Makes and engine sizes that they're interested in. Either way, after each retrieval, the Customer is shown the results as a collection of matching CarModels (U2), along with basic information such as CarModel name. The

**Case Study (cont'd)**

Customer can then choose to view extra information about particular CarModels such as a description and an advert (U3).

Customers come in two varieties, Members and NonMembers.

Customers who have become Members can log on (U5) and gain access to extra services. The extra services are: making a Reservation (U7), canceling a Reservation (U11), checking membership details (U6), viewing outstanding Reservations (U10), changing their log-on password (U9), viewing their outstanding Rentals (U8) and logging off (U12).

Assistants are involved in the life cycle of Reservations, moving Cars to and from the reserved area, for example.

Browsing the index and searching for CarModels are two different ways of looking for CarModels (U13). In order to view CarModel details, a Customer must be viewing the results of looking for models (via the browsing or searching route).

In order to reserve a CarModel, a Member must be viewing its details (NonMembers can't make reservations, even when they're viewing details).

In order to cancel a Reservation, a Member must be viewing their outstanding Reservations.

## 6.5.3 System Use Case Details

Once we've identified use cases and how they fit together, we need to show the details. Since UML doesn't specify what the use case details should include or how they should be arranged, a choice has been made here based on taste and experience. For Ripple, **system use case details** include:

- The use case number and title.
- Whether the use case is abstract.
- relationships to other use cases.
- Any **preconditions** (conditions that must be satisfied before the use case is carried out).
- The steps themselves (where we can assume that the preconditions have been met).
- Any **postconditions** (conditions that are guaranteed after successful completion of the use case).
- Any **abnormal paths** and what to do in each case (although the paths are abnormal, we include them if it's important for us to specify the system's reaction).
- Any **nonfunctional requirements** that relate to this use case.

Figure 6.8 shows the format of use case details used in this book; of all the items, only the number, title, preconditions, steps and postconditions are mandatory – the others can be left out if they're empty.

```
Number, Title (relationships)
Preconditions
Steps
Postconditions
Abnormal paths
Nonfunctional requirements
```

**Figure 6.8: Format for system use case details**

Figure 6.9 shows four of the iCoot use cases in the specified format.

These system use cases are significantly more detailed than the business use cases we saw earlier. This reflects the fact that we're now trying to be prescriptive rather than merely descriptive: we want to be precise about the services the system will provide in order to remove the guesswork from our analysts and designers.

For the purposes of this book, we use a sequence of steps written in natural language. As a matter of personal preference, you may prefer to add a more algorithmic structure with conditionals and loops (if–then–else and repeat–until, for example).

When writing use case details, it's important that we specify the *function* of the system but not the way that function is *delivered*: for example, if we were to include steps such as 2. Customer clicks on the Details… button, we would be restricting the user interface designer. Unless it's an absolute requirement, you should always try to use neutral words like select, initiate, indicate and display.

Any reasonable designer will be able to make informed decisions about exactly how specific the requirements-gatherer is trying to be: for example, the designer may implement steps in a different order, or in parallel, as long as the end result is the same. We can see where something like this might happen in U5:Log On: the first three steps could be implemented in any order and it would make no difference to anyone.

## 6.5.4 Preconditions, Postconditions and Inheritance

Since we have considered inheritance between use cases, we must concern ourselves with how specialization affects preconditions and postconditions. (Although it's recommended that you only inherit from abstract uses cases without steps, such use cases can still have preconditions and postconditions, as you can see from Figure 6.9.) Here are the rules:

U1: Browse Index. (Specializes U13, includes U2.)
Preconditions: None.
1. Customer selects an index heading.
2. Customer elects to view CarModels for the selected index heading.
3. Include U2.
Postconditions: None.

U3: View CarModel Details. (Extends U2, extended by U7.)
Preconditions: None.
1. Customer selects one of the matching CarModels.
2. Customer requests details of the selected CarModel.
3. iCoot displays details for the selected car model
   (makes, engine size, price, description, advert and poster).
4. If Customer is a logged-on Member, extend with U7.
Postconditions: iCoot has displayed details of selected CarModels.
Nonfunctional Requirements:
r1. Adverts should be displayed using a streaming protocol
    rather than requiring a download.

U5: Log On. (Extended by U6, U8, U9, U10 and U12.)
Preconditions: Member has obtained a password from their local Store.
1. Member enters their membership number.
2. Member enters their password.
3. Since iCoot must enforce one logon for a Member, Member can choose
   to steal (invalidate and thus take over from) an existing session.
4. Member elects to log on.
5. Extend with U6, U8, U9, U10, U12.
Postconditions: Member is logged on.
Abnormal Paths:
a1. If the membership number/password combination is incorrect,
    iCoot informs Member that one of the two is incorrect
    (for security, they're not told which one).
a2. If the membership number/password combination is correct,
    but Member is already logged on and they have not elected to
    steal, iCoot informs Member.

U13: Look for Car Models (Abstract, specialized by U1 and U4.)
Preconditions: None.
Postconditions: Customer has been presented with summaries of
    retrieved CarModels.

**Figure 6.9: Details for some iCoot system use cases**

1. When one use case specializes another, it inherits the parent's preconditions as a starting point. Any new preconditions added by the child must only *weaken* the inherited ones (they're combined using 'or').
2. For postconditions, the child's starting point is the postconditions of the parent. Any postconditions added by the child must only *strengthen* the inherited ones (they're combined using 'and').
3. Preconditions and postconditions added by children have no effect on the parent's preconditions and postconditions.

In the above list, rule 3 should be obvious from what you already know about object-oriented theory (children don't affect the behavior of the parents), but rules 1 and 2 may be surprising to you. Informally, the reason we can only weaken preconditions and strengthen postconditions is that the child use cases have an obligation to readers of the parent use case not to spring any nasty surprises. For example, U13:Look for CarModels has no preconditions, so if U4:Search had a precondition that said Don't do this on Tuesdays, anyone prevented from searching for car models on a Tuesday would have legitimate cause for complaint – 'Excuse me, but according to "Look for Car Models", I can look at any time.'

A postcondition on a parent provides a guarantee to users and it wouldn't be reasonable for the child to try and water down that guarantee. For example, U4:Search has a postcondition Customer has been presented with matching CarModels; it wouldn't be reasonable for a child to add or a randomly-selected CarModel.

Rules 1 and 2 imply that if a parent has Preconditions: None (there are no restrictions on when the use case may be applied), its children must also have Preconditions: None; if a parent has Postconditions: None (there are no guarantees about the outcome), the child can specify any postconditions it likes.

In summary, when one use case specializes another, you must carefully consider the preconditions and postconditions of the parent.

## 6.5.5 Supplementary Requirements

Most of the time, it's possible to associate nonfunctional requirements with a particular use case. For example, a nonfunctional requirement of Adverts should be displayed using a streaming protocol rather than requiring a download fits neatly with U3:View CarModel Details, the use case that makes adverts available to customers in the first place.

Nonfunctional requirements that don't fit with any use case can be recorded in a **supplementary requirements** document, as shown in Figure 6.10.

## 6.5.6 User Interface Sketches

Thinking about the user interfaces for the system can help us to clarify the use cases. The interfaces can be brainstormed with our sponsors at an early stage and the results recorded

```
Supplementary Requirements
--------------------------

s1. The client applet must run in Java PlugIn 1.2 (and later versions).
s2. iCoot must be able to cope with a catalog of 100,000 car models.
s3. iCoot must be able to serve a million customers simultaneously
    with no significant degradation in performance.
```

**Figure 6.10: Supplementary requirements for iCoot**

as **user interface sketches**. These sketches should be regarded as a functional guide rather than a professional GUI design: they help us to identify and partition functionality in a way that can be implemented according to personal preference.

For example, Sketch 1 in Figure 6.11 shows a user interface that allows the user to select one or more categories, manufacturers and engine sizes; on clicking the Retrieve button, we're referred to Sketch 2 which shows a list of matching car models; clicking the < Go Back button returns us to Sketch 1; clicking the Details… button takes us on to Sketch 3 (not shown); and so on. (Obviously, these are not the original sketches that were hand-drawn on a whiteboard; they're the versions that had been agreed by the end of the brainstorming session, which were then mocked up using a drawing package.)

Since use cases and user interfaces both represent a partitioning of system functionality, it's a good idea to maintain a clean mapping between the two, a mapping that survives through to implementation. For example, with iCoot, we have three broad categories of access: member access, nonmember access and assistant access. This suggests three separate user interfaces.

Within each user interface, we should provide a window or a panel that corresponds to each of the use cases (the choice of window, panel, or some other widget is, of course, a design issue). For example, the sketches in Figure 6.11 show a notebook-style widget representing the nonmember interface. Nonmembers can search the catalog and browse the index, so each of these use cases is assigned its own page in the notebook. Both of these use cases include viewing the results – another use case that gets its own panel. We would expect the Search, Index and Results panels to be reused in the member interface. (For easier migration, the assistant interface will resemble the existing Auk interface.)

## 6.5.7 Prioritizing System Use Cases

It's a good idea, especially in the context of an incremental development process, to rank system requirements in order of their implementation priority. With use case modeling, the obvious thing to do is to rank the use cases – each can then be given a score to indicate its

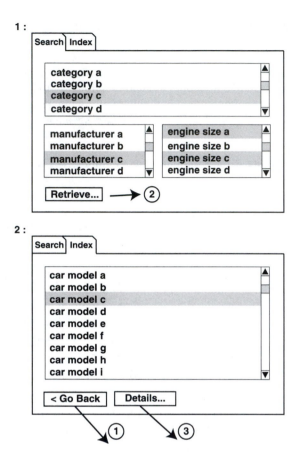

**Figure 6.11: User interface sketches for iCoot**

urgency. The priorities and urgencies can be used to help plan the rest of the development and any further increments.

One useful scoring technique is **traffic lights**:

- **Green** use cases must be implemented in the current increment; failure to do so means that the project has failed to reach its minimum goals.
- **Amber** use cases are optional for the current increment and should only be attempted once the green use cases have been completed (they're added bonuses that we can use to impress our sponsors). Any amber use case that is incomplete by the delivery date must be dropped completely (partial implementations look unprofessional).
- **Red** use cases won't be implemented in the current increment, even if time permits: they're outside the scope of the current increment and proper allowances are unlikely to have been made for them.

In practice, use case priorities (and urgencies) will be based not only on desirability, but also on how much of the system architecture and coding effort individual use cases will pull into the current increment: choosing priorities requires a certain amount of skill, experience and crystal-ball gazing. There's nothing wrong with putting easier use cases first: they will help us to learn more about the system as we iterate, with less risk.

If you're lucky enough to have time available at the end of the increment (after finishing the green use cases and all the amber use cases), you should:

- Review the project status.
- Finalize planning for the next increment (re-prioritizing unimplemented use cases, for example).
- Do some unrelated work.
- Have an office party.
- . . .

---

**Case Study**

*iCoot use case priorities*

- Green:
    - U1:Browse Index
    - U4:Search
    - U2:View Results
    - U3:View CarModel Details
    - U5:Log On
- Amber:
    - U12:Logoff
    - U6:View Member Details
    - U7:Make Reservation
    - U10:View Reservations
- Red:
    - U11:Cancel Reservation
    - U8:View Rentals
    - U9:Change Password

U1:Browse Index is both essential and simple (because it doesn't involve rentals or reservations), so it goes at the top of the list; U5:Log On is essential before any of the member services can be made available, so it must appear before the member services; U6:View Member Details is attempted before U7:Make Reservation because it is simpler (reservations turn out to have a complicated life cycle); and so on.

Assigning priorities and urgencies to system use cases is another indication that we should develop for extensibility and reuse. Here's a summary of how the traffic lights fit in with the other stages of development, after business modeling:

- Green: System requirements, analysis, system design, subsystem design, specification, implementation and testing should be complete for use cases in this group.
- Amber: System requirements should be complete and analysis and system design should be complete, or nearly complete, for use cases in this group; subsystem design, specification, implementation and testing are optional.
- Red: System requirements should be complete for use cases in this group; analysis is optional; system design should support these use cases; subsystem design, specification, implementation and testing should *not* be performed.

Of course, 'complete' is a relative term in a spiral, iterative and incremental process.

## 6.6 SUMMARY

In this chapter, we looked at:

- The importance of specifying functional requirements (what the system must be able to do, such as 'browse the catalog') and nonfunctional requirements (how the system must run, such as the specific Web browsers that must be supported) in a requirements phase before any coding begins.

- Modeling the business context and system functionality using high-level business use cases and identifying actors.

- Modeling the system requirements with a complete use case model comprising use cases, use case diagram, supplementary requirements, user interface sketches, use case priorities and urgencies. Although communication diagrams and activity diagrams were considered optional at this stage, a glossary is always essential.

## FURTHER READING

Although it doesn't cover UML, a mine of useful information on the theory of business process modeling is [Bustard *et al.* 00].

Ivar Jacobson's original book on the Objectory method [Jacobson *et al.* 92], describes the original justification for use cases and the kind of information that they should contain – it's always a good idea to see how an important technology came about in the first place. Alistair Cockburn is a widely respected authority on use cases. As well as a book on the subject [Cockburn 00], Cockburn has his own web site at www.usecases.org.

For more advice on communication diagrams and activity diagrams, Martin Fowler's book [Fowler 03] is a good place to start. As ever, [OMG 03a] has comprehensive coverage of the notation.

# REVIEW QUESTIONS

1. With reference to Figure 6.12, what are X1, X2 and X3? Choose only one option.

   (a) Roles.
   (b) Prima donnas.
   (c) Actors.
   (d) Sticks.

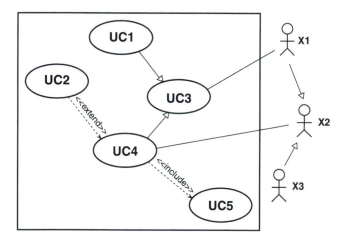

**Figure 6.12: For use with Review Questions 1, 2 and 5**

2. With reference to Figure 6.12, which of the following statements are true? Choose all options that apply.

   (a) X3 can interact with the system using UC4.
   (b) X1 can interact with the system using UC1 and UC4.
   (c) X3 and X1 are different kinds of X2.
   (d) UC3 is an abstract use case with no steps of its own.

**PizzaBase Case Study**

The PizzaBase restaurant wants to automate the ordering of pizzas by customers. Each table will be fitted with a touch-sensitive screen which customers can use to browse the pizzas on offer and select their choice.

Two basic types of pizza will be offered: the Do-it-Yourself will have a base with tomato sauce only and then customers can choose any number of toppings, at a fixed price per topping; the Prefab will come in several varieties, each with a fixed set of toppings. Every pizza can be ordered with a deep crust or crispy base, and three sizes are available: 6 inch, 9 inch and 12 inch.

Customers will also be able to order from a fixed set of drinks, such as cola and lemonade flavors, each in large or small size. Once customers have confirmed their order, they will be shown the final price and, thereafter, the screen will display the progress of their food as it is being prepared and cooked. At the end of a meal, payment will be made in the conventional way.

3. With reference to the PizzaBase case study, which of the following options are likely business use cases? Choose all options that apply.

   (a) Customer pays for meal.
   (b) Restaurant prepares meal.
   (c) Customer sees progress of food.
   (d) Customer chooses pizza.
   (e) Customer selects drink from display.

4. Which of the following UML artifacts is used to show the steps involved in getting value from a system? Choose only one option.

   (a) User interface sketches.
   (b) Glossaries.
   (c) State machine diagrams.
   (d) Use cases.
   (e) Class diagrams.
   (f) Deployment diagrams.

5. With reference to Figure 6.12, which of the following statements are true? Choose all options that apply.

   (a) UC5 is a compulsory part of UC4.
   (b) UC4 is an optional part of UC5.
   (c) UC1 is unused.
   (d) UC2 is an optional part of UC4.
   (e) UC4 is a compulsory part of UC2.

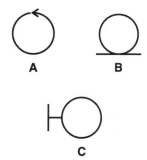

**Figure 6.13: For use with Review Question 6**

6. With reference to Figure 6.13, what kind of objects are A, B and C? Choose only one option.

   (a)  A is an entity, B is a controller, C is a boundary.
   (b)  A is a boundary, B is an entity, C is a controller.
   (c)  A is an entity, B is a boundary, C is a controller.
   (d)  A is a controller, B is an entity, C is a boundary.
   (e)  A is a boundary, B is a controller, C is an entity.
   (f)  A is a controller, B is a boundary, C is an entity.

# ANSWERS TO REVIEW QUESTIONS

1. In Figure 6.12, X1, X2 and X3 are c. Actors.
2. With reference to Figure 6.12, all of the statements are true:

   (a)  X3 can interact with the system using UC4.
   (b)  X1 can interact with the system using UC1 and UC4.
   (c)  X3 and X1 are different kinds of X2.
   (d)  UC3 is an abstract use case with no steps of its own.

3. The following options are likely business use cases:

   (a)  Customer pays for meal.
   (b)  Restaurant prepares meal.
   (d)  Customer chooses pizza.

4. d. Use cases show the steps involved in getting value from a system.
5. With reference to Figure 6.12, the following statements are true:

   (a)  UC5 is a compulsory part of UC4.
   (d)  UC2 is an optional part of UC4.

6. With reference to Figure 6.13, d. A is a controller, B is an entity, C is a boundary.

# 7

## Analyzing the Problem

In this chapter, we'll be looking at the classical analysis phase and how to do it in a modern, object-oriented way. Analysis is an essential bridge between requirements capture and design, leading us from a clear statement of what the system must provide to a clear understanding of the objects that we'll be dealing with. Once we understand the objects that we must deal with, we stand a much better chance of producing an elegant solution.

# Learning Objectives

**Understand what analysis is.**

**Build a static analysis model.**

**Understand how dynamic analysis can help us to verify the static model.**

# Chapter Outline

**7**

# 7.1 INTRODUCTION

Analysis is about discovering *what* the system is going to handle, rather than deciding *how* to do the handling. We need to decompose a complex set of requirements into the essential elements and relationships on which we will base our solution. Analysis is our first opportunity to get to grips with modeling the real world as objects.

An analysis model has both static and dynamic parts. We can depict the **static analysis model** using a **class diagram**. A class diagram shows the objects that the system will handle and how those objects are related to each other. For the **dynamic analysis model**, we can use **communication diagrams** to demonstrate that our static model is feasible. As before, rather than all the intricacies of UML notation, you'll see only the essential parts here: the parts that will suffice for most purposes.

There are two inputs to analysis:

- The **business requirements model** (see Section 6.4) contains descriptions of the manual and automated workflows of our business context, described using business-oriented versions of actors, use cases, objects, the glossary and, optionally, communication diagrams and activity diagrams.
- The **system requirements model** (see Section 6.5) contains an external view of the system, described as system-oriented versions of actors, use cases and use case diagrams, user interface sketches, an enhanced glossary and nonfunctional requirements.

These inputs must be transformed into a model of the objects that will be processed by the proposed system, along with their attributes and relationships. These objects will exist within the system itself or at the system boundary, accessible via one or more interfaces. Most of the objects that we discover at this stage will correspond to physical objects or concepts in the real world (lower-level, solution-oriented objects won't appear until design). Once we have a model of the system objects, we will put them through a verification process to convince ourselves that they would support a solution.

# 7.2 WHY DO ANALYSIS?

So, why do we do analysis in the first place? Because analysis stops us designing a solution before we understand the problem. Although, in principle, we could jump straight into design and then implementation, hoping to draw out an understanding of the problem through trial and error, the analysis techniques we'll look at here are much more efficient. (Some well-chosen prototyping or proof-of-concept work is still permitted, if you feel the situation calls for it.)

We can't expect to have a complete understanding of the problem from the business requirements model, because it describes *existing* practices: by adding software, we expect to be introducing *new* practices. Also, we have not separated manual workflows and automated (or potentially automated) workflows: for example, reserving a car model, as described in Chapter 6, involves both human-to-human and human-to-computer interaction. Even when we have a system use case model, our understanding of the problem is still incomplete, because the focus of use cases is external: use cases deal with the interactions between actors and the boundary of our system – the system itself is regarded as a **black box**, with only the outside visible. Use cases are imprecise: in order to make them easy to produce and easy to understand, use cases are written in natural language – therefore, they rely on our ability to understand language and to make certain assumptions. Business requirements modeling and system requirements modeling must still be done, of course: the former allows us to understand the business context; the latter forms a contract with our sponsors.

Once we've completed **static analysis**, our sponsors will be able to confirm that our understanding of the business objects is correct, before we let the objects influence our design. After **dynamic analysis**, we will be confident that our analysis objects support the required system functionality. In keeping with the philosophy of spiral development, dynamic analysis will also help us to build the static model. The static analysis model is also valuable when it comes to designing a database schema (for those business objects that need to be stored).

# 7.3 OVERVIEW OF THE ANALYSIS PROCESS

In the case of Ripple, analysis has the following steps which you repeat until you and your sponsors are happy:

1. Use the system requirements model to find **candidate classes** that describe the objects that might be relevant to the system and record them on a **class diagram**.
2. Find **relationships** (association, aggregation, composition and inheritance) between the classes.
3. Find **attributes** (simple, named properties of the objects) for the classes.
4. Walk through the system use cases, checking that they're supported by the objects that we have, fine-tuning the classes, attributes and relationships as we go – this **use case realization** will produce operations to complement the attributes.
5. Update the glossary and the nonfunctional requirements as necessary – the use cases themselves should not need updating, although perhaps they will need some correcting.

The term 'realization' means 'making real'. Operations discovered during use case realization should be disregarded during design – at this stage, we're trying to build our confidence not design the solution.

You will need to show class diagrams, complete with attributes, to your sponsors, so that they can look for mistakes (those sponsors that understand the business probably understand it better than you do). A member of your team should summarize the information shown in the class diagram while the sponsors look on. This, coupled with the fact that class diagrams are relatively easy for nonprogrammers to understand, will elicit useful comments such as 'Hang on, did you just say that nonmembers can't reserve cars? You know, they can if they pay a deposit . . .' Deciding when to present the class diagram to sponsors is up to you (and your team), but you will generally do so at least twice: once to look for mistakes and once to verify that you've fixed the mistakes.

Generally, it's not a good idea to show object operations or communication diagrams to your sponsors, because:

- They add a lot of complexity.
- They're superfluous, as far as nonprogramming sponsors are concerned, because you've already demonstrated the dynamic behavior with the system use cases.
- They imply code, something that's definitely taboo for nonprogrammers.
- They will be discarded before design anyway.

Some sponsors, such as technical managers, may like to be shown a little of the dynamic analysis in order to increase *their* confidence: fine, but do this in separate, technical, meetings.

In the rest of this chapter, we'll look in detail at static and dynamic analysis, respectively.

# 7.4 STATIC ANALYSIS

Static modeling involves deciding on the logical or physical parts of the system and how they should be connected together. Roughly speaking, it describes how we construct and initialize the system.

## 7.4.1 Finding Classes

In the previous chapters of this book, classes were not identified systematically. Because we have now gone through the processes of business requirements modeling and system requirements modeling, we have a good source of candidate classes in the form of system use cases.

Candidate classes are often indicated by **nouns** in the use cases. With a little practice, we can quickly cross out those nouns that represent:

- The system itself, for example, 'system' or 'iCoot': As far as we're concerned, the system is just a boundary for the development effort.
- Actors, for example, Assistant or Head Office: An exception to this is when we need to store information about an actor internally (for example, for Member, we need to store a password). Most of the time, actors are anonymous driving forces for our boundaries.
- Boundaries, for example, 'customer applet' or 'head office link': At this stage, we're trying to identify business-related objects with interesting information and behavior. Boundaries are particular pieces of software that allow actors to get at our objects.
- Trivial types (for example, strings and numbers): We can assume that these will be provided by the implementation language or its libraries.

Short descriptions for the candidate classes that are left after this filtering process should be added to the glossary. If you can't write a *short* description for any class, maybe you're expecting it to represent too much: consider splitting it into more than one class.

## 7.4.2 Identifying Class Relationships

Once we have a list of candidate classes, we can try to draw **relationships** between them. There are four possible types of relationship:

- Inheritance: A subclass inherits all of the attributes and behavior of its superclass(es).
- Association: Objects of one class are associated with objects of another class.
- Aggregation: Strong association – an instance of one class is made up of instances of another class.
- Composition: Strong aggregation – the composed object can't be shared by other objects and dies with its composer.

Inheritance is a different kind of relationship to the other three: inheritance describes a compile-time relationship between classes while the others describe a run-time connection between objects. According to the UML standard, all run-time relationships come under the umbrella term **association**. However, most people use the term 'association' to mean 'an association that isn't aggregation or composition'.

Choosing between relationships can be tricky – you need to use intuition, experience and guesswork. During analysis, you should expect the frequency of these kinds of relationship to be:

association > aggregation > inheritance > composition

As far as design and implementation are concerned, the differences between association, aggregation and composition can be difficult to spot.

### 7.4.3 Drawing Class and Object Diagrams

A **class diagram** shows us what classes exist and how they're related. (Officially, class diagrams can also show attributes and operations, but that requires a lot more space.) In the case of aggregation, composition and association, the class diagram shows *permitted* run-time relationships rather than *actual* ones.

Figure 7.1 shows a UML class diagram for iCoot. Every class is represented as a box with the class name inside (in bold, if not drawing by hand). If the class is abstract, the class name is italicized. If you're labeling an abstract class by hand, you can add the keyword {abstract} above or to the left of the class name instead of using italics.

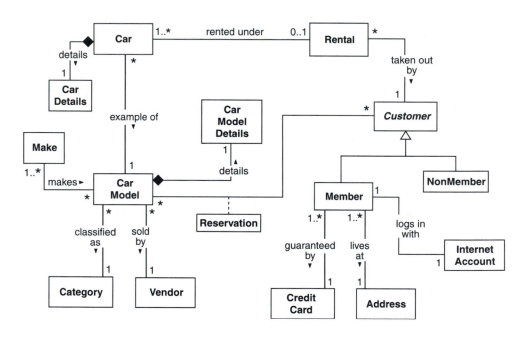

**Figure 7.1: An analysis class diagram for iCoot**

Relationships between classes are shown as lines with various annotations. Even without particular knowledge of UML, its easy to pick information out of a class diagram, just from the text. For example, we can see that 'A Car can be rented under a Rental', 'A Rental can be taken out by a Customer', and so on.

Although the relationships on a class diagram are usually drawn between classes, the run-time relationship is actually between objects: for example, according to Figure 7.1, we would expect to see instances of Car connected to instances of Rental at run time. UML allows us to draw run-time objects as well as compile-time classes, as shown in Figure 7.2 Although UML allows us to mix classes and objects on the same diagram, people generally use the

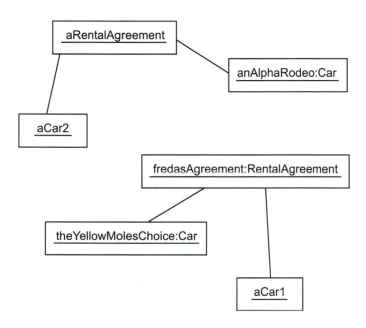

**Figure 7.2: Depicting objects in UML**

term class diagram if there are no objects and **object diagram** if there are no classes (it's up to you what you call a diagram that has both).

In object diagrams, objects are shown as boxes connected by **links** – the links are 'realized' associations. So that we can easily spot the difference between classes and objects, object labels are underlined. As well as the object's name, a label can include the object's class, after a colon, as in fredasRental:Rental. We can show either the object's name, or the object's class, or both. If we show only the object's class, we have to include the colon, to distinguish a class name from an object name, as in :Rental.

Figure 7.2 shows two rentals: under the first, aRentalAgreement, aCar2 and anAlphaRodeo have been rented; under the second, fredasRentalAgreement, theYellowMolesChoice and aCar1 have been rented. As you can see, object names correspond to the kind of variable names we would use in our programs.

Object diagrams are useful for illustrating a particular run-time scenario, but they're optional. For clarity, we would prefer to avoid putting classes and objects on the same diagram.

## 7.4.4 Drawing Relationships

Figure 7.3 shows how inheritance is depicted on a class diagram: a white filled arrowhead on a solid line is drawn from the subclass to the superclass. In order to emphasize hierarchies of

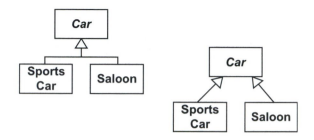

**Figure 7.3: Depicting inheritance in UML**

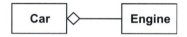

**Figure 7.4: Depicting aggregation in UML**

**Figure 7.5: Depicting composition in UML**

**Figure 7.6: Depicting association in UML**

subclasses, the arrows can be combined in the style shown on the left. Thus, SportsCar and Saloon are both subclasses of Car.

Aggregation is drawn as a line between two classes with a white diamond on the aggregator's end. So, Figure 7.4 shows that an Engine is part of a Car.

Composition is drawn in a similar way to aggregation, but with a black diamond on the composer's end – see Figure 7.5, which shows that a Body is always part of the same Car.

Association is shown as an undecorated line (see Figure 7.6). Thus, a Driver is associated with a Car, but the Driver is not part of the Car (that would be aggregation) and the Driver is not always part of a single Car (that would be composition).

When developing your analysis class model, for the sake of simplicity, make sure that information can only be deduced in one way. For example, the iCoot class diagram shown in Figure 7.1 allows us to calculate how many Cars a particular member is renting, from the

Rental class, the rented under association and the taken out by association. Thus, it would be redundant to show a hasOutForRent association from the Member class to the Car class, even if our use case model implied that such an association were needed.

## Multiplicity

All relationships except inheritance can indicate at either end the number of run-time objects that are allowed to take part in the relationship (the **multiplicity** of the relationship):

- n: Exactly n.
- m..n: Any number in the range m to n (inclusive).
- p..*: Any number in the range p to infinity.
- *: Shorthand for 0..*.
- 0..1: Optional.

For composition, the multiplicity at the composer's end is always 1 because, according to the UML rules, a composed object can't be shared among composites – thus a multiplicity would be redundant in this case. In other cases, if no multiplicity is shown, we must assume that it has not been specified, or that it is simply not known at this stage. It would be wrong to assume that a missing multiplicity implied some default value, such as 1.

Looking at Figure 7.7, we can deduce the following:

- A Car has one Engine.
- An Engine is part of one Car.
- A Car has four or five Wheels.
- Each Wheel is part of one Car.
- A Car is always composed of one Body.
- A Body is always part of one Car and it dies with that Car.
- A Car can have any number of Drivers.

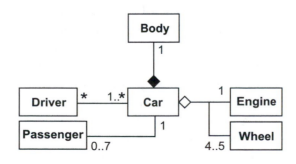

**Figure 7.7: Depicting multiplicities in UML**

- A Driver can drive at least one Car.
- A Car has up to seven Passengers at a time.
- A Passenger is only in one Car at a time.

Even though the notation we've seen so far appears to be unambiguous, things are never that easy, because we're still dealing with natural language and assumptions about the real world that the reader will make. For example, the association between Car and Passenger, rather than being read as shown in the list above, could be read as the following pair of statements:

- For each Car, there are only seven Passengers that could ever be in the Car.
- A Passenger is only allowed in one particular Car.

You may well argue that our initial interpretation is more obvious, based on what the modeler is likely to be trying to say (although we frequently talk about how many people a car can carry, when would we ever want to dictate who was allowed to ride in a particular car?). If the distinction is not obvious, or we wish to be pedantic for the sake of it, we can provide a verbose description – a **class survey**, if you like. Or, we could provide further annotation for our diagram using **comments**.

The difference between aggregation and composition is subtle. In Figure 7.7, why is the Engine aggregated while the Body is composed? The differences relate to object sharing and object lifetimes. Recall that a composed object can never be part of more than one composite and dies with the composite, while an aggregated object can be shared and can outlive its aggregator. Although a car trundles out of the factory with a brand new engine inside, the engine may later be replaced, because it's worn out, so the engine doesn't necessarily die with the car; in contrast, the body of the car is an intrinsic part of the car – it's the soul of the car, if you like, you can't destroy the car without destroying the body (but you could always take the engine out first). The issue of sharing is not important in this example: although the body could never be part of two cars (not legally, anyway), the engine couldn't either.

All this may seem a little confusing. The existence of composition in UML is really just a result of the properties of programming languages like C++. In C++, an object can be part of the same piece of memory as another object: in this case, the sub-object certainly dies with the larger object. This language property also leads to the second part of the rule: a composed object can't be part of two objects at the same time. Even if the composed object is separate, we have no garbage collector in C++, so the composer may want to delete the composed object when the composer itself is deleted, which reinforces the danger of sharing. It would be neater if UML also required the composite to *create* the composed object (that would work well for our body example); however, that would prohibit us from creating the composed object first and then passing it into the composite's constructor.

The fact that composition is really a programming issue implies that it is more common in design than analysis. As a matter of analysis style, it's recommended that you use aggregation when there is an obvious part–whole relationship (as in the engine example) and save composition for those rare cases when there is an obvious shared lifetime (as in the body example).

For design purposes, composition is also useful when you wish to add behavior to an object by hiding a delegate object inside, rather than by inheriting from another class (we saw an example of this in Chapter 3 with Stack and LinkedList).

From an implementation point of view, one-to-many and many-to-many relationships often result in the use of collection objects (lists, trees, sets, etc.) at run time. For example, Car may employ some kind of List object to hold on to its passengers. One advantage of using multiplicities on class diagrams is that we do not need to be specific about such messy implementation details until much later.

## Association Labels, Roles and Comments

All relationships, except inheritance, can be given an **association label**, indicating the nature of the association. If it's not obvious which way the association name should be read, a black arrowhead can be used. For example, in Figure 7.8, we can see that there is at least one Wheel that turns the Car.

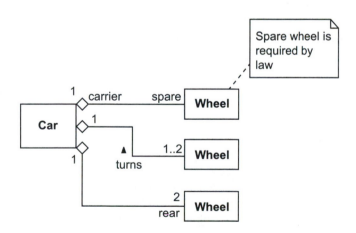

**Figure 7.8: Association labels, roles and comments in UML**

As well as association names, we can show **roles**. A role indicates the part played by an object in the association – the role is shown as a label near the object that plays the role. For example, Figure 7.8 indicates the following roles:

- A Car has one Wheel acting as a spare.

- The spare Wheel has one Car acting as its carrier.
- A Car has two rear wheels.

In principle, association names and roles can be combined on the same association, but most of the time they should be considered alternatives (in order to avoid clutter).

Figure 7.8 also shows a UML **comment**, an arbitrary piece of text enclosed in an icon that looks like a piece of paper, connected to the relevant part of the diagram by means of a dashed line. If the target of the dashed line is unclear, we can put a small white circle with a black border at the end – this is useful when the target is another dashed line, for example. A comment, which can appear on any diagram, can be used to provide extra information that would be difficult or messy to show using other UML notation.

## 7.4.5 Attributes

An attribute is a property of an object, such as its size, position, name, price, font, interest rate, or whatever. In UML, each attribute can be given a **type**, which is either a class or a primitive. If we choose to specify a type, it should be shown to the right of the attribute name, after a colon. (We might choose not to specify attribute types during analysis, either because the types are obvious or because we don't want to commit ourselves yet.)

Attributes can be shown on a class diagram by adding a compartment under the class name. To save space, we can document them separately instead as an **attribute list**, complete with descriptions. If we were using a software development tool, we would expect to be able to zoom in to see attributes (and their descriptions) or zoom out to see class names only. If you can't provide a *short* description for an attribute at this stage, perhaps it should be several attributes, or even a class in its own right.

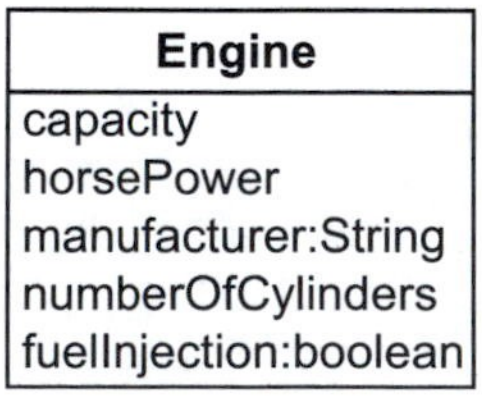

```
+------------------------+
|        Engine          |
+------------------------+
| capacity               |
| horsePower             |
| manufacturer:String    |
| numberOfCylinders      |
| fuelInjection:boolean  |
+------------------------+
```

**Figure 7.9: Depicting attributes in UML**

Figure 7.9 shows the attributes of an Engine: capacity, horsePower, manufacturer, numberOf-Cylinders and fuelInjection. This diagram is specific about the type given to manufacturer (String) and fuelInjection (boolean); the implication is that we've decided that we will never be interested in finer details of the manufacturer – address, for example – or the particular variety of fuelInjection (we just want to know whether or not it's there).

As soon as we start showing attribute types, we open a can of worms: what is a String? What is a boolean? If the type is the name of one of our own classes, there's no problem. Other than that, we don't want to tie ourselves to a particular programming language or set of libraries. Therefore, it's recommended that you stick to ubiquitous primitives (such as int, boolean and float) and one or two obvious classes (for example, it's fairly obvious that String indicates an object containing a sequence of characters).

Although UML does allow us to define our own primitives in language-independent notation – Integer, Real and Boolean, for example – you might like to avoid using this facility because, when you come to design, you will have to be language-specific. (Another reason to avoid this issue is that, in Java, types such as Integer are classes, *not* primitives.)

You may also like to avoid using the array type, which is usually a cross between an object and a primitive, even though most object-oriented languages support it. The reason is that your classes are likely to be more elegant if you use collection classes such as List and Set exclusively. During the design phase, you may find yourself using arrays more, but you will need to be careful not to compromise good style for the sake of a slight improvement in performance.

For simplicity, you should avoid including derived attributes in your artifacts. For example, a circle's attributes include radius, diameter, circumference and area. However, we could store any one of these attributes and calculate the rest at run time, so we only need to show one of the four attributes on our class diagram. In this case, radius seems the obvious choice, because it's probably going to be accessed more than the others (so we'd rather not calculate it) and the other attributes can be calculated using multiplication (which is faster than division).

As far as UML is concerned, attributes and associations (all three varieties) are just properties of a class. In other words, every attribute can be shown as an attribute or as an association with the attribute's name as the role (although an association to a *primitive* value or an array would look odd). This means that we can add multiplicities to attributes, after the type name, as in *, for a multi-valued attribute, or [0..1], for an optional attribute. This is UML's way of avoiding the thorny issue of whether we should show an attribute or an association in any particular case. In this book, multiplicities won't be shown for attributes, except in the case of optional attributes.

Figure 7.10 shows a full set of attributes for the analysis objects discovered while examining the iCoot system use cases. For completeness, some of the attributes shown are from the full Coot system (totalAmount, for example). In order to avoid manipulating images and video in the system, adverts and posters are simply attributes that specify a location elsewhere (using a URL, for example).

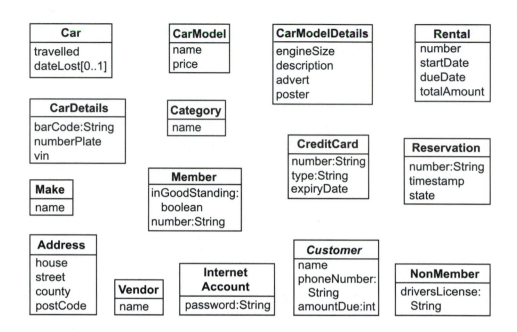

**Figure 7.10: Attributes for iCoot**

The dateLost attribute is optional (indicated by its [0..1] multiplicity): if the Car is lost, we record the date it was lost, otherwise we record nothing. In programming terms, we could use a null pointer to indicate that a particular Car is not lost. If an optional attribute has a primitive type, such as int, we have to reserve one value to indicate 'no value here': for example, our model might allow us to set aside 0 or -1.

Occasionally, you'll find attribute multiplicities to be useful, but don't overuse them. For example, only one attribute in this entire book (dateLost) required a multiplicity (even then, it could be argued that a more general notion of 'car state' would have proved better in the long run).

As we saw earlier, UML allows us to draw run-time objects as well as compile-time classes. Figure 7.11 shows how we can specify run-time attribute values on object diagrams.

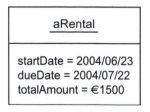

**Figure 7.11: Depicting attribute values in UML**

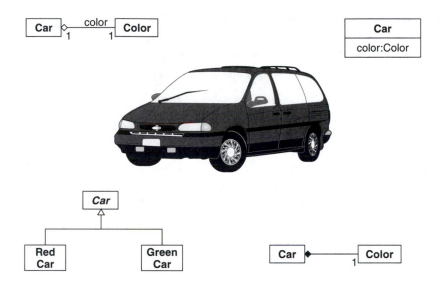

**Figure 7.12: Choosing between attributes and relationships**

## Attribute or Relationship?

Often, we need to make choices between alternative ways of modeling information. For example, how would you choose to model the color of a Car, for the benefit of customers? Figure 7.12 shows four alternatives:

1. Introduce an aggregation between Car and a class called color.
2. Add an attribute to Car called color, with type color.
3. Introduce a subclass of Car for each possible color.
4. Introduce a composition between Car and color.

All of these options make sense, although some of them may seem counter-intuitive. But how would we choose?

The central issue is this: which modeling option fits the situation best? Or, to put it another way, which is the most natural? As far as option 1 goes, it seems a little heavy-handed to say that the color is part of the Car. Option 2 seems pretty good: as far as Car buyers are concerned, the color is just one of a Car's attributes. Option 3 definitely seems to be over the top – do we really want a new type of Car for every available color, especially when there might be dozens? Option 4 seems a little more sensible than option 1 – a Car comes out of the factory sprayed a particular color; even if we change the color later, the original color is likely to remain underneath. Overall, option 2 would seem to be most appropriate in the context of buying cars.

But would the choice be different if we were modeling cars on behalf of a car manufacturer? In that case, the manufacturer of the paint would probably become important – we would need to know where to get more if we ran out. So, we would need to model the color as a separate class with its own relationships and attributes; therefore, option 4 might be the best choice.

Could we ever justify option 3? Perhaps. For example, if we were psychologists seeking to model the effect of a car's color on the behavior of the driver – maybe red cars incite dangerous driving while green cars encourage caution. In that case, red and green cars may be sufficiently different to justify modeling them as separate classes.

The moral of this story is that the analysts must choose whichever representation seems to fit the current situation best: there is no *correct* answer. The best advice is probably not to worry about the philosophy too much. Instead, use common sense, experience, intuition, spirals and iterations to press forward to a successful implementation.

In order to avoid confusion, you should ignore the fact that UML doesn't distinguish between an attribute and an association-plus-role. Be guided by your model: if it seems to be an attribute, draw it as an attribute; if it appears to be an association, draw it as an association.

## 7.4.6 Association Classes

Occasionally, an association has some information or behavior related to it. An **association class** can be introduced alongside the association, as depicted in Figure 7.13. This diagram indicates that a CarModel can be associated with any number of Customer objects and a Customer can be associated with any number of CarModel objects. For each link, there is a corresponding Reservation object that has a number, time-stamp and state. There is no name given to the association in this case, because it is implicit in the name of the association class.

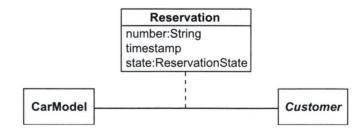

**Figure 7.13: An association class from iCoot**

An association class represents attributes and operations that exist only because the association exists: the attributes and operations are not tied to the objects at either end of the association. In the example above, when a customer makes a reservation, a new link is created at run time between the Customer and the corresponding CarModel. During requirements capture and analysis, it was determined that the reservation number, time-stamp and state must all be recorded. However, there is no sense in which these attributes fit with the Customer or with the CarModel, they're somewhere in between. Therefore, an association class is appropriate.

When we come to design, we will have to replace association classes with something more concrete, because they're not supported directly in most programming languages. However, they are useful during analysis.

## 7.4.7 Tangible versus Intangible Objects

Often, you will find yourself modeling an **intangible** object, such as a product described in a catalog, and a separate **tangible** object, such as the actual item that is delivered to your door. The object in the catalog describes the properties of something that you *could* order from the supplier, but which hasn't necessarily been manufactured yet. The object that arrives at your door definitely *has* been manufactured, it is an instance of the type of product described in the catalog. Typically, there are many tangible objects for each intangible one.

It is a common mistake to model tangible and intangible pairs as a single object. For example, if we were writing a sales system for a car dealership, we would discover during analysis that we were dealing with 'catalogs' describing the cars available for sale, 'cars' that we sell to customers, and 'customers' that buy the cars. It would be easy to conclude that we should produce the three concrete classes shown in Figure 7.14. However, in reality, we have two 'car' concepts here: the car that appears in the catalog is intangible, it describes the features of all cars of that type, but there may not be any such car in existence; in contrast, the car that is owned by a customer is tangible, it definitely exists, because it can be driven – it is separate from any similar car owned by a different customer.

### Getting it Wrong

To reinforce the issue of tangibility, let's assume that, as well as selling cars, our dealership services customer cars on request. The information relating to sales includes:

- modelNumber: This identifies the production process for making a car of this type.

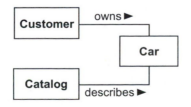

**Figure 7.14: Buying cars**

- availablecolors: The colors that cars of this type can be painted before they leave the factory.
- numberOfCylinders: The number of combustion cylinders in the engine fitted to this type of car.

The information relating to services includes:

- owner: The registered owner of the vehicle.
- vehicleIdentificationNumber: A unique number stamped on a plate and riveted to the car's body when it is manufactured that identifies the car for registration purposes and helps the police to trace the owners of stolen cars.
- mileageAtLastService: The number of miles the car had driven at the time of its last service – this allows us to calculate how many miles it's covered since it was last serviced.

Using the single concept of Car shown in Figure 7.14, we would have no choice but to put all of these attributes on one class, as shown in Figure 7.15. From what you already know about object modeling, the introduction of a class with two distinct sets of responsibilities should be ringing alarm bells already – such classes are said to have **weak cohesion**: their responsibilities do not form a single clump.

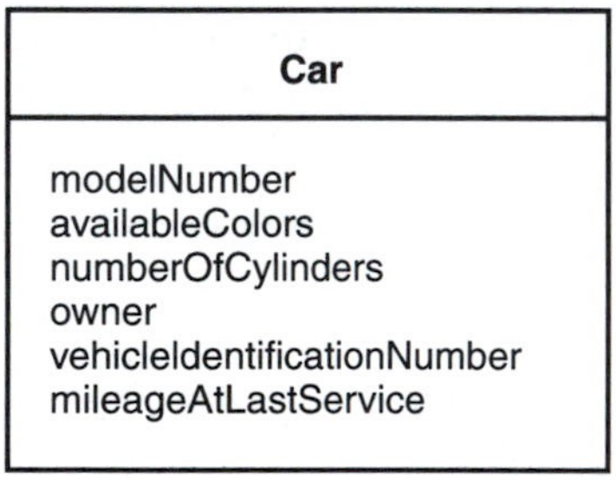

```
┌─────────────────────────────────┐
│              Car                │
├─────────────────────────────────┤
│  modelNumber                    │
│  availableColors                │
│  numberOfCylinders              │
│  owner                          │
│  vehicleIdentificationNumber    │
│  mileageAtLastService           │
└─────────────────────────────────┘
```

**Figure 7.15: A Car class, showing its attributes**

Let's suppose that we're going to offer for sale the 'Alpha Rodeo 156 2.0': we would have to create a Car and set its attributes appropriately. This would give us the situation shown in Figure 7.16. (Possible attribute values have been shown as a list enclosed in braces – not strictly UML, but convenient for our purposes.)

Now let's suppose that a customer brings their 'Alpha Rodeo 156 2.0' in for its first service. We now have two choices: we can create a new Car to represent the car owned by this particular customer, giving us the situation shown in Figure 7.17A, or we can use the existing Car, giving us the situation shown in Figure 7.17B.

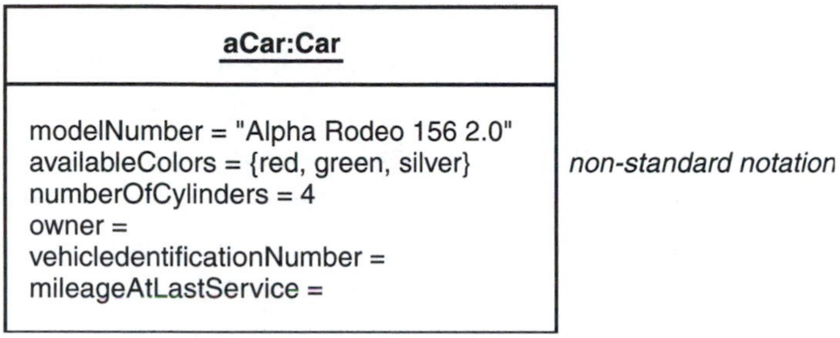

```
                aCar:Car

modelNumber = "Alpha Rodeo 156 2.0"
availableColors = {red, green, silver}        non-standard notation
numberOfCylinders = 4
owner =
vehicledentificationNumber =
mileageAtLastService =
```

**Figure 7.16: A car for sale**

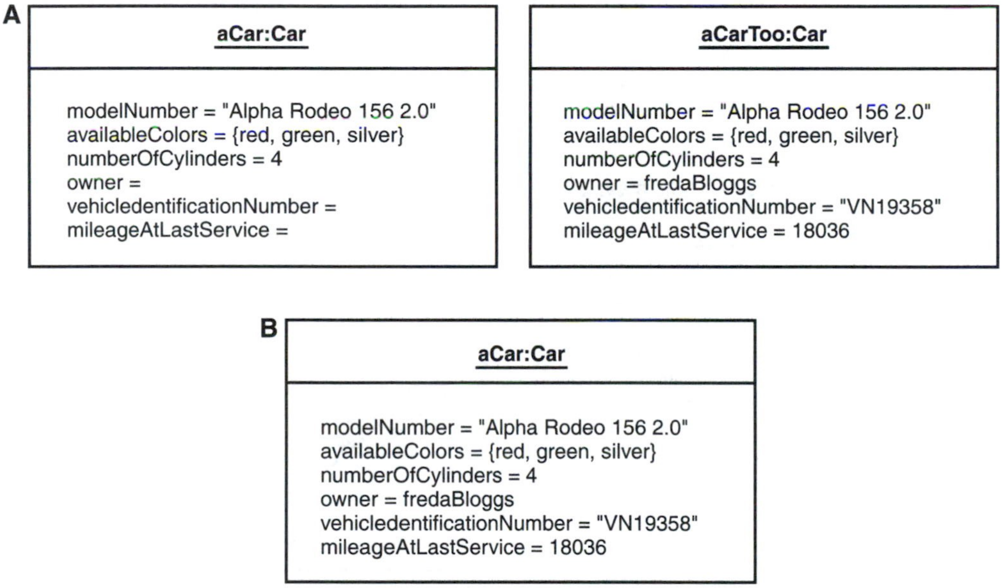

**A**
```
              aCar:Car                             aCarToo:Car

modelNumber = "Alpha Rodeo 156 2.0"    modelNumber = "Alpha Rodeo 156 2.0"
availableColors = {red, green, silver}  availableColors = {red, green, silver}
numberOfCylinders = 4                   numberOfCylinders = 4
owner =                                 owner = fredaBloggs
vehicledentificationNumber =            vehicledentificationNumber = "VN19358"
mileageAtLastService =                  mileageAtLastService = 18036
```

**B**
```
                aCar:Car

modelNumber = "Alpha Rodeo 156 2.0"
availableColors = {red, green, silver}
numberOfCylinders = 4
owner = fredaBloggs
vehicledentificationNumber = "VN19358"
mileageAtLastService = 18036
```

**Figure 7.17: Servicing a car**

If we choose option A, half the attributes remain unused on the first car object and we have redundant information on the second object. If we choose option B, we can only service one 'Alpha Rodeo 156 2.0' at a time (otherwise information about the first one we started servicing will be lost).

Although the original model shown in Figure 7.14 appeared natural and reasonable, the practical implications show that the model is nonsense. What we should have spotted early on is that we have an intangible concept, responsible for the first set of attributes, and a tangible concept, responsible for the second set.

### Getting it Right

Let's discard the model shown in Figure 7.14, replacing it with a new intangible concept called CarModel and a tangible concept called Car. This gives us the class diagram shown in Figure 7.18. Now we can place the attributes modelNumber, availableColors and numberOfCylinders on CarModel, while owner, vehicleIdentificationNumber and mileageAtLastService remain on Car. Applying this new model to the example scenario we saw earlier, we create the run-time objects shown in Figure 7.19. Here we have one CarModel representing the 'Alpha Rodeo 156 2.0' and two Car objects representing the separate instances of this type of car that have been brought in for service. With this new model, we don't care how many cars of

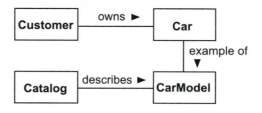

**Figure 7.18: A tangible car and an intangible car model**

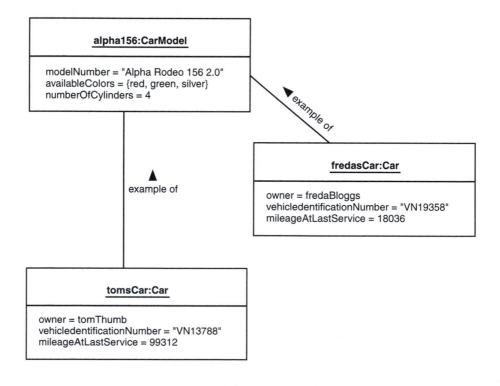

**Figure 7.19: Car models for sale and cars that have been sold**

a particular type are sold, nor how many are returned for service, nor how many are serviced simultaneously, because the model can cope, logically and concisely, with all possibilities.

Usually, a single intangible object will give rise to many tangible ones. Also, the attributes of intangible objects tend to be fixed, while those in tangible objects tend to change over time. In our example, there is one CarModel, representing any number of 'Alpha Rodeo 156 2.0' Car objects that we might sell. The attributes of CarModel do not change over time (the manufacturer *may* occasionally change the specification, by adding new colors, for example, but that doesn't happen very often). The model shows two Car objects, each representing a particular 'Alpha Rodeo 156 2.0' that's been returned for service, at least once, by its owner. The attributes of Car are changeable: the owner changes when the car is sold and the mileageAtLastService changes every time the car is serviced. The vehicleIdentificationNumber doesn't change, but this is a special case of an **identity attribute**, a property that distinguishes this object from all other similar objects, throughout its lifetime.

**ACTIVITY 4**     Before we leave the subject of tangibility, consider a video rental system. Which of the two class diagrams shown in Figure 7.20 is correct, do you think?

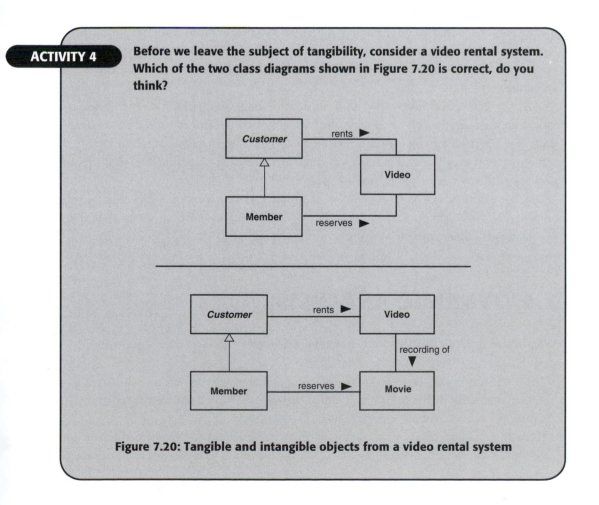

**Figure 7.20: Tangible and intangible objects from a video rental system**

### 7.4.8 Good Objects

It's all very well being able to draw class diagrams in perfect UML notation. It's quite another thing to be able to find good objects, attributes and relationships.

In this book, the recommended starting point is nouns in use cases, a combination of the obvious with the valuable work of Jacobson. Beyond that, a lot of your success will come from hard thinking and growing experience. Domain experts (customers and colleagues) can help here, since they should be invited to comment on your class model. Using spirals and iterations will also help, a lot.

If you find yourself struggling to decide what should be an object and what shouldn't, remember that objects are cheap – if something you're thinking about or talking about sounds like an object, it probably *is* an object: don't be afraid to put it down on paper, look at it and see what it can do – at this point, you're a long way off the heavy investment of writing code. If you find yourself thinking about the properties of an object, you have attributes; if you're thinking about what an object should be able to do, you have operations. In this book, it's recommended that you don't worry too much about operations until dynamic analysis, but there's no harm in noting some down in the meantime – dynamic analysis is used to *verify* that you have at least the operations you need in order to satisfy the use cases, but a few more won't hurt.

Another good trick, if you can't seem to find the right objects from the use cases, is to talk to an independent colleague about the business or the system in question. Ask them to note down everything you mention that seems to be an important concept, in exactly the same way as if they were taking notes at a lecture. This way, any unhelpful anxieties and prejudices that you have will be side-stepped.

The practical advice you've seen on choosing between attributes and relationships, considering the tangible and the intangible, and identifying association classes should help you to avoid common pitfalls.

## 7.5 DYNAMIC ANALYSIS

We perform **dynamic analysis** for the following reasons:

- To confirm that our class diagram is complete and accurate, so that we can fix it sooner rather than later: this may involve adding, deleting or modifying classes, relationships, attributes and operations.
- To gain confidence that our modeling up to this point can be implemented in software: we're not the only ones that should be confident before we proceed, our sponsors are just as important.

- To verify the functionality of the user interfaces that will appear in the final system: it's a good idea to partition access to the system into separate interfaces, along use case lines, before we dive into detailed design.

According to Jacobson, the most important part of dynamic analysis is **use case realization**, i.e. making our use cases real by demonstrating how they can be implemented as collaborating objects. Use case realization has the following steps:

1. Walk through the system use cases, simulating the messages sent between objects and recording the results on communication diagrams.
2. Introduce operations on the objects that receive the messages.
3. Add classes to represent boundaries (system interfaces) and controllers (placeholders for complex business processes or for the creation and retrieval of objects), as necessary.

## 7.5.1  Drawing Use Case Realizations

As we simulate the messages sent between our analysis objects, we need to record our results. UML communication diagrams and sequence diagrams are designed for this purpose. Although we can pretty much record the same information on communication diagrams and sequence diagrams, communication diagrams are better for use case realization because they're simpler to produce and they focus on the objects and their connections, rather than on the order in which the messages are sent.

We saw a simple business-level communication diagram in Section 6.4.4. Unlike our business requirements example, which had a rather free-form mix of actors, objects and systems, the analysis example (Figure 7.21) is cleaner. An informal description of the information shown in Figure 7.21, from a member of the iCoot team, might read as follows:

A Member actor asks the MemberUI to reserve a particular CarModel; the Member is warned that there is a fine if the corresponding car is not collected when it arrives; once the Member confirms that they do wish to make a reservation, the MemberUI asks the ReservationHome to create a new Reservation, passing in the CarModel and the Member (which the user interface already has, as a result of logging on); finally, the MemberUI gets the number from the new Reservation and passes it to the Member.

In general, analysis-level communication diagrams can show:

- Actors interacting with boundaries (for example, the Member interacts with a MemberUI).
- Boundaries interacting with objects *inside* the system (for example, the MemberUI interacts with a ReservationHome, a Member, a CarModel and a Reservation).

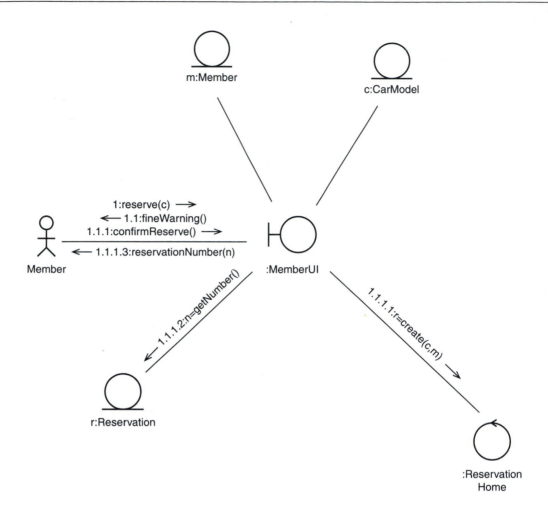

**Figure 7.21: A communication diagram for U7:Make Reservation**

- Objects inside the system interacting with boundaries to external systems (we might imagine an internal ReportGenerator object interacting with a HeadOffice boundary, for example).

We do not need to show any business objects that lie outside the system, nor do we need to show actors that don't interact with the system directly.

Rather than two-way interactions, we can now use a more computer-oriented, client–supplier style: actors initiate interactions with boundary objects; boundary objects initiate interactions with system objects; system objects initiate interactions with other system objects, and boundaries to other systems.

## 7.5.2 Boundaries, Controllers and Entities

A plain communication diagram shows objects as labeled boxes. For extra expressiveness, UML allows the developer to use **icons**, instead of boxes, to indicate the nature of the object. Figure 7.22 shows the UML meanings of the icons in Figure 7.21:

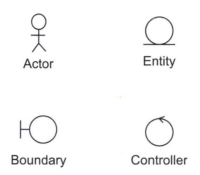

**Figure 7.22: Jacobson's icons for communication diagrams [Jacobson** *et al.* **92]**

- Actor: A person (usually) or system (occasionally) existing outside the system.
- Boundary: An object at the edge of the system, between the system and the actors. For system actors, boundaries provide a communication path. For human actors, a boundary means a user interface, capturing commands and queries and displaying feedback and results. Each boundary object usually corresponds to a use case, or a group of related use cases. More specifically, such a boundary usually maps to a user interface sketch (in which case it may be an entire interface or just a sub-window). It is quite reasonable for boundary objects to survive through to design.
- Entity: An object inside the system, representing a business concept such as a customer, a car or a car model and containing useful information. Typically, entities are manipulated by boundary and controller objects, rather than having much behavior of their own. Entity classes are the ones that appear on our analysis class diagram. Most entities survive through to design.
- Controller: An object inside the system that encapsulates a complex or untidy process. A controller is a service object that provides the following kinds of service: control of all or part of a system process; creation of new entities; retrieval of existing entities. Without controllers, our entities would become polluted with messy details. Since controllers are just a convenience for the benefit of analysis, we do not expect many of them to survive through to design; an important exception to this is the idea of a **home**. A home is a controller that is used for the creation of new entities and the retrieval of existing ones. A home may also have utility messages as in carModelHome.findEngineSizes(). Since a home is such a clean concept, they often survive through to design.

The RUP approach is to retain all controllers for the design phase, complete with all the operations that we discover during dynamic analysis. With RUP, there is no distinction between the analysis model and the design model – we simply start with the analysis model and enrich it again and again, until it is transformed into an implementable design model. For the purposes of this book, and in general, this approach is considered too optimistic.

The valuable outputs from analysis are:

- good entity objects with validated attributes;
- high-level boundary objects that mirror the use cases;
- confidence that our model is correct;
- homes (ignoring any utility messages).

The designer should not have the opportunity to modify these fundamental outputs for the sake of implementation. The flip side to this is that the analyst should not be considering programming details, such as how to implement object attributes, relationships or operations.

It's recommended that designers begin with a fresh class diagram that is seeded with the entity objects that were discovered during analysis. Selected boundaries and homes can then be added to this diagram, as appropriate.

## 7.5.3 Communication Diagram Elements

Figure 7.23 shows the analysis communication diagram again, with annotations that explain the individual pieces of notation. The details of the notation are as follows:

- Actors are shown in the same way as they are on use case diagrams.
- Objects are shown as labeled icons or labeled boxes.
- A line between two objects indicates a link, as on an object diagram.
- A message is shown as a sequence number (indicating the message's position in the communication), a message name (in the usual format) and a parameter list (in parentheses).
- An open-ended arrow shows the direction the message is being sent (this arrow doesn't have to be positioned at the end of the message, some developers place it below, for example).
- Labels, used to identify objects and parameters, can be shown as name, name:Type, :Type or literal (for example, carModel, m:CarModel, :CarModel, 10 or "abc").
- Assignment of a reply value to a name can be shown like this: n = getNumber().
- A conditional message can be shown as a **guard** (a condition in brackets), next to the message, for example, 4:[Only on Saturday]readPaper().
- Iteration can be indicated with a * next to the part of the sequence number that iterates.

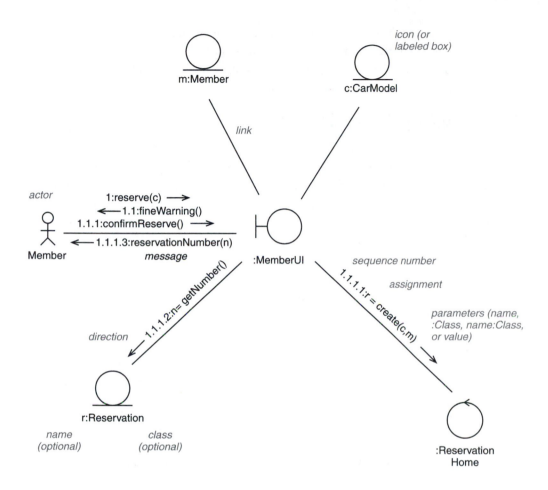

**Figure 7.23: Elements of a UML communication diagram**

Although, in reality, no actor would literally 'send a message' to a boundary object, the message metaphor is a convenient and concise way of representing an interaction. Unlike object diagrams, object labels on communication diagrams are not underlined (partly because classes can't be present to cause confusion).

A few words about sequence numbers. Initially, a message is sent to an object, causing the execution of a method. Within that method, further messages can be sent: these are given sequence numbers that show the level of the interaction. For example, message 1 causes method 1 to execute; its first message is 1.1, the second is 1.2, and so on. The first message sent within method 1.2 is 1.2.1. As in Figure 7.23, when a communication diagram shows the implementation of a single top-level message (reserve), the first number in the sequence is never higher than 1. Although this numbering scheme can lead to many levels of nesting (especially where we have a two-way interaction), it does at least allow us to be precise.

If we're dealing with concurrent communications on a single diagram, we can give each communication – or thread – a name, as part of the sequence number. For example, we might use a and b as the names of two separate threads; 2.2a and 2.2b would happen at the same time, while 2.3a would happen later on thread a.

## 7.5.4 Adding Operations to Classes

Every message on a communication diagram corresponds to an operation on a class, so we should record the operations in order to have a complete set of use case realizations. Operations can be shown on a class diagram in a separate compartment below the attribute compartment, as shown in Figure 7.24. Alternatively, they can be documented as a separate **operation list**, to save space. The style you choose is likely to be dictated by whether you're using a development tool, paper or a whiteboard; however you do it, be sure to include descriptions of the operations too.

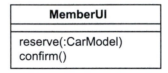

**Figure 7.24: Some operations from iCoot**

The general form of a UML operation is:

```
opName(paramName1:paramType1,paramName2:paramType2):ReturnType
```

Each parameter name, parameter type and return type is optional. (If the parameter name is omitted, the colon must be retained in front of the parameter type, to avoid confusion.) For an empty parameter list, the parentheses can be omitted, but they're retained in this book, so that operations are instantly distinguishable from attributes.

## 7.5.5 Responsibilities

Whenever you add detail to your objects, you should consider **responsibility** as described in [Wirfs-Brock and McKean 02]. This will help you to find and correctly assign operations and attributes. (Although you will have discovered many of the attributes during static analysis, during use case realization you will discover the need for more.) Whenever you discover some information or behavior that needs to be in the system, think to yourself 'Which object is *responsible* for this?' Information ends up as attributes (and objects); behavior ends up as operations (and collaborations).

Taking the idea of responsibilities a step further, make sure that no object is responsible for more than one job (or role, if you prefer): if you have an object that is responsible for getting order details from a customer *and* processing the order, you probably want two objects (a boundary and a controller, perhaps). Objects with a single set of responsibilities are said to have **strong cohesion**, a desirable goal.

Also, remember to think of your objects as clients (who ask questions and give commands) or suppliers (who provide answers and perform services). The alternative, two-way collaboration, leads to greater complexity and more difficult maintenance. A supplier is said to be **loosely coupled** to its client. Two-way collaborations lead to **strong coupling** in both directions. The fact that each use case realization described in this book involves an actor as initiator talking to a boundary that talks to entities, should help you to produce client and supplier objects. Of course, going deeper into the system, a supplier may also be a client and a client may also be a supplier.

## 7.5.6 State Modeling

Sometimes, an entity will have a life cycle that's complex enough to be shown on a **state machine diagram**. For example, Figure 7.25 shows a model of the complex life of a Reservation in the iCoot system. In this diagram, a box with rounded corners indicates a **state**, with a label giving its name. An arrow indicates a **transition** to another state – the label on the arrow indicates the **trigger** that causes the transition. A black circle with an arrow coming out of it points to an **initial state** – a state into which an object can be born. An arrow pointing to a ringed black circle indicates that the source is a **final state** – a state where an object can end its life.

As a result of the start and stop states, Figure 7.25 shows that, when a Reservation is created, it is Waiting and, once it has reached the Concluded state, it plays no further part in the system. As for the other parts of the diagram, rather a lot is being said. Below is a full description – a **state machine survey**, perhaps. This description alone should convince you of the need for a diagram.

> When a Member reserves a CarModel over the Internet, the Reservation is initially Waiting to be processed by an Assistant (this is so the Customer can make a Reservation without the intervention of an Assistant). The Reservation becomes Notifiable if, some time later, an Assistant finds a suitable unreserved Car in the display area of the car park, or if one is returned by a Customer. In this case, the Car is moved to the reserved area.

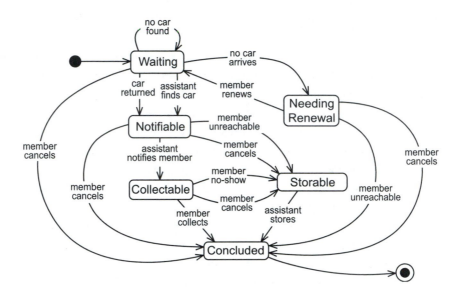

**Figure 7.25: State machine diagram for a reservation**

If no Car becomes available for a particular Reservation within a week, the Reservation becomes NeedingRenewal: the Member must be contacted, by phone or in person, so that they can cancel the Reservation, or ask for it to be renewed for another week. If the Member cancels or can't be contacted within five days, the Reservation is Concluded.

Once a Reservation is Notifiable, the Member must be notified by an Assistant, in person or by phone, within three days; if the Customer can be reached, the Reservation is Collectable otherwise it becomes Displayable (a Car that was moved to the reserved area must be returned to the display area).

Once a Reservation is Collectable, the Member must collect the Car within three days: if they do collect, the Reservation is Concluded; otherwise, the Reservation becomes Displayable.

Once a Displayable Reservation's Car has been put back in the display area, the Reservation is Concluded.

At any time, the Member may cancel the Reservation over the Internet, by phone or in person.

The system will keep Assistants informed as to the state of current (not yet concluded) reservations, so that they can take appropriate action.

As well as **behavior state machines**, such as the one we've just seen, UML has **protocol state machines**. The latter are used to show the order in which messages can legally be sent to an object, but otherwise they're similar.

# 7.6 SUMMARY

In this chapter, we've looked at:

- How to perform the analysis phase of software development.

- How to build a static analysis model showing the business-oriented objects of our proposed system, along with their attributes and relationships, on a class diagram.

- How dynamic analysis can improve and verify the static model, using communication diagrams, and how we can model complex life cycles, using state machine diagrams.

# FURTHER READING

Finding good objects, attributes and relationships comes partly from good thinking, partly from talent and partly from experience. Despite this being a rather philosophical activity, there are places to look for help. Three popular books that are worth investigating are [Fowler 96], [Larman 01] and [Martin and Odell 98]. Fowler gives many examples of analysis models from the real world. The other two books, although they cover a much broader range of topics, do address the issue of finding conceptual objects.

For finding responsibilities, [Wirfs-Brock and McKean 02] is the foundation.

The original ideas on breaking a system up into boundaries, controllers and entities are due to Jacobson [Jacobson *et al.* 92].

In this book, state machine diagrams are covered at a conceptual level only – Martin Fowler provides more detail in [Fowler 03] and the full picture can be found in the UML Specification [OMG 03a].

# REVIEW QUESTIONS

1. With reference to Figure 7.26, what do you think is the most likely implementation of the relationship between Car and Engine? Choose only one option.

    (a)  A field, of type Car, in Engine.
    (b)  A class called CarEngine with one field of type Car and another field of type Engine.
    (c)  A field, of type Engine, in Car.
    (d)  A field, of type Engine, in Car and a field, of type Car, in Engine.

2. With reference to Figure 7.26, which of the following statements are true? Choose all options that apply.

    (a)  A car always has the same body.

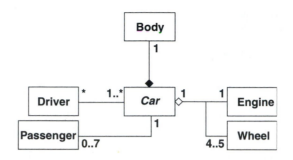

**Figure 7.26: For use with Review Questions 1 and 2**

(b)  Some cars have spare wheels.

(c)  A car has one engine, and engines are not shared between cars.

(d)  All cars have either four or five wheels.

(e)  A car must have at least one driver.

(f)  Passengers cannot be drivers.

---

### PizzaBase Case Study

The PizzaBase restaurant wants to automate the ordering of pizzas by customers. Each table will be fitted with a touch-sensitive screen which customers can use to browse the pizzas on offer and select their choice.

Two basic types of pizza will be offered: the Do-it-Yourself will have a base with tomato sauce only and then customers can choose any number of toppings, at a fixed price per topping; the Prefab will come in several varieties, each with a fixed set of toppings. Every pizza can be ordered with a deep crust or crispy base, and three sizes are available: 6 inch, 9 inch and 12 inch.

Customers will also be able to order from a fixed set of drinks, such as cola and lemonade flavors, each in large or small size. Once customers have confirmed their order, they will be shown the final price and, thereafter, the screen will display the progress of their food as it is being prepared and cooked. At the end of a meal, payment will be made in the conventional way.

---

3.  With reference to the PizzaBase case study, which of the following is most likely list of attributes at the analysis stage? Choose only one option.

(a)  cola, base, price, size, lemonade, payment.

(b)  flavor, variety, payment, final, display, meal, tomato.

(c)  progress, variety, flavor, price, touchSensitive, size, drink.

(d)  base, price, variety, size, progress, flavor.

4.  With reference to Figure 7.27, which diagram is the best model of Pizzas in the PizzaBase restaurant? Choose only one option.

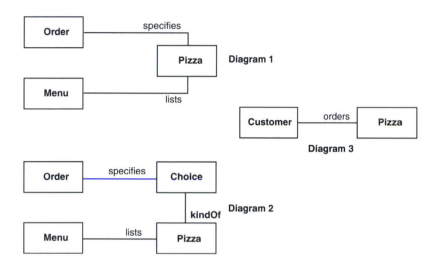

**Figure 7.27: For use with Review Question 4**

(a)  Diagram 1.

(b)  Diagram 2.

(c)  Diagram 3.

5.  With reference to the PizzaBase case study, which of the following is the most likely list of analysis classes? Choose only one option.

(a)  Payment, Order, Drink, Topping, Pizza, Order, Restaurant, Base, Sauce.

(b)  Customer, Table, Pizza, Topping, Drink, Restaurant, Order.

(c)  PizzaBase, Cola, Restaurant, Lemonade, Customer, Do-it-Yourself, Prefab, Table, Order.

(d)  Restaurant, Pizza, Topping, Display, Order, Payment, Touch.

(e)  Screen, Order, Offer, Topping, Size, Meal, Pizza, Restaurant.

(f)  Pizza, Customer, Cook, Table, Crust, Topping, Drink, Restaurant.

6.  In UML, which diagrams are used to show messages sent between objects? Choose all options that apply.

(a)  Activity diagrams.

(b)  Object diagrams.

(c) Communication diagrams.

(d) State machine diagrams.

(e) Sequence diagrams.

(f) Deployment diagrams.

7. With reference to Figure 7.28, which kind of icon would you use to represent a business object containing useful information? Choose only one option.

(a) A.

(b) B.

(c) C.

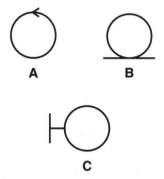

**Figure 7.28: For use with Review Question 7**

8. What is an association class? Choose only one option.

(a) It describes the various kinds of relationship that can exist between classes.

(b) It adds attributes and/or behavior to an association between two other classes.

(c) It associates an object with the class of which it is an instance.

9. With reference to Figure 7.28, which kind of icon would you use to represent a communication path between systems or between a human and a system? Choose only one option.

(a) A.

(b) B.

(c) C.

10. With reference to Figure 7.28, which kind of icon would you use to represent an object that coordinates a system process, creates objects or retrieves objects? Choose only one option.

    (a) A.
    (b) B.
    (c) C.

# ANSWERS TO ACTIVITY 4

The lower option in Figure 7.20 is correct. If there's any doubt in your mind, consider the placement of the attributes barCode and title. A title belongs to a Movie and every recording of it will have the same title. However, every physical Video copy of a Movie will have its own barCode. This illustrates that, sometimes, the name of an intangible class can be completely different to that of its tangible partner.

# ANSWERS TO REVIEW QUESTIONS

1. The most likely implementation of the relationship between Car and Engine is c.
2. With reference to Figure 7.26, the following statements are true:
   a. A car always has the same body. c. A car has one engine, and engines are not shared between cars. d. All cars have either four or five wheels.
3. The most likely list of attributes at the analysis stage is d. base, price, variety, size, progress, flavor.
4. With reference to Figure 7.27, b. Diagram 2 is the best model of Pizzas in the PizzaBase restaurant.
5. The most likely list of analysis classes is b. Customer, Table, Pizza, Topping, Drink, Restaurant, Order.
6. In UML, c. Communication diagrams and e. Sequence diagrams are used to show messages sent between objects.
7. I would use icon B to represent a business object containing useful information.
8. An association class b. Adds attributes and/or behavior to an association between two other classes.

9. I would use icon C to represent a communication path between systems or between a human and a system.

10. I would use icon A to represent an object that coordinates a system process, creates objects or retrieves objects.

# Designing the Solution

# Designing the System Architecture

**T**his chapter considers how to move from analysis into design and concentrates on the system architecture elements of design.

# Learning Objectives

**Understand the steps involved in system design and how a system can be decomposed into physical and logical components.**

●

**Illustrate architectural decisions on UML deployment diagrams.**

**Understand the concurrency and security issues that arise in networked systems.**

●

**Understand how to partition a system and add partitioning decisions to a UML deployment diagram.**

# Chapter Outline

# 8.1 INTRODUCTION

Analysis and design are very different ideas, although the boundaries are sometimes blurred. This blurring can happen intentionally, as in the case of RUP, or accidentally, resulting from poor software development. A clear separation between analysis and design is a good idea, to make sure that the problem is well understood before a solution is considered. With that separation in mind, analysis is about investigating the problem while design is about inventing a solution. Or, to put it succinctly, 'Analysis = What; Design = How'.

There are no strict rules for transforming an analysis model into a design model. Anyone who tells you otherwise is ignoring the human factors and creativity involved in software development – if we could be systematic, software development would be just like engineering, an idea that's already been debunked in Chapter 5. The design process is driven by the need to produce a finished system; the experience of the team; reuse opportunities; personal preference. Once the designer has studied the requirements and analysis artifacts, he or she can start with a clean sheet of paper: we don't care whether there is a close correspondence between analysis objects and design objects, as long as the design leads to an effective solution.

During the design phase, we make certain technology choices (for example, programming languages, protocols and database management systems). We must decide how much impact we want these choices to have on our design. Our technology choices will influence the libraries, patterns and frameworks that are available to us and even the detailed UML notation that we use.

The more general we can make our design, the less we are tied to a particular technology – this will reduce the need for developers to be experts in multiple technologies and it will protect us from technologies that become obsolete or unsupported. The downside of being general is that we may not get the maximum benefit from any particular technology (reuse and performance being the important factors here).

History suggests that individual technologies appear and disappear more frequently than the theories that underpin those technologies. For example, programming languages have included COBOL, Fortran, Pascal, Ada, Modula, PL/1, C, C++, Smalltalk, Eiffel, C# and Java, but the use of these technologies has been governed by only two theories: structured programming and object-oriented programming. Therefore, it's reasonable to conclude that being general is safer than being specific.

With respect to the reuse penalty of a general design, we must accept that some investigation will be needed to discover new reuse opportunities for each implementation. As for the performance penalty, we would hope that keeping our design general would not lose us more than, say, 10% of the maximum possible performance. (By adding extra capacity to our system, using more machines or faster machines, we should be able to make that last 10% irrelevant.)

On the whole, apart from a discussion of the common technologies available today, the discussion will be as general as possible for the rest of this book, relying purely on object-oriented theory and generic UML notation. One exception to this is that where primitive types must be added to diagrams, Java primitives will be used: this is to avoid confusion when looking at the Java code fragments and because some Java classes have primitive-looking names. (Although this is not a strictly generic use of UML, the UML standard does allow the relaxation.) For most of this book, Java arrays will be avoided in favor of collection classes, since the latter are more elegant.

# 8.2 DESIGN PRIORITIES

Since object-oriented software development is incremental, we mustn't expect to design the whole system in one pass. So, at the start of each design phase, we need to plan which parts of the system we will design. The use case priorities will help here; so will the use case urgencies that we indicated using the traffic light analogy during the requirements phase: anything green must be fully designed; anything amber doesn't have to be designed, but it must be supported; anything red must not be designed, but it should still be supported ('designed' means that a solution has been invented; 'supported' means that a reasonable solution is possible, which requires some foresight on our part).

In practice, we seek a system architecture that will support a practical, efficient solution for all the use cases. Within that architecture, we perform detailed design for the most important use cases and partial design for the less important ones. Between increments, we adjust the priorities, the urgencies and the design, as appropriate.

# 8.3 STEPS IN SYSTEM DESIGN

Design can be thought of as having two distinct activities: system design and subsystem design. System design forces us to take a high-level view of the task ahead before we dive into the detail of subsystem design (see Chapter 10). Of course, in good object-oriented tradition, we can blur the boundaries and we can spiral and iterate, but the idea of having two activities is still essential.

System design includes the following activities:

- Choosing a **system topology**: how the hardware and processes will be distributed, perhaps over a network.
- Making **technology choices**: selecting programming languages, databases, protocols and so on (see Chapter 9); some decisions may be deferred until later in the design phase.

- Designing a **concurrency policy**: concurrency means many things happening at once – multiple processes, users, machines; these must be coordinated by our software in order to avoid chaos.
- Designing a **security policy**: security has a number of aspects, each of which must be properly addressed and controlled; as an example, consider a customer's personal data – we must ensure that the data is not stolen by criminals and we must ensure that it can't accidentally be shown to other customers.
- Choosing **subsystem partitions**: often, it is impractical to produce a single piece of software that solves all of our problems; instead we need to produce separate pieces of software and then make sure that the pieces communicate effectively.
- Partitioning the subsystems into **layers** or other subsystems: typically, each subsystem will need to be decomposed further into manageable chunks before we can do detailed design.
- Deciding how machines, subsystems and layers will **communicate**: communication decisions usually happen as a side-effect of the other steps.

# 8.4 CHOOSING A NETWORKED SYSTEM TOPOLOGY

System topology indicates how a system is decomposed into separate physical and logical components. In this section, we see an overview of the history of network architectures and then discuss current architecture issues: thin versus fat clients; networks; and client–server applications versus distributed applications. We'll also see how we can use UML deployment diagrams to illustrate architectural decisions.

## 8.4.1 The History of Network Architectures

Most modern, networked, systems have a **three-tier architecture**. To see what 'three-tier' means and to understand why it's a good idea, we need to take a look at the historical alternatives.

Back in the 1940s, computers were large monolithic devices capable of running only one program at a time. These monolithic machines evolved into **mainframes** that were capable of running multiple programs simultaneously, typically one program per user or one program per **batch** (a batch comprises sets of similar data that are run through a program in sequence, to process electricity bills, for example). Mainframes were able to handle multiple programs simultaneously because they employed a **time-slicer** to run each program on the CPU bit-by-bit, each program taking it in turns to perform a little more processing.

To begin with, users and batch administrators would access a mainframe via a **teletype** unit – an electric typewriter that the operator would use to send one line of text to the mainframe at a time (the text would represent program commands or program data). The program running on the mainframe would then send back one or more lines as a response. As technology improved, teletypes were replaced with **dumb terminals** (also known as **green screens**) that used a Cathode Ray Tube (CRT) instead of paper for textual input and output. With a dumb terminal, the operator could prepare an entire screen of commands or data before dispatching it all at once to the program running on the mainframe (see Figure 8.1).

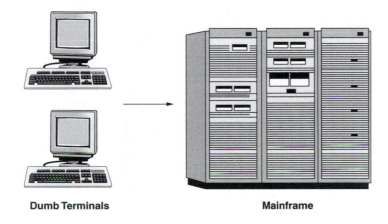

**Dumb Terminals**                    **Mainframe**

**Figure 8.1: Mainframe computing: a one-tier architecture**

The mainframe model, still in use today for large-scale business tasks, is a **one-tier architecture**. This means that, for any given program, there is only one level of computing activity running on one machine (teletypes and dumb terminals do not perform any processing). Or, to put it another way, one-tier architectures have no network: although there is a thin wire from each terminal to the mainframe, possibly over a phone line, that doesn't constitute a network in the modern sense.

The main advantage of a mainframe is that it's simple to set up; the main disadvantage is that we can only increase computing power by buying a new mainframe, or by upgrading the existing one.

The next architectural generation, popularized in the 1970s, was the **two-tier architecture** (although it wasn't called that at the time). The idea was to have processing power on each client, with an optional hard drive, so that large central machines would not have to do all the processing. Thus, we could add, or replace, client machines as a cheaper alternative to changing the central machine. **Mini computers** and **workstations** were introduced as clients that accessed **midi computers** and **file servers**, respectively (see Figure 8.2). The mini–midi combination shown here (for example, VT100 and PDP/11) is really the same as the workstation–file server combination (for example, Solaris workstation and Solaris file server), they just came out of different communities.

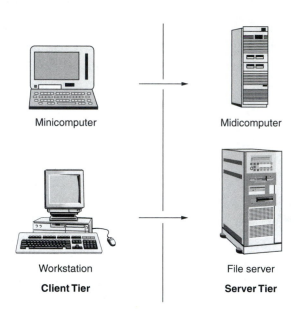

Minicomputer                    Midicomputer

Workstation                     File server
**Client Tier**                 **Server Tier**

**Figure 8.2: Two-tier architectures**

With the two-tier architecture, programs and data must be shipped from the large central machine to the client machines; this requires fast connections, leading to the modern idea of a **network**. A network is an arbitrary number of **host** machines connected together using fast communication links. (We don't need to worry about the different network topologies that are possible; suffice to say that a network allows us to get a piece of information quickly from one machine to another.)

Once we have a network, we can replicate the large central machines as well as the clients, so it's much easier to add computing power. Owners of client machines with hard drives also have the flexibility to manage their own data and programs without having to go through the system administrators. If we allow client machines to hang on to programs and data, we have a maintenance headache: as data changes and programs are upgraded, the clients get out of step. It is quite reasonable, therefore, to prohibit the long term storage of programs and data on client hard drives.

Two-tier architectures brought sophisticated graphics capabilities and **window systems** to clients, replacing the text-only model of teletypes and dumb terminals. Two-tier architectures are still widely used today, mostly in the form of Unix workstations and **file servers**.

## 8.4.2 Three-Tier Architecture

The three-tier architecture (see Figure 8.3) became popular in the 1990s, as a way of separating user interfaces, program logic and data in networked systems, for reasons that

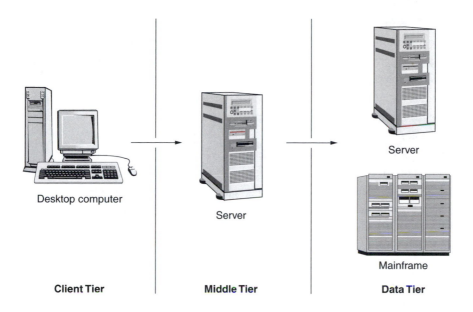

Client Tier     Middle Tier     Data Tier

**Figure 8.3: Three-tier architecture**

will shortly become clear. In a three-tier system, any one program involves at least three machines: the **data tier** stores the data and provides safe concurrent access to it, typically with the help of a database management system (DBMS); the **middle tier** – also known as the **business logic tier** or **server tier** – runs multi-threaded program code using large processors and lots of memory; the **client tier** presents the user interface to the user, so that they can enter data and view results.

The three-tier architecture has many benefits:

- Separation of concerns: Any large system has to deal with secure, efficient management of bulk data; high-throughput programming logic; and simple user interfaces. By programming each of these concerns separately, we make the developer's job easier and we can access the optimizations that have been designed for each particular concern.
- Using the right machine for the job: There is no such thing as a 'one size fits all' computer. Running a user interface is a simple task that doesn't require a mainframe or even a file server; executing programming logic uses CPU and memory intensively but doesn't require huge amounts of disk space, so a powerful server machine can be used; managing bulk data (for example, a million electricity customers) requires as much computing power and disk space as you can lay your hands on, so this calls for large server machines or mainframes.
- Improved performance: We can replicate machines in the data tier or the middle tier, to spread the computing load (**load balancing**), and each tier is specialized and thus easier to optimize.

- Improved security: Frequently, a three-tier system will be deployed in such a way that the client machines are running over the Internet. Therefore, we must have a rigorous security policy in place to protect our internal machines, our programs and our data. With the three-tier architecture, we can make the middle tier secure – impervious to accidental or malicious attack from the outside. Since our data tier is behind the bomb-proof middle tier, we do not have to secure its communications or hardware; this means that our data tier is easier to program and it runs faster. (However, there is a growing feeling that internal tiers need to be protected from employees.)

- Protection of our investment: For situations where we have an existing mainframe that has been performing bulk data storage and batch processing for years, we would prefer not to throw everything away and start again, just to get the benefits of a network and a three-tier architecture. (In general, it's a bad idea to rewrite software: we end up with another 'Version 1.0' with the usual lack of features, performance problems and faults.) Instead, as long as our mainframe manufacturer can make the mainframe network-accessible (most have already done so, because of the 'client–server' revolution), our middle tier can act as a client to the mainframe and as a server to the real clients. This allows us to transform our **legacy system** into a modern marvel.

- Flexibility: As well as the obvious flexibilities of being able to add and remove machines at will, if we design our system with a three-tier architecture, we get deployment flexibility as well. For example, as long as the logical partitioning is correct, we can develop the system on one tier and then deploy it to three tiers, two tiers (middle and data tiers combined) or one tier (all three tiers combined), as the need arises.

- Accommodation of different types of client: Since the client-tier machines only have to capture user input and display system results, we can provide different interfaces for different kinds of device: personal computers, PDAs, set-top boxes, mobile phones, etc. The middle and data tiers can work unchanged in all contexts.

Because of the many advantages of the three-tier architecture, it is recommended that you use it for all your systems, even small ones. After all, even the most humble one-tier program is eventually put to the test of 'Can it be accessed over the network?' You should only choose a two-tier or one-tier architecture for exceptional cases, such as if you need to optimize application size or speed for special purposes, for example, washing machine controllers or operating systems.

## 8.4.3 Personal Computers

In the 1970s, computer enthusiasts working in their garages began building computers that could be used at home. These self-contained, one-tier machines really took off when endorsed in the early 1980s by IBM – the **Personal Computer (PC)** design was meant to result in 'a computer on every desk'.

By the end of the 1980s, it was obvious that PCs were more useful if they were attached, via a corporate network, to file servers and mainframes. The result was a two-tier architecture, with PCs performing complex tasks such as spreadsheet editing and document production, while machines on the corporate network provided e-mail and, to a lesser extent, access to corporate data.

Since the 1990s, PCs have become increasingly popular. In the corporate sector, they benefited initially from endorsement by IBM, and then from their facilities and their low cost (compared to workstations). PCs have also made home-working more practicable. In the home market, there has really been no competition: the high cost of workstations and the low speed of home access to external networks has meant that there is no realistic alternative.

Nowadays, the PC design has displaced all other competitors that emerged from the work of those early garage enthusiasts, with the exception of offerings from Apple (especially popular with graphic designers).

## 8.4.4 Network Computers

By the mid-1990s, as mainframes, Unix boxes and PCs jostled for position in the corporate space, the maintenance cost of PCs was becoming a headache. As mentioned earlier, if you give someone a machine with a hard drive, data and programs on that drive will differ from the central data and programs. This leads to errors – customer data being out of date, for example – and huge extra cost – every client machine has to be returned to central administration for the installation of new releases of e-mail programs, word processors, and so on.

As a result, the concept of a **network computer** was created. A network computer gets *all* of its data and programs on demand from large central servers or mainframes. This requires a fast network (tens or hundreds of megabits per second). In order to prevent individuals polluting the model, network computers do not have a hard drive. (Well, they *can* have a hard drive, but only if it's used by the operating system to cache data and programs.) As you may already have worked out, a network computer is really just a disk-less workstation, typically running some flavor of Unix, because Unix is good at handling on-demand loading of programs over fast networks.

Network computers were a very good idea. Not surprising really, since disk-less work-stations had been successful for many years. But network computers failed to break the stranglehold of PCs. They even failed to break the stranglehold of workstations with disks, in areas where these were popular. (Even professionals like to keep some autonomy, regardless of the cost to themselves and their employer in frustration and wasted time.)

Network computers were used by Java enthusiasts to spread Java in corporations. Since network computers were naturally Unix machines and Java programs can run on Unix, the hope was that Java and Unix would suddenly appear everywhere. However, the network computer has struggled to catch on. Network computers have never been practical for home use because Internet connections, even broadband, are too slow. In order to move beyond PCs, home users need Web browsers that access three-tier architectures.

The terms **thin client** and **fat client** emerged at about the same time as **network computer**. The intention was to emphasize the advantages of the lean, mean client machine, typified by the network computer, over the obese, disk-full PC attached to a network. Thin clients are a good idea: whether you sit in front of a PC or a workstation, all nontrivial work should be network-centric. In the corporate sector, this can be achieved using Java applets accessing a three-tier system. In the home, the best alternative is a Web browser accessing a three-tier system.

## 8.4.5 The Internet and the World Wide Web

By the mid-1980s, many researchers and government employees were making use of a world-wide network of computers, now referred to as the **Internet**. The Internet owes its origins to US research and defense agencies who had put together **ARPAnet** decades before. The Internet is characterized by free access to central servers that allow machines and people to locate other machines by their **Internet address**. Internet addresses have a literal **dotted decimal** form, e.g. 100.99.88.32, and a symbolic **dotted ASCII** form, e.g. www.nowherecars.com. Under the covers, the Internet relies on a low-level protocol called **TCP/IP**: any machine that understands TCP/IP has access to all the facilities of the Internet.

In the early 1990s, when the Internet was firmly established in the research community (as a tool for e-mail and file transfer), Tim Berners-Lee, working at the Swiss research institute CERN, came up with the idea of documents that contain **hyperlinks** to other documents on the Internet. Berners-Lee made his ideas practical by inventing a document layout language called **HyperText Markup Language** (HTML) and a protocol called **HyperText Transfer Protocol** (HTTP). HTTP allows any machine to load a document via a hyperlink from any other machine. The location of a document can be specified using a **Uniform Resource Indicator** (URI) of the form http://www.nowherecars.com/index.html.

Berners-Lee's invention was christened the **World Wide Web** (of information). By the mid-1990s, anyone wanting to make documents available for others to read could deploy them on a **Web server** and anyone wanting to read documents could run a **Web browser** on their client. Once **Internet Service Providers** appeared, providing access to the Internet from home, the World Wide Web spread everywhere. Nowadays, the distinction between the Internet and the World Wide Web is blurred. You may hear any number of terms used more or less interchangeably, such as Internet, Net, World Wide Web, Web or Information Super-Highway.

## 8.4.6 Intranets

The Internet has two major problems: it is slow and it is insecure. The performance problems come from the fact that information might have to travel thousands of kilometers before it reaches its destination, often encountering slow connections and servers on the way. Also, the information has to compete for delivery with all the other information that's in transit. The insecurity of the Internet results from the fact that everyone has access and, therefore, anyone can intercept and read information in transit – even if we encrypt the information, there is still potential for someone to decrypt it.

As a result, the concept of an **intranet** was invented, to mean a 'mini Internet' running behind closed doors. **Intranet** means 'network inside', as opposed to **Internet**, which means 'network between'. An intranet is typically controlled by a single corporation or government. By preventing access to an intranet from outside, we can improve performance (using powerful machines with no competition from outside traffic) and we don't need to worry so much about security. For global intranets, information may still travel long distances, so, on the whole, we still have to forego the performance of a local area network.

As far as security is concerned, we need to make sure that no unauthorized person comes to one of our sites and connects their own computer, of course; beyond that, we have to deal with all the usual problems of industrial espionage, disgruntled or careless employees, spies monitoring the electro-magnetic emissions from our machines and networks – rumor has it that one government organization makes its employees use their computers inside Faraday cages, supplying mains power by induction from outside the cage: it's all a question of how paranoid you want to be.

For most intranets, we can retain the local performance and security benefits and still give our employees access to the Internet (for e-mail, information gathering and monitoring competitors' Web sites). To do this, we need to employ an **Internet firewall**. A firewall is a piece of software that allows machines on an intranet to access any TCP/IP address, while making intranet addresses invisible from the outside. Internet firewalls can perform other tasks too: for example, we can make sure that only Web browsers can access the Internet from employees' machines – this prevents rogue programs from sneaking in and communicating secrets to the outside world; we can configure our Internet firewall to allow e-commerce requests from outside to **tunnel** through on their way to our e-commerce servers; at home, we can use a **personal firewall** to protect our PCs from hackers and viruses.

## 8.4.7 Extranets and Virtual Private Networks

So how can we exploit the performance and security benefits of intranets for business-to-business communications? Easy – we use an **extranet**, a secure connection between one or more intranets. The term extranet is a pun on intranet, short for 'external intranet'. The easiest way to make an extranet is to run a piece of software on the Internet firewalls at the edge of each intranet, which does two things:

- Allows information to pass from firewall to firewall.
- Uses strong encryption to protect that information as it passes over the Internet.

An extranet is also referred to as a **Virtual Private Network (VPN)**. The simplest form of VPN, even older than the idea of an extranet, is a worker dialing in to their corporate LAN from home using purpose-built software.

Figure 8.4 illustrates how intranets, extranets and the Internet fit together.

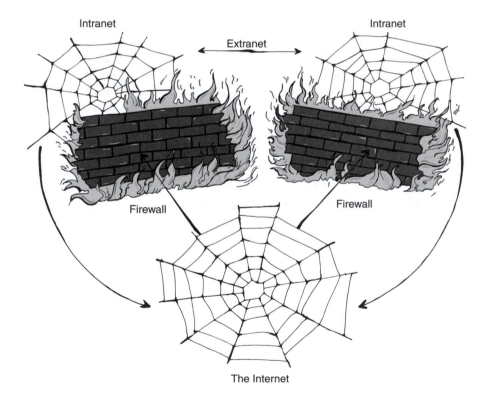

**Figure 8.4: How the different kinds of net fit together**

## 8.4.8 Client–Server versus Distributed Architectures

Whenever we connect multiple machines or software systems, we have to choose between **client–server** and **distributed** styles, as illustrated in Figure 8.5. Despite its origins in the mainframe arena, these days 'client–server' simply means that we have a large number of

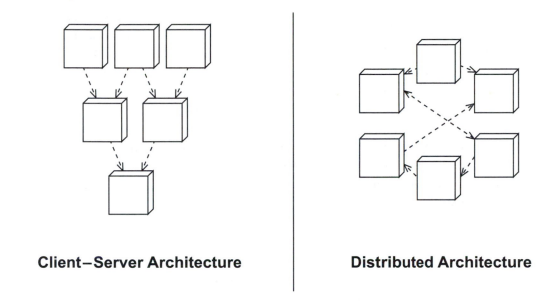

**Client–Server Architecture**     **Distributed Architecture**

**Figure 8.5: Client–server and distributed architectures**

small, simple clients sending requests to a few large, multi-threaded servers that process the requests. A distributed (or **peer-to-peer**) architecture, on the other hand, is characterized by a collection of autonomous peers, communicating in any direction, as the need arises.

The most common example of a client–server architecture is the e-commerce model: customers' Web browsers issue requests to company Web servers, which in turn issue instructions to back-end systems. Most two-tier and three-tier systems are client–server.

A good example of a distributed architecture is when a massive computing task is spread over many Internet machines. If we have a very large amount of data or processing that needs to be performed and we can partition the data or the processing, we can distribute the problem over independent machines.

One example is SETI@home, a nonprofit organization that looks for alien radio signals. The search for extra-terrestrial intelligence (SETI) started out as a NASA project with radio telescopes scanning the heavens and recording anything they came across. This data was then processed to see if it contained evidence of coherent radio transmissions from aliens. Eventually, the SETI project was canceled (because of lack of funds or lack of belief) and was reborn as SETI@home. The enthusiasts who developed SETI@home take the same radio data and distribute it to machines on the Internet: each participating machine analyzes its data using a piece of software that runs as a screensaver; any interesting results are sent back to the central server for further analysis. For more information, see the SETI@home Web site at setiathome.ssl.berkeley.edu.

Although SETI@home has a central repository of data, it is still a distributed architecture because most of the processing is carried out by independent nodes. The idea of bringing together huge numbers of machines to solve a complex task has also been used for prime-number searches and cancer research. The basic idea is now being researched under the heading of **grid computing**.

The terms 'client–server' and 'distributed' (or 'peer-to-peer') are also used to describe software architectures, independently of how the software is deployed on physical machines and networks. Objects running in a program are a good example: normally, we write our objects as servers that can be reused in different contexts with different client objects; but, for special purpose applications, we might also write groups of objects that collaborate in a distributed manner.

Network communication links tend to be bi-directional, meaning that although the link may be opened initially by the client, the server can also send information to the client (whether the client takes any notice is up to the designer of the client software). Thus, strictly speaking, the distinction between client–server and distributed is an artificial one, used by designers to structure their solutions in one way or another.

As a general rule, client–server architectures are easier to develop, but they may not provide maximum theoretical performance (for example, the client is usually idle when the server is processing one of its requests). Distributed architectures are, usually, harder to develop but they may provide better performance. Often, the choice of architecture is obvious. For example, making a purchase is a step-by-step process (customer asks for product details, supplier provides product details, customer elects to purchase product, supplier provides purchase form, customer submits purchase form, and so on), and thus is a natural client–server interaction. In contrast, a multiuser flight simulator requires each pilot's computer to perform complex real-time rendering of the cockpit, scenery and other aircraft – the only communication needed is the periodical broadcast by each machine of its plane's current position. Thus, a multiuser flight simulator is a natural distributed architecture.

## 8.4.9 Depicting Network Topology in UML

System architectures can be depicted in UML on a **deployment diagram** (see Figure 8.6). This simple deployment diagram shows only **nodes**, **communication paths** and multiplicities. Each node, in this diagram, represents a host machine (indicated with the UML keyword `<<device>>`). A communication path shows that two nodes communicate in some way. Nodes can be given multiplicities to indicate how many might exist at run time: thus, in this diagram, we have nodes that are duplicated (`CootServer` and `DBServer`) and nodes that are multiplied (`CootHTMLClient` and `CootGUIClient`).

Deployment diagrams are similar to class diagrams and object diagrams in that they can show *possible* architectures (node types) and *actual* architectures (node instances). When

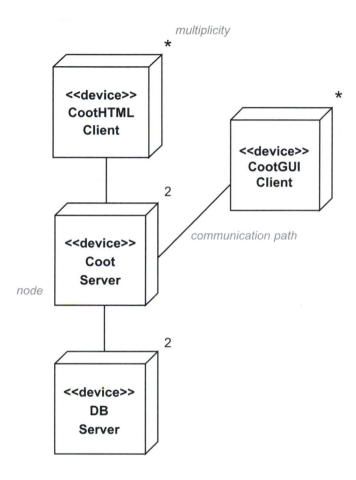

**Figure 8.6: A basic deployment diagram for Coot**

showing node instances, just like objects on an object diagram, the node label takes the form name:Type, and should be underlined.

Most deployment diagrams need an accompanying description if they're to make any sense. We might call this a **deployment survey**, in Jacobson style.

---

**Case Study**

*iCoot deployment survey*

This description could accompany Figure 8.6:

The iCoot data tier comprises two database servers (which we have called DBServer). Having two such nodes improves throughput and reliability.

> **Case Study (cont'd)**
>     The middle tier, which communicates with the data tier, consists of two server machines (CootServer), again duplicated for the sake of reliability and throughput.
>     Each CootServer can be accessed simultaneously by any number of CootHTML-Client nodes.
>     Eventually, we will also provide access from CootGUIClient nodes.

# 8.5 DESIGNING FOR CONCURRENCY

Most systems, especially networked systems, have many things happening at once; that is, they are **concurrent systems**. This has implications for the system as a whole and also for the individual processes running as part of the system. Although it would be much easier to develop systems if we could rely on all users and processes to form an orderly queue, in reality we have to turn chaos into order with our own programming efforts.

Concurrency introduces the same issues, time and again:

- How to ensure that information is updated completely before anyone can act on the update; for example, to stop anyone accessing the details of a new car model until all the details have been added.
- How to ensure that information is not updated while it's being read; for example, don't delete a car model while its details are being viewed.

At a low level, database transactions and thread monitors are used to protect data inside individual processes, for example. At a higher level, we need to use system rules and business rules to control concurrent activity.

The easiest approach to concurrency is to constrain the system or introduce extra business rules, especially if the user experience doesn't diminish significantly. For example, for iCoot, rather than trying to cope with updating the car catalog while customers are accessing it, we could update the catalog in a separate database and switch databases once a day; this way the Internet subsystem can assume that the catalog is read-only, which makes our code much easier to write. (The user experience diminishes slightly – in rare cases they will have to be told that a car model they've just tried to reserve has been discontinued – but we choose to live with that.) This is an *artificial* constraint on the system.

Business rules can also make the developer's life easier. Indeed, business rules are sometimes introduced because there is simply no off-the-shelf way to solve the problem. For example, consider a purchasing system for concert tickets. Customer Fred walks into a booking office in Paris at about the same time that customer Beryl walks into another booking office in New York. Both customers have decided that they want a ticket to the same concert in London. Unfortunately, there is only one ticket left. How do we decide who gets the ticket? Both customers will ask 'Is there a ticket available?' Both sales clerks will check on the system and both will reply 'Yes'. Now we have a race: the first customer who says 'Okay, I'll take it.' will win, subject to the efficiency of the clerks and the network delays from Paris and New York to the location of the actual server.

In the ticket scenario, we must ensure, at the very least, that we don't inadvertently sell two tickets when there's only one seat left. This is a process-level concurrency issue, because it can be controlled by the server process (the requests are serialized: the first to arrive gets the ticket, the second gets an error message). But that may not be good enough from the business point of view, because we end up with one disgruntled customer who was told there was a ticket only to be told a few seconds later that there wasn't one after all.

To avoid disgruntled customers, we can introduce an extra business rule: when a clerk queries the availability of a ticket, if one is available, it is *temporarily* reserved – the reservation lasts until the clerk cancels the enquiry or the reservation times out (for example, the temporary reservation lasts for ten minutes if the clerk doesn't cancel it first). With this new business rule, we can ensure that only the first customer who makes the virtual trip to the ticket server is told that there's a ticket available (the ticket server can combine the query and the reservation into a single business service).

Let's assume that Fred is successful. The clerk serving Fred has ten minutes to persuade him to pay for the reserved ticket, or the clerk can cancel within that time if Fred changes his mind. (The clerk would also cancel if Fred's method of payment failed, which is another reason for having temporary reservations in the first place.) Beryl now thinks that the concert sold out before she got to the booking office, so she has no reason to blame the booking agency for providing incorrect information. (If the last ticket is not bought by Fred and Beryl later discovers that the concert was not sold out, she can simply be told 'Somebody must have canceled'.)

Detailed consideration of concurrency problems and their solution is beyond the scope of this book. In any case, there is no real substitute for sitting down and thinking (hard) about it. For now, here are some observations:

- The look and feel of a well-designed concurrent system is no different to the single-user version.
- Our business services are the same for concurrent and single-user cases.

- To make a business object concurrent-safe, it's only necessary to *add* messages and supporting objects; therefore, business messages (and associated attributes) can be designed separately.

If you can think of a concurrent situation that might cause difficulties for your system, do not proceed to implementation until you can guarantee that that situation is no longer a problem. Be tough on your system, because reality will be tougher.

# 8.6 DESIGNING FOR SECURITY

Detailed consideration of security, although fascinating, would require a book in itself. Therefore, only an overview will be provided here.

A secure system is one that is protected from misuse, regardless of whether the misuse is accidental or malicious. Security is a rather broad term that can be broken down into the following five aspects:

- Privacy: We must be able to hide information, making it available only to those who are authorized to read it (or change it).
- Authentication: We need to know where each piece of information came from, so that we can decide whether or not to trust it.
- Irrefutability: This is the flip-side of authentication, ensuring that the originator of information can't deny that they're the source; this is helpful to us if anything goes wrong.
- Integrity: We must be sure that information hasn't been damaged, accidentally or maliciously, on its way from the source to us.
- Safety: We must be able to control access to resources (such as machines, processes, databases and files). Safety is also known as **authorization**.

In this context, information means not only data, such as business documents and user passwords, but also pieces of executable code. Code is an issue because it may be loaded dynamically over the network.

The first four requirements above can be satisfied using **digital encryption** (more on this in the next section). The safety requirement is rather more complex. Normally, when a piece of code is running, the operating system will exert some kind of control over what the code is able to do; typically, this means controlling access to files, to directories and to other programs. Operating systems have faults and security holes (some more than others). In addition, the control provided by operating systems is inflexible: for example, we have no easy way for the user or the developer to invent their own abstract controls such as 'Only Freda and Ben can join my virtual game of poker' or 'Only members of my family can turn the microwave on using their mobile phone'.

If our system operates over a network, the safety aspect becomes even more important. This is because, in a networked world, hackers can try to hijack programs running on our machines to get them to misbehave. To make matters worse, courtesy of Java and ActiveX, code fragments can travel around the network, executing on different machines as they go. Java is the only mainstream technology that adds the required level of safety for code traveling around a network and the flexibility to invent our own controls, regardless of the operating system being used. The practical implication of this is that if you're not using Java, you should prevent code from moving around the network: install code on each client or server as needed and rely on the operating system and your own programming efforts to make things safe.

## 8.6.1 Digital Encryption and Decryption

This is an aside to give you some idea how digital encryption and decryption – **cryptography** – can be used to provide privacy, authentication, irrefutability and integrity. First, the basic idea: to **encrypt** information means to scramble it so that it's useless if anyone manages to steal it. For this to make sense, the scrambling method must be reversible and it must be known to the intended recipient. The reverse of encryption is **decryption**.

As kids, most of us played with the so-called **Caesarian Cipher** (although we probably didn't call it that). What we do is to take a message and then scramble it by shifting each letter a number of places down the alphabet, wrapping round if we fall off the end. For example, if we choose to shift four places, the message 'Mister Watson, can you hear me?' would be encrypted as 'QMWXIVAEXWSRGERCSYLIEVQI'. (We leave out punctuation, letter case and spaces in the encrypted version in order to avoid giving clues to spies.) As long as the recipient knows that the algorithm is Caesarian and the offset is four, they can decrypt the original message.

The Caesarian Cipher is a general form of encryption: it involves an extra piece of information that the recipient must know (4) as well as the algorithm itself (Caesarian). The extra piece of information is called a **key**, because it unlocks the code: it's not enough to know that unlocking a door involves turning a key, you need to have the key too.

The success of an encryption mechanism boils down to two things:

- How difficult it is to **crack** the encryption, by trial and error or by hard work.
- Safe distribution of the key to the intended recipient.

Both of these can have their problems. The Caesarian Cipher, for example, is easy to crack: a wrong-doer only has to guess that the Caesarian method is being used and then try a maximum of 26 possible offsets before the message materializes in front of their eyes. As for safe distribution, we might try whispering the details of the key into the ear of every intended recipient: however, as well as being inconvenient, this approach is doomed to failure – if any recipient with a defective memory writes the key down on a piece of paper, we might have a security breach.

Although it's possible to come up with an **uncrackable** encryption algorithm – **one-time pads** and **quantum cryptography** are examples – these algorithms are either inconvenient (code books) or very expensive (quantum cryptography, at least for the time being). So, for everyday use, especially in the context of network programming, we normally choose the level of security that we want and then select an efficient algorithm that provides that level. This works because no self-respecting criminal would bother to eavesdrop our encrypted credit card details if it might take them, say, a million years to decipher the details: they would just burgle our house or pick our pocket instead.

**Digital encryption** and **digital decryption** are simply an extension of the ideas above to encrypt the digital information passed between computers, where software can do all the hard work. The level of digital encryption is normally expressed in **bit strength**: 128-bit encryption is considered minimum these days and 1024-bit encryption is desirable.

Digital keys are based on prime numbers, hence cracking them is difficult, because it involves trying to find prime factors, which is an intensive process. The keys themselves are distributed using **digital certificates**. A certificate, with the help of a trusted **certificate authority**, authenticates the key, so that we can't be fooled by hackers.

Below is an indication of how four of the security aspects identified earlier can be implemented using cryptography:

- Privacy: In digital encryption and decryption, safe distribution of keys is achieved using **public/private key pairs**, **certificates** and **certificate authorities**.
- Authentication: This relies on being able to prove the origin of the key, using certificates and certificate authorities; roughly speaking, if we can successfully decrypt the information, and we know the origin of the key, we know that the information must have come from the same place as the key.
- Irrefutability: Since authentication relies on proving the origin of the key, once we've authenticated a piece of information, our authentication is irrefutable.
- Integrity: First, we transmit the encrypted information *and* the unencrypted information to the client. Next, the client decrypts the encrypted version and compares the result with the unencrypted version – obviously, the two should match (the chance of them matching by accident is tiny). Therefore, we're confident that we have received the correct information.

There are two problems with integrity-checking as just described: first, we've sent the information unencrypted; second, we've sent the information twice (the encrypted version is just as big as the unencrypted version). The first problem can be overcome by sending everything over a secure line. The second problem can be overcome by an optimization based on **message digests** – a digest is a small string of bits generated from a piece of information using an irreversible algorithm. Without going into detail, we end up sending the encrypted digest, but not the encrypted information. The end result is that we get the same degree of integrity checking, but the information is sent only once. (For the record, an encrypted digest is called a **digital signature**.)

## 8.6.2 General Security Rules

As with concurrency, when designing a secure system, there is no way to avoid sitting down and thinking hard about it in order to make sure that no-one can abuse the system. Here are a few things to bear in mind when trying to secure your (networked) system:

- Protect your servers from unauthorized access, whether accidental or malicious.
- Confine sensitive information to your internal network: sensitive information includes details of business deals with other companies; business strategy; personnel details; details of the credit reference agencies you use; information relating to national security; and so on.
- Prevent the eavesdropping of exported information: ensure that information you pass outside your intranet can only be read by the intended recipient.
- Protect employee and customer passwords, which are not only the foundation of your entire security policy, they're often highly personal.
- Prevent server code accessing unneeded resources.
- Prevent client code accessing unneeded resources: we want to protect the client against unauthorized access to their resources and against accidental damage (because we want to offer a high quality of service and because we don't want them to sue us if something goes wrong).

If you're really brave, you might consider hiring **ethical hackers**, consultants who do everything they can to break into your system. Once the ethical hackers have certified your system, you're less likely to get a nasty surprise when it goes live.

# 8.7 PARTITIONING SOFTWARE

For any large business, it's impractical to lump all the business entities and business processes into a single software system – the result would be far too complex and difficult to use. We can, and should, partition software into systems, then into autonomous subsystems if necessary, then into layers (which can also be considered to be subsystems).

## 8.7.1 Systems and Subsystems

Consider how the simple concept of Customer is viewed differently by the departments in a large organization, sales, marketing, billing, procurement, dispatching and so on. If we tried to put together a single software system that supported all of these departments, our Customer would have hundreds of attributes and hundreds of operations: a recipe for disaster.

Instead, a business should have a number of separate systems, each implemented by a different development team so that the temptation to reuse objects inappropriately is minimized. Then, where information needs to be passed between systems, it should pass in a well-defined, controlled manner via well-defined interfaces. In order to reduce complexity further, each system should be broken down further into separate subsystems.

Figure 8.7 shows a company's systems as independent trees in a forest. Underneath each tree is the database of information that the systems need to access and at the top is the user interface. Communication takes place along narrow, constrained pathways (rope bridges), from business logic to business logic via purpose-built interfaces. Although each system has its own independent data, we can still use a single DBMS for deployment, since a DBMS will happily manage multiple databases.

**Figure 8.7: Coordinating multiple systems**

For the case study, we have a single system called Coot which comprises two subsystems: iCoot provides access for members and nonmembers; the other subsystem provides access for assistants and resembles the existing Auk interface. The latter subsystem will not be considered in detail.

## 8.7.2 Layers

Inside a software system, we usually employ multiple **layers** of code (see Figure 8.8). Each layer is a cluster of collaborating objects dependent on the facilities offered by lower layers. Layers don't have to contain objects. For example, the Unix system library provides access to low-level operating system facilities via a layer of C functions.

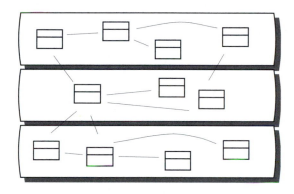

**Figure 8.8: Objects in layers**

Layers help to reduce complexity by breaking the implementation up into more manageable chunks. Layers also increase the chance of reuse, since each layer is written to be independent of the layers above. As Bertrand Meyer put it in [Meyer 97]:

> A serious software system, even a small one by today's standards, touches on so many areas that it would be impossible to guarantee its correctness by dealing with all components and properties on a single level. Instead, a layered approach is necessary, each layer relying on lower ones.

Often, regardless of the total number of layers, the top layer represents the user interface and the bottom layer represents the operating system, or a network connection. In the following diagrams, the lowest layers have been omitted for simplicity, stopping at a well-known layer that's documented elsewhere. In the following sections, we'll see examples of common layers used in systems that have one, two or three tiers.

Layers may be **open** (exposing some of the objects from lower layers for use by layers above, i.e. it manages the objects below but doesn't completely hide them) or **closed** (completely encapsulating the layers below, i.e. objects from lower layers are hidden from those above). There is no easy rule for deciding whether a particular layer should be open or closed. You have to use your skill, judgment, experience and foresight. Generally speaking, a closed layer requires more coding and may run more slowly than an open layer (because there's more copying and translating of information to be done). On the other hand, an open layer is generally not as safe (because lower layers are unprotected) and harder to maintain (because each layer has more than one dependent layer above it).

To a certain extent, we can swap layers in and out without disturbing other code. For example, we can always throw away the top layer and replace it with another. Furthermore, we can replace a closed intermediate layer with one that has the same interface, without affecting the layers above. Most often, layers are re-implemented at the bottom, when we move our system to another platform, or at the top, when we move the user interface to a new device.

Some of the technologies in the following discussion are explained further in Chapter 9.

### Layers for Single-Tier Systems

Figure 8.9 shows a simple layering scheme as might be employed in a single-tier system. At the bottom, we have the database layer, whose job it is to ship data back and forth between the DBMS and the business layer. The assumption has been made that most applications have data storage requirements, so that data doesn't evaporate if the system is shut down for any reason. If we had a simpler system that stored data in files, the database layer would be a file system instead of a DBMS. On top of the database layer, we have the business layer, which consists of the entity objects and supporting implementation objects. Finally, on top of the business layer, we have the user interface layer, which contains objects whose job it is to present available options to the user, to pass user commands and data on to the business layer and to display data coming back from the business layer.

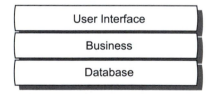

**Figure 8.9: Layers in a single-tier system**

### Layers for Two- and Three-Tier Systems

Two-tier and three-tier systems employ a network to get from the user interface running on the client to the business layer running on the server. We can cope with this by employing two more layers, as shown in Figure 8.10. The network layer contains objects that make the network transparent to the user interface. As far as the user interface is concerned, it may just as well be accessing the server objects directly. The server layer contains objects that simplify use of the business layer into a manageable set of **business services**. As well as

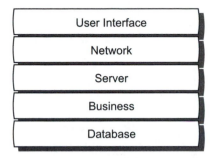

**Figure 8.10: Layers in a two tier or three-tier system**

simplifying the client, this allows us to localize security measures in the server layer without polluting the business layer and to accommodate different kinds of client.

For a two-tier system, the database layer is on the same machine as the server and business layers. For a three-tier system, the database layer spans a network, but the details are hidden from us by the DBMS.

If we use HTML forms to get from the client to the middle (or server) tier, the user interface–network situation is less clear cut. In this case, the user interface is partly on the client (as HTML pages and forms) and partly on the server (as servlets and JSPs). If we prefer, we can adjust the diagram to reflect this.

## Translation Layers

As illustrated in Figure 8.11, different layers have different focus. For example, when designing a user interface, we're concerned with menus, dialogs, notebooks, windows, usability, intuitiveness, and so on. For the network, we're worried about protocols, bandwidth and different types of hosts. When we move on to the server, we should concern ourselves with security, multi-threading and throughput. In the business layer, the part that flows most directly from our business analysis, we're most interested in abstraction, attributes, operations, polymorphism, reuse and the other fundamentals of object-oriented modeling. Finally, we arrive at the database layer where, traditionally, we expect to deal with keys, tables, SQL, locking, functional dependencies and all the other aspects of database theory. In short, if we try to connect these differing worlds together directly, we will end up with too much complexity and too much coupling (strong coupling, when one object's implementation is closely dependent on another's, makes code harder to maintain).

We can reduce complexity and coupling by introducing extra layers to act as translators. **Translation layers** are particularly useful for translating the business layer (in the single-tier case) or the network layer (when we have multiple tiers) into the minimal

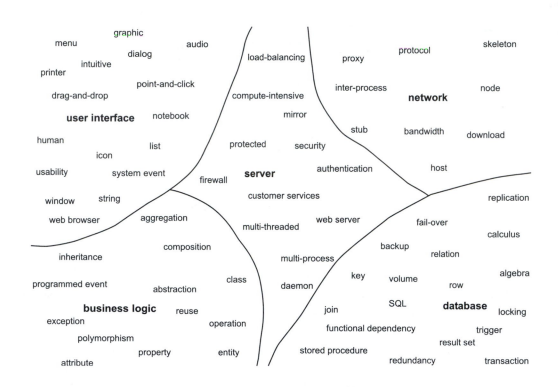

**Figure 8.11: Differing concerns in a large system**

functionality needed by the end user – such layers are often referred to as **controllers**. Controllers manage the user interface's communication with the rest of the system. (This fits well with Jacobson's idea of a controller.) Another common translation layer is the so-called **persistence layer** that sits between the business layer and the database layer: by removing the business layer's dependence on the actual storage mechanism in use, it becomes easier to change the storage mechanism later (from files to a DBMS, for example). Figure 8.12 shows a multi-tier system with the addition of control and persistence layers.

## 8.7.3 Java Layers: Applet plus RMI

In order to illustrate a Java client with a proper GUI, Figure 8.13 shows a complete set of layers for a three-tier system with an RMI applet as the front end. RMI is a Java network protocol.

In this illustration, the user interface layer is implemented using the Swing library (Java's portable library of GUI components). Underneath the user interface layer, we have a control layer that contains all the code for accessing the business services; this code would otherwise

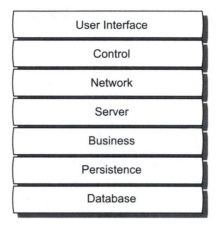

**Figure 8.12: Translation layers in a multitier system**

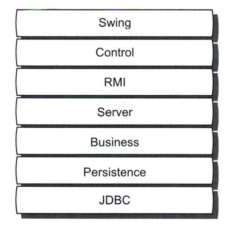

**Figure 8.13: RMI applet layers**

have to be buried in the user interface objects and re-implemented for every new interface that we add later (mobile phones, for example).

95% of the network layer is provided for us by the RMI framework – we just have to follow a few simple rules in the control layer and the server layer to make our server objects accessible from any client.

The server layer, business layer and persistence layer are just like the ones described in the previous subsection. Last, but not least, we have the database layer provided by the Java DataBase Connectivity (JDBC) library. JDBC allows us to access any relational database using dynamic or precompiled SQL. Because we have included a persistence layer, we could replace JDBC with an object-oriented database, or the file system, without disturbing the business objects.

---

**Case Study**

*iCoot layers*

As an illustration of the HTML/CGI-with-servlets configuration, Figure 8.14 shows the layers that are used for iCoot.

For iCoot, there is no persistence layer, because a relational database, accessed via JDBC, is expected to serve the purposes of the system throughout its life. The JDBC layer itself is provided by classes from the standard Java library. For the user interface, there are two styles: CGI-with-servlets and RMI-plus-applets. For the first increment, HTML/CGI-with-servlets will be used (using JSPs for the dynamic page content) in the ServletsLayer. For later releases, an RMI-plus-applets mechanism will be provided, for desktops, using the SwingLayer, and then small devices, such as PDAs and mobile phones, using the MicroLayer. The MicroLayer is implemented using the **Java 2 Micro Edition (J2ME)**.

For the sake of the first increment, the control layer is provided by servlets, with the help of JSPs. For the RMI version, on the other hand, the ControlLayer is designed for a proper GUI. Oddly enough, this means that the control layer is *below* the network for HTTP/CGI, but *above* the network for RMI. In either case, the controllers are translating (or coordinating) the ServerLayer. Thus, everything from the ServerLayer down is reused without change. (The ControlLayer is also reused, by the two styles of GUI.)

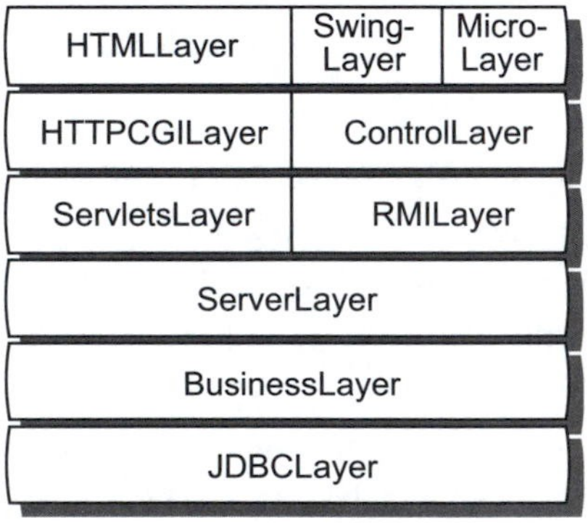

---

**Figure 8.14: Layers for iCoot**

## 8.7.4 Message Flow in Layers

In a layered system, each layer is a client of the layer immediately below it. Thus, we expect messages to be sent from the upper layer to the lower layer, as shown in Figure 8.15. Each message is either a question (retrieving some information, for example, getAddress) or a command (an instruction to do something, for example, setAddress).

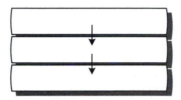

**Figure 8.15: Messages flow downwards in a layered system**

Many commands sent into a layer will have an effect on the information managed by that layer – otherwise there would be little point in issuing the commands in the first place. But, what if the upper layer needs to know what information has changed? The upper layer might, for example, be a user interface that needs to update its display with the new information. We have two choices:

- Add knowledge to the upper layer about which commands change which information.
- Get the lower layer to send messages to the upper layer whenever the information changes.

The problem with the first option is that it pollutes the upper layer with knowledge that, logically, belongs in the lower layer – this makes the coding of the upper layer more complicated and couples the upper layer more tightly to the lower layer. The problem with the second option is that the lower layer has to know something about the upper layer so that it knows which objects to send messages to – thus, the lower layer is polluted with knowledge about the upper layer, making it more complicated and also coupling it to the upper layer. (Ideally, lower layers should not be coupled to upper layers at all.)

### Events

So, is there some way that a layer can notify the layer above when something interesting has happened, without increasing complexity or coupling in either direction? The answer is 'Yes, **events**'. Figure 8.16 shows the real-world analogy that we use for events. An **event source** detects when something interesting has happened (an **event**) and shouts out the details (**broadcasts**) to anyone who might be listening (the **event listeners**). An event might be an **attribute event**, indicating a change in the value of one of the event source's attributes,

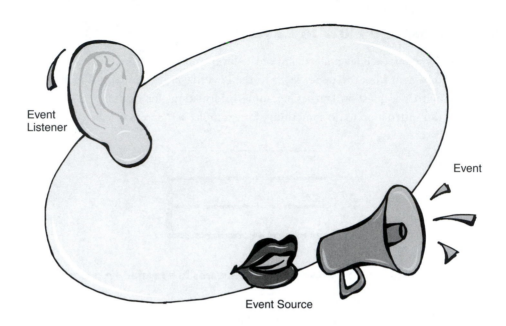

**Figure 8.16: The event analogy**

or it might be a **pure event**, not related to any attribute value. For example, consider a Clock entity: it could broadcast an attribute event when the time changes – say, every second – and it could broadcast a pure event when the alarm goes off.

As the phrase 'broadcast an event' suggests, we would like the event source to detect when the event happens and just shout it out to anybody who is listening: this way, the event source won't be complicated by knowledge of the listeners and the event listeners won't be complicated by knowledge of when the events might occur. In our layering scheme, we can use event sources in each layer to broadcast events to listeners in the layer above, thus achieving our goals of keeping knowledge in the right place and minimizing coupling.

But how do we implement such an idea using messages? As a first step to understanding how this might work, Figure 8.17 shows an example collaboration between a Clock, the event source, and a ClockUI, the event listener. In this diagram, the special name self is UML notation for 'the current object' (it corresponds exactly to the special name this in Java).

As part of the initialization process, the ClockUI registers itself with the Clock by sending it the addClockListener message. Next, the ClockWatcher sets the alarm in the ClockUI, which passes the alarm setting on to the Clock. As the clock sends itself the tick message periodically, eventually it will detect that it is time for the alarm to go off. When this happens, the Clock creates a ClockEvent (with the help of the ClockEventHome), with information about the event (in this case, the only information is the source of the event). The Clock then sends the alarm message to the ClockUI with the ClockEvent as a parameter. (The event object records the

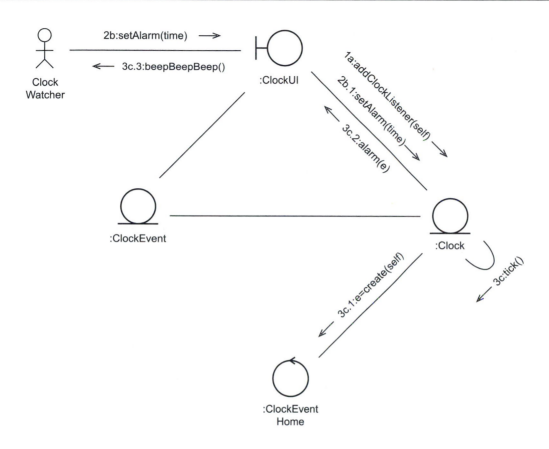

**Figure 8.17: A communication diagram showing how events work**

event source; if the ClockUI is listening to more than one clock, it can find out which one has just sounded the alarm.) Finally, the ClockUI beeps at the ClockWatcher.

You may be wondering why the sequence numbers in this communication diagram have letters in them. The reason is that we have three independent sequences in our scenario: adding the clock listener; setting the time; and sounding the alarm. (As long as adding the clock listener happens first, the other two sequences can happen multiple times, in any order.) The clock has to run independently of the ClockUI and the ClockWatcher, otherwise, when the alarm has been set, control returns to the ClockWatcher and the Clock is not able to tick. A name as part of a UML sequence number shows that the message in question is dependent on messages that include the same name, but independent of others. We can still show the ordering of independent messages, by the careful use of numbers: for example, it is implicit that message 2b happens *before* message 3c in our scenario; it would also be implicit that messages numbered 99x and 99y happen *at the same time*.

The class diagram for the alarm clock scenario is shown in Figure 8.18 (for simplicity, ClockEventHome and ClockWatcher have been omitted). From this diagram, we can see that ClockEvent has a getter for the source attribute. Also, the ClockUI has a message that allows the ClockWatcher to set the alarm – setAlarm – and another message for detecting the alarm event – alarm. Finally, the Clock class has a message for setting the alarm – setAlarm and a message for registering a listener – addClockListener. (There are some new pieces of UML notation in this diagram which will be explained shortly.)

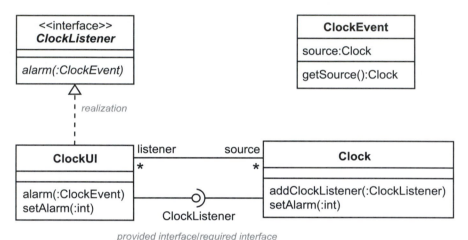

**Figure 8.18: Events as a class diagram**

Because object-oriented languages generally don't have a true broadcast mechanism, the Clock in Figure 8.18 must maintain an internal list of interested listeners and then send a message to each one when the event occurs. The listeners, for their part, must make sure that they register for the event. It may have occurred to you that the Clock is now coupled to the ClockUI, something that we were trying to avoid in the first place. We can solve this problem by introducing an abstract class – called ClockListener – that only lists the messages required for detecting Clock events. As long as ClockUI inherits from ClockListener, we will be able to register a ClockUI with a Clock and the ClockUI will be able to receive the alarm message. Thus, although Clock *is* coupled to ClockListener, it is *not* coupled to ClockUI. (ClockListener resides in the same layer as Clock, while ClockUI floats independently in the layer above.)

An **interface**, denoted by the <<interface>> keyword, is a pure abstract class – a class that has no concrete methods and no attributes. Since interfaces are so useful, for specifying communication with reduced coupling, they have some special UML notation shown in Figure 8.18. The dashed arrow with a white head (labeled realization) indicates inheritance, for the special case where the superclass is an interface. The ClockListener notation, labeled provided interface/required interface, allows us to indicate that one class uses another class via a particular interface. In this case, the part that looks like a lollipop indicates that ClockUI realizes (is a kind of) ClockListener, while the cup-shaped part indicates that Clock only depends on the fact that ClockUI is a ClockListener. As you've probably spotted, there is redundancy in Figure 8.18. It's up to you when you use the 'dashed inheritance' or 'lollipop-and-cup' styles in your own diagrams.

### Message Flow using Events

Figure 8.19 shows how messages should flow when using layers. Ordinary messages are shown flowing down through the layers, while event messages are shown rising up. (The event messages have been shown as dashed arrows to indicate that the lower object has no knowledge of the recipient.)

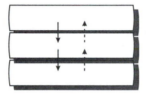

**Figure 8.19: Control flow using events**

Events are most often used in client code, because they're a convenient way of keeping a user interface up to date with the information in the layer below. Events are rarely used on the server side, because server code tends to be multi-threaded, which complicates event-driven programming significantly (there is increased potential for deadlock, for example), and because events should not be broadcast over a network: we don't want the server held up while it sends event messages to lots of clients, some of which might have perished or be difficult to contact.

Therefore, it's recommended that you avoid event-driven programming on the server side. If you wish to broadcast over a network, use machine-to-machine messaging instead, such as that provided by the Java Messaging Service (JMS).

## 8.8 SUMMARY

In this chapter, we've looked at:

- The steps involved in system design and how a system can be decomposed into physical and logical components, with particular attention paid to network topologies.

• How to illustrate architectural decisions on UML deployment diagrams.

• The concurrency issues that arise in networked systems: how to ensure that information is updated completely before anyone can act on it and how to ensure that information is not updated while it's being read.

• How to ensure that a system is protected from accidental and malicious misuse, by ensuring privacy, authentication, irrefutability, integrity and authorization.

• How a company's software can be broken down into multiple systems, subsystems and layers.

# FURTHER READING

Full details of the HTML specification can be found in [W3C 99]. For a more readable description, see [Raggett *et al.* 97]. Raggett is one of the main forces behind the UML standard.

For more information about the history of cryptography, take a look at [Singh 00], an approachable book by Simon Singh, a science journalist rather than an academic.

# REVIEW QUESTIONS

1. Why are layers important in subsystem design? Choose all options that apply.

   (a) They make it easier to change the implementation
   (b) They reduce the number of classes in the implementation
   (c) They increase reuse
   (d) They reduce complexity

2. If two customers, on opposite sides of the world, wish to purchase the last ticket available for a concert, what would be a good approach for allocating the ticket? Choose only one option.

   (a) Introduce an extra business rule that combines a query for ticket availability with a temporary reservation.
   (b) Make the customers take part in a software 'race' to get the ticket.
   (c) Don't allow the last ticket to be sold, because that would be unfair to one of the customers.

3. With reference to Figure 6.13, what is Z? Choose only one option.

   (a) A class.

   (b) An event.

   (c) An interface.

   (d) A boundary.

   (e) A property.

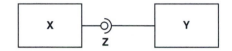

**Figure 8.20: For use with Review Question 3**

# ANSWERS TO REVIEW QUESTIONS

1. Layers are important in subsystem design because:
   a. They make it easier to change the implementation
   c. They increase reuse
   d. They reduce complexity

2. If two customers, on opposite sides of the world, wish to purchase the last ticket available for a concert, a good approach would be to a. introduce an extra business rule that combines a query for ticket availability with a temporary reservation.

3. With reference to Figure 8.20, Z is c. An interface.

# Choosing Technologies

This chapter identifies the major technologies available for the client side and the server side and helps to ensure that you know how to make informed choices.

# Learning Objectives

**Understand client-side technologies.**

**Understand server-side technologies.**

**Understand protocols for connecting clients and servers.**

**Understand network technologies.**

# Chapter Outline

# 9.1 INTRODUCTION

Although we have a full set of requirements and analysis documents and even an initial architecture diagram, we still haven't made any choices about the implementation technologies that we're going to use. As already mentioned, the longer we delay this decision, the less sensitive our system will be to changes in the future. On the other hand, the longer we wait before we choose technologies, the less chance we will have of exploiting the finer points of those technologies.

Making technology decisions at this stage in the development (before detailed design) is a good compromise. Once we have made the decisions, we can still make informed choices as we move forward about how much we want to tie ourselves to the unique features of any particular technology. All the diagrams in this book stick to language-independent UML. For example, the standard UML operation signature has been used, rather than switching to something more specific, such as Java syntax. In contrast, Java primitives have been shown in the diagrams, rather than UML primitives, because they're more compact and because it is clearer that we're using a primitive value rather than an object value.

# 9.2 CLIENT TIER TECHNOLOGIES

Let's look at the software that runs on clients in a multi-tier system (the main focus of this book). We have two main choices: we can launch either a purpose-built application (program, executable, or whatever you prefer to call it) or a Web browser that hosts the client software. The kind of client applications that we can run include:

- Human to human communications: e-mail, instant messaging, USENET news, chat.
- File transfer or file swapping.
- Remote login.
- Proprietary applications (anything that doesn't fit into a more general category, for example, a multiuser flight simulator).

Clients hosted in a Web browser can use the following technologies:

- HTML forms.
- JavaScript.
- Proprietary plug-ins (anything that isn't one of the other general categories, for example, interactive animation using Flash).
- ActiveX controls.
- Java applets.

All of the above technologies use some kind of protocol (for example, IMAP for e-mail, AIM for instant messaging and HTTP/CGI for HTML forms) to communicate with at least one other machine (mail server, messaging server or Web server). Generally speaking, applications and browser plug-ins can be written in whichever language you prefer (Java, C++, Eiffel, Fortran, or COBOL). This was always the case for applications; for browser plug-ins, you need a compiler for your chosen language that's willing to put the machine code into a DLL (Windows) or shared library (Unix).

Client applications have the disadvantage that they require installation of software on the client machine before they can be used. However, for some purposes (such as desktop publishing) they're a good choice. A Web browser, an application in its own right, is especially useful for client software because it can be enhanced by the multi-tier developer to behave in ways never dreamt of by the developer of the browser itself. For example, a Web browser can be used to read news bulletins, as HTML pages, from a global broadcaster; it can also be used to check bank account details using a Java applet. And all this is done without any prior installation on the client machine (apart from the browser itself of course).

For a large client tier written in Java, it may be impractical to load an applet over the network – in such cases, local installation of the applet (or a Java application) may be necessary. Section 8.4.4 suggested that network computers were a good idea, regardless of the size of application loaded over the network. The reality is rather more subtle. Normally, a network computer uses Internet technology (over an intranet) to get hold of its software. Internet-style networks, by their very nature, have bottlenecks that make the frequent loading of large programs impractical. Although this problem can be alleviated by having a good local cache, the best kind of network computer is still a disk-less Unix workstation, which suffers far fewer bottlenecks. For the time being, this means that 'If you want to load a large program over the Internet, don't. If you want to load a program over an intranet, make sure it's not very large (<2 MB)'. All is not lost, however: it turns out that a useful thin-client GUI can be squeezed into a 100KB Java applet, which is practical even for the Internet.

Each browser technology has its own advantages and disadvantages. For example:

- HTML is visually rich and widely supported, but HTML forms are primitive and they're not automatically validated on the client. Also, being forced to step through a dozen pages, each of which flashes to white before it's drawn, is not the nicest way of interacting.
- JavaScript permits some client-side programming (for example, data validation in HTML forms). But JavaScript is interpreted (and therefore slower than compiled code), is not pure (in the object-oriented sense) and different browsers provide different levels of support (which makes coding awkward).
- In theory, plug-ins can provide any kind of client interaction you wish to implement. However, plug-ins often need to be downloaded and installed the first time they're used; each one requires different programming expertise; and they must be ported by the

supplier to each new platform (operating system/CPU combination) so they may not be supported by every client.

- ActiveX controls are 32-bit Windows binaries hosted by a Web browser. Although this gives them the same possibilities as plug-ins and Java applets, they can only run on Windows.

- Java is a simple, pure, object-oriented language, so potentially it offers the best solution. Java also provides a measure of safety because it prohibits access to resources on the local machine without explicit and detailed authorization by the user. Partly because of corporate chicanery, at the time of writing most Web browsers only support an old version of Java – for a full-featured version of Java, you need the Java PlugIn from Sun (Java masquerading as a browser plug-in) or you need to buy a PC with Java preinstalled.

In principle, Java is the best choice for implementing clients in a three-tier system. Because of the lack of out-of-the-box support in Web browsers, most developers opt for HTML forms. (To be fair, the problem of browser support also plagues other client options, such as plug-ins and ActiveX – HTML forms are only practical because they have been around for so long.) Many Web browsers can also host older client applications, including file transfer, e-mail and USENET news.

Most of the important technologies are migrating onto newer devices such as personal digital assistants (PDAs) and mobile phones. TCP/IP is ubiquitous, even on small client devices – it even works over wireless connections. Thus, porting a three-tier system to new kinds of devices will normally just involve redesigning the user interface to make it smaller (and more primitive).

# 9.3 CLIENT TIER TO MIDDLE TIER PROTOCOLS

Client software, whether running as an application or inside a Web browser, has to communicate with a server using some kind of protocol. Most protocols are layered: at the bottom we have a low-level protocol such as TCP/IP and on top of that we build further protocols, specialized for particular tasks. For example, on top of TCP/IP, we can put the **Secure Sockets Layer (SSL)** which encrypts and decrypts the information for the sake of privacy and integrity. On top of SSL we might run **Secure HTTP (HTTPS)**, a secure protocol that allows a client to request a document by URI and get back the contents of that document.

It's quite reasonable to have multiple layers. For example, Java has a mechanism called **Remote Method Invocation (RMI)** that allows an object to send a message to an object running on a separate machine – the message is sent using a protocol called **Java Remote Method Protocol (JRMP)**. In order to get through Internet firewalls, RMI is prepared to piggyback HTTP if necessary. So, when an object sends an RMI message to another object, we may end up with the run-time situation shown in Figure 9.1 – this shows a message being encoded using JRMP, then HTTPS, then SSL, then TCP/IP; on the server side, the message is unwrapped and sent to the intended recipient. The reply is sent back via the reverse path.

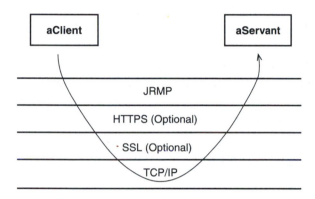

**Figure 9.1: How RMI can use a network**

Commonly-used protocols fall into two categories: specialized and general. Specialized protocols include:

- IMAP (e-mail).
- AIM (AOL Instant Messaging).
- NNTP (USENET news).
- HTTP/CGI (HTML forms).
- FTP (file transfer).
- Telnet (remote login).

General protocols (adaptable to many tasks) include:

- TCP/IP (low level transport, also known as **sockets**).
- JRMP (for Java-to-Java communications).
- IIOP (for CORBA communications, similar to RMI but multiple implementation languages).

Developers usually use a higher level abstraction, courtesy of their run-time system and libraries. For example, RMI and CORBA programmers just send messages to objects – the RMI or CORBA code does all the wrapping and unwrapping invisibly; programmers of HTML forms simply design the layout of their forms – the Common Gateway Interface (CGI) mechanism arranges for the form data to be passed to executable code on the server.

# 9.4 MIDDLE TIER TECHNOLOGIES

Having seen the ways of getting to the first line of servers, we need to decide what kind of software will take over from there. Server applications are typically multi-threaded pieces of code, designed for high throughput (capable of handling thousands, or millions, of clients simultaneously). A server application **listens** on some **port** (connection point) for clients to **connect**.

As far as styles of software are concerned, the server situation is similar to that on the client. On the client, we can run stand-alone applications or code hosted by a Web browser. On the (middle tier) server, we can run stand-alone applications or we can run a Web server and put our code inside that. Stand-alone applications include:

- Mail, messaging, news and chat servers.
- FTP daemon.
- Telnet daemon.
- RMI Registry (a look-up mechanism for RMI objects).
- CORBA naming service (a look-up mechanism for CORBA objects).
- Java Naming and Directory Interface (JNDI) server (a general name-to-thing mapping service that can be used instead of an RMI registry, a CORBA naming service, a user registry, etc.).
- Proprietary server (for example, a process hosting CORBA or RMI objects, an EJB client, a .Net client)

Server code that can be hosted by a Web server includes:

- Java Server Pages (JSPs), for building Web pages on-the-fly.
- Active Server Pages (ASPs), similar to JSPs but coding is typically Visual Basic rather than Java.
- CGI scripts (these can be interpreted files, written in languages such as PERL, or executable programs).
- Servlets (Java server objects that can be accessed by Java applets, JSPs or HTML forms).

**RMI registries** and **CORBA naming services** allow RMI and CORBA clients to find their server objects by name (or they can use JNDI).

**CGI scripts** are either textual files written in some command language, such as PERL, or native executables, compiled from a programming language in the normal way. A CGI script is normally invoked by an HTML form: the Web server strips the data out of the form and passes it to the CGI script as environment variables; the script places its result on standard output, which is returned to the client browser and displayed according to its type (HTML page, image, audio file, etc.).

**Servlets** are Java objects instantiated on-demand by a Web server. A servlet is usually passed data from an HTML form for processing: as with CGI scripts, the result returned by the servlet specifies what the user sees next in their browser. A servlet is a platform-independent, fast alternative to a CGI script.

**JSPs** are text files containing raw HTML interspersed with Java code. When first invoked a JSP is translated into a servlet: the raw HTML is replaced with print statements and the Java code is included verbatim; the servlet is then compiled and invoked. JSPs are normally used to personalize Web pages – by inserting a bank statement for the customer who's currently logged in, for example. They can be invoked directly or via servlets.

**ASPs** are similar to JSPs but they use Microsoft technologies, so they're not as portable.

# 9.5 MIDDLE TIER TO DATA TIER TECHNOLOGIES

So far, we have run some code on the client, launched ourselves onto the middle tier via some protocol and invoked some code on the middle tier. What do we do next? Well, the usual answer, in a three-tier context, is that we access the data tier. There are a number of ways of doing this:

- Include database-client code on our middle tier so that we can access a DBMS running on the data tier. With Java, we can do this generically with the help of the Java Database Connectivity (JDBC) mechanism [Campione *et al.* 98].
- Communicate with the data tier using any of the client-to-middle-tier technologies already discussed. After all, as far as the data tier is concerned, the middle tier is just another client.
- Do something proprietary, such as access a server running on a data-tier machine or run some code directly on the middle tier (a two-tier configuration).
- Access the data tier using some non-TCP/IP protocol (we will usually only do this in order to access a legacy system).
- Include Enterprise Java Beans (EJB) client code in our middle-tier server, then access the data tier via EJBs (Java objects that are typically used to provide data and process services on an intranet).
- Include .Net client code in our middle tier server. The .Net framework is Microsoft's competitor to the EJB framework (and other parts of J2EE). Since this book uses Java-centric examples, no further detail of .Net is given.

Figure 9.2 shows how all the technologies discussed so far fit together, in terms of where they normally sit in a three-tier system.

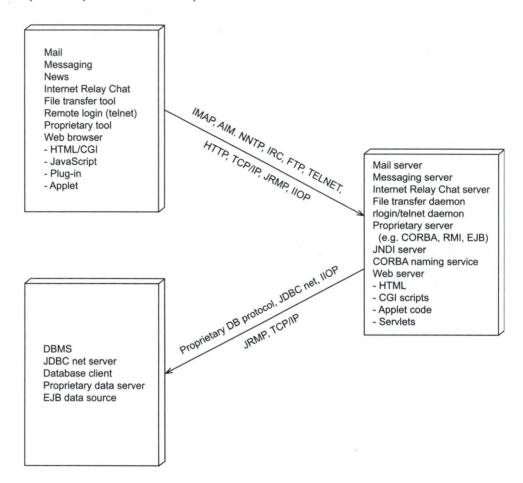

**Figure 9.2: Summary of three-tier technologies**

# 9.6 OTHER TECHNOLOGIES

There are a number of other technologies that deserve a mention at this point. These technologies have been excluded from the discussion so far, either because they're relatively new and may not survive or because they simply provide alternatives to what has already been discussed.

- Authentication: When users are accessing a system over a network, it is desirable to verify who they are. We can either invent our own mechanism for doing this or we can use existing techniques – for example, a servlet can instruct a Web browser to display a login screen before proceeding. However, what we would really like is a mechanism that forces the user to log in and then preserves their identity throughout the system: from the Web browser, through the middle tier services and onto the back end. This desirable goal is referred to as **single sign-on** (or **global sign-on** if we can cross to other domains). Single sign-on for Java is part of J2EE. For global sign-on, emerging technologies include Microsoft .Net Passport (www.microsoft.com) and those under development by the Liberty Alliance (www.projectliberty.org).

- XML: With networked systems, we frequently need to transmit business data from one machine to another. The **eXtensible Markup Language** (XML) [Yergeau *et al.* 99] is a textual language for describing data as structured name–value pairs. Since XML documents are simply streams of characters, they can be transmitted over whichever protocol we happen to have chosen for our system, HTTP or RMI, for example. For our XML documents, we can invent whatever structure and name–value pairs we like. For XML to be truly useful, when one of our documents arrives at another machine, the target machine has to be aware of the *meaning* of the data, not just its structure. For example, if we define an XML document with a value called NETAMOUNT, our document will be of little use unless the recipient knows that the document is an invoice and that NETAMOUNT is the amount to pay before sales tax. For this reason, standards work is underway to define XML document types for common business information. In the absence of standard document definitions, XML is still useful because it allows us to use the same libraries for parsing and generating all our documents (libraries are available for Java, for example). XML can be used for storing textual information, as well as transmitting it; for example, we can store spreadsheet documents in XML format.

- Events and messages: Events are a common mechanism for broadcasting information to interested parties. The trouble with events is that they don't work well over a network, because it can be tricky to make them thread-safe and because they're inefficient (from the server point of view). A better way to broadcast over a network is to use **machine-to-machine messaging**. Messages are nuggets of information that can be broadcast to interested clients: once the server has initiated the broadcast, it plays no further part in the delivery of the information; failure to deliver to a particular client has no adverse effect (messages can also be sent in guaranteed-delivery mode). For more information on messaging, investigate the **Java Messaging Service** (JMS) [Bodoff *et al.* 02].

- SOAP: The **Simple Object Access Protocol** (SOAP) [W3C 03] is similar to RMI and CORBA. What sets it apart, however, is its use of a protocol based on XML, which makes it a good candidate for becoming the *de facto* standard of the future.

- Web services: The idea with web services is that customers (at home or in business) will pay to have their information stored and processed on fat servers, accessible over the Internet or extranets. A simple example of a Web service is browser-based e-mail;

a more complex example is the processing, managing and printing of digital photos. Web services are deployed as Internet-based three-tier systems, using TCP/IP and XML-related technologies, such as SOAP. For more information check out the Web Services Interoperability Organization (www.ws-i.org) and the Java-related efforts led by Sun (java.sun.com).

# 9.7 TYPICAL FRONT-END CONFIGURATIONS

Having seen the many technologies available for tiers in a multi-tier system, let's take a look now at some typical configurations for communication between the client tier and the middle tier. While reading the next few topics, bear in mind that getting from the client tier to the middle tier is a user interface exercise: by keeping all the complicated business logic on the middle tier, we can happily choose any or all of these front-end configurations, according to personal preference or the time available. In Chapter 10, we'll see how to design the middle and data tiers so that we can swap our front ends in and out as we wish.

## 9.7.1 HTML/CGI-with-Scripts

Originally, HTML was a simple page markup language for multimedia documents with embedded hyperlinks [W3C 99]. A Web browser session would be started by a user typing in a destination URI, such as http://www.blueskyuniversity.com/salespitch.html, and hitting the return key (or by selecting a bookmark or favorite). The browser would then parse the URI, detect that HTTP is being used to connect to the Web server and pull out the Web server's IP address (www.blueskyuniversity.com). The browser would then contact the Web server and pass it an HTTP request to fetch the file salespitch.html. The Web server would retrieve the corresponding file, a Web page in this case, and return it to the browser for display.

This basic HTTP mechanism was fine for browsing distributed multimedia documents, but it provided no way for the user to enter data, such as which book they would like to purchase. The **Common Gateway Interface (CGI)** addresses this issue. With CGI, the HTML displayed in a browser contains one or more **forms** (text fields, drop-down lists and buttons) for the user to fill in. All the user has to do is enter data into the form and click a button (typically labeled Submit or Proceed to Checkout). When the button is pressed, the Web browser extracts name−value pairs from the form and passes them to the Web server with the name of the **CGI script** (command file, interpreted file or executable) that should process the data. All the information about the script and the name−value pairs can be parceled up by the Web browser as a URI:

```
http://www.blueskyuniversity.com/cgi-bin/buy.pl?b=Gemma&q=2
```

(The name–value pairs can also travel across in the body of the HTTP request, but the end result is the same.)

When the Web server receives the request, it detects that it's being asked to run a process because of the /cgi-bin part of the URI – this specifies a location on the server where the scripts are kept. The Web server finds the script to run (a PERL script called buy.pl in this case), starts it up and then passes it the name–value pairs as environment variables (operating system values that can be retrieved by a process). In the book example, above, we have two name–value pairs representing a book and a quantity, respectively, b=Gemma and q=2.

The script can now do any processing it needs to do, based on the values it was passed (presumably, in this case, arranging for the delivery of two books and the debiting of the customer's credit card, using details already entered). Once the script has finished, anything that it writes to standard output is passed back to the client browser as the result of the interaction – for example, it could be a new HTML page, a picture or a sound clip. In the book example, we would probably send back an order confirmation page.

The HTML/CGI configuration is summarized in Figure 9.3. This shows a Web server providing access to HTML files, scripts and other media files, while the client hosts a Web browser that displays HTML pages and provides data capture via CGI forms.

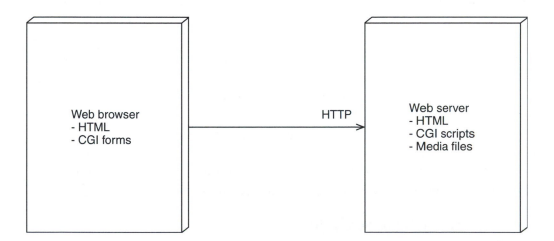

**Figure 9.3: Configuration using HTML/CGI-with-scripts**

Thus, CGI allows us to collect form data from the client for processing on the middle tier. The main advantage of CGI is that it's supported everywhere, regardless of how old the client's Web browser is. Thus, any machine can be a client in a three-tier system simply by having a Web browser installed.

CGI has a number of disadvantages:

- Poor interactivity: CGI forms have a limited number of input components: text entry fields, lists, drop down lists and buttons. The sophisticated modern user will be used to notebooks, toolbars, spin buttons, menus, and so forth. Using a client-side scripting language such as JavaScript can alleviate some of these problems, at great cost in time and effort to the developer. But, even then, the end result is not perfect. Worse still, each click of a Submit button might take the user to another page, which causes the whole of the browser window to be cleared to the background color and repainted. In contrast, a proper GUI paints much more quickly.
- Slow speed: The user has to wait for the contents of the form to be dispatched to the server, for the process to be started and run to completion, and for the results to be brought back and painted. Thus, the user gets the impression of slow interaction.
- No data validation on the client: We can use JavaScript on the client to improve things a little by validating the form before dispatch. However, we still have to do checks in the server to protect ourselves from hackers, so all we can hope to do with client-side validation is to increase the number of correct forms that hit the server.
- Overloaded server: On the server, we have a serious problem because we're trying to start one process per form. This problem is so serious that we simply couldn't contemplate processing thousands of forms simultaneously. We can use a tool called **FAST-CGI** that allows us to keep a process in memory to avoid starting one for each request but we still need a separate copy of the program's data area for each request.
- Scripts may not be portable: Historically, programming languages, scripting languages and command languages have not been entirely portable. Therefore, if we decide that we want to change our middle tier servers from, say, Windows to Unix, there will be some porting effort.
- No security: By default, name–value pairs are passed to the Web server unencrypted, so personal information can be read in transit. To get round this, we can run HTTP over SSL (look for https:// at the start of the URI before you submit your form). But this is extra configuration that we must do ourselves (and perhaps pay money for).

## 9.7.2 HTML/CGI-with-Servlets

Courtesy of some clever design by Sun and partners, the HTML/CGI-with-servlets configuration is nearly identical to the HTML/CGI-with-scripts configuration (see Figure 9.4). The client has the same Web browser, HTML pages and CGI forms. The difference is in the URI: rather than nominating a script to run, we specify a servlet (a Java object) to instantiate:

```
http://www.blueskyuniversity.com/servlet/BuyServlet?b=Gemma&q=2
```

Here, the Web server spots that we want to run a servlet because of the /servlet part of the URI. Next comes the class name of the servlet (BuyServlet). The first time the Web server

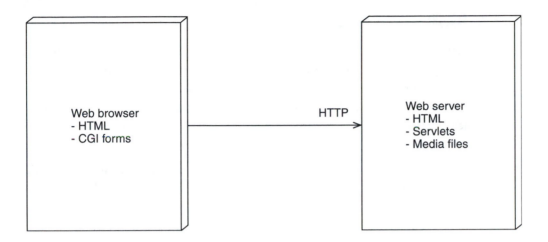

**Figure 9.4: Configuration using HTML/CGI-with-servlets**

receives a request for a particular servlet, the servlet is instantiated and told to process the request. Thereafter, the servlet stays alive and all subsequent requests go through the *same* servlet. (Each request is run through the servlet in a separate **thread** of execution. So, rather than running scripts as separate processes, we have the Web server passing multiple client requests through a single Java object.)

To pass a request to a servlet, the Web server uses one of a handful of standard messages, doPost(:HttpServletRequest,:HttpServletResponse) being the most common; the name–value pairs are inside HttpServletRequest. When the doPost method has finished its back-end processing, the response is put into HttpServletResponse. The Web server extracts the contents of HttpServletResponse and dispatches it back to the Web browser in the normal way.

Servlets have the following advantages over scripts:

- Performance: A servlet handles multiple requests simultaneously without multiple processes or multiple data areas, so requests are serviced more efficiently. Also, servlets normally run faster than interpreted programs written in languages such as PERL.
- Scalability: Since multiple servlets can be handled by a single (Web server) process, we can manage millions of simultaneous client requests without overloading the server.
- Portability: If we change our operating system, the only porting effort is to install the appropriate version of Java on the new platform. The servlets themselves remain unchanged.
- Ease of use: Since servlets are standard Java objects, servlet developers have access to a huge library of reusable objects for common computing tasks, so there's less coding to do than with scripts.

## 9.7.3 RMI

Remote Method Invocation (RMI) [Campione *et al.* 98] is a fancy term that means 'Java objects sending messages to other Java objects over a network'. RMI is part of the standard Java libraries, so it's available to anyone who installs Java 2 Standard Edition (J2SE) or Enterprise Edition (J2EE). The RMI designers have worked hard to make RMI simple to use and remote objects are almost as easy to use as local objects. The only differences are that:

- Server objects must be deployed on the machines that are to be contacted over RMI; they may provide all the services needed by remote clients or they may simply be factories for other objects.
- Any machine hosting server objects must run a **naming service**, a server process running on a well-known port that allows remote machines to look up server objects by name. RMI has its own naming service called a **registry**; however, it is better to employ the pluggable **Java Naming and Directory Interface (JNDI)**, so that you can exploit whatever naming service is available.
- Any message sent over the network may throw an exception, RemoteException: this ensures that client programmers can't ignore the fact that they're stepping outside of their local Java process.

Apart from these minor restrictions, the developer can use RMI to set up any client–server or distributed architecture.

Each host in an RMI configuration can be implemented as an applet or an application. The applet scenario has the advantage that, as long as we deploy a Web server somewhere on the network, the client doesn't need any of our system software installed beforehand – all the client software can be loaded as it is needed via the Web browser and Web server. For applications, we have to do one of the following:

- Deploy the client software to each client machine. Whenever we update the client software, we need to redeploy on all clients. This option is best left for situations where the system software for the client is large (what large means depends on the speed of the network you're using).
- Deploy a Web server and then use a small piece of bootstrap software to load the client code. The bootstrap software still needs to be installed on each client, but at least we guarantee that the client gets the latest version of the software on each startup.
- Use Java WebStart to load the client software as needed. Java WebStart is a tool provided by Sun to enable the dynamic loading of Java applications (a mechanism normally reserved for applets). To use Java WebStart, we need to deploy a Web server and then make sure that each client has a Web browser with Java WebStart and the Java PlugIn (part of J2SE)

installed. This is the simplest option if we want to run clients as applications rather than as applets.

Figure 9.5 shows the front-end configuration for an RMI applet client. On the middle tier, we must run some kind of server process that contains our system-specific code in addition to the generic code that runs as part of the naming service.

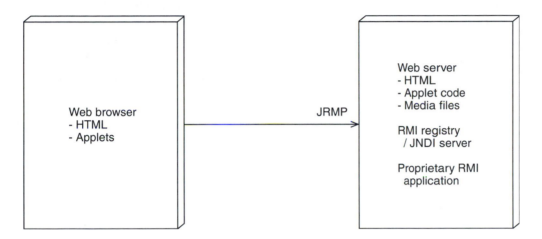

**Figure 9.5: RMI used from applets**

## 9.7.4 CORBA

The **Common Object Request Broker Architecture (CORBA)** [OMG 04] was developed by the Object Management Group, the industry consortium dedicated to the development of open object standards that also owns UML. CORBA is similar to RMI but it predates RMI, so it has a stronger foothold in industry. The main differences between CORBA and RMI are:

- CORBA is multi-language: host software can be written in C++, Eiffel, C#, Java and even non-object-oriented languages such as C or COBOL (the server software will still appear object-oriented to clients).
- CORBA has its own dedicated naming service (although this can be used via JNDI).
- Java hosts receive **unchecked exceptions** from CORBA but **checked exceptions** from developer code – this can cause confusion. (A checked exception must be handled by the programmer, whereas an unchecked exception need not be.)
- CORBA costs money (the free implementation that comes with Java is suitable for development and testing purposes).
- RMI has access to the entire Java 2 platform (Standard Edition, at least). This is useful for gaining access to media files, for example.

CORBA, because of its generality, is more complicated than RMI. RMI, on the other hand, is more powerful (it supports the dynamic exchange of object graphs and compiled classes). Also, RMI performance can be optimized for each new application. Other than that, the Java programmer should regard CORBA and RMI as alternatives. Non-Java programmers should regard CORBA as the best choice for simple message-sending over the network (it is preferable to proprietary, non-portable alternatives). Sun has developed a bridging protocol called **RMI-over-IIOP** that allows RMI hosts to be mixed with CORBA hosts, with a few restrictions.

Figure 9.6 shows the front-end configuration for applets accessing CORBA. For non-Java hosts, CORBA client software must be deployed on each client (and redeployed for each new release). CORBA hosts written in Java have the same deployment options as RMI hosts.

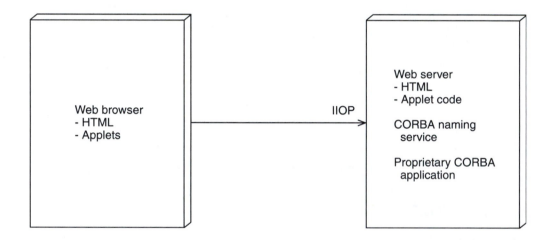

**Figure 9.6: CORBA used from applets**

## 9.7.5 EJB

**Enterprise Java Beans (EJB)**, part of J2EE [Bodoff *et al.* 02], is a framework for distributed Java systems with full transaction management, security and persistence support. In Java terms, a **bean** is an object with a well-known style of interface. EJB implementations are available from many industry leaders such as IBM, Sun and BEA Systems. There is also a reference implementation available from Sun, so that you can develop and test EJB software without buying an implementation. The EJB framework is, in many ways, a competitor to Microsoft's .Net strategy (especially if we include all the other facilities of J2EE). .Net, of course, is proprietary and not very portable, whereas EJB is open and portable.

Detailed discussion of the EJB framework is beyond the scope of this book. Suffice to say that EJBs come in three main varieties:

- Entity beans, which correspond to entity objects in the Jacobson/UML sense: business objects that have business information and business behavior. Entity beans can be stored automatically by an EJB implementation, using a relational database of your choice, or the developer can elect to store the beans using proprietary code (for integration with legacy systems and object-oriented databases). Access to entity bean data is subject to transactions: the developer can settle for the default or choose from a variety of options (representing different speed/accuracy trade-offs). For the sake of portability, all transaction semantics are specified by the framework while the implementor of each EJB run-time system has to make sure that the semantics are supported by the implementation. For efficiency reasons, messages are sent to entity beans locally, rather than over the network.
- Session beans, which manage business tasks on behalf of EJB clients. A client sends a message over the network to a session bean, which satisfies the request using entity beans and other session beans. A session bean provides default transaction behavior for all the entity beans and session beans that it accesses. Alternatively, the client can control when transactions start and finish (and, to a limited extent, how they should be propagated to other beans).
- Message-driven beans, which integrate seamlessly with industrial strength machine-to-machine messaging implementations. Messages can be sent peer-to-peer or broadcast to several machines at once, under full transaction control.

Figure 9.7 illustrates the configuration for an EJB application front end. In order for EJBs to work, they must be dropped into an **Enterprise Java Server** (**EJS**), often referred to using the more general term **application server**. This is different from the RMI and CORBA cases,

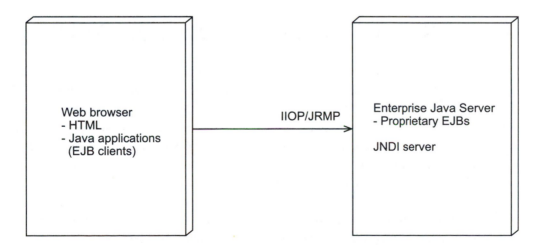

**Figure 9.7: An EJB application front end**

where we had to provide our own server to contain our business objects. As with RMI and Java-based CORBA, various alternative configurations are possible.

## 9.8 BACK-END CONFIGURATIONS

So far, we've seen how clients of a three-tier system can be implemented using CGI, RMI, CORBA or EJBs. For Internet applications, the most common choice is HTML/CGI. For intranets, we can choose our preferred mechanism, although, for the sake of maintenance, we should strive to keep the middle tier in a three-tier system applicable to all types of client, regardless of which type of access is implemented first. (If we have a controlled user base – users who are prepared to install the correct level of Java – we can choose whichever front-end technology we prefer, even for Internet use.) Any of the configurations described can be used as the front end for a two-tier system.

So, what happens when we arrive at the middle tier? The simplest solution is to install a DBMS client on the middle tier and access it from whatever server software we have chosen to deploy (scripts, servlets, RMI server, CORBA server or Enterprise Java Server). Access to the database client may be possible within the same process as our middle-tier code, or it may have to be in a separate process. Alternatively, we can arrange for our server software to act as a .Net client or an EJB client. Since the Enterprise Java Server or .Net server that we access from the middle tier provides business services, logically it belongs in the middle tier; however, all of these technologies permit deployment across multiple machines in many different ways so it doesn't matter where the server actually resides.

## 9.9 JAVA E-COMMERCE CONFIGURATION

Because e-commerce systems need to attract the most casual of Internet users, we're really stuck with the HTML/CGI front end as the default mechanism. If we deploy any other kind of front end, we risk losing customers: most customers, when confronted with 'You must install such and such to use this site' will simply go elsewhere. Front ends not hosted by a Web browser are also out of the question: it is not reasonable to expect e-commerce customers to install software for our benefit.

With the help of JSPs (or ASPs, for the Microsoft-minded), we can produce an interaction that is tailored to each user (although we can't solve the repainting and slow-round-trip problems inherent in browsers). Once we've reached the middle tier, we can choose any technology we like to access the data tier and other parts of the middle tier.

So, how do we combine CGI, JSPs, servlets, EJBs and DBMSs into a coherent, scalable whole? The basic idea is that we use CGI to access servlets that provide the business services;

the servlets rely on reusable EJBs to do most of their work; the EJBs rely on a DBMS to store enterprise data; finally, the servlets pass the result data to JSPs to build the personalized Web pages that are sent back to the client. The full picture is illustrated in Figure 9.8. (Nonstandard, UML-style keywords have been used to show how each object fits into the EJB framework.)

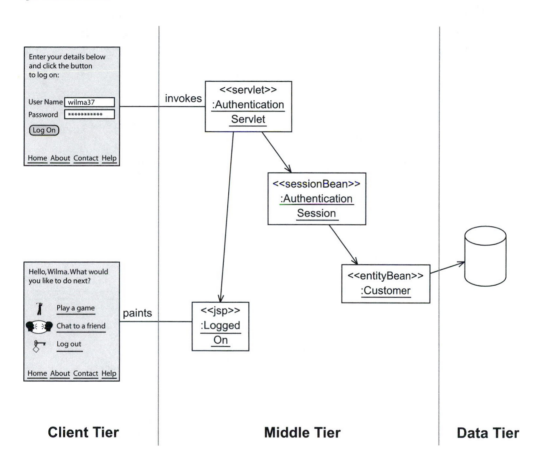

**Figure 9.8: Java e-commerce technologies in action**

In the scenario illustrated, Wilma navigates to the logon page of our site, so that she can access services that are only available to registered customers. Wilma fills in her user name – Wilma37 – and password and clicks the Log On button. Wilma's form data is passed to the AuthenticationServlet for processing. The AuthenticationServlet invokes an EJB session bean – the AuthenticationSession – to check the user name and password. The AuthenticationSession bean asks the EJB run-time system to find the CustomerEntity bean that has the user name Wilma37 (if there is no such customer, an error is signaled to the servlet). The AuthenticationSession then compares the CustomerEntity's password with the one passed in by the servlet. If the passwords match, the AuthenticationSession returns a session token (a unique identifying value) to the AuthenticationServlet; if they don't match, the AuthenticationSession signals an error to the servlet.

In the case of a successful logon, the AuthenticationServlet associates the session token with the browser session (usually as a **cookie**, a small piece of information that gets passed back to the browser), along with any other relevant information (such as the key of the CustomerEntity). Next, the servlet forwards the request to a JSP, passing it a Java object

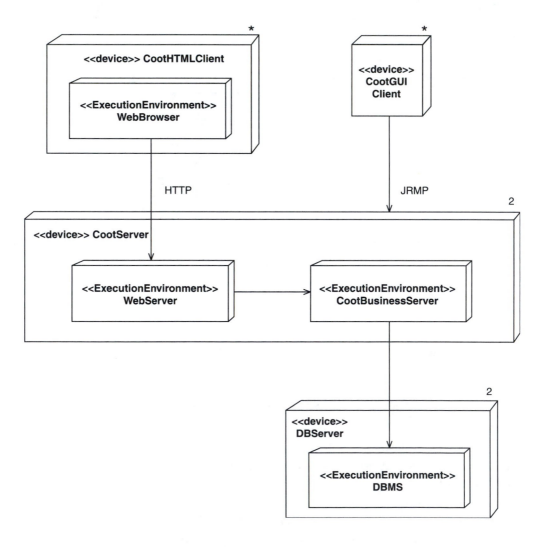

**Figure 9.9: A more detailed deployment diagram for iCoot**

containing result data (such as the real name of Wilma37). The JSP runs its embedded Java code to interleave personalized data with the static HTML. Once the completed page has been sent back to the browser and displayed, the business transaction (use case) is complete.

In the event of an unsuccessful logon, the error raised by the AuthenticationSession is detected by the AuthenticationServlet. The servlet forwards this request to an error page, which might be a static HTML page containing a generic message, such as User name or password incorrect, or a dynamic page (built by a JSP) with something more specific, such as The password you entered was incorrect. Returning an error page to the browser marks an alternative end to the business transaction (use case).

---

**Case Study**

*iCoot configuration*

Because of its simplicity, portability and light loading of the client, the HTML/CGI-with-servlets configuration will be used for the first increment of iCoot. A later increment will also provide a proper Java client so that customers can use a GUI for elegant and fast access to the system via RMI. On the server side, a proprietary business server that accesses a relational database using JDBC will be used. The business server will use EJB session beans to provide access to Java transactions but it won't use EJB entity beans because the developers have not yet been trained in their use.

We can add these architectural decisions to the topological deployment diagram that we saw earlier (in Section 8.4.9). Figure 9.9 shows processes as subnodes, each marked with the UML keyword <<ExecutionEnvironment>>. The communication paths now show navigability – the path name can be used to indicate the communication protocol.

The deployment survey for this extended picture is:

The iCoot data tier comprises two database servers (which we have called DBServer). Having two such nodes improves throughput and reliability. Each DBServer hosts a DBMS process for managing access to data.

The middle tier, which communicates with the data tier, consists of two server machines (CootServer), again duplicated for the sake of reliability and throughput. Each CootServer hosts a CootBusinessServer (for handling business requests) and a WebServer (for handling static HTML content and forwarding business requests to the CootBusinessServer). Data access for the CootBusinessServer is provided by the DBMS. Because they're proprietary to the products that we select, the communication protocols between the WebServer and the CootBusinessServer and between the CootBusinessServer and the DBMS are not specified.

> **Case Study (cont'd)**
>
> Each CootServer can be accessed simultaneously by any number of CootHTML-Client nodes. Each CootHTMLClient hosts a WebBrowser, which accesses one of the WebServer nodes using HTTP.
>
> Eventually, we will also provide access from CootGUIClient nodes. Each Coot-GUIClient will access one of the CootServer nodes, using JRMP. Because the mechanism that allows such requests to get into the CootBusinessServer is the subject of a future increment, no details are given. Nor is any detail given for the CootGUIClient processes.

# 9.10 UML PACKAGES

The UML concept of a **package** allows us to group related classes. The **package diagram** in Figure 9.10 shows each package as a box with a tab at the top left corner. The package name appears in bold, either in the middle of the box or, if we want to show the contents of the package, inside the tab. The contents of a package can be classes or other packages. Figure 9.10 also shows a dependency (the dashed open-ended arrow) from one package to another: the implication is that the source package uses something inside the target package.

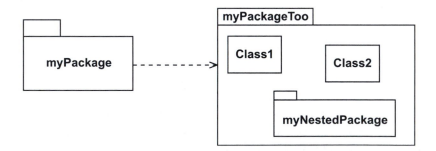

**Figure 9.10: UML package diagram**

A package can be used to represent:

- a layer
- a subsystem
- a reusable library
- a framework

- classes that should be deployed together
- ...

From a programming point of view, packages map conveniently to existing language constructs such as Java packages and C++ namespaces. But bear in mind that packages are simply a compile-time concept: they help us to organize code for the benefit of development, deployment and maintenance.

---

**Case Study**

*iCoot packages*

Figure 9.11 shows the package design for iCoot. In this case, each layer in the system has been mapped to a distinct package. Dependencies on packages in the standard Java library such as java.sql, which is used by the business package for access to the database, have not been shown. If all dependencies had been included, the diagram would have been much larger and much more cluttered.

The main iCoot package is labeled com::nowhere. This is shorthand for 'package nowhere is nested inside package com'. UML borrows this notation for the **namespace operator** from C++ (when writing Java source code, the '::' is replaced with '.'). Despite the use of events in iCoot, there is no dependency from the control package to the packages above. This is because the event listener and event types reside in the control package. The protocol package contains definitions of the lightweight copy objects, exported by the server layer for simplifying network access to the BusinessLayer. (This is explained further in Chapter 10.)

---

Many developers will use a package diagram to show layers. However, there are a couple of problems with this approach. Firstly, layers are chosen before any decision about how to organize source code into packages has been made (and the organization may well be different). Secondly, a package diagram doesn't allow us to show some important information; for example, the existence of the HTTPCGILayer in iCoot is important, but it doesn't map to any package that we might implement or borrow from a library (it's simply an indication that we use the HTT P protocol with the CGI extras). Thus, for iCoot, a special-purpose layer diagram, with an accompanying document describing the **layer interaction policy**, is more appropriate (see Figure 8.14).

Package diagrams are also not good at showing horizontal partitions (subsystems); a deployment diagram should be used instead. Figure 9.12 shows the iCoot deployment diagram after system design has been completed, detailing the content of the CootServer processes in terms of UML **artifacts** and packages.

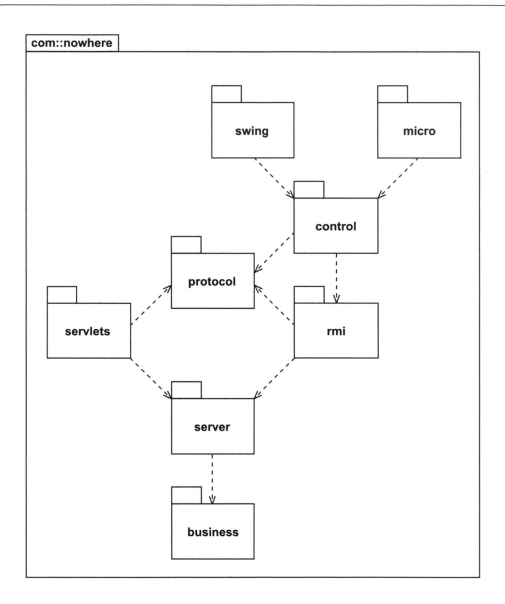

**Figure 9.11: Packages for iCoot**

An artifact, in UML, is something that can be deployed, usually a file. (A file can be almost anything: for example, a program, a DLL, a folder, some XML data or a README document.) Artifacts are indicated by either a sheet-of-paper icon or the <<artifact>> keyword. The artifacts in Figure 9.12 are iCoot, a folder of static HTML pages; icoot.ear, a compressed archive of servlets, JSPs and EJBs (the Java naming convention .ear is short for 'enterprise archive'); and cootschema.ddl, a proprietary script for creating the database.

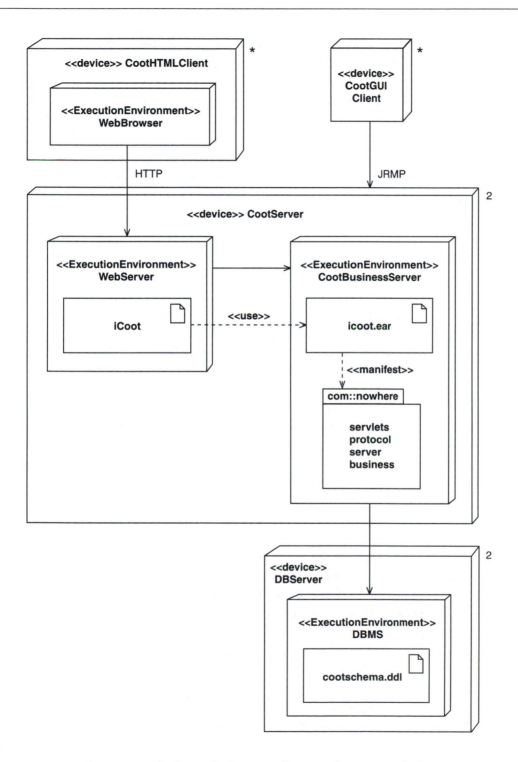

**Figure 9.12: The iCoot deployment diagram after system design**

We can show which elements from our model give rise to a particular artifact by adding a dependency from the artifact to the group of elements, labeled <<manifest>> (the artifact is a manifestation of the elements). Here, icoot.ear has been shown as a manifestation of four of the com::nowhere packages. We can show other dependencies on a deployment diagram. For example, with the help of the <<use>> keyword, it's been shown that iCoot uses icoot.ear.

---

**Case Study**

*Updated iCoot deployment survey*

The iCoot data tier comprises two database servers (which we have called DBServer). Having two such nodes improves throughput and reliability. Each DBServer hosts a DBMS process for managing access to data.

The cootschema.ddl artifact contains commands for creating database tables, in a format specific to the database being used. This is deployed to each DBMS process, using database-specific tools (no detail given here). Note that cootschema.ddl contains the schema for the full Coot system, since iCoot and Coot use the same data.

The middle tier, which communicates with the data tier, consists of two server machines (CootServer), again duplicated for the sake of reliability and throughput. Each CootServer hosts a CootBusinessServer (for handling business requests) and a WebServer (for handling static HTML content and forwarding business requests to the CootBusinessServer). Data access for the CootBusinessServer is provided by the DBMS. Because they're proprietary to the products that we select, the communication protocols between the WebServer and the CootBusinessServer and between the CootBusinessServer and the DBMS are not specified.

Within each CootServer, the iCoot folder, containing static HTML pages, is deployed to the WebServer, while the icoot.ear archive is deployed to the CootBusinessServer. The icoot.ear archive contains servlets, JSPs, business objects and (eventually) RMI decorators, from the com::nowhere package.

Each CootServer can be accessed simultaneously by any number of CootHTMLClient nodes. Each CootHTMLClient hosts a WebBrowser, which accesses one of the WebServer nodes using HTTP. No artifacts need to be deployed to the CootHTMLClient nodes.

Eventually, we will also provide access from CootGUIClient nodes. Each Coot-GUIClient will access one of the CootServer nodes, using JRMP. Because the mechanism that allows such requests to get into the CootBusinessServer is the subject of a future increment, no details are given. Nor is any detail given for the Coot-GUIClient processes. The artifacts deployed to the CootGUIClient nodes, if any, are not specified.

# 9.11 SUMMARY

In this chapter, we've looked at:

- The major technologies available on the client and server.

- The middleware protocols that can be used to connect clients and servers.

- Popular technology choices for the front ends to networked systems.

- How UML packages can be used to show clusters of related classes on a deployment diagram.

# FURTHER READING

For an HTML/CGI client tier, accessing servlets on the middle tier, the **Struts** framework [Robinson and Finkelstein 04] from the open source Apache Software Foundation is well respected. Struts takes most of the drudgery out of implementing an interactive HTML front end. To download Struts and view the documentation, go to www.apache.org.

If you're interested in serious CORBA programming, a comprehensive book that covers both Java and C++ is [Bolton 01]. As usual, the last word on anything technical is the CORBA Specification [OMG 04].

For an overview of key multi-tier Java technologies, see [Campione *et al.* 98], which covers RMI, JDBC, servlets and Java IDL (the Java interface to CORBA). The contents of this book are also available on-line at java.sun.com.

In order to learn more about J2EE, including JSPs, servlets, EJBs, transactions, security, XML, XSL, SOAP, JMS and Java ServerFaces (for interactive HTML interfaces) see [Bodoff *et al.* 02] and the on-line version at java.sun.com. Sun's web site also has details of the latest Java angle on Web Services.

# REVIEW QUESTIONS

1. What are some of the advantages of Java as an implementation technology? Choose all options that apply.

   (a) Object-oriented purity.
   (b) Invented by Microsoft.
   (c) Network readiness.
   (d) Portability.
   (e) Scalability.
   (f) Security.

2. Servlets are a direct replacement for what? Choose only one option.

   (a) XML.
   (b) Applets.
   (c) ActiveX controls.
   (d) CGI scripts.
   (e) CORBA.

# ANSWERS TO REVIEW QUESTIONS

1. Some of the advantages of Java as an implementation technology are:

   (a) Object-oriented purity.
   (c) Network readiness.
   (d) Portability.
   (e) Scalability.
   (f) Security.

2. Servlets are a direct replacement for d. CGI scripts.

# 10

## Designing the Subsystems

In this chapter, we'll be looking at **subsystem design** (also known as **detailed design**). Having chosen our network topology, our implementation technologies, our subsystems and our layers, it's time to decide exactly what is going to go inside each subsystem and layer.

# Learning Objectives

**Understand how to design the business layer.**

**Understand how to map run-time objects to storable data.**

**Understand how to design user interfaces.**

**Understand multi-threading.**

# Chapter Outline

# 10.1 INTRODUCTION

Because of the size of the subsystem design task, and the creativity that's unique to every project, we couldn't hope to write down a step-by-step guide to designing a professional, object-oriented, multi-tier system. Instead, this chapter contains an overview of each of the major tasks. In practice, if you place these tasks at the center of your design effort, everything else will fall into place.

First of all, we'll consider how to design the business layer. This normally involves deciding what objects will populate the layer, how they will be connected and what their interfaces will be. We must transform the business-oriented class model that we developed during analysis into implementation-oriented classes for our chosen programming language.

For the purposes of this book, the subsystem design discussion is more or less independent of the programming languages and other technologies that are chosen. However, for the sake of illustration and convenience, some bias is shown towards Java and relational databases. (Despite the Java bias, the design presented is portable to any language that includes pure object-oriented facilities; similarly, the relational database bias won't tie us to any particular DBMS.)

Subsystem design involves transforming a conceptual analysis model into implementable classes, following the strategy laid out in the system design model. In keeping with the system design principles already discussed, subsystem design can proceed as follows:

1. Design the classes and fields of the **business layer**, using the analysis class model as a guide. The business layer consists of the entities from our problem domain and the various supporting classes that they need.
2. Decide how any **persistent data** will be stored and design the storage layout. Persistent data is data that must not vanish when the system is shut down.
3. Finalize the look and feel of the user interface, with reference to the sketches that were produced during the analysis phase.
4. Walk through the system use cases, with reference to the user interface design, noting the **business services** that must be supported by the middle tier. Business services are questions and commands that a client can send to the server, such as 'buy a book' or 'reserve a car model'.
5. Develop the business services into **server objects**, whose messages are available over the network. Server objects implement the business services using the business layer, in such a way that different kinds of client can be accommodated.
6. Finalize the measures that are needed to ensure **concurrency control** and **thread safety**. concurrency control means using business rules to control access to the system: user names and passwords, reserving tickets before purchase, and so on. Thread safety means making sure that data within a process is not corrupted and that parallel activities do not get in each other's way.

# 10.2 MAPPING THE ANALYSIS CLASS MODEL INTO THE DESIGN CLASS MODEL

In moving from analysis to design, some classes will be discarded (controllers, for example) and others will be introduced (such as collection classes that implement multiplicities). For the purposes of this book, designers have freedom to decide how the business objects, boundaries and homes developed up to this point should be turned into implementable code. (This is different from the RUP approach where the analysis class model is massaged into an implementable design model.)

For each design class that we come up with, we need to choose the names and types of its fields. Often, fields are derived from the attributes or associations discovered during analysis. There is no way we can tell, just from looking at source code, whether a particular field started out as an attribute, a composition, an aggregation or an association. This is one reason why the high-level artifacts produced during requirements capture and analysis are important.

As well as attributes and associations, we need to consider inheritance. Inheritance relationships don't need to be mapped into anything new, we just need to decide whether or not to keep them. Because of the complexities involved, inheritance should be handled with care: it is quite reasonable to produce a system with little or no inheritance among its classes. (Any inheritance that we do use is more likely to be introduced during design rather than analysis.)

## 10.2.1 Mapping Operations

But what about the operations? Up to this point, operations have been introduced merely as a way of recording use case realizations – in other words, as the system use cases were simulated, operations were discovered as a side-effect of verifying that the analysis classes would support an implementation. These analysis operations should be ignored for the purposes of design. So, where do our design operations come from? Now that we're switching to design, we can stick to the programming terms 'message' and 'method', rather than the UML term 'operation'. So, where do the messages come from? For most of our objects, regardless of the layer in which they reside, messages will be added for one or more of the following reasons:

- To allow client objects to read or change the values of fields.
- To allow client objects to access derived data (for example, as well as a message to read the radius of a Circle, we would expect to be able to read the diameter).
- Because our experience or intuition tell us that a particular message might be useful.

- Because some framework or pattern that we have decided to use requires certain messages to be present.

In addition, when we design the business services for our middle tier, we invent messages for the server objects. As we work out how the business services can be satisfied using the business objects, we're likely to come up with even more messages. In short, as we map the analysis classes, attributes and relationships, into their design counterparts, messages will start to appear from all directions.

## 10.2.2  Variable Types

When we introduce a field, we need to decide what type it is: a primitive or a class. For most purposes, we can restrict ourselves to the following types:

- The primitive types and simple classes that we would expect to find in every object-oriented programming language (for example, int, float, boolean, String, List, Set and array, or []).
- Classes that we ourselves are designing.
- Classes from the patterns and frameworks that we have chosen to use.

In some languages, arrays and collections do not mix well – arrays tend to be fixed-size and may not be objects at all. Therefore, base your choice on elegance (collections) or a slight improvement in performance (arrays).

## 10.2.3  Visibility of Fields

As well as providing the names and types of fields, we must declare their **visibility**. The visibility of a field specifies which pieces of code are allowed to read or modify the value. The following visibilities are enough for most purposes:

- Private (shown by - in UML): Only visible within the defining class.
- Package (shown by ˜ in UML): Visible within the defining class and to all classes in the same package.
- Protected (shown by # in UML): Visible within the defining class, to all classes in the same package, and to all subclasses of the defining class (whether inside or outside the package).
- Public (shown by + in UML): Visible everywhere.

Normally, if the language permits, developers will make fields private: apart from the encapsulation benefits, this gives the compiler more optimization opportunities. Sometimes, developers will make fields protected instead, so that developers of subclasses have more opportunities for modifying the behavior of the superclass (although this does increase the coupling between the subclass and the superclass).

Fields with package visibility are a bad idea, because they can be accessed by any piece of code in the package without the knowledge of the owning object. Occasionally, for pragmatic reasons (performance and brevity), a developer will give a field package access, but only if the chosen language provides some way of making the value read-only (for example, using the keyword final in Java). This argument applies even more strongly to public fields, since they're also visible outside the package.

Visibilities can be applied to *messages* too. In this case, each message will be:

- public, if it's part of the interface of the package;
- package, if it's implementation code to be used by the class itself and by classes in the same package;
- protected, if it's implementation code to be used by the class itself, by its subclasses and by classes in the same package;
- private, if it's implementation code for use by this class only (which decreases coupling and allows the compiler to do more optimizations, as with fields).

Not all languages support the four styles of visibility used in UML, but Java does.

## 10.2.4 Accessors

It's a good idea to provide **accessor** messages for fields. Accessor messages come in two varieties: **getters** which return the value of a field and **setters** which set the field to a new value (see Implementation Point 5 for an example). Accessors allow us to centralize access

---

**Implementation Point 5**

This fragment of a Java class shows one field with a pair of accessors:

```
...
private int count;

public int getCount() {
    return count;
}
public void setCount(int c) {
    count = c;
}
...
```

to fields, making maintenance easier. Accessors are also easy for a compiler to optimize (especially if the associated variable is private). Within the class itself, we may relax the rule slightly: it is common to read a field directly but to set it using a setter.

## 10.2.5 Mapping Classes, Attributes and Compositions

In UML, the same notation is used for analysis class diagrams and design class diagrams. However, you will find yourself using more of the available notation in your design diagrams.

The notation for class fields is the same as for instance fields, except that class fields are underlined. Similarly, class messages use the same notation as instance messages, except that class messages are underlined. You could be forgiven for thinking that this underlining policy is inconsistent with the policy for class names (on a class diagram) versus object labels (on an object diagram) – class names are not underlined while object labels are. Yes, it is confusing. The justification is that it's better to underline whichever version is drawn less often.

Figure 10.1 shows a fragment of the analysis class diagram from iCoot being converted into a design class diagram. In mapping to the design diagram, three major issues have been resolved: the classes to be implemented; the attributes' types; and how to map the composition. In this case, the decision has been made to retain both analysis classes, with no new supporting classes required (apart from the trivial class String). As for the attributes, all of them have survived as private fields of some appropriate type. An optional attribute

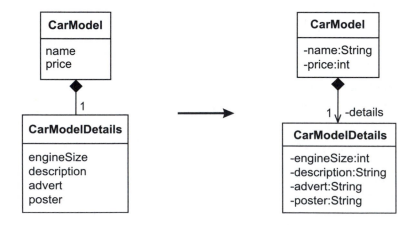

**Figure 10.1: Mapping attributes and compositions from analysis**

would have been mapped in the same way – the only difference would be that, at run time, the corresponding field might take a null value. The composition relationship takes a little more thought. For analysis purposes, compositions are bi-directional: starting from either object we can easily find the object at the other end. When we come to design, however, we have to deal with the fact that fields can only point one way (at run time, we can get from the owning object to the object at the far end, but we can't get back). So, we need to decide whether we want a field at each end of the relationship or just at one end (and, if so, which end).

We would expect a composition's primary relationship to be from the composer to the composed. This reflects the fact that the composer is the owner of the relationship. It also reflects the fact that a composition is similar to an attribute: normally, the owning object uses the services of the attribute or the composed object, but not the other way round. Bear in mind, though, that there are no absolutes: if we felt it suited our particular system better, we could put a field inside the composed object or inside both the composer and the composed. (UML also has the notion of a **data type**, which is designed specifically for embedded attributes [OMG 03a].)

Once we have decided the direction of a composition, we can add an arrow-head to the class diagram to show it, along with a role and a visibility to indicate how the composition maps to a field (see Figure 10.1). At run time, messages can only flow in the direction of the arrow. We could also remove the composition altogether and show a -details:CarModelDetails field inside CarModel instead. Most UML authoring tools allow the developer to expand and collapse such information at will.

In Figure 10.1, the advert and poster fields are both of type String. This is because we don't need to manipulate or store raw media in the iCoot system itself. Instead, we can deploy these complex types as files – *.ram and *.png files, for example – under the control of a Web server and then store the relative URIs as attribute values. For example, a CarModel could have "/adverts/mcgs.ram" as the value of its advert field.

## 10.2.6 Mapping Other Types of Association

Having dealt with compositions, let's look at the mapping of other types of association. Recall that there are three kinds of association: (plain) association, aggregation (stronger) and composition (stronger still). For mapping purposes, we don't need to make any distinction between aggregation and association because object-oriented programming languages make no distinction. So, the term association will be used for the rest of this topic.

Most of the associations that we decide to retain from analysis, along with any new ones that we add solely for design purposes, end up as fields on objects. Some may end up as class fields instead. Either way, since fields only permit navigation in one direction, we need to decide whether we want to go both ways, or whether one way will do. The way we implement an association depends on the multiplicities at each end: one-to-one, one-to-many or many-to-many.

## One-to-One Associations

Take a look at the fragment of analysis class diagram at the top of Figure 10.2. Three ways of implementing the association have been shown: we could put a field called account into Member, pointing to the InternetAccount; we could put a field called member into InternetAccount, pointing to the Member; or we could combine the two, effectively implementing a two-way association.

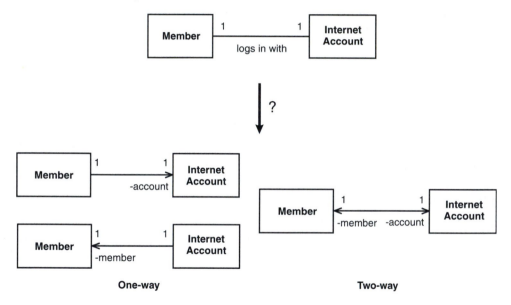

**Figure 10.2: Mapping a one-to-one association**

If we go for the two-way alternative, we would need to add code to make sure that the association doesn't get out of step. For example, it would not make sense to change an InternetAccount's member field to point to another Member if we didn't also inform the original Member that its account had changed (perhaps to null, meaning 'no value'). It is certainly possible to do this synchronization, using appropriate methods in Member and InternetAccount, but it's awkward. Therefore, most of the time, we select a one-way alternative. In this case, it's likely that the natural alternative will work best: let the Member refer to the InternetAccount, but not vice versa.

If we choose a one-way alternative, as long as we have a relational database underneath our business layer, we can always derive the complementary information at run time: for example, if we choose to put a field only into Member, any InternetAccount can, if necessary, ask the database where its Member is.

An optional association – with a multiplicity of 0..1 on one end (or on both) – is similar to the one-to-one case, except that the field (or fields) can take the value null (i.e. 'no object at the far end').

## One-to-Many Associations

Figure 10.3 shows an example of a one-to-many association. For this case, we still have to decide whether to put a field in one end or in both. The same arguments apply as in the one-to-one case. As before, we may decide that there is a natural solution, but we're still free to use our skill and judgment as designers to do it another way.

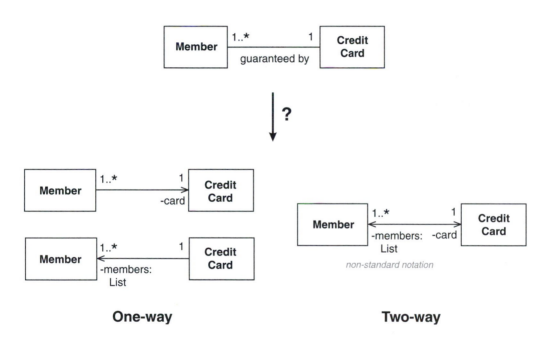

**One-way**                    **Two-way**

**Figure 10.3: Mapping a one-to-many association**

Unlike the one-to-one case, if we decide to put a field in the 1 end this time, we must be prepared to store more than one associated object. For example, if we add a members field to CreditCard, the field will have to store one or more Member objects. Thus, the CreditCard would need to employ some kind of collection class for holding on to its Member objects (or perhaps an array, according to personal preference). In Figure 10.3, a List has been used. We have something of a dilemma here: the natural choice of collection seems to be Set; however, when you add an object to a Set, most implementations will check whether the object is already there, so that it doesn't appear twice, potentially an expensive operation. Therefore, if you can be sure that you won't try to add an object twice, you should use a Bag. If you can't *always* be sure, consider using a Bag anyway and performing the duplication test manually in the exceptional cases. If your implementation language doesn't provide something like a Bag, as Java doesn't, a List will do, especially if the items are kept in order, which makes for faster searching.

The notation shown in Figure 10.3, with regard to the collection-valued fields, is not quite legal UML. Although we can certainly show a field as a navigable association with a role indicating the visibility and field name, the :List part is nonstandard. The alternative ways of showing this relationship in UML are more complicated and less informative – the version shown here is compact and it allows us to draw relationships to the type of object inside the collection.

## Many-to-Many Associations

This is the most complicated case. Consider the example shown in Figure 10.4. Here, we have a Make that can manufacture any number of CarModel objects, while each CarModel can be made by one or more Make objects. Each of the three mapping possibilities is labeled A,

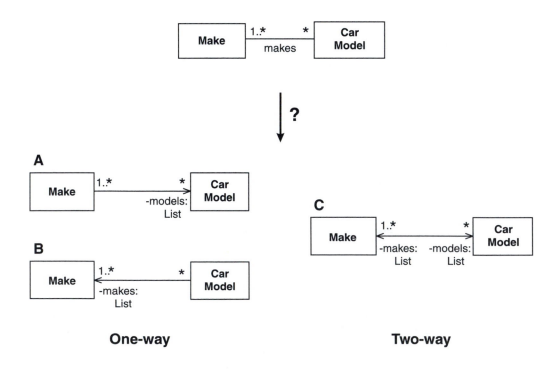

**Figure 10.4: Mapping a many-to-many association**

B or C – List objects have been chosen again, which, this time, allows us to place the Make objects in order of importance.

In common with a lot of many-to-many associations, there is really no owner of the association in this case. If we decide, based on our problem domain, that we're more likely to start with a Make and then navigate to its CarModel objects, option A would work well. Conversely, if we decide that we're more likely to start with a CarModel, option B would be better. If, however, we decide that we're just as likely to start with a Make or a CarModel, we're really stuck with option C.

With option C, the synchronization problem is worse than it was in the one-to-one and one-to-many cases: we're going to have to search through collections to find objects, rather than just accessing individual objects directly. In such cases, it can be worth introducing an **association class** to deal with the complexity, as described next.

## Association Classes

We first encountered association classes in the analysis section. An association class is necessary if there is data related to an association. The fragment of analysis class diagram at the top of Figure 10.5 shows an example of an association class.

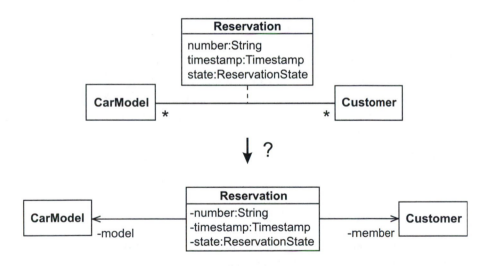

**Figure 10.5: Mapping an association class**

From this diagram, we know that Customer objects can reserve any number of CarModel objects and that CarModel objects can be reserved by any number of Customer objects; but, for each Reservation link, we need to record the reservation number, the time-stamp and the state; this data doesn't belong to the Customer or to the CarModel, rather it belongs to the association itself. Therefore, we should introduce Reservation as an association class, with appropriate attributes.

When we come to designing an association class, the easiest thing to do is to create a design class with fields for all the attributes, and two extra fields to point at the associated objects, as shown at the bottom of Figure 10.5. Then, we can create an instance of the association class for each link.

If we wanted to be able to navigate from a CarModel to its Reservation objects, we would have to add a field to CarModel, with all the associated synchronization problems. (A similar argument applies to Customer.) Alternatively, we can provide a findAllReservations-For(:CarModel) message on the ReservationHome class. (A **home** allows us to create and find objects of a particular class, usually by dipping into the underlying database; each home object is a **singleton**: we write code to guarantee that only one instance of the home exists.)

An association class is the most general way of mapping any association from analysis to design. Therefore we could, if we wished, introduce an association class to represent every association from our analysis class diagram. This would alleviate some of the synchronization problems we saw earlier. Although some code generation tools do indeed operate this way, you may feel that it is too much trouble if you're writing the code by hand.

---

**Case Study**

*iCoot BusinessLayer class diagram*

In Figure 10.6, all the analysis classes of the iCoot BusinessLayer have been mapped into design classes that can be implemented directly in any popular object-oriented language. This class diagram has been enclosed in a UML **frame**, the name of the package being shown in the top left-hand corner. Details of the fields for these classes are given in Section B.5.

---

# 10.2.7 Universal Identifier

Most business objects, at some point in their life, need to be retrieved by **key**. A key is an attribute value, or a combination of values, that is unique to each instance. For example, a bank account is uniquely identified by the combination of its account number and sort code.

Handling different types of keys in a software system can be cumbersome. Therefore, it's worth considering the introduction of a unique number to distinguish each business object from other objects of the same class. This helps to synchronize copies of the objects, to track their movements as they travel around a network (their universe) and to handle keys uniformly and efficiently (via home objects, for example). Such **universal identifiers** are also

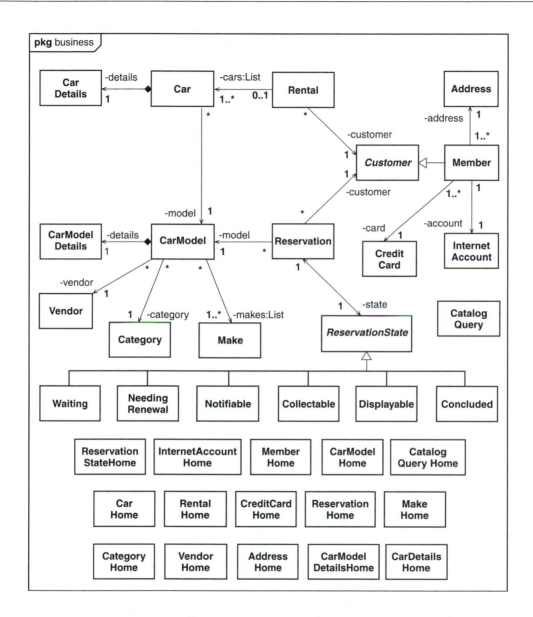

**Figure 10.6: BusinessLayer classes for iCoot**

useful when objects and links are stored in a database – the universal identifier takes the place of a memory address when the system is shut down.

A suitable type for a universal identifier is an integer. The specific type of integer depends on how many unique objects of each class you want to be able to accommodate: a 16-bit integer (short in Java) allows 65 thousand unique instances; a 32-bit integer (int in Java) allows four billion unique instances. If four billion proves inadequate, there is always the 64-bit integer (Java long) which allows a virtually unlimited number of instances (about 18 quintillion).

If you do use a universal identifier, it should be set during the construction of the object and it should remain fixed thereafter. Figure 10.7 illustrates the implementation of a universal identifier for the CarModel class. The UML <<create>> keyword has been used to indicate that the CarModel operation creates instances of CarModel. This is good practice in UML since, without the keyword, the reader would have to assume that an operation with the same name as the class is a 'constructor' but the fact that constructors exist at all, let alone that their names follow some rule, is language-specific. (It may be common, but it is still language-specific.) Therefore, in this book, although the term constructor is used as shorthand for 'operation used to create instances of the class', the <<create>> keyword is still used in diagrams.

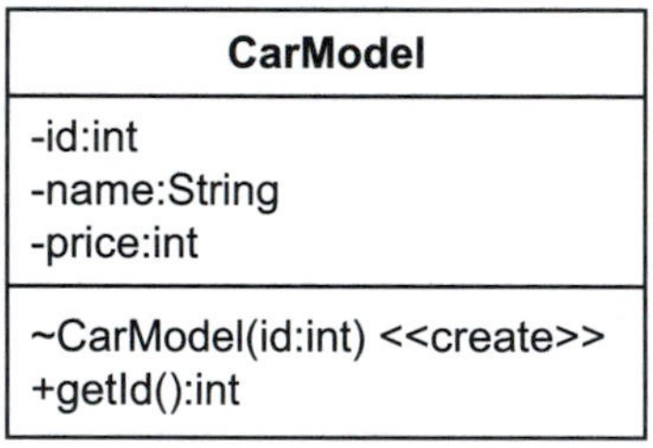

| CarModel |
| --- |
| -id:int<br>-name:String<br>-price:int |
| ~CarModel(id:int) <<create>><br>+getId():int |

**Figure 10.7: Implementing a universal identifier**

Normally, the constructor would not be public: this would allow the developer to control which universal identifiers actually get assigned, using homes for example. (If the constructor were public, any client would be able to create a CarModel using an identifier that was already in use elsewhere.) In Figure 10.7, the constructor has package access, so that the objects can be created by a CarModelHome class living in the same package.

# 10.3 HANDLING PERSISTENCE WITH A RELATIONAL DATABASE

Since most systems have data storage requirements, we'll look next at how graphs of run-time objects can be mapped into storable data, concentrating on how to use a relational database for this task, since relational databases are by far the most popular in industry. Once we've designed our business layer and our database schema, we can think about what code needs to be written to translate from one to the other.

## 10.3.1 Database Management Systems

Often, an application's data is stored separately, so that the data doesn't evaporate when the application is shut down – such data is said to **persist**. A **database management system** (**DBMS**) manages arbitrary amounts of data in separate **databases** – a database is a fenced-off area of data. The terms DBMS and database are often used interchangeably. We use a DBMS to:

1. Invent a **schema** that describes the data that we're going to store, using a **Data Definition Language** (**DDL**).
2. Add, remove and update the data in our database using a **Data Manipulation Language** (**DML**).
3. Retrieve the data from our database using a **Data Query Language** (**DQL**).

Ideally, the DDL, DML and DQL should all be **declarative**. With a declarative language, we specify *what* we want rather than *how* to do it. For example, we don't know, and we don't want to know, how the DBMS organizes data physically on a disk; instead, we would like to state what kind of data is stored, what the data values should be and what we would like to retrieve.

Over the last four decades, many varieties of DBMS have been invented – **indexed file**, **hierarchical**, **network**, **relational** and **object-oriented**, to name a few. There is always a **semantic gap** (difference in meaning) between the programming language we use to write our code and the way we access data in our database. Therefore, we need to perform some kind of run-time mapping between the software system and the database. Some tools (such as EJB implementations) will generate the mapping code for us. However, even if we wish to use such tools for our project, we still need to understand the underlying principles in order to use them effectively (and in order to understand the run-time error messages).

A relational database is often used to store the data in a multi-tier Internet system. The relational model has been chosen here because:

- Relational databases are the most common. Although object-oriented databases do exist, they're much less widely used, especially in the business world. (Most relational databases have **object-oriented extensions**, but we can ignore those, for the sake of simplicity.)
- All relational databases support the same core model, based on rigorous mathematics. This makes them unique among varieties of DBMS.
- All commercial relational database implementations support the same hybrid DDL/DML/DQL language: the **Structured Query Language** (**SQL**).
- Java has a comprehensive, portable, library for connecting to relational databases, known as **Java Database Connectivity** (**JDBC**).

To be fair, the reasons given above for sticking to a relational database are a little optimistic. Some relational DBMSs use nonstandard versions of SQL – always check first. The ANSI **SQL-92** standard (on which JDBC is based) is also not a particularly rigid specification, for example:

- With some databases, semi-colons are optional in SQL statements, while in others, they're compulsory.
- You may find that your chosen DBMS folds several data types into one: for example, DATE, TIME and TIMESTAMP might all be implemented as TIMESTAMP.
- Some data types may not be supported by your DBMS.
- The number of bits devoted to a particular data type is not in the standard: an INTEGER might be 16 bits in one DBMS and 32 bits in another.

These issues cause some difficulties for portable libraries such as JDBC. If you're not worried about the finer details of accuracy and performance, a relational schema will pretty much work on any of the popular commercial systems, although there may be some porting effort if you switch a completed system from one DBMS to another.

## 10.3.2 The Relational Model

The relational model is a mathematical model, which makes it clean, reliable and easy to optimize (easy for the DBMS, that is). However, the relational model resembles a filing cabinet containing indexed cards, rather than a repository of complex, highly-connected objects. So, the semantic gap is large.

Although an object-oriented model can be mapped easily onto a relational schema, it's difficult to predict which of several possible mappings will be the most efficient for any particular software system (with respect to storage efficiency and access speed). Therefore, you may need to experiment, preferably with the help of a mapping tool or a persistence layer, to find which mapping works best for your system.

Here, we'll look at one possible mapping: a straightforward, pure mapping. This way, you should be convinced that it's possible to store object-oriented data in a relational database. For this mapping, we can assume that we have control over how the data is stored. In real life, we may not be so lucky: the schema may be under the control of Database Administrators (DBAs) or the database may already exist as a legacy system that we can't modify – in these cases, we would have to 'reverse engineer' our mapping.

We won't look at how to write the code to ship data between a software system and its database, because that is probably the single most difficult piece of code in the whole system. If you use a framework such as EJB, the tools will generate all of the code you need for the basic mapping described here. To do anything manually requires lots of effort and study of your database's programming interface. For our purposes, it's enough to say that the underlying techniques involve using SQL statements (via a library such as JDBC) to read data from the database into run-time objects and then to write new data back out.

Since the database layer is encapsulated by the business layer, we're free to tune the business layer for the benefit of client programmers and the database layer for the benefit of the database – the mapping code can do the rest.

## Tables

The relational model is based on **tables** of data (also known as **relations**) which contain **columns** and **rows**. Figure 10.8 shows a table called ADDRESS, with four columns of string data (HOUSE, STREET, COUNTY and POSTCODE) and one of integer data (ID). As you can see, the ADDRESS table has three separate addresses stored in it. Each column stores the values for one of the address attributes – thus, the address with ID 2 represents '8 Yewbrook Rd, Cheshire, SK4 3QT'.

**ADDRESS**

| ID | HOUSE | STREET | COUNTY | POSTCODE |
|----|-------|--------|--------|----------|
| 2 | 8 | Yewbrook Road | Cheshire | SK4 3QT |
| 9 | Dunroamin | Dairy Avenue | Greater Manchester | M19 4IK |
| 6 | 74 | Old Ladbroke Grove | Lancashire | M20 7HJ |

**Figure 10.8: An ADDRESS table**

Each column can store values of one particular type. The SQL standard defines a couple of dozen types that we can choose from. For the purposes of this book, we can make do with the following:

- VARCHAR(X): A string, up to a maximum of X characters.
- INTEGER: A whole number which is often, but not always, 32 bits.
- DATE: A day in the Gregorian calendar.
- TIMESTAMP: A combination of date and time of day.
- BOOLEAN: True or false.

For example, for the ADDRESS table above, we might specify INTEGER, VARCHAR(20), VARCHAR(40), VARCHAR(40) and VARCHAR(10) as the types of ID, HOUSE, STREET, COUNTY and POSTCODE, respectively.

With the relational model, every row must be unique. For the ADDRESS table, this is achieved by introducing a unique ID attribute. Since every row is unique, each table is actually a *set* of rows. The rows in Figure 10.8 could have been shown in any order.

### Keys

A **key** is a value, or a combination of values, that uniquely identifies a row. Some tables contain obvious keys: for example, an insurance policy always has a policy number. Other tables need to have keys invented for them: for example, a customer table would need to include a customer number to identify unique people who buy our products. A key that combines several values (such as a bank account's number and sort code) is referred to as a **compound key**.

Some tables have more than one **candidate** key: for example, a car has a license number as well as a Vehicle Identification Number (VIN) that appears on a plate riveted to its body. In such cases, we have to choose one candidate to act as the **primary** key – the DBMS will assume that the primary key is the one most often used to find a particular row and it will perform optimizations accordingly.

Finding a row using a compound key is slower than finding a row using a simple key. For example, considering the ADDRESS table, we could use (HOUSE and POSTCODE) as the key, because the combination is unique for every house. However, a combination of strings is inconvenient and slow to use. Thus, in the ADDRESS example, an artificial key (ID) has been introduced that uniquely identifies each dwelling. This also allows us to record the fact that two customers live at the same address (we could store the ID twice, but the address only once).

On the schema diagrams in this book, primary keys are shown in bold. If you are sketching such a schema by hand, you can add a '+' next to the column name instead.

### Mapping an Object Model to a Relational Model

When mapping an object model into tables, we can start with either the analysis class diagram or the design class diagram. The analysis diagram is closer to a relational model, because it shows no commitment to the direction of associations, so it would seem to be a good choice. However, the design class diagram has types assigned to fields, which we need to know when designing the tables. To solve this paradox, we will use the analysis model to drive the design of the tables, but pick up the types from the design model. Any discrepancy between the actual design model and the database tables can be removed by the mapping code that we write.

## 10.3.3 Mapping Entity Classes

In order to map an entity (business object) from an object-oriented model into a relational schema, we need to introduce a table with the same name as the entity's class. (We've already seen an example of this with the ADDRESS table.) Every row in an entity table represents a unique object from the business domain.

For each simple field (primitive or string) we can add a column to the table with the same name as the field and an appropriate SQL data type. Entity fields that point to (non-string) objects must be treated differently, as we will see shortly when we look at the mapping of associations.

For the sake of object-oriented programming, it's important to introduce an integer attribute, such as ID, to use as the primary key. This is because it simplifies the mapping code (important if we're writing the code manually) and it makes navigating from one object to another easier and more efficient (especially important since objects tend to form complex graphs). It also provides the benefits associated with universal identifiers. From here on, an INTEGER column called ID will be added to every entity table, even though it is not shown in the accompanying class diagram fragments.

## 10.3.4 Mapping Associations

When we looked at how to map an analysis class model into a design class model, we saw that we had to transform the two-way analysis associations into one-way pointers. A relational database stores two-way associations directly, so we don't have the same problem: if our database schema allows us to navigate from entity A to entity B, the DBMS and the query language will allow us to navigate just as easily from entity B to entity A. Therefore, our database schema will resemble the analysis class model more closely than the design class model. (We should still design the business layer before producing the database schema though, because the design process will harden the analysis model and help us to choose attribute types.)

### One-to-One Associations

For a one-to-one association, we can add a **foreign key** to one of the entity tables. A foreign key is an entry in one table that refers to a primary key in another table. In other words, a foreign key is a reference from a row in one table to a row in another table. To emphasize which columns represent foreign keys, the column names are shown in italics here. (When drawing by hand, you can add a '>' next to the column name instead.)

In Figure 10.9, the CARMODEL table contains a foreign key called CARMODELDETAILSID that allows us to find a CarModel's details in the CARMODELDETAILS table. (The fragment of class diagram shown here uses analysis notation, without navigability, but universal identifiers have been added to each table, even though they're not analysis-level attributes.) We could equally well add a foreign key called CARMODELID to the CARMODELDETAILS table – the choice made reflects the logical nature of the composition relationship that we're dealing with. Because of the bi-directional properties of relational databases, we don't need to put a foreign key in both ends.

As an alternative to foreign keys, we could combine the two tables into one. For ease of maintenance, tables should only be combined when one of the tables doesn't represent an entity in its own right. For example, if CarModelDetails were just a composite attribute of CarModel, budded off for the convenience of programmers, it would be reasonable to add the

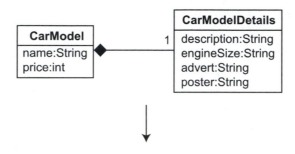

**CARMODEL**

| ID | NAME | PRICE | CARMODELDETAILSID |
|----|------|-------|-------------------|
| 111 | Grey Shadow | 19500 | 37 |
| 39 | Fly | 25000 | 19 |
| 14 | Dooby 9 | 35000 | 18 |

**CARMODELDETAILS**

| ID | ENGINESIZE | DESCRIPTION | ADVERT | POSTER |
|----|-----------|-------------|--------|--------|
| 19 | 3500 | Pure luxury... | arf.ram | arf.jpg |
| 18 | 3000 | Power and... | amd9.ram | amd9.jpg |
| 37 | 4800 | Smooth but... | rcgs.ram | rcgs.jpg |

**Figure 10.9: Mapping a one-to-one association to a foreign key**

RELEASEDATE, CATALOGDATE, CLIP and POSTER columns to the CARMODEL table and discard CARMODELDETAILS altogether. In this case, we can tell that the developers have decided to regard CarModelDetails as an entity because it has been given a universal identifier.

For the special case of an optional association (multiplicities of 1 and 0..1), we can add a foreign key to the optional end. Incidentally, relational databases support **nullable** columns. A nullable column is one that allows a cell to contain the value NULL, meaning 'there is no value here'. Thus, we could also store an optional association as a nullable foreign key in the 1 end. However, for reasons of simplicity and elegance, it's better to avoid nullable values.

## One-to-Many Associations

For a one-to-many association, we can add a foreign key to the 'many' table, as shown in Figure 10.10. In this example, each CreditCard can guarantee more than one Member. Thus, each row in the MEMBER table has a reference to its card (CARDID). (This assumes that each member only has one card recorded in the system.) In the finished system, this MEMBER table also has a foreign key to indicate the member's address.

## Many-to-Many Associations

For many-to-many associations, one foreign key is not enough to identify the many entities at each end of the association. Consider the fragment of analysis class diagram shown at the

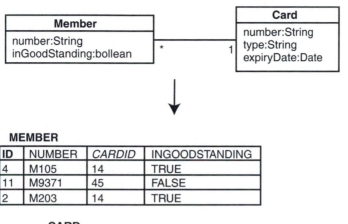

**Figure 10.10: Mapping one-to-many associations to foreign keys**

top of Figure 10.11. Here, a Make can manufacture many CarModel objects and a CarModel can be manufactured by many Makes (the Make objects are collaborating in the manufacture of the CarModel). In the pure relational model, every value in a table must be atomic – i.e. not a collection of values. So, we wouldn't be able to record all of a CarModel's Make objects as a MAKEIDS column in the CARMODEL table.

Since we can't have multi-valued attributes, we need to use a **link table**. As its name suggests, each row in a link table represents a link between an entity in one table and an entity in another table. The bottom half of Figure 10.11 shows a link table called MAKECARMODEL that links CarModel objects to Make objects. For example, we can see that Make 8 and Make 9 are both manufacturers of CarModel 39, and that Make 8 also manufactures CarModel 111. Technically, a link table has a compound primary key consisting of two foreign keys.

We could also use a link table to store one-to-one and one-to-many associations. However, they're probably best left for the special cases of many-to-many associations and association classes (see next).

## Association Classes

Association classes, since they have data of their own, must be mapped to link tables, regardless of the multiplicities at each end of the association. Unlike plain link tables, tables representing association classes have attribute columns – they may even have an ID column (if the association class represents an entity in its own right).

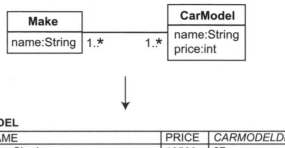

**CARMODEL**

| ID | NAME | PRICE | *CARMODELDETAILSID* |
|----|------|-------|---------------------|
| 111 | Grey Shadow | 19500 | 37 |
| 39 | Lacrosse | 25000 | 19 |
| 14 | Dooby 9 | 35000 | 18 |

**MAKECARMODEL**

| *MAKEID* | *CARMODELID* |
|----------|--------------|
| 8 | 111 |
| 65 | 14 |
| 9 | 39 |
| 8 | 39 |

**MAKE**

| ID | NAME |
|----|------|
| 65 | Astra Marten |
| 9 | Alpha Rodeo |
| 8 | Rolls Choice |

**Figure 10.11: Mapping a many-to-many association to a link table**

For example, Figure 10.12 shows a table representing the association class called Reservation. The RESERVATION table has a primary key for the reservation itself, two foreign keys referencing the objects at each end of the association and two attribute columns.

## 10.3.5 Mapping Object State

For business objects that have an associated state machine, such as might be shown on a state machine diagram, we need to record the state that each object is in. In the business layer, our business object might have a simple field indicating its state, a String or an int perhaps, or we might have a complex field pointing to a state object (as described by the State pattern).

If we choose to use a String or an int, we need to make sure that the field can only take on certain values: for iCoot, Reservation has six possible states, so we would have to choose six Strings ("waiting", "notifiable", "collectable", "needingRenewal", "storable" and "concluded", for example) or six integers (0 to 5 perhaps). From the database point of view, we could also take a simple approach: add a column called STATE to the RESERVATION table and set its type to VARCHAR or INTEGER, as appropriate. (We would expect the INTEGER version to be faster, but harder to debug.) This approach is illustrated in Figure 10.13.

Or, we could take a more complex approach: introduce a new table for each possible state and use foreign keys to indicate which reservations are in which states. For example, Figure 10.14 shows two of the six state tables that we would need, indicating that reservations

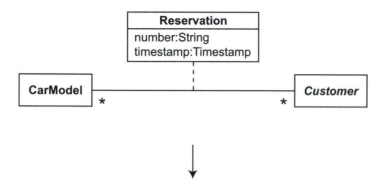

**RESERVATION**

| ID | CARMODELID | CUSTOMERID | NUMBER | TIMESTAMP |
|----|-----------|-----------|--------|-----------|
| 7 | 33 | 4 | R187a | 2004-12-06 14:23:16.543 |
| 1 | 22 | 2 | R7b | 2004-12-03 00:03:21.872 |
| 99 | 72 | 4 | R459b | 2004-12-05 09:45:07.210 |

**Figure 10.12: Mapping an association class to a link table**

**RESERVATION**

| ID | CARMODELID | CUSTOMERID | NUMBER | TIMESTAMP | STATE |
|----|-----------|-----------|--------|-----------|-------|
| 7 | 33 | 4 | R187a | 2004-12-06 14:23:16.543 | 0 |
| 1 | 22 | 2 | R7b | 2004-12-03 00:03:21.872 | 2 |
| 99 | 72 | 4 | R459b | 2004-12-05 09:45:07.210 | 0 |

**Figure 10.13: Mapping object state to a column**

**WAITINGRESERVATION**

| RESERVATIONID |
|---------------|
| 7 |
| 99 |

**COLLECTABLERESERVATION**

| RESERVATIONID |
|---------------|
| 1 |

**Figure 10.14: Mapping object state to state tables**

7 and 99 are waiting and reservation 1 is collectable. The complex approach is arguably more elegant. Whether or not it's more efficient than the simple approach depends on the usage patterns within our system, a difficult thing to predict.

When storing states, we sometimes have to deal with **state attributes** – data associated with a business object when it's in a particular state. For example, when a reservation is in the waiting state, we need to know when the reservation was last renewed (because, after a week in the waiting state, the reservation needs to be renewed). Similarly, for a collectable reservation, we need to know when the car was made collectable (because, if the customer doesn't collect it within three days, the car becomes storable).

With the state-table approach, we can store state attributes as extra columns. This is illustrated, for our two example states, in Figure 10.15. With the state-column approach, we would have to add a column for every state attribute to the business object table, which could be many columns. Each column would have to be nullable so that the data could be omitted when the object was not in the relevant state. This approach is illustrated for our two example states in Figure 10.16. Since it's better to avoid nullable columns, the state table approach wins in this case.

**WAITINGRESERVATION**

| *RESERVATIONID* | LASTRENEWEDDATE |
|---|---|
| 7 | 2004-16-10 |
| 99 | 2004-10-18 |

**COLLECTABLERESERVATION**

| *RESERVATIONID* | DATEPUTASIDE |
|---|---|
| 1 | 2004-12-04 |

**Figure 10.15: Adding state attributes to state tables**

**RESERVATION**

| ID | *CARMODELID* | *CUSTOMERID* | NUMBER | TIMESTAMP | |
|---|---|---|---|---|---|
| 7 | 33 | 4 | R187a | 2004-12-06 14:23:16.543 | ... |
| 1 | 22 | 2 | R7b | 2004-12-03 00:03:21.872 | |
| 99 | 72 | 4 | R459b | 2004-12-05 09:45:07.210 | |

| STATE | LASTRENEWEDDATE | DATEPUTASIDE |
|---|---|---|
| 0 | 2004-16-10 | NULL |
| 2 | NULL | 2004-12-04 |
| 0 | 2004-10-18 | NULL |

... (to the left of the STATE table)

**Figure 10.16: Mapping state attributes to nullable columns**

## Mapping Inheritance

In order to map an inheritance hierarchy onto tables, we can introduce a table for each class, with columns for the attributes added by that class. So that we can find all the attributes for an object, the tables must share the same primary key. For example, Figure 10.17 shows the Customer class hierarchy mapped to three tables: the CUSTOMER table has three columns for the attributes defined by the Customer class; the NONMEMBER table has one column for the attribute defined by the NonMember class; and the MEMBER table has two columns for the attributes defined by the Member class.

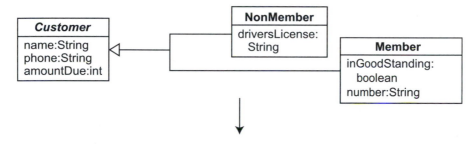

**CUSTOMER**

| ID | NAME | AMOUNTDUE | PHONE |
|----|------|-----------|-------|
| 4 | Helen Meeder | 0 | (0452)94983 |
| 11 | Alice Tara | 0 | (0161)898349 |
| 2 | George Milo | 3980 | (07968)14599 |
| 33 | Mary Smith | 0 | (07968)14599 |

**MEMBER**

| ID | NUMBER | INGOODSTANDING | CARDID | ADDRESSID |
|----|--------|----------------|--------|-----------|
| 4 | M105 | TRUE | 14 | 9 |
| 11 | M9371 | FALSE | 45 | 2 |
| 2 | M203 | FALSE | 14 | 9 |

**NONMEMBER**

| ID | DRIVERSLICENSE |
|----|----------------|
| 33 | DUCK MH8L3 7324 |

**Figure 10.17: Mapping inheritance to multiple tables**

As usual, the universal identifier (which will have been added to Customer class) is used as the primary key: this time it appears as the primary key in all three tables. When we come to retrieve the data for Customer 33, for example, we pick up NAME, AMOUNTDUE and PHONE from the CUSTOMER table; next, we have to test whether there is a row with key 33 in either of the subclass tables (if there is, we know that Customer 33 is actually an instance of a subclass); in our example, we detect that Customer 33 has NONMEMBER data, so we pick up its License. The end result is the NonMember shown in Figure 10.18.

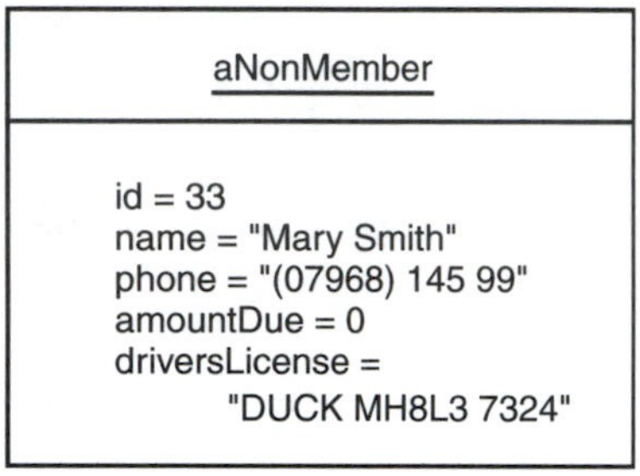

```
┌─────────────────────────────────┐
│           aNonMember            │
├─────────────────────────────────┤
│  id = 33                        │
│  name = "Mary Smith"            │
│  phone = "(07968) 145 99"       │
│  amountDue = 0                  │
│  driversLicense =               │
│          "DUCK MH8L3 7324"      │
└─────────────────────────────────┘
```

**Figure 10.18: A reconstituted nonmember**

As with the mapping of object states, we could instead put all the attributes into a single table (this would reflect the fact that an object being an instance of a class is similar to an object being in a particular state). For example, in Figure 10.19 we have a single CUSTOMER table with a CLASS column, specifying the class of each individual row. In addition, the table has a nullable column for each of the attributes in the hierarchy.

As ever, the choice of mapping to multiple tables or a single table will be based on personal preference, experience, crystal-ball gazing and experimentation.

**CUSTOMER**

| ID | NAME | AMOUNTDUE | PHONE | |
|----|------|-----------|-------|---|
| 4 | Helen Meeder | 0 | (0452)94983 | |
| 11 | Alice Tara | 0 | (0161)898349 | ... |
| 2 | George Milo | 3980 | (07968)14599 | |
| 33 | Mary Smith | 0 | (07968)14599 | |

| | NUMBER | INGOODSTANDING | *CARDID* | *ADDRESSID* | |
|---|--------|----------------|----------|-------------|---|
| | M105 | TRUE | 14 | 9 | |
| ... | M9371 | FALSE | 45 | 2 | ... |
| | M203 | FALSE | 14 | 9 | |
| | NULL | NULL | NULL | NULL | |

| | DRIVERSLICENSE | CLASS |
|---|----------------|-------|
| | NULL | 0 |
| ... | NULL | 0 |
| | NULL | 0 |
| | DUCK MH8L3 7324 | 1 |

**Figure 10.19: Mapping inheritance to a single table**

**ADDRESS** (**ID**:INTEGER,HOUSE:VARCHAR(99),STREET:VARCHAR(99),COUNTY:VARCHAR(99), POSTCODE:VARCHAR(99))

**CAR** (**ID**:INTEGER,TRAVELLED:INTEGER,DATELOST:DATE,*CARDETAILSID*:INTEGER)

**CARD** (**ID**:INTEGER,TYPE:VARCHAR(99),NUMBER:VARCHAR(99))

**CARDETAILS** (**ID**:INTEGER,BARCODE:VARCHAR(99),NUMBERPLATE:VARCHAR(99),VIN:VARCHAR(99))

**CARMODEL** (**ID**:INTEGER,NAME:VARCHAR(99),PRICE:INTEGER,*CARMODELDETAILSID*:INTEGER, *CATEGORYID*:INTEGER,VENDORID:INTEGER)

**CARMODELDETAILS** (**ID**:INTEGER,ENGINESIZE:VARCHAR(99),DESCRIPTION:VARCHAR(256), ADVERT:VARCHAR(99),POSTER:VARCHAR(99))

**CATEGORY** (**ID**:INTEGER,NAME:VARCHAR(99))

**COLLECTABLERESERVATION** (*RESERVATIONID*:INTEGER,DATENOTIFIED:DATE)

**CONCLUDEDRESERVATION** (*RESERVATIONID*:INTEGER,REASON:VARCHAR(99))

**CUSTOMER** (**ID**:INTEGER,NAME:VARCHAR(99),PHONE:VARCHAR(99),AMOUNTDUE:INTEGER)

**DISPLAYABLERESERVATION** (*RESERVATIONID*:INTEGER,REASON:VARCHAR(99))

**INTERNETACCOUNT** (**ID**:INTEGER,PASSWORD:VARCHAR(99),SESSIONID:INTEGER)

**MAKE** (**ID**:INTEGER,NAME:VARCHAR(99))

**MAKECARMODEL** (*CARMODELID*:INTEGER,*MAKEID*:INTEGER)

**MEMBER** (**ID**:INTEGER,NUMBER:VARCHAR(99),INGOODSTANDING:BOOLEAN,*CARDID*:INTEGER, *ADDRESSID*:INTEGER)

**NEEDINGRENEWALRESERVATION** (*RESERVATIONID*:INTEGER,DATERENEWALNEEDED:DATE)

**NONMEMBER** (**ID**:INTEGER,DRIVERSLICENSE:VARCHAR(99))

**NOTIFIABLERESERVATION** (*RESERVATIONID*:INTEGER,*DATEPUTASIDE*:DATE)

**RENTAL** (**ID**:INTEGER,NUMBER:VARCHAR(99),STARTDATE:DATE,DUEDATE:DATE,TOTALAMOUNT:INTEGER)

**RENTALCAR** (*RENTALID*:INTEGER,*CARID*:INTEGER)

**RESERVATION** (**ID**:INTEGER,NUMBER:VARCHAR(99),TIMESTAMP:TIMESTAMP,*CUSTOMERID*:INTEGER, *CARMODELID*:INTEGER)

**VENDOR** (**ID**:INTEGER,NAME:VARCHAR(99))

**WAITINGRESERVATION** (*RESERVATIONID*:INTEGER,LASTRENEWEDDDATE:DATE)

**Figure 10.20: Database schema for iCoot**

> **Case Study**
> *iCoot database schema*
> The finished database schema for iCoot is shown in Figure 10.20. Each table is shown
> as a name followed by column types in parentheses. As before, primary keys are
> shown in bold and foreign keys are shown in italics (with primary–foreign keys in
> bold–italic). For completeness, this schema includes a few pieces from the full Coot
> system, such as NONMEMBER and DATELOST.

# 10.4 FINALIZING THE USER INTERFACES

Next, we'll look at the design of our user interfaces. We have a handful of vague sketches
that we used while fleshing out the system requirements. This section includes hints and
tips on how to produce good, simple, interfaces for thin clients.

In the early stages of development, during requirements capture and analysis, it's useful
to consider the functionality of the user interfaces. This makes sense because, with a use-
case-driven methodology, the way that actors interact with the system is paramount and
most actors are human. To this end, we already have the following:

- User interface sketches. These were used to help us produce system use cases during
  requirements capture, with the help of our sponsors.
- Boundary objects in communication diagrams. During dynamic analysis, we used communication diagrams to show the realization of the use cases; in these diagrams, every actor
  was shown interacting with the system via boundary objects.

But, we still need to *design* the user interfaces: we have to take the coarse boundary
objects, the vague user interface sketches and the precise use cases, and transform them into
user interface descriptions that can be implemented directly. (We expect system-to-system
interfaces to be designed as part of our layers – for systems that are accessed by us – or as
part of our business services – for systems that access our system.)

You may have been surprised by the fact that most of a software system can be designed
successfully without considering the user interfaces in detail (having completed the system
use cases, we concentrated almost entirely on the objects inside the system). There are two
main reasons for this:

- The correct behavior of a system depends on its internal construction, not on the way that
  people interact with it. To use an analogy: a car consists of an engine, four wheels and a

body; depending on which interfaces we use, and how we use them, we can get a car to transport people from A to B, or we can get it to tow a caravan, or we can get it to knock down a wall; however we choose to interact with a car, it still behaves as a car.

- We would prefer to write reusable code. If we focus on the needs of a particular set of interfaces, we risk producing a system that *only* works for those interfaces – this is one of the problems of traditional development: 'Solve today's problem today, forget about tomorrow'. Being use-case driven might seem to be against the principle of reuse; however, as far as the internals of the system are concerned, use cases are just a good way of ensuring that the developers don't wander off into irrelevant areas.

Rather than delving into the theory of human–computer interaction, we'll look at some basic principles for good user interface design (especially for thin clients accessing multi-tier systems).

## Be Guided by Use Cases

From the system point of view, use cases simply keep the developers on track. To the users, on the other hand, the use cases are everything. Thus, use cases should be used to give structure to the user interfaces.

In general, we should try to keep our use cases simple: they should not contain too much functionality or they will be difficult to manage. Therefore, although we would expect each user interface to represent a number of use cases, the interfaces themselves can still be simple.

We would expect the grouping of related use cases to be reflected in the structure of the user interface. For example, iCoot customers are presented with a single, Web-based, user interface that includes a dozen or so use cases. Within that single interface, we would expect to find activities grouped into 'reservations', 'rentals', 'browsing the catalog' and so on.

We should also avoid splitting a single use case, or a chain of related use cases, into more than one interface. For example, a customer who had homed in on an interesting car model would be annoyed if they had to go to a different interface to reserve it.

## Keep it Simple

Keeping things simple is a good principle in its own right. But also, many of our users will be novices, especially those users accessing our system over the Internet, so simplicity is even more important. There's a strong argument for keeping user interfaces simple and uncluttered for expert users too: we don't want the overwhelming functionality of our user interface to hamper their productivity.

In an e-commerce context, we don't want a learning barrier in front of the goods that we have to sell. When a customer comes across our site, if they're presented with long instructions on how to use it, they'll leave immediately. So that customers can use our site immediately, we must limit ourselves to trivial, step-by-step, guidance, as in Click here to buy or Enter your credit card details below and click Next.

The simpler the interface, the easier it will be to port to more primitive platforms (for example, mobile phones, set-top boxes, personal digital assistants, home appliances). The need to produce portable user interfaces is a strong argument for using a control layer in your design.

## Use Notebooks

You should use notebooks to group related use cases. A notebook is a set of pages that shows only one page at a time – the other pages are available via tabs along the edge. The advantage of a notebook is that, because its size and location stays the same, the user can focus on a single area of the screen, even for long interactions that involve more than one use case. This improves the **user experience** and also **user productivity**. Notebooks are supported by most GUI libraries, such as Java's Swing (Figure 10.21 shows iCoot running as a Swing applet). For HTML/CGI interfaces, we can only simulate a notebook – the end result is similar, but

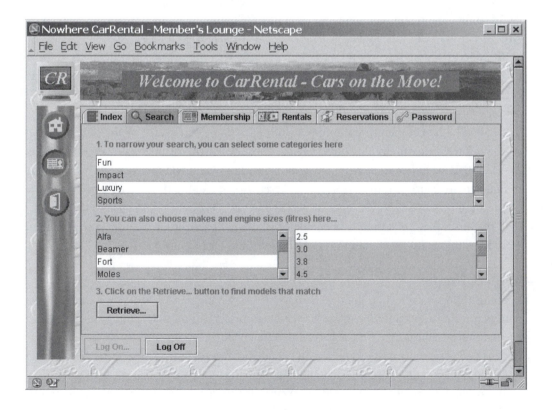

**Figure 10.21: iCoot using a Swing notebook**

the user has to tolerate the flashing-to-background-color and longer delays when moving to a new page (Figure 10.22 shows iCoot running as a simulated HTML/CGI notebook).

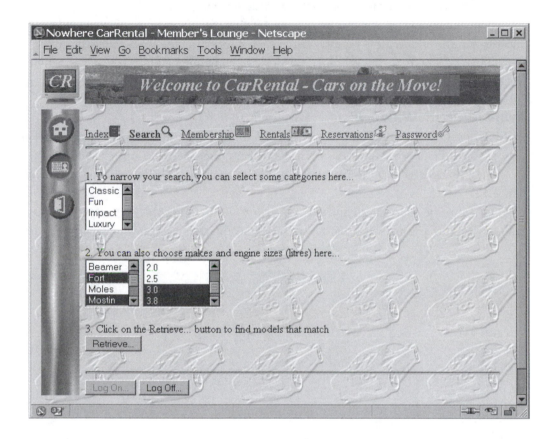

**Figure 10.22: iCoot using a simulated notebook**

Often, a use case will map cleanly to a single page. With the help of a wizard, even a complex use case can be followed inside a single panel.

## Use Wizards

A **wizard** is a sequence of pages that guides a user, step by step, through a complex activity. When the user selects an activity, they're presented with a page representing step 1; the user completes step 1 and clicks the Next button to go on to step 2; and so on. Before completing an activity, a user can revisit the earlier steps, using the Back button. Each page of the wizard contains fields, lists and other widgets that the user employs to enter the data needed for the current step. Normally, each page will have simple instructions, such as Type your old password into the box below and then click Next.

The step-by-step nature of the wizard and the simple instructions allow the user to perform a complex activity without having to remember how to do it. Also, a wizard, like a notebook, keeps the user's focus on one area of the screen.

As with notebooks, if we're using a pure HTML/CGI interface, we can only simulate wizards, but the end result is probably better than if we didn't use them at all. (In this case, the alternative would be one very long HTML page containing all the steps of the activity: rather inconvenient for the user to have to scroll down through the steps.)

## Avoid Multiple Windows

Multiple, overlapping windows were invented for the benefit of computer experts rather than novice users. Even if our user is sufficiently computer-literate to open a Web browser, we should not expect them to be able to cope with multiple browser windows or pop-up dialogs.

Apart from the inherent complexity, we also have to accept that, on some platforms, multiple windows just don't make sense. In iCoot, the user navigates to a particular car

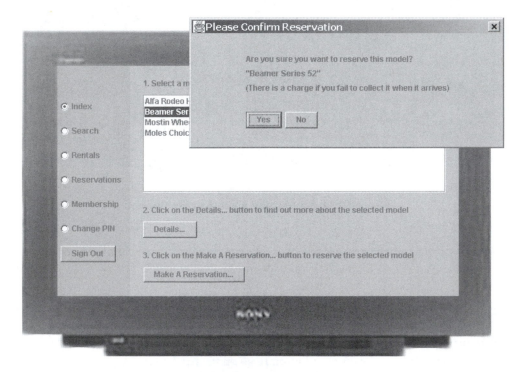

**Wrong**

**Figure 10.23: Problems with multiple windows**

model and clicks the Make a Reservation button to reserve it. Since there is a potential fine associated with reserving a car model, the system needs to ask the user for confirmation. The natural thing for a developer of multi-windowed systems to do is to pop up a dialog. However, iCoot may be running on a TV (with the help of a set-top box). Due to limited screen resolution and space, set-top boxes don't support dialogs, so there's nowhere for the message to go (see Figure 10.23). It is possible to avoid multiple windows (see Figure 10.24) by overlaying the previous page with the contents of the dialog. If the user clicks No, the system returns to the previous page (equivalent to canceling the dialog); if the user clicks Yes, the reservation is made and the system returns to the previous page.

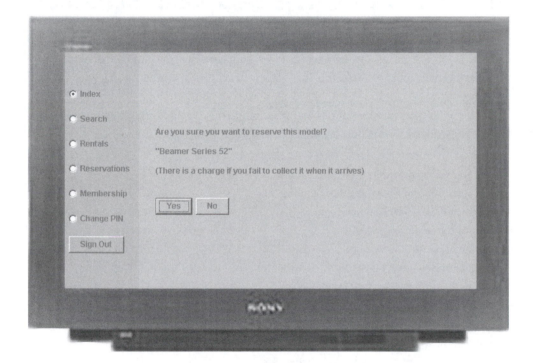

# Right

**Figure 10.24: Avoiding multiple windows**

The interface shown in Figure 10.24 is a **wizard running inside a notebook**: the radio buttons down the left-hand side of the screen correspond to the tabs of the notebook, allowing the user to switch between major use cases; within the notebook page, we see a wizard guiding the user through the U7:Make Reservation use case (which is an extension of U1:Browse the Index).

So, notebooks and wizards can be used together to confine complex interactions to a single area of the screen, so that the user doesn't get tired or confused. This all works well as long as we stick to the 'Do one thing at a time' rule; even when we design our user interface according this rule, we can still allow the user to switch between half-finished activities. For example, in Figure 10.24, the user can ignore the question for the time being and switch to the Change PIN page. When the user eventually returns to the Index page, the same question will be waiting to be answered.

# 10.5 DESIGNING THE BUSINESS SERVICES

Once we've decided on the look and feel of the user interface and the interface of our business layer, we can design our server layer: this consists of a number of server objects, collaborating with objects in the business layer, providing a simple interface for the benefit of clients.

**Business services** are the queries and commands that a middle tier makes available to its clients. For example, for iCoot, we might derive the following set of business services:

- Read the index headings from the Catalog.
- Read CarModel for a given index heading.
- Read every CarModel Category.
- Read all CarModel engine sizes.
- Read all Makes of CarModel.
- Read CarModels for a given set of Category, engine size and Make.
- Read details for a given CarModel.
- Reserve a CarModel.
- Read details for a given Member.
- Change a Member's password.
- Read the Cars rented by a given Member.
- Read the Reservations made by a given Member.
- Cancel a Reservation.

The business services represent a concise summary of the information flow between the user interfaces on the client and the business logic on the middle tier. Business services can be derived by walking through the use cases, with reference to the user interface design and the system architecture. (The idea of breaking a server's interface down into the services it provides can be applied to any kind of communication; for example, we could extend the ideas discussed in this section to the problem of deciding how the layers within a subsystem should communicate.)

For business services to make sense in the context of HTML/CGI interfaces, we have to assume that user interfaces are spread between client tier and middle tier: the combination of HTML forms, servlets and JSP result pages comprise a single user interface, despite the fact that some pieces run on the middle tier. We can even execute servlets on a separate middle tier machine to the one that's performing the business processing, to reduce the load on the business objects – in this case, the servlet machine is really a client of the middle tier rather than part of the middle tier itself. Therefore, in the following sections, the term client, means either:

- A piece of code, such as an applet, running on a separate machine to the business layer.
- Servlets running in a separate process or on a separate machine to the business layer.

Implementing client–server communication in terms of business services allows us to:

- Simplify the client code. Since most client interfaces only need a subset of the system's capability, each one can be given a cut-down view.
- Complicate the business layer. We can make the business layer as complex, powerful or reusable as we like, or even change it altogether, without worrying about the impact on the client.
- Build a pluggable server layer. We would like to provide various kinds of interface to cope with different user preferences or client capabilities – applet/RMI versus HTML/CGI-with-servlets, for example – without having to re-implement the middle tier services every time.

## 10.5.1 Using Proxies and Copies

When a client requests a business service, the result may include one or more business objects. For example, if the client request is 'Read all Make objects of CarModel', the result will be a list of makes. As well as retrieving business objects, a client may send business objects to the server. For example, if the client request is 'Cancel a Reservation', the reservation will need to be specified.

So, logically at least, business objects flow back and forth between client and server. If we were dealing with a one-tier system, there would be no problem: we would just pass object pointers around our run-time system and send messages to the objects according to our needs. However, when we're dealing with a network, things are not that simple.

We can, with the help of technologies such as RMI, arrange for messages to pass between objects over the network: each object lives inside a single run-time system, but messages can arrive from outside. Alternatively, we can pass copies of objects around the network: each run-time system has a copy of the objects it needs and sends messages to them locally. In the case of communication between layers in a subsystem, we have a similar choice: do we pass object references between layers or object copies? (We would expect an open layer to pass references across its boundary while a closed layer might pass copies.)

To be more precise, we have two basic strategies to choose from: **proxies** are client objects that know how to forward the messages they receive to a real business object sitting elsewhere; **copies** are client objects containing a copy of the real business object's data.

The main advantages of using proxies are that:

- All clients see the same objects, so they're always working with the same information.
- All the run-time systems merge into a single universe: distributed objects are treated in the same way as local objects.

The main disadvantages of proxies are that:

- The business layer objects must be secured. For example, we must be sure, when we receive a message from a client, that the client has permission to send the message. This complicates the business layer. (The alternative security model, where the business objects are accessed only by the server layer and the server layer only has to secure its business services, is much easier to implement.)
- Network traffic increases. In an object-oriented system, we normally get hold of the object and then send it messages; with the proxy technique, initial retrieval of the object is quick but sending messages to the object is slow (because each message must travel over the network).
- The burden on the middle tier increases: the business layer, running on the middle tier, executes all of the methods all of the time.

The main advantages of using copies are that:

- Network traffic reduces: we retrieve more information to begin with (all the object's data) but methods execute quickly (because they run locally).
- Processing doesn't all take place in the middle tier, because some business methods execute on the client.
- Direct access to business methods doesn't have to be secured because only the server layer has direct access and the server layer is secure in itself.
- The object's implementation doesn't have to be concurrent-safe: once a copy has been created on behalf of a client, the client has exclusive access to it.

The main disadvantages of copies are that:

- Too much data may be copied. For example, if we copy a CarModel, we might end up copying all of its CarModelDetail objects, all of its Make objects, all of its Reservation objects, all of the Member objects that have made those reservations, and so on.

- The copies can get out of step because each client has an independent copy of every object that it uses.

For some applications, it may be quite reasonable for a client copy to become out of date. For example, if a user issues a search engine request from a Web browser, the results page that is displayed will age as Web pages are added, updated and removed. The user has to accept that, strictly speaking, the results were only accurate at the moment the query was executed.

By careful coding, we can alleviate some of the problems of proxies and copies. For example, when using proxies, we could cache some of the object's data locally to reduce network traffic, taking care to ensure, by some complicated mechanism, that the objects didn't get out of step. With the copying approach, we can copy any referenced objects on demand, thereby reducing the copy-too-much problem: for example, when we read a CarModel, the client can be given the top-level attributes only – any referenced objects would stay as null unless the client actually navigated to them (using encapsulation, this process could be made transparent to the client code).

If we're lucky, we will have access to a framework or a library that supports configurable proxies, configurable copies and hybrids of the two. However, even with such technologies, the developer still has to choose which variety they want to use.

Alternatively, as long as we're prepared to accept a little hand-crafting, we can take a simpler approach: **lightweight copies**. With this approach, when a client asks for a business object, it is given only the essential information it needs and information is not passed to the client if the client must already have that information. Going the other way, when a client needs to identify a business object to the server, the client passes just the universal identifier of the object to the server.

For lightweight copies to work, we need business services (so that we can reason about what information is needed by the client) and universal identifiers (so that clients have an efficient way of passing objects back). The information passed to a client will consist of copies of the business object's simple attributes (numbers, strings, and so on) and universal identifiers for any reference attributes, in case the client needs to navigate further.

## 10.5.2 Classifying Business Services

We would expect business services to form groups of related behavior, in other words, messages on objects. We would expect these **server objects** to have few attributes of their own and we wouldn't expect them to record state on behalf of the clients (each client must remember its own state). Server objects reside in the server layer of a multi-tier system.

The server objects that have been designed for iCoot are shown in Figure 10.25. The business services have been classified as reservations, authentication, membership information,

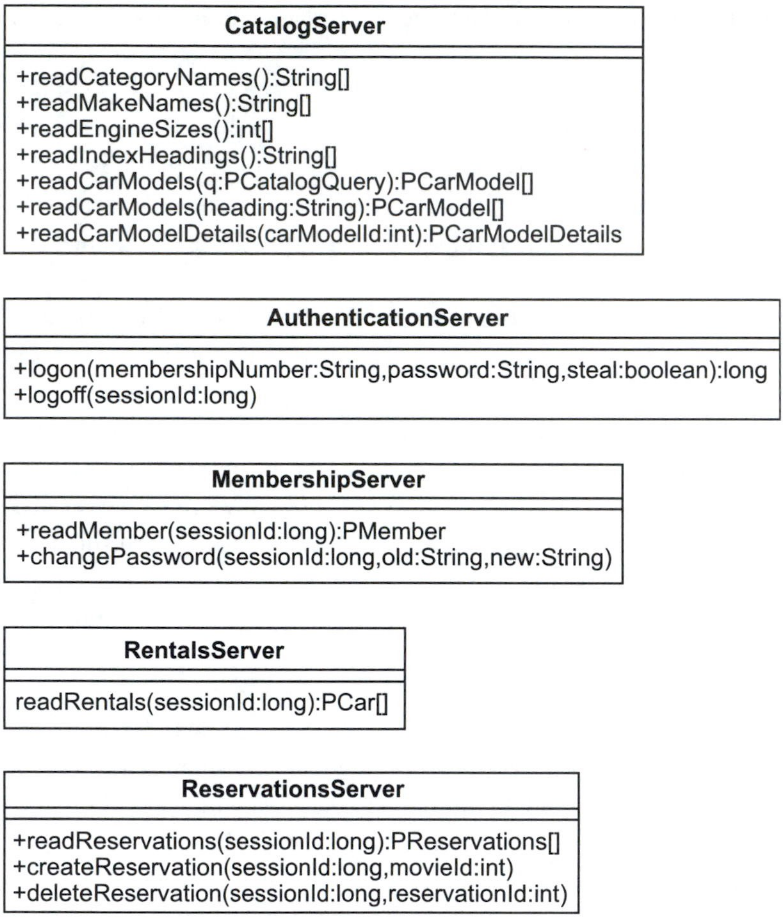

| CatalogServer |
|---|
| +readCategoryNames():String[]<br>+readMakeNames():String[]<br>+readEngineSizes():int[]<br>+readIndexHeadings():String[]<br>+readCarModels(q:PCatalogQuery):PCarModel[]<br>+readCarModels(heading:String):PCarModel[]<br>+readCarModelDetails(carModelId:int):PCarModelDetails |

| AuthenticationServer |
|---|
| +logon(membershipNumber:String,password:String,steal:boolean):long<br>+logoff(sessionId:long) |

| MembershipServer |
|---|
| +readMember(sessionId:long):PMember<br>+changePassword(sessionId:long,old:String,new:String) |

| RentalsServer |
|---|
| readRentals(sessionId:long):PCar[] |

| ReservationsServer |
|---|
| +readReservations(sessionId:long):PReservations[]<br>+createReservation(sessionId:long,movieId:int)<br>+deleteReservation(sessionId:long,reservationId:int) |

**Figure 10.25: Server objects for iCoot**

catalog information and rentals (ReservationsServer, AuthenticationServer, MembershipServer, CatalogServer and RentalsServer, respectively).

The business service messages shown in Figure 10.25 have been tuned to ensure that neither the client nor the server will pass information to the other side unnecessarily. For example, consider the CatalogServer. In order to search for car models, the client must first retrieve all the category names, engine sizes and make names. These come back from the server as String objects and int objects.

The client then allows the user to build a query ('All sports models made by Alpha Rodeo or Beamer', for example). The client passes the query to the server as a PCatalogQuery. Inside the PCatalogQuery are three array attributes that identify the category names, engine sizes and make names that the user is interested in. The server returns an array of matching PCarModel objects. (The P stands for protocol – it helps the developers of the server objects to avoid any name clashes with heavyweight business objects. Arrays are used because they're more compact than collections.)

In order to reduce the amount of information returned to the client, the PCarModel objects do not contain any details, just the price, model number and universal identifier. When the user asks for the details of a particular car model, rather than passing over the whole PCarModel, whose attributes the server must already have, the client passes over just the universal identifier, as a parameter to the readCarModelDetails message.

## 10.5.3  Session Identifiers

Often, in order to frustrate hackers, we need to restrict client access to privileged services. For example, for iCoot, we have privileged services, such as 'Reserve a CarModel', that require the client to have logged in and non-privileged services, such as 'Read the index headings from the Catalog', that are available to everyone, even hackers.

Some client–server protocols, such as HTTP, have a standard **challenge** mechanism for displaying a log-on screen to the user: the user name and password typed in is validated on the server; if successful, the client is given a unique session identifier. However, if we want to provide pluggable business services, i.e. services that will work with any kind of front end, we have to implement a mechanism ourselves. Figure 10.25 shows one way to do this. All the privileged services take a long number as their first parameter: this must be a session identifier created by the server layer, or use of the privileged service will fail. To get hold of a session identifier, clients must use the logon message on the AuthenticationServer. (The steal parameter is used by the client to specify whether any existing session for this member should be terminated – this is part of the single-log-on mechanism.)

When the logon method is called, the AuthenticationServer checks the membership number and password using the business layer. If the client's credentials are correct, the AuthenticationServer generates a random number and associates it with the corresponding Member in the business layer. Subsequently, whenever a privileged service is invoked, the relevant server object can use the session identifier to look up the Member before proceeding. Naturally, if the original credentials or the session identifier are invalid, the client receives an error message. The session identifiers must be difficult to fake – a randomly-generated 64-bit number will suffice. Hackers generally do not bother trying to guess 64-bit random numbers because their chances of success are tiny.

Another way of providing a portable privileged/non-privileged mechanism would be to make the session identifier an object. Through encapsulation, this would give us more flexibility in the kind of difficult-to-fake information that we chose to employ.

## 10.5.4 Business Service Realization

Now that we have designed the business services (the messages on our server objects), we need to work out how they're going to be implemented in terms of the business layer. To do this, we need to walk through the use cases, drawing sequence diagrams that show which messages need to be sent. For want of a better name, we'll call this process **business service realization**. This is similar to the use case realization that we did during analysis, walking through the use cases and drawing communication diagrams to demonstrate that the business objects would support an implementation. We should use sequence diagrams to document our business service realization rather than communication diagrams, because sequence diagrams are more compact (we're being specific about the implementation, so we have more information to show).

Figure 10.26 shows a sequence diagram for the AuthenticationServer's logoff method. Along the top are the objects involved in the interaction. Unlike objects in communication diagrams and object diagrams, the objects shown in sequence diagrams do not have underlined labels. Time flows down the page, so, starting at the top, the Member actor is shown initiating the log-off via the AuthenticationServlet, which in turn sends the logoff message to the AuthenticationServer, which sends the findById message to the MemberHome, and so on.

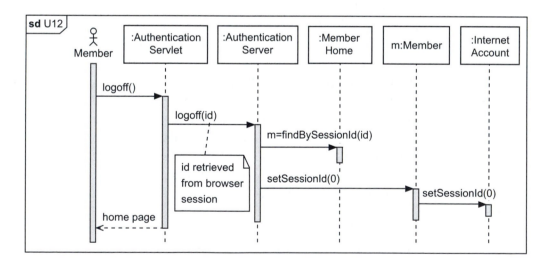

**Figure 10.26: Depicting business service realization**

The dashed vertical lines on a sequence diagram are called **lifelines** (the lines don't have to be dashed on a hand-drawn diagram). The vertical grey rectangles are called **activation bars**; they indicate when an object is executing a method. (The bars may be white or omitted altogether on a hand drawing). Each sequence diagram can be enclosed in a **frame** – a box with an **operator** in the top left corner, like the one we saw earlier for our design class diagram, but with a different operator. (All UML diagrams can be enclosed in a frame, the operator indicating the context for the diagram.) In the case of a sequence diagram, the operator is sd followed by the sequence diagram name. For a class diagram, we use the pkg operator, indicating the package that contains the classes. In this book, frames are only placed around the sequence diagrams and design-level class diagrams from iCoot. Frames can also be used to enclose loops and references to other sequence diagrams (see Appendix 3).

---

**Case Study**

*iCoot sequence diagram*

A member of the iCoot team describes the interaction shown in Figure 10.26 as follows:

When a Member actor elects to log off, their browser tells the AuthenticationServlet to logoff. The AuthenticationServlet then sends the logoff message to the AuthenticationServer, along with the Member's id, which it retrieves from the browser session.

The AuthenticationServer uses the id to retrieve the corresponding Member from the MemberHome. The AuthenticationServer then sends the setSessionId message to the Member, with 0 as parameter, which is passed on to the Member's InternetAccount. The InternetAccount stores the session identifier 0, to indicate that the Member has logged off.

Finally, the Member actor is presented with the home page so that they can access customer services or log on again.

---

For business service realization, we need to show the messages that flow between the server objects and the business layer objects, but we don't need to show the inner workings of the business layer objects themselves. Depending on the size of the system, it may or may not be feasible to show every business service on a sequence diagram. In general, we should expect to show the most important **scenarios** – the use cases will help us to decide which ones are the most important. Within each use case, there may be several normal scenarios and several abnormal ones: for our purposes, it is enough to show the normal path for the most common scenario.

As we draw sequence diagrams, we will discover more and more messages on the interfaces of our business layer objects. The resulting messages on the business layer objects are fed into the specification phase, along with any others that we come up with using intuition, experience, libraries, patterns, frameworks and guesswork. In the specification phase, we try to complete the object interfaces and describe the required behavior (see Chapter 12).

# 10.6 USING PATTERNS, FRAMEWORKS AND LIBRARIES

A **pattern** (see Chapter 11) is a portable solution to a small programming problem – in the object-oriented sense, a pattern is a handful of collaborating objects. Patterns allow developers to work faster and produce better code by not duplicating effort. Some fundamental patterns have been mentioned at other points in this book: singletons (where a class has only one instance); factories (for creating objects); homes (for creating objects and finding existing ones); and states (representing an object's life cycle). Each pattern has a name, a description and some examples of its use. Every developer should familiarize themselves with the common patterns.

In some ways, a **framework** is similar to a pattern: it's a way of putting together part of a system. Frameworks, however, have two important differences: firstly, they tend to be much larger; secondly, some of the code is already written for you (this may take the form of partially implemented classes or code-generation tools). Just as with patterns, you should seek out frameworks that have been designed for your particular problem domain, so that you can avoid writing unnecessary code.

One of the most comprehensive and popular frameworks is Enterprise JavaBeans. The EJB framework allows developers to construct middle-tier business logic without having to write any code to deal with persistence, transactions, security, concurrency, distribution or thread safety. Although it's a large framework, it's certainly worth studying.

A **library** is a collection of prewritten classes that can be used off-the-shelf. You should make yourself aware of the libraries available for your problem domain, so that you can avoid writing new classes when suitable ones already exist. The Java 2 Platform library is a good example. It comes in three varieties, Enterprise Edition, Standard Edition and Micro Edition, targeted, respectively, at large-scale systems (for example, e-commerce), medium-scale systems (for example, desktop publishing) and small-scale systems (for example, PDA e-mail clients).

# 10.7 TRANSACTIONS

Every concurrent system, if it's going to be robust, must be built around **transactions**. A transaction, also known as a **unit of work**, is used to fence off a number of database accesses.

(A **database access** means 'reading some data' or 'writing some data'.) Transactions are fairly complicated, so a detailed discussion is beyond the scope of this book.

Transactions are used to guarantee that:

- Information in the database doesn't become corrupted by system problems. We want to make sure that the database moves from one consistent state to another: data is never partly updated; it's either completely updated or not updated at all.
- Clients don't get hold of out-of-date information. We want to avoid situations such as the following: client A reads a customer's address, client B modifies the customer's address, client A takes some action based on the old address.

A database client **starts** a transaction, accesses some data and then **commits** the transaction. If the commit is successful, all updates made since the start of the transaction are flushed to the database (while the transaction is active, the updates are merely pending) and the client can be sure that it acted on up-to-date information. If the commit fails, because of a system problem or a clash with another transaction, the client can **roll back** the transaction, discarding any pending updates (and, therefore, any data that was updated on the basis of out-of-date information will remain unchanged). Because the DBMS guarantees that the accesses within a transaction *all* succeed or *all* fail, we know that the database will move from one consistent state to another. Obviously, the DBMS must ensure that all accesses take place inside a transaction.

Transactions can be short – wrapped around access to a single row – or long – wrapped around several accesses to related rows. A DBMS generally allows the client to choose between short and long transactions: by default, every access to the database is wrapped inside a new (short) transaction; alternatively, the client can opt to start, commit and rollback a (long) transaction manually. In theory, transactions can be **nested**: this allows us to wrap small units of work inside larger ones. In practice, however, most relational DBMSs do not support nested transactions.

## 10.7.1 Pessimistic and Optimistic Concurrency

Concurrency control (using transactions to control simultaneous access to data from multiple clients) can be **pessimistic** or **optimistic**. With pessimistic concurrency, the DBMS guarantees that no other transactions can perform conflicting accesses while a transaction is active. With optimistic concurrency, transactions access at will but, when a transaction is committed, the DBMS checks that no other transactions have performed conflicting accesses in the meantime.

By default, relational databases use pessimistic concurrency. Optimistic concurrency is more common in object-oriented databases, although it is sometimes provided as an option by object-oriented frameworks that sit on top of relational databases. (One way to implement optimistic concurrency for a relational database is to reread a row before updating it: if data in the row has changed, we know that another transaction modified it; however, this is only a partial solution.)

To implement pessimistic concurrency, a relational DBMS **locks** data accessed within a transaction until the transaction has finished. For example, if a transaction modifies the balance of account 123, the DBMS locks the row containing the new balance; other transactions are prevented from reading the row until the first transaction finishes (and the lock is released). Locks apply to reads as well: for example, if a transaction reads the balance of account 456, other transactions won't be allowed to modify the row containing the old balance until the first transaction finishes (otherwise, the first transaction might do half of its work relative to the old value and half of its work relative to the new value, which wouldn't make sense).

For performance reasons, relational DBMSs allow the client to relax the locking scheme, at the expense of some semantic accuracy.

## 10.7.2 General Guidelines for Using Transactions with Objects

When mapping from an object-oriented model to a relational database, we have a conflict of interest. On the one hand we have a complex object graph, whole chunks of which we might want to process inside a single long transaction. On the other hand, we have a relational database with a pessimistic locking scheme by default and object data spread over many tables: this suggests that we should use short transactions, in order to avoid locking up large parts of the database. (This is why optimistic concurrency is popular with object-oriented databases and object-oriented frameworks.)

Getting around this conflict requires skill and experience. If you're lucky, you'll be using a sophisticated framework such as EJB that solves most of the problems for you. If you're performing the mapping by hand, consider the following advice:

- Organize objects and access paths to reduce overlap. For example, with iCoot, we can make sure that each member is logged on only once. Thus, overlaps will only occur on the rare occasion that an assistant accesses a member's data while that member happens to be logged on.
- Use primary keys so that database accesses are well focussed. The trouble with most relational DBMSs is that they lock an entire table if they can't be sure which rows are being accessed. For example, if ID is a primary key in the CUSTOMER table, a focussed query such as 'Get me the name of customer 789' will lock one row; a query involving non-primary columns, such as 'Get me customers with the surname "Bloggs"' might lock the whole table. So, make sure that you choose a primary key for every entity and tell the database about it; then, base your database accesses on primary keys whenever possible.

- Keep transactions short. Although you may want to control the start and end of a transaction, so that you can make several object accesses in one go, don't overdo it.

### 10.7.3 Transactions in Upper Layers

Transactions have a ripple effect: the fact that they're in the database layer usually becomes obvious in the persistence layer; once they're obvious in the persistence layer, they usually become obvious in the business layer; and, once they're obvious in the business layer, developers of the server layer must understand them and how to use them properly.

Generally, we can't hide transactions until we get out to the client: to do this, the server layer must encapsulate transactions inside simplified requests (business services).

## 10.8 HANDLING MULTIPLE ACTIVITIES

Normally, when we use a computer, we want to be able to do several things at once – write a letter, read e-mail, run a lengthy computation and browse the Web, for example. We may want a server to do thousands of things at once (handling simultaneous requests from multiple clients). To this end, most operating systems permit **multitasking**: each program runs as an independent **process** with its own protected area of code (program instructions) and data (program variables).

Some programming languages allow us to execute multiple tasks *within* a single process. These tasks are usually referred to as **threads of execution** or just **threads**. Normally, each thread represents an activity within the program, running alongside other activities.

In this section, we'll examine the issues surrounding multi-threading and how we can make our code thread-safe (this turns out to be most important for the business layer).

### 10.8.1 Controlling Multiple Tasks

Each process managed by the operating system can be idle (waiting for user input perhaps) or active (performing some computation). Because we usually have more processes than CPUs, the operating system must share the CPU time between the active processes: the operating system allows each process to run for a small amount of time and then moves on to the next. This **time-slicing** is controlled by a piece of software called a **scheduler**. We don't need to know the details of the algorithm the scheduler uses to distribute the CPU's time among processes – we can just assume that each process gets its fair share. As an extra facility, most operating systems allow us to assign a **priority** to each process, so that some processes get more of the available time than others. For example, we might give a high priority to the detection of mouse clicks and a lower priority to user applications.

Although any decent operating system will prevent processes from accessing each other's code and data, it's the programmer's job to make sure that access to external resources (such as files and databases) is managed sensibly. For example, when a word processor opens a file, it can **lock** the file to prevent other processes from editing it at the same time; concurrent access to a highly shared resource such as a database is usually controlled through a combination of transaction management and business rules.

From the perspective of an individual user, multitasking allows us to have multiple applications open at once on our desktop. We can switch between the applications at will, doing one thing at a time, or set off several tasks at once, each of which appears to finish independently. Multitasking also has the advantage that, having set off a lengthy computation, we don't have to wait until it finishes before we do something else: for example, while we're waiting for an Internet search to complete, we can check the time or collect our messages.

From the server perspective, as well as being able to serve many clients simultaneously, multitasking gives us better throughput (the server deals with clients more efficiently). For example, imagine that a script called search.pl is used to execute Internet searches over HTML/CGI. Some searches issued by clients will execute quickly, in milliseconds perhaps, while others will take several seconds. If a client starts a long search and then a simpler search comes in from another client, the second search can execute immediately, without waiting for the first one to complete.

## 10.8.2 Controlling Multiple Threads

Threads are different from processes in that they all share the same data area within their process. Therefore, as well as protecting external resources, the programmer has to protect internal data. (The code area inside each process is normally hidden from threads by the run-time system, so we don't need to take any special steps to protect it.) In all other respects, threads are just mini-processes: they're controlled by a scheduler and we can assign different priorities to them.

From a client point of view, multi-threading has the following advantages:

- The user can run many applications at the same time and do many things within a single application: for example, in a single e-mail process, we can edit a message, be notified when new mail arrives, view a real-time clock, and so on.
- The user can interact with the user interface even if the application is busy. For example, imagine a database querying tool where the user types in a query and presses the Retrieve button; then, while the query is executing, the user notices that they have made a spelling mistake in the query. If the query tool has only one thread, the user can't edit the query until the useless results have been returned and displayed. If, on the other hand, we

arrange for the user interface and the database query to run in separate threads, the user can issue another search before the first one has finished: the application can kill the incorrect thread immediately and the incorrect results are never displayed.

- The user interface can be updated even when the application is busy. Consider a query tool, running as a single thread. If the user initiates a search and then, before the results are displayed, resizes the application window, what happens? Well, grabbing the corner of the window and moving it across the screen is performed by the operating system (the desktop), so the window boundary will move as expected. However, the *inside* of the window has to be painted by our application: since the application is busy, the inside of the window won't be repainted until the query results come back. The user sees a rather amateurish user interface that repaints at unexpected times. If we use a separate thread for the query, the user can resize the window while they're waiting and the repainting will happen immediately.

From a server point of view, multi-threading is good because:

- It allows us to serve many clients simultaneously without the overhead of multiple processes. Processes are much more expensive to set up, execute and tear down than threads. For example, a machine that crashes when you ask it to run 1000 processes simultaneously may be perfectly happy running four processes with 250 threads each. For certain kinds of networked application, this is critical: for example, servlets run in a single process with multiple threads but CGI scripts, by default, run in multiple processes; thus, if we want the benefits of servlets, we have to have multi-threading.
- It reduces **latency** (idle time) in the server. For example, if a middle tier machine accesses a database server using a single server thread, the middle tier machine is idle while the query is executed on the data tier machine. With multiple threads, the middle tier machine can be doing other work while the query is executing.
- It reduces time-outs. With some protocols, a client request will fail automatically if the server doesn't respond within a certain length of time (say, two minutes). If all client requests have to queue, waiting to be served by a single server thread, we will get more time-outs (each request is lengthened by the time it takes to serve the requests that were already in the queue). With multi-threading, short requests have a faster turn-around: time-outs will only happen for network problems, server overloading and overly-complex requests.

Ideally, the programming language and its run-time system handle the messy details of multi-threading – scheduling, priorities, time-slicing, etc. This way, the programmer just has to write the code that will be run by the threads and start them up.

## 10.8.3 Thread Safety

Multi-threading causes problems, because threads can be **interrupted** before they're finished (to allow other threads to run). For example, consider the following scenario:

Two threads A and B are accessing an object O.

Thread A starts to read one of O's fields, F, using a getter method.

When A has read half of the value, the scheduler interrupts it so that B can run for a while.

B starts to modify F, via its setter.

The scheduler allows B to finish its modification before it wakes up A.

When A wakes up, it reads the rest of F.

Thread A has now read half of the old value and half of the new value, which is clearly nonsense. This kind of data corruption applies to external resources too (imagine if A were reading a text file and B were modifying it).

When we access data in a database, the DBMS provides us with a sophisticated transaction mechanism to make sure that data isn't corrupted. However, inside multi-threaded code, we have to protect the data ourselves. The key to protecting data in an object-oriented program is to make sure that each piece can only be accessed via a single object that manages the data. Then, as long as we ensure that only one thread accesses the object at a time (**mutual exclusion**), we know that the data will be safe. Preferably, our programming language will allow us to enforce mutual exclusion (we'll see how it's done in Java shortly).

Code that is safe for multi-threaded use is said to be **thread-safe** or **MT-safe** (as opposed to 'not thread-safe' or **MT-hot**). Generally speaking, we would like to make all of our objects thread-safe and multi-thread all of our applications.

### Immutability

An **immutable** object is an object whose data can't be changed. Here the term data means:

* The values of the object's fields.
* The values stored in external resources managed by the object (such as text in files).
* The values inside any objects pointed to by the object.
* . . .

In other words, for an object to be truly immutable, it must be impossible to change the object's own fields and any data that can be reached by the object, directly or indirectly, internally or externally.

Immutable objects have the advantage that they're always thread-safe – since there's no data that can be changed, there's no data that can be corrupted. They're also more efficient (they can be shared transparently and kept in read-only areas of memory).

Some languages provide facilities for ensuring immutability – C++'s const keyword and Java's final keyword are common examples. These facilities, however, tend to be partial. A better approach is to enforce immutability by programming style (not providing setters, locking files, and so on).

Although immutable objects are a nice idea, most objects need to be mutable: for example, a Customer that didn't allow us to change its address attribute wouldn't be much use. Thus, we have to know how to make mutable objects thread-safe.

## Fixed Values

Working out how to make objects thread-safe is a challenge. To make matters worse, we usually have to reason about whole families of objects and how they will be used together. One reason for this is **deadlock**. Deadlock refers to the situation where thread A is waiting for thread B to do something while thread B is waiting for thread A to do something: both threads end up waiting for ever. In order to avoid deadlock, we have to think about how our objects collaborate and how threads will wander through them.

One simple trick we can use to help achieve thread safety is to look for **fixed values** in our objects. A fixed value is an immutable field: for example, a Math object might have a Pi value inside it that never needs to be changed. Fixed values, being immutable, are automatically thread-safe, so scenarios like the 'interrupted read' that we saw earlier, are not a problem.

Having decided which of an object's fields are fixed, we can divide our object into two halves: fixed values, which don't need special code to protect them, and changeable values, which do. Fixed values only have to be immutable *after* the object in question has been created. In other words, we can manipulate fixed values inside an object's constructors: as long as we don't change the value after the constructor has finished, everything will be fine. The reason for this is that only one thread can get inside a constructor: the thread that asks the run-time system to create the object; no other thread can get inside the object while it's being constructed, because it doesn't exist yet. (This assumes that the constructor doesn't make the object available to other threads while it is executing.)

## Synchronization in Java

We can solve most multi-threading problems by encapsulating each shared resource inside a single object. It is then the object's responsibility to make sure that only one thread is allowed in at a time. Preferably, the programming language should support this mutual exclusion.

For example, in Java, a method can be marked as synchronized: the run-time system guarantees that only one thread at a time can be active inside any of an object's synchronized methods. This is achieved by associating a **lock** with each object, under the control of a **monitor**. The first thread to arrive at one of the object's synchronized methods is allowed in by the monitor, but other threads are locked out of the synchronized methods until the first thread departs. Java's mutual exclusion does *not* apply to unsynchronized methods: threads are free to run in and out of them at any time.

Figure 10.27 shows a snapshot of a Java object in use, with four threads trying to get inside. This object has MT-hot values, which need protecting, and fixed values, which don't. The three threads that we've called T1, T2 and T3 are currently active; T2 is suspended outside method M2 because T1 has already entered the object through another synchronized method (M1). For this scheme to work, the programmer must ensure that only the code inside M1 and M2 accesses the MT-hot values. The fixed values, on the other hand, can be accessed from any method.

Thus, in order to make a Java object thread-safe, we need to synchronize access to all the MT-hot values. In practice, this requires experience and hard thinking in order to avoid deadlock and unnecessary synchronization (this is important because mutual exclusion can reduce an object's throughput).

---

### Case Study

*Thread safety in iCoot*

So, how do we address the thread-safety of iCoot? We can consider each layer separately (another advantage of using layers):

- In keeping with servlet programming style, our servlets (part of the distributed interface) are state-less, and therefore MT-safe. Session data (such as the PMember for the current user) is stored in one HttpSession per client and is protected using Java's synchronization mechanism (using **synchronized blocks**). (As part of the standard HTML/CGI-plus-servlets mechanism, the Web server stores the session objects and the Web browsers store the session identifiers.)
- Our pluggable server objects are also state-less and therefore thread-safe: each individual business service returns a response (as protocol objects) that is detached from the business layer and used only by the client that requested it.
- The business layer has to be made MT-safe, by careful programming, so that multiple threads can run through it from the server layer without corrupting cached data read from the database layer.

   Incidentally, the database layer is concurrent-safe by default, courtesy of its transaction mechanism – the programmer simply has to make sure that a transaction is created at the start of each business service and committed at the end.

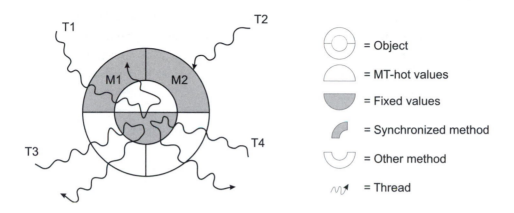

**Figure 10.27: Synchronization in Java**

# 10.9 SUMMARY

In this chapter, we looked at subsystem design – the process of deciding exactly what objects we are going to implement and what interfaces they should have:

- We considered the design of the business layer and how to derive it from the analysis class model.

- We saw how an object model could be mapped onto a relational database schema. For the sake of simplicity, we didn't look in detail at how we would write the code to perform the actual mapping at run time.

- After a brief look at tips for designing user interfaces, we discussed how to group the facilities offered by the middle tier into business service classes that hide the complexities of the business layer (for the benefit of different kinds of user interface).

- We considered the importance of looking for patterns, libraries and frameworks to avoid writing fresh code.

- We looked at the issues surrounding database transactions and multi-threading (intra-process concurrency), the concepts involved and an example of mutual exclusion in Java.

# FURTHER READING

When considering how to map an analysis class model into design, it's important to keep good theory and practice in mind. For a theoretical discussion by Bertrand Meyer (but which is readable nonetheless), see [Meyer 97]. Martin Fowler's popular book [Fowler 03] explains some of the fancier parts of class diagram notation; more can be found in the UML Specification [OMG 03a]. For a discussion of best practices for writing Java source code, see [Bloch 01].

Scott Ambler, an agile methodology enthusiast, provides comprehensive coverage of object-to-relational mapping in [Ambler 03].

In [Constantine and Lockwood 99], you will find advice from Larry Constantine on how to design user interfaces according to the way the system is used (based on use cases, of course).

J2EE covers all parts of multi-tier design and implementation, from GUIs and HTML front ends, through to servlets and EJBs on the middle tier and an object-to-relational mapping generated automatically by tools. Patterns for use with J2EE are described in [Alur *et al.* 03].

For a discussion of thread safety in Java, and some reusable patterns, see [Lea 99].

# REVIEW QUESTIONS

1. What kind of diagram is shown in Figure 10.28? Choose only one option.

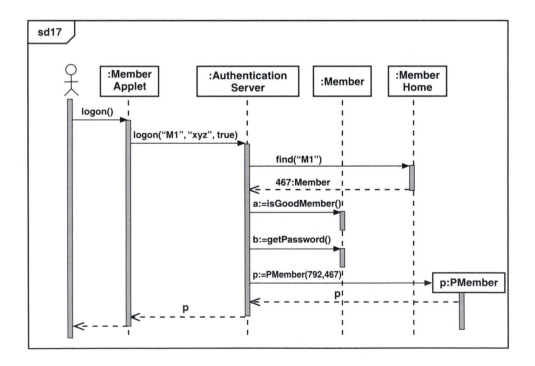

**Figure 10.28: Used with Review Question 1**

(a) State machine diagram.

(b) Activity diagram.

(c) Class diagram.

(d) Use case diagram.

(e) Sequence diagram.

(f) Communication diagram.

(g) Deployment diagram.

2. Currently, what is the most common type of database management system? Choose only one option.

(a) Network.

(b) Relational.

(c) Object-oriented.

(d) Hierarchical.

(e) Indexed file.

3. In UML diagrams, how are class messages distinguished from instance messages? Choose only one option.

(a) Class messages are shown in brackets.

(b) Class messages are shown in italics.

(c) Class messages are underlined.

(d) Class messages are shown with the keyword ⟨⟨ static ⟩⟩.

4. What is meant by the term 'deadlock'? Choose only one option.

(a) Two processes or threads refuse to talk to each other.

(b) An object's monitor allows its lock to terminate early.

(c) An object is waiting for a resource, which is being used by an object waiting for a resource used by the first object.

5. What is a 'thread'? Choose only one option.

(a) An independent process running on a node, with its own memory and IO.

(b) An activity within a process that shares memory with other activities.

(c) A designer's thought process.

# ANSWERS TO REVIEW QUESTIONS

1. The diagram in Figure 10.28 is e. Sequence diagram.
2. The most common type of database management system is b. Relational.

3. In UML diagrams, class messages are distinguished from instance messages because c. Class messages are underlined.

4. The term 'deadlock' means c. An object is waiting for a resource, which is being used by an object waiting for a resource used by the first object.

5. A 'thread' is b. An activity within a process that shares memory with other activities.

# 11

## Reusable Design Patterns

**W**hen writing software, as with any discipline, it's important to avoid duplicating effort – if somebody has discovered a perfectly good solution to a problem, we want to exploit their knowledge and experience, rather than waste time producing another solution. Always remember, object-oriented programming is about *not* writing code: the more we reuse, the more skilled we are.

# Learning Objectives

**Understand what a pattern is and what it means to a developer of object-oriented software.**

**Identify patterns that apply to our own software and how to use them together.**

**Examine some of the more common patterns.**

# Chapter Outline

11

# 11.1 INTRODUCTION

**Design patterns** are one way that developers can avoid duplicating effort: they allow us to apply the knowledge and experience of other developers to our particular problem. Patterns also allow us to communicate our own knowledge and experience to others. Each pattern is a description of a particular way of doing something that has proved effective in the real world.

When design patterns were introduced to the software community, they created a lot of interest. As a result, they have now been applied to many other areas:

- Human–computer interaction
- Concurrency
- Reuse
- Teaching/learning object technology
- Distributed computing
- Project management
- Web sites
- Risk management
- Anti-patterns (things going wrong)
- Problem-solving
- Organizations

## 11.1.1 A Brief History of Patterns

Originally, patterns had nothing to do with software. In the 1960s, Christopher Alexander, an architect of buildings, started writing about patterns in architecture and urban planning. Having studied human language, Alexander considered a sentence to be made up of reusable pieces or **patterns** that are employed by all of us to record knowledge, construct complex communications and solve problems. Because of its patterns, Alexander considered natural language to be a **pattern language**.

Alexander believed that architecture and urban planning could be improved if a pattern language could be developed for them. Some of the improvements would result from having concise descriptions of the knowledge of experts, while more still would result from the improved communication, allowing members of the public to be involved in the process: it seemed reasonable that, to ensure a successful outcome, the eventual inhabitants of a space should influence its design [Alexander *et al.* 77].

In the late 1980s, when object-oriented programming was becoming more and more popular among researchers and practitioners, experts including Kent Beck, Ward Cunningham, Erich Gamma, Bruce Anderson and Richard Helm started to think about how patterns could be applied to software. As experienced designers (and Smalltalk programmers), these experts were well placed to start identifying and recording patterns of collaborating objects, ones that had shown themselves to be useful over time. The work of these enthusiasts eventually became centered around the Object-Oriented Programming, Systems, Languages and Applications (OOPSLA) conferences in the early 1990s.

Ultimately, this effort led to a seminal book [Gamma *et al.* 95], which contained a general discussion of patterns, along with a catalog of 23 patterns ready for wider use – it's a mark of the importance of this book that, a decade later, its 23 patterns are still considered to be fundamental. The authors are often referred to as the **Gang of Four**.

## 11.1.2 Software Patterns Today

Today, as a result of the original book, the term 'design pattern' is mostly used to refer to software design patterns. Often, once the context is obvious, developers simply refer to **patterns**. Real enthusiasts still use the term **pattern language** to describe existing patterns and the way that they're used to record knowledge, to communicate and to construct solutions.

The original inventors of design patterns were true to Alexander's vision, involving end users in the development process. However, patterns are not normally used in that way today. This may be because software design, even small pieces of software design, can't easily be understood by non-programmers. Or, it may be because we don't yet know enough about software to produce patterns that are simple enough for the lay-person. (Involving end users is still desirable, but we tend to use other artifacts such as use cases, analysis class diagrams and GUI sketches.)

We've seen before how software is an inexact science, if a science at all. The gaps between the patterns are much larger than the gaps between any patterns that might exist in natural language or architecture. This may be because software design is too difficult to condense into a set of interlocking patterns, or it may simply be that we don't know how to do it yet.

Patterns can certainly be used by software developers to record knowledge, so that other developers don't have to duplicate their effort. Identifying and describing a pattern takes skill and experience; even experts should not try to describe a new pattern until they have demonstrated its effectiveness in several different applications.

As well as recording knowledge, a pattern can be used as a pre-fabricated part of a new design. Because patterns are independent of programming language and application domain, they can't be used simply as they are, in the same way that a framework or a library can. Patterns need to be fine-tuned for each particular situation. Nevertheless, they still save us a lot of time.

Patterns are also used widely to document a solution. For example, rather than trying to describe how 'messages that are sent to this object are forwarded over the network to the real implementation object, which has a similar interface', we can simply record that 'this object is a network Proxy'. For a complicated pattern, the name of the pattern can be worth a thousand words.

# 11.2 A PATTERN TEMPLATE

Since patterns are meant to be used widely, they need to be presented in a widely accepted format. Ideally, the format will be easy to read and understand; but, in the name of completeness and correctness, each pattern description may end up being rather formal. This is the case with [Gamma *et al.* 95]: although each pattern is essential and well described, the end result is more of a reference work than a tutorial. In this book, the pattern descriptions are informal, showing the purpose, the structure and the mechanism, with code examples and illustrations.

[Gamma *et al.* 95] describes a **template** that can be filled in by pattern authors. In order to give you a flavor of how full-blown patterns should be described, the template headings are reproduced below along with a few words of explanation for each:

- Pattern Name: A short name for the pattern (usually one or two words), Memento for example. Obviously, this name should be indicative of the pattern's purpose. It should also be unique within the application area.
- Classification: Each pattern is classed as **creational** (concerned with how objects are created), **structural** (concerned with putting objects together into a larger structure), or **behavioral** (concerned with collaborations between objects to achieve a particular goal).
- Intent: A short description (one or two sentences) summing up what the pattern is for, for example, 'Without violating encapsulation, capture and externalize an object's internal state so that the object can be restored to this state later'.
- Also Known As: Aliases for the pattern.
- Motivation: A description of a design problem that is solved by use of the pattern.
- Applicability: Areas where this pattern can be applied and how to recognize those areas.
- Structure: One or more class diagrams and sequence diagrams that illustrate how the pattern works. [Gamma *et al.* 95] uses OMT (a predecessor of UML); obviously, UML will be used here.
- Participants: Short descriptions of the objects involved and what each one does (what its responsibilities are).
- Collaborations: Description of the collaborations between the participants.
- Consequences: Benefits and shortcomings of the pattern (plus advice on what to do about the shortcomings).
- Implementation: Advice on implementing the pattern, including useful tricks and things to avoid.

- Sample Code: Full implementations of the pattern. In [Gamma *et al.* 95], the implementations are in C++ or Smalltalk – Java is used in this book.
- Known Uses: Where the pattern has been applied in the real world.
- Related Patterns: The patterns that are similar to this one and exactly how they differ. Also, which patterns can be valuable when used with this one.

# 11.3 COMMON DESIGN PATTERNS

As a general principle, we must be familiar with the core patterns before trying to implement anything other than a trivial program. This section gives informal descriptions of the most common patterns. Complete, formal descriptions are available elsewhere but the information here is enough to provide a good grounding. You are encouraged to investigate other patterns for yourself, at least the other well-known ones (Prototype, Bridge, Builder, Memento, Command, Decorator, Chain of Responsibility, Interpreter, Mediator and Visitor).

## 11.3.1 Observer

> Define a one to many dependency between objects so that when one object changes state, all its dependents are notified automatically. [Gamma *et al.* 95]

Often, the state of one object depends in some way on the state of another – a common case is a GUI component displaying the state of an entity. For example, Figure 11.1 shows a tool for previewing a car that a customer is considering buying. As each of the car's attributes are varied by the customer, the picture of the car and the displayed price vary accordingly. The GUI object itself, which is an instance of class CarView, is composed of three panels, each displaying some information about the car. Under the covers, the GUI is supported by a Car object which has a field for each of the possible options (with corresponding getters and setters). The price is derived from the other attributes and made available with getPrice.

Where should we put the logic to detect when the car display needs updating? If we put it in the GUI, the GUI programmer must have knowledge of the way a Car operates – the sunroof affects the price but the color doesn't, for example. This approach would make the GUI programmer's life more difficult. It would also spread knowledge around the system, making it harder to manage. If we put the knowledge in the entity instead, how can we make sure that the GUI is updated at the appropriate time? We could make the car entity aware of the GUI; however, we want the entity to be developed independently of the GUI so that it can be reused in many car applications – coupling it to a particular GUI would limit its usefulness.

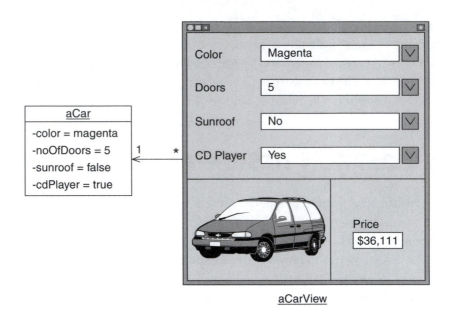

**Figure 11.1: A GUI for car buyers**

So we seem to have a paradox: we want the knowledge about changing attributes to be in the entity, where it belongs; however, we can't put it in the entity, because then the entity would be coupled to the GUI. We can solve this paradox with the **Observer** pattern. The basic idea behind Observer is to give all GUIs a simple interface that allows an entity to signal a change of state: this means that there is only a light coupling between the entity and the GUI. (The analogy is that the entity goes about its business, more or less oblivious to any object that happens to be watching what it's doing.)

Let's look at Observer in detail, an abstract definition first followed by an implementation of the car example. In Figure 11.2, the object with changing attributes is referred to as the **subject**, while an object that observes the changes is called an **observer**. The Observer class has a simple interface consisting of one update message – this message, which will be sent by the subject when an attribute has changed, provides an opportunity for an observer to refresh itself. The subject, for its part, maintains a collection of Observer objects that have registered an interest in changes – registration is achieved using the addObserver message. (If necessary, observers can be unregistered at a later date using the removeObserver message.) The subject also has a protected notify message that iterates over the observers, sending the update message to each one (for the sake of predictability, we can ensure that the update messages arrive in the same order that the observers were registered).

The Subject class, despite having a complete implementation, is designed to act as a superclass – the reusable implementation is not much use without some attributes to

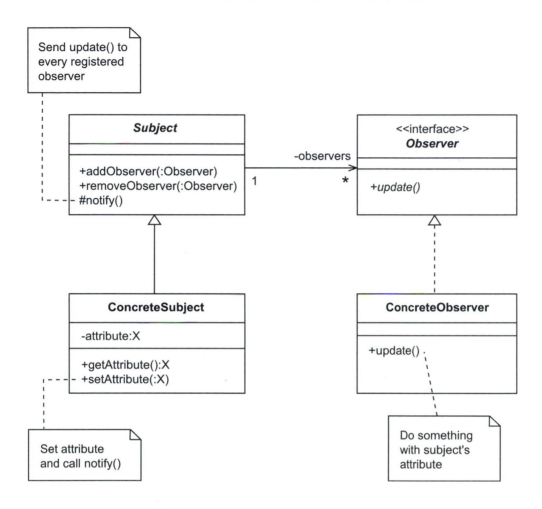

**Figure 11.2: Observer class diagram**

modify – so we mark the class as abstract. Anyone wishing to implement an observable object can make their class inherit from Subject, as has been done here with ConcreteSubject. The implementor of ConcreteSubject must ensure that notify is called whenever attribute values are changed – inside setAttribute for example – so that the update message is sent to every observer. (In order to avoid unnecessary notifications, the implementor must make sure that this only happens when the new attribute value is different to the old value – most of the time, because we're dealing with attributes, different means not equal, rather than not identical.)

The Observer class has no concrete methods (because we don't know what an Observer will need to do to refresh itself). Thus, Observer can be an interface (a pure abstract class). When we write an Observer class, it needs to inherit from Observer and implement the update

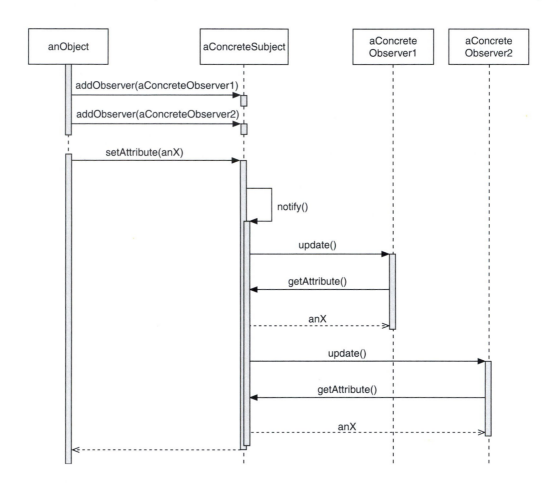

**Figure 11.3: Observer sequence diagram**

method to refresh its contents in some way – this is illustrated by the class ConcreteObserver in Figure 11.2. Typically, a ConcreteObserver will use ConcreteSubject getters to retrieve new attribute values during the execution of the update method.

The sequence of messages for the Observer pattern is illustrated in Figure 11.3. Initially, anObject registers two observers with aConcreteSubject. Some time later, anObject modifies aConcreteSubject's state using setAttribute. Having recorded the new value internally, aConcreteSubject sends itself the notify message. (A stacked activation bar has been used, in official UML style, to show the duration of the notify method.) Inside the notify method, the update message is sent to aConcreteObserver1 and then to aConcreteObserver2. Inside the update methods, each observer uses getAttribute to discover the current state of the subject.

The ConcreteSubject knows that it's dealing with Observer objects, but not ConcreteObserver objects. (The parameter to each of addObserver and removeObserver is an Observer.) Thus, the

ConcreteSubject is coupled to the Observer class but not to ConcreteObserver: the two abstract classes provide the glue that makes the subject independent of the observer. Obviously, the observer is tightly coupled to the subject, but since the observer is usually in the layer above (in the subsystem design sense), that's not a problem. The abstract classes, since they're generic, can be added to a class library.

Applying Observer to the car display tool in Figure 11.1 gives us the class diagram shown in Figure 11.4. A single observer, aCarView, registers itself with the subject and also acts as the source of updates. The message flow is illustrated in Figure 11.5. Initially, the addObserver message is used for registration. Then, some time later, the user elects to add a sunroof: this results in the setSunroof(true) message being sent to aCar. Assuming that the sunroof attribute had been false, the update message is sent to aCarView inside notify. Inside the update method on aCarView we read the current attribute values using the getters.

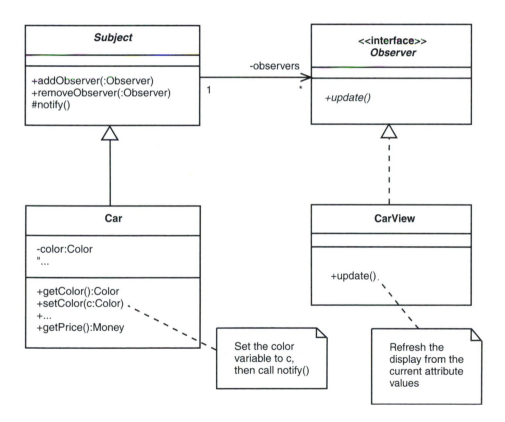

**Figure 11.4: Car observer class diagram**

Although Observer is often used to allow a GUI to update itself when an entity changes, we can use the pattern elsewhere too, especially in a layered system. For example, entities

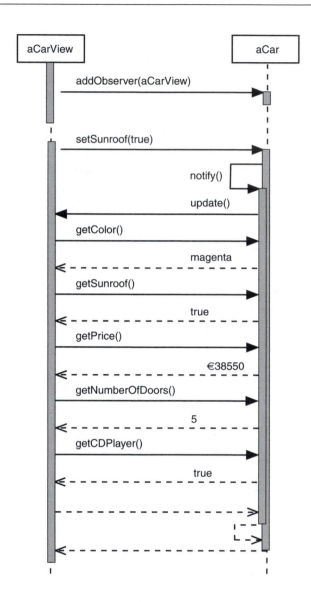

**Figure 11.5: Car observer sequence diagram**

in the business layer may be observed by controllers in the control layer (controllers act as translators between the business layer and the user interface layer). In turn, the controllers can be observed by GUI components. (See Chapter 8 for an alternative way of signaling between layers, using events, that has the same effect as Observer.)

In a multi-tier system, with a real GUI (as opposed to an HTML-based interface), Observer is invaluable on the client side. However, on the server side, we often have to deal with multiple threads and the extra complexity makes it difficult to employ Observer. In theory, we could also use Observer to signal updates from the server to the client; however, in this case, the problems of multiple threads are exacerbated by multiple machines and network issues (such as time-outs and crashed clients). In short, it's best to restrict our use of Observer to the client side, and then only to use it as a means of passing notifications from one layer to the layer above. In all other cases, we should avoid Observer, for the sake of simplicity and safety. (Exceptional cases on the server can be dealt with by other means, such as callbacks from the operating-system clock and machine-to-machine messaging, as exemplified by the Java Messaging Service.)

## 11.3.2 Singleton

> Ensure a class has only one instance, and provide a global point of access to it. [Gamma
> *et al.* 95]

From time to time, it's useful to have an object that is the only instance of its class. Often, this will be because the object represents a unique component in the system or in the application domain – for example, in a system that stores data in a database, the database itself can be represented as a single instance of a class DB. Another common case is where the singular instance needs to be shared between separate parts of the system, saving memory space and creation time – for example, we might use a single Calendar to answer all questions such as 'How many days are there in February?', rather than creating lots of Calendar objects.

In the field of design patterns, an object that is the sole instance of its class is called a **Singleton**. In order for a singleton to be useful, it should satisfy the following three criteria:

- It must be easy to find.
- It must be impossible for anyone to create another one.
- It should not be created until it's needed.

In order to make the singleton easy to find, we can store it in a class field, accessed via a class message. This is reasonable since, in object-oriented programming, classes have long been used as the entry point for shared data and services. To ensure that only one singleton can be created, we can make sure that the code used to create the singleton is inaccessible to ordinary code by making it private.

It is less important that the singleton is not created until it is needed but it is still desirable, in order to avoid creating and initializing an object that is never used. Client programmers won't issue instructions to 'create the object now', so we can choose between creating the object when the system starts or creating it on-demand – typically, we choose the latter and use a simple technique called **lazy initialization** where conditional logic is used to check, at the point of access, whether the singleton has yet been created.

Figure 11.6 shows a Singleton implementation as a class diagram. Here, we have a private class variable called instance which points to the Singleton object – this object is created on-demand by the getInstance class method (remember that UML distinguishes class elements from object elements by underlining them). We also have a constructor, indicated with the <<create>> keyword. Since the constructor is private, it can't be used anywhere outside the class. Finally, the Singleton class includes definitions of the instance methods, instanceMethod1, instanceMethod2 and so on. (Of course, our Singleton could also have fields, just like any other object.) In Figure 11.7, you can see a less abstract example of a singleton in the form of a calendar. Despite the new class name, the naming convention getInstance has been retained.

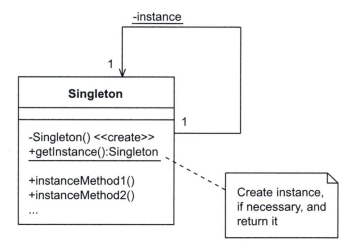

**Figure 11.6: Singleton class diagram**

You may be feeling, at this point, that the class diagrams you've just seen are difficult to understand, because they mix instance and class concepts in the same box. This is a sad fact of life for class diagrams in general, but one which it is worth getting used to. However, for the sake of clarifying the Singleton pattern, we can take an alternative view of what's going on (see Figure 11.8), which you may find easier to appreciate. Here, we consider the class to be a separate object in its own right, hosting the constructor (Calendar), the class field (instance) and the class method (getInstance). Meanwhile, the singleton object hosts instance fields and instance methods. (Some programming languages, such as Smalltalk and

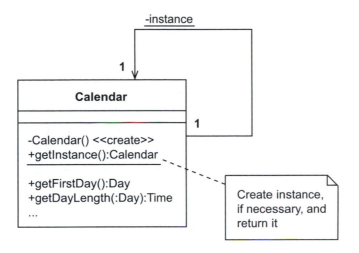

**Figure 11.7: Calendar class diagram**

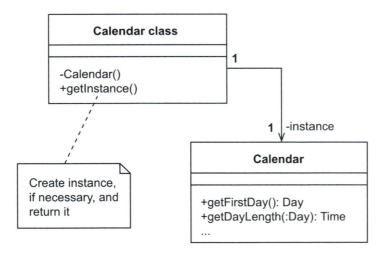

**Figure 11.8: Calendar as a class object**

Java, do indeed model each class as a distinct object.) In UML terms, the class that has been labeled Calendar class is a **metaclass**: rather than using the official UML keyword, the naming rules have been bent a little, to make things clearer. Figure 11.8 gives rise to the object diagram in Figure 11.9. Here, creation of the singleton and access to it is managed by the class; the singleton itself is like any other object: it has a name, a type and, usually, some fields.

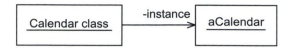

**Figure 11.9: Calendar object diagram**

In programming terms, the implementation of the Singleton pattern is easy. In order for programmers to make use of a singleton, they must first identify the class and then invoke (getInstance). The way this is done varies from language to language. Here it is in Java:

```java
public class Calendar {

    private static Calendar instance; // static means "class field"

    private Calendar() { // Must declare a private constructor
        // Initialize any fields here
    }
    public static getInstance() {
        if (instance == null) {
            instance = new Calendar();
        }
        return instance;
    }

    // Declare any instance fields here...

    // And now for the instance methods:
    public Day getFirstDay() { ... }
    public Time getDayLength(Day aDay) { ... }
    ...
}
```

The Java code fragment below shows the calendar being used to discover the first day of the year, so that we can print it out for the user:

```java
Date d = Calendar.getInstance().getFirstDay();
System.out.println("The first day of the year is: " + d);
```

In Chapter 2, class fields and class messages were identified as a way of managing centralized data and services. As you can see from the calendar example, Singleton also provides access to centralized data and services. So which is better? Generally speaking, Singleton is the better choice, for two reasons:

• Class elements are not very object-oriented because most programming languages do not support inheritance and redefinition for them. This makes it difficult to craft a hierarchy of different kinds of Calendar, such as Calendar, GregorianCalendar, JulianCalendar, IslamicCalendar, and so on.

- As designers and programmers, it's quite enough for us to have to deal with objects at run time, why should we have to deal with classes too? (Okay, so Singleton does use one class field and one class method, but that's as far as it goes.)

If you find yourself wanting to use class elements, you should say to yourself 'Perhaps what I really need is a singleton'.

## 11.3.3 Multiton

Singleton is undoubtedly useful and you should expect to encounter it often. However, there is a related pattern, dubbed **Multiton**, that doesn't appear in [Gamma *et al.* 95] (a form of it does, however, appear at www.patterndigest.com). The term multiton is a pun on 'multi-valued singleton' although that is, admittedly, an oxymoron. If you prefer, a multiton is any type with a restricted set of values. (This is similar to an **enumeration** in languages like C or in UML, except that each value of such an enumeration is a primitive rather than an object, which makes them less useful.)

For example, we are designing a sales system for a car showroom that has cars available in the following five colors: sunset red, midnight blue, morning orange, noon yellow and afternoon grey. In object-oriented terms, we would like each color to be represented as an independent object with its own data and behavior (for example, the amount that this color adds to the cost of the car). We would like the five objects to be easily accessible. Furthermore, in order to avoid mistakes, we would like to stop programmers creating their own colors. This design begins to sound rather like Singleton but with every occurrence of 'one' replaced with 'five'.

Figure 11.10 shows a class called CarColor containing a lazily-initialized Map of Car-Color objects, each retrievable by name. (A Map is a collection that allows us to insert and retrieve objects by name.) Our getInstance method now takes a String parameter allowing us to specify which of the five instances we're interested in. CarColor also has a retrieveAllInstances message that we can use to get a list of all the instances – this would be useful for displaying the available colors in a GUI. Figure 11.11 shows CarColor separated from its contents, so we can see clearly what is going on: the class has a reference to the Map which, in turn, has references to five CarColor objects. Because the constructor is private, we know that client programmers can't create their own CarColor objects.

Multitons are useful in languages that don't provide a special syntax for declaring types with a restricted set of values. Java has a form of multiton within the syntax of the language itself, so you don't have to write your own.

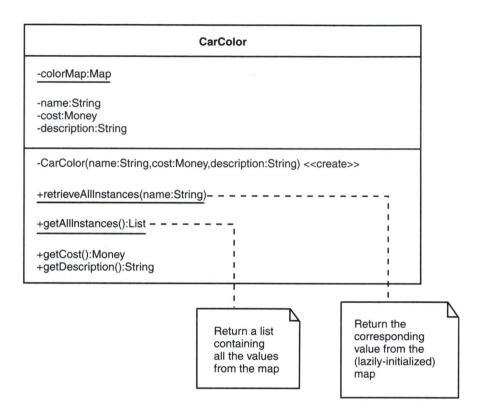

**Figure 11.10: Car colors using Multiton**

## 11.3.4 Iterator

> Provide a way to access the elements of an aggregate object sequentially without exposing its underlying representation. [Gamma *et al.* 95]

Often, we need to be able to do something for every object in a collection. For example, if we have a collection of items in a warehouse, we might want to add the value of all the items together to calculate the total value of the warehouse contents – in other words, we would need to 'add this value to the total' for every item in the warehouse. We don't normally have direct support for this kind of task in our programming language, so we must use objects and messages instead.

**Iterator** is a simple pattern that allows us to retrieve items one at a time from any kind of collection, using a standard loop – once we have a reference to an object inside the loop, we can perform the desired operation. For unordered collections, we don't care about the order in which the objects are retrieved, as long as each is retrieved exactly once; for

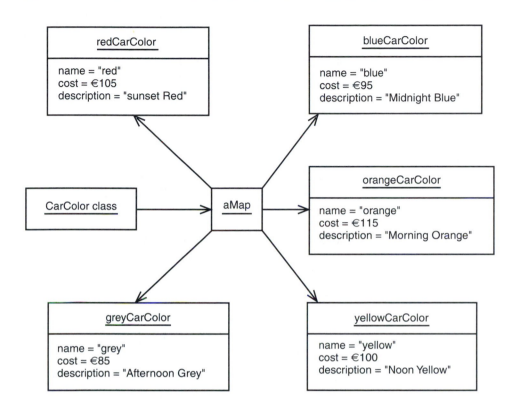

**Figure 11.11: Multiton object diagram**

ordered collections, we would expect the objects to be retrieved in order. Iterator requires the collaboration of collection-class implementors, which must provide at least a method to create and return an iterator.

Figure 11.12 shows the Iterator pattern, represented by the Iterator interface (since we don't expect to be able to provide a reusable implementation at this level, the class can be an interface). Alongside Iterator is a basic hierarchy of collections: the top level class, Collection, has an abstract method called createIterator that creates and returns an iterator of the appropriate type; underneath Collection, we have an unordered variety called Bag and an ordered variety called List.

We expect to have to provide more than one concrete implementation of Iterator, because it's unlikely that we could write a single iterator that would work for every kind of collection (although some iterators may work for more than one). Let's assume that each concrete collection has its own concrete iterator, hence the classes BagIterator and ListIterator in Figure 11.12. We have to rely on the cooperation of collection-class implementors, who must find or implement an iterator that will work for their collection and return it from createIterator. Given the class model in Figure 11.12, and appropriate method

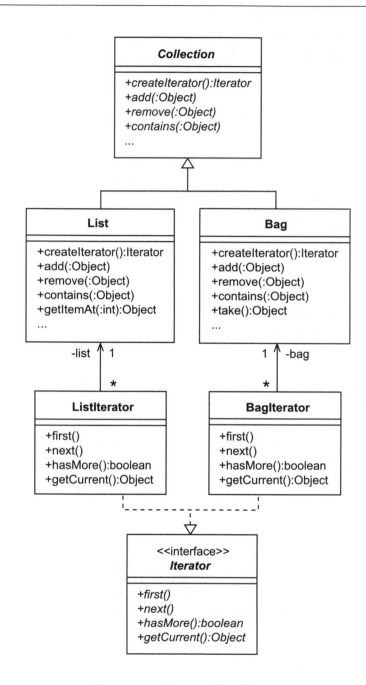

**Figure 11.12: Iterator class diagram**

implementations, the client programmer can write uniform iterating code, as in the following Java example:

```
Collection items = new Bag(); // "new List()" would work just as well

items.add(new Widget());
items.add(new FDoobrie());

Iterator i = items.createIterator(); // Iterator now at first element
while (i.hasMore()) {
   Object item = i.getCurrent();
   ... // Do something with item
   i.next();
}
```

It turns out that the implementation of ListIterator is straightforward. Here's how it looks in Java:

```
public class ListIterator implements Iterator {
   private List list;
   private int index; // Automatically set to 0

   protected ListIterator(List l) { // Constructor
      list = l;
   }
   public void first() {
      index = 0;
   }
   public void next() {
      index = index + 1;
   }
   public boolean hasMore() {
      return index < list.getSize();
   }
   public Object getCurrent() {
      return list.getItemAt(index);
   }
}
```

To complete the picture for ListIterator, we need to persuade the implementor of List to add the following method to their class:

```
public Iterator createIterator() {
   return new ListIterator(this); // "this" means "the current object"
}
```

It is common practice to provide some kind of two-way iterator for collections that keep their elements in order, so that clients can iterate in reverse order if they want to. We can achieve this with a sub-interface of Iterator, called TwoWayIterator, that adds messages called last and previous. Then, given concrete implementations such as ListTwoWayIterator, each ordered collection can provide a factory method called createTwoWayIterator, to complement createIterator.

## 11.3.5 Factory Method and Abstract Factory

Define an interface for creating an object, but let subclasses decide which class to instantiate. Factory method lets a class defer instantiation to subclasses. [Gamma *et al.* 95]

**Factory Method** should be mentioned at this point because of its importance. A new description isn't needed, because we've already seen this pattern being used in the implementation of Iterator (with createIterator and createTwoWayIterator).

At its simplest, a factory method creates and returns an object of some type. Factory methods are convenient for client programmers because:

- The client doesn't need to know the concrete type of the object being created. Instead, they work with a higher-level abstraction (always a good idea with object-oriented programming). In our example, client programmers would need to know about the Iterator and TwoWayIterator interfaces but not the concrete types ListIterator, BagIterator and ListTwoWayIterator.
- The type can be changed from time to time, or from platform to platform, without affecting existing client code as clients don't know the actual type of object being created (another example of loose coupling).
- Clients don't need to be concerned with the creation details of concrete classes (fiddly constructor parameters, for example).

Factory Method 'lets a class defer instantiation to subclasses'. This allows the implementor of Collection to work with a mechanism that hasn't yet been defined. In other words, Collection can provide an abstract createIterator method which has separate definitions in List and Bag.

In a related pattern, called **Abstract Factory**, a class contains multiple factory methods – this is used to provide a single point of creation for whole families of objects. (The **Abstract** part indicates that we can build a hierarchy of factories.)

## 11.3.6 State

Allow an object to alter its behavior when its internal state changes. The object will appear to change its class. [Gamma *et al.* 95]

As we saw in Chapter 7, objects sometimes have a complicated life cycle, one that is complicated enough for us to want to use a state machine to model their behavior. When we come to implement such an object, it's a good idea to avoid coding all the details of the corresponding state machine inside the object's own methods; otherwise the complexity would be spread throughout the code, where it would be difficult to manage. The **State** pattern is a convenient way of implementing a state machine separately from the original object, allowing us to see and modify the state-related behavior easily.

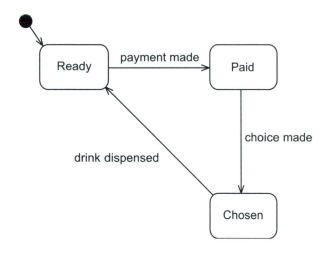

**Figure 11.13: State machine diagram for a vending machine**

Consider the state machine diagram in Figure 11.13, showing the activities of a typical vending machine that dispenses one of a number of cans of drink, all at the same price. When the machine is powered up and ready to go, it is in the Ready state, waiting for the price of a drink to be inserted by the customer. A customer walks up to the machine and puts in some money; when the money reaches the price of a drink (the payment made event), the vending buttons light up – the machine is now in the Paid state. Next, the customer presses one of the buttons (the choice made event) and the machine is in the Chosen state while it retrieves the drink. Finally, when the drink has been dropped into the collection tray (the drink dispensed event), the machine is ready for another payment. So, how can we turn this state machine into objects, using the State pattern?

The general form of the State pattern is shown in Figure 11.14. Here, the object with the interesting life cycle is called Context. There are two events in Context's state machine that have been translated into messages on Context – someEvent and anotherEvent. To avoid coding the effect of these events inside Context, a separate object (called ContextState) has been added to do the work: any message that is sent to Context will be passed on to ContextState. ContextState is just a superclass, however: the real activity is added in subclasses, one for each state that appears in the state machine diagram (StateA and StateB in this case). The basic idea is that, when Context is in state A, its state variable will be an instance of StateA and when it is in state B, its state will be an instance of StateB. Since all state messages sent to Context are delegated to the state object, programmers can put state-related activity in the subclasses of ContextState, where it's easier to find.

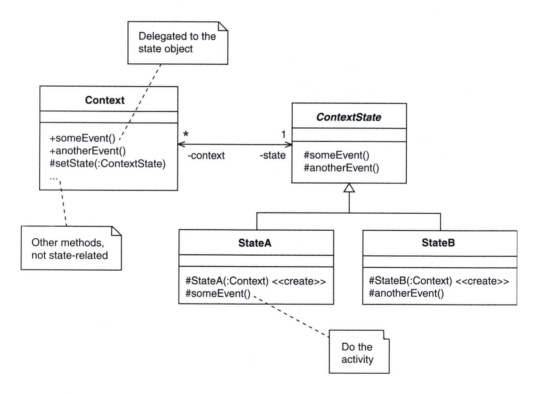

**Figure 11.14: State class diagram**

When a Context is created, it sets its state variable to an instance of StateA or StateB, depending on which is the start state. During this initialization, the state object's context variable will also be set. For example, for a Context class written in Java, we could have:

```
public Context() { // Constructor
   new StateA(this);
}
```

And, for a ContextState, we could have:

```
public ContextState(Context c) { // Constructor
   context = c;
   c.setState(this);
}
```

Now, for each event that happens to cause a transition to another state, the implementor of the event method can use Context's setState message to get the context into the new state, as in:

```
public void anEvent() {
   ... // State activity, followed by:
   new StateB(context);
}
```

Although the scheme described above means that we have two links, one from Context to ContextState and another from ContextState to Context, it does keep the state-transition behavior inside the state objects, where it belongs. All methods and constructors on the state classes are protected, because they should not be accessible to clients. The ContextState class is abstract, because only instances of its subclasses should be created.

Now look at Figure 11.15, showing the vending example implemented using State (the constructors and setState have been omitted, for simplicity.) Anyone wanting to work with a vending machine simply needs to create a VendingMachine object and send it the pay, choose and dispense messages at the appropriate times. Internally, the VendingMachine starts with an instance of Ready, which is replaced with an instance of Paid when the pay message arrives, then with an instance of Chosen when the choose message arrives, and then reverts to Ready when the dispense message arrives. This entire process, including creation of the objects, is illustrated in Figure 11.16. Inside each of the state methods, on the concrete subclasses, we can implement any behavior we like. This could take the form of manipulations of the states themselves, or manipulations of the VendingMachine context (since we have a reference to the context, we can easily send it messages).

You may think that the methods on a class such as VendingState would be abstract. However, if we make them abstract, implementors of the concrete subclasses have to redefine methods that are not relevant to them (because each event can only occur in certain states). Thus, in our vending example, the writer of Ready would have to provide an implementation for choose and dispense, even though these events could never happen (because the drink-selection buttons are inactive until enough money has been inserted and because the machine won't dispense a drink until a choice has been made). Although some sort of implementation

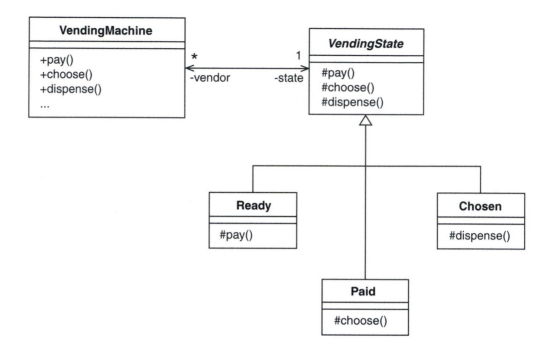

**Figure 11.15: Vending machine class diagram**

could be provided for the irrelevant methods, reporting an error for debugging purposes perhaps, the end result would be inconvenient and clumsy. A better approach is to provide an implementation for every method on VendingState that reports an error – this way, writers of subclasses only have to override the methods that can occur in that state.

Figure 11.16 contains some new UML notation which deserves explanation. A **lifeline** shows how long an object survives in the sequence. We can show an object (such as Ready) at the point where it is created. If the object is created by another object, we can indicate that with a message sent from the creator's activation bar to the new object's perimeter (optionally labeled with the constructor details). It is also possible to indicate the end of an object's useful life by putting a large black X at the end of its lifeline, perhaps with an incoming message such as close. This marker, a **stop** in UML, indicates that the object can be deleted or that it must not be used beyond this point.

Another issue that often has to be addressed with state machines is state data, i.e. attributes that are relevant to particular states. The amount of money that has been paid and the drink that has been selected are examples from our vending machine. State data also fits neatly into the State pattern: all we have to do is add the getters and setters to the Context and ContextState classes, just as we did with state methods. The fields and concrete getters

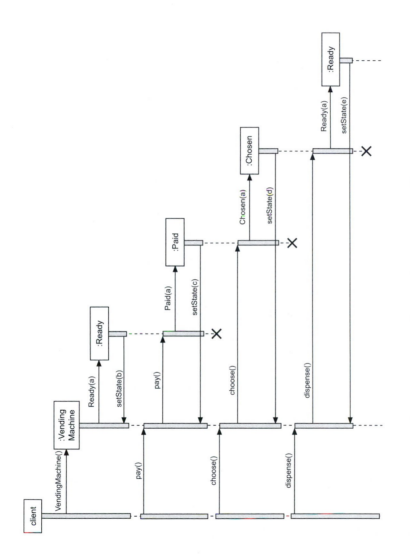

**Figure 11.16: Vending machine sequence diagram**

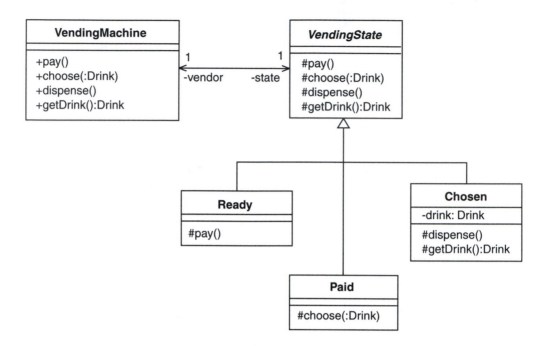

**Figure 11.17: Vending machine with state data**

and setters can then be added to the subclasses that actually use the data. For example, Figure 11.17 shows the effect of adding the customer's choice of drink to our vending machine (again, constructors and state-setting methods have been omitted, for the sake of simplicity). Here, the choice made by the customer is passed in as a parameter to choose and then passed on to Chosen via its constructor. The Java implementation of choose for the Paid class would be something like:

```
public void choose(Drink d) {
    new Chosen(vendor, d);
}
```

## 11.3.7 Facade

Provide a unified interface to a set of interfaces in a subsystem. Facade defines a higher-level interface that makes the subsystem easier to use. [Gamma *et al.* 95]

When implementing a subsystem or layer using objects, the number of objects involved can be relatively large. For example, for a system like iCoot, the business layer runs to dozens of classes, both new ones and ones that we've re-used from elsewhere. This is reasonable, because we try to break down the complexity of a sizeable programming task into manageable objects that collaborate as necessary. The alternative would be fewer, larger, objects: such large objects would be more difficult to implement correctly and many would end up being multi-purpose (i.e. they would have weak cohesion). However, having produced lots of sophisticated objects with many connections, the clients of our layer or subsystem have a problem: how do they use the rich set of objects to perform a simple task without intimate knowledge of the internal interfaces and collaborations?

The **Facade** pattern comes to the rescue here: each facade translates the complexity of some part of a subsystem or layer into a single object with a subset of the available services. In our iCoot system, for example, half a dozen server objects were introduced to translate the multi-threaded, transaction-oriented business objects into a much simpler 'request–response' protocol that can be used by all manner of networked clients. In the request–response protocol, when a simple request comes in from a client (Web browser or applet), the relevant server object uses whatever combination of business objects and messages is necessary to generate a simple reply. This way, the task of the programmers of the user interface is made easier, with the added bonus that the facades can be used in different kinds of interfaces with minimal extra coding.

Figure 11.18 shows two facades providing a limited number of services for clients of a complex subsystem, alongside the more complicated alternative where clients use the subsystem objects directly.

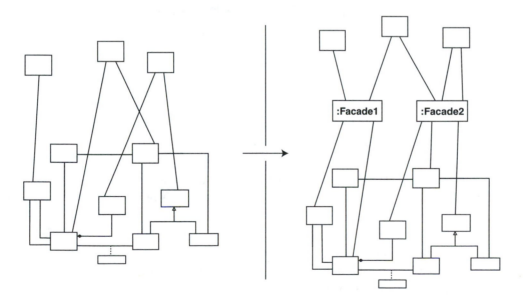

**Figure 11.18: Subsystems with and without the Facade pattern**

## 11.3.8 Adapter

Convert the interface of a class into another interface clients expect. Adapter lets classes work together that couldn't otherwise because of incompatible interfaces. [Gamma *et al.* 95]

**Adapter** wraps one object inside another so that the first object can be used in a different context. Often, we need to do this in order to connect objects that weren't designed to be used together. The basic form of Adapter is shown in Figure 11.19. Here, the client and the adaptee were designed separately, but, in the name of reuse, we would like them to work together. To do this, we interpose an adapter that has the interface expected by the client – inside the adapter, we forward incoming messages to the actual messages on the adaptee, translating message names, parameters and return types as necessary. Inside each adapter method, we can also provide any behavior that the adaptee lacks or modify the existing behavior.

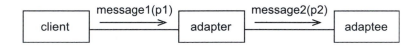

**Figure 11.19: Adapter object diagram**

In Figure 11.20, we have a simple application of Adapter. Here, the design requires a class called Queue that holds a queue of objects and allows us to add an object to the end, remove an object from the beginning and find out how many objects are queued (getCount). Someone has already implemented a List class that allows us to add an object to the end, remove the first object (using removeFirst) and ask how many objects there are (using getSize) – exactly the kind of messages needed for Queue, but with different names. We don't want to force our clients to use the List class because it has the wrong name and messages and because the client would be able use it for non queue-like behavior (such as removing an object from the middle of the queue with removeElementAt).

One solution, which avoids writing lots of code but still gives clients what they need, is to implement the queue object as an adapter (see Figure 11.21). When finished, our Queue translates its three messages into the corresponding List messages but omits all of the unwanted List behavior, as shown in the following Java implementation:

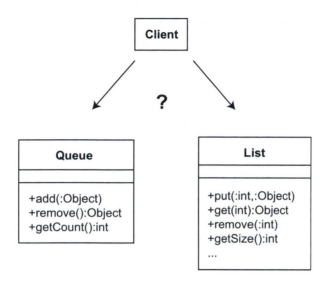

**Figure 11.20: Queues and Lists**

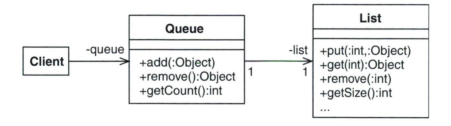

**Figure 11.21: Queue class diagram**

```
public void add(Object o) {
    list.add(o);
}
public Object remove() {
    return list.removeFirst();
 }
public int getCount() {
    return list.getSize();
}
```

## 11.3.9 Strategy and Template Method

> Define a family of algorithms, encapsulate each one, and make them interchangeable. Strategy lets the algorithm vary independently from clients that use it. [Gamma *et al.* 95]

Sometimes, a family of tasks differ in some minor detail. For example, driving a car is similar to driving a van or a lorry, but each has its own detailed characteristics such as stopping distance, all-round visibility and driver height.

To take a smaller example, how about the problem of keeping a list of objects in sorted order? We can make sure that the elements of a list remain sorted by inserting each new one into its correct location, just as we would do with physical index cards. To be more specific, when a new element comes along, we scan down the existing list to find the first element that is 'bigger' than the new one, then we insert the new one in front of the one that we just found. (If we get to the end of the list without finding a bigger element, we know that we have to add the new element at the end.) Although the general task is the same each time, the detail is different: if the list contains numbers, 'bigger' means 'further from zero'; if the list contains names, 'bigger' means 'further from A'.

In software terms, we now have a problem: because the detail is different every time, we can't easily implement a SortedList class that works for every kind of element. Here are a couple of things that we could try:

- Make the add(:Object) method use an if statement to work out what to do (if o is a number, do this; otherwise, do that). The trouble with this is that the varying logic is buried inside a method, where it's difficult to find. Worse still, clients can't use our class to deal with lists of customers sorted by credit rating, or products sorted by price, or anything else they might think of.
- Provide an abstract method called biggerThan(:Object,:Object) that returns true if the first parameter is bigger than the second (this method would be invoked by a generic algorithm inside add). Then, we would need to provide a SortedNumberList subclass that implements biggerThan in one way and a SortedNameList subclass that implements it another way. (This is actually another pattern called **Template Method**.) Although the kernel of the sorting algorithm is now easy to get at, we've disturbed the collection hierarchy: what if SortedList needed subclasses called SortedLinkedList and SortedArrayList? We could end up with SortedNumberLinkedList, SortedNameLinkedList, SortedNumberArrayList, SortedNameArrayList – a complete mess. (Any alternative solution using multiple inheritance would probably not be any easier to use.)

**Strategy** is designed to solve this problem. Essentially, we take the detail (the **strategy**) and separate it completely from the main task (the **context**). In this case, we separate the biggerThan method from the SortedList class, as shown in Figure 11.22. Here, SortedList

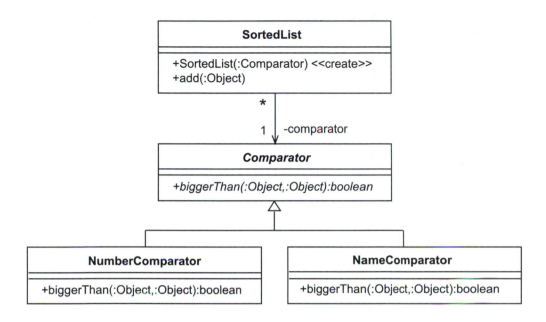

**Figure 11.22: Class diagram for a SortedList using the Strategy pattern**

has an add method as before, but now biggerThan is inside an interface called Comparator. Comparator represents an object that knows how to compare two values of a similar type: it has subclasses for each type of object that we're interested in (NumberComparator and NameComparator). Each SortedList must have a Comparator available when objects are added. Therefore, we give SortedList a comparator attribute, set by the constructor. Now, if we want to build a sorted list of numbers we do the following (see the sequence of messages in Figure 11.23):

```
Comparator c = new NumberComparator();
SortedList l = new SortedList(c);
l.add(aNumber);
l.add(anotherNumber);
```

If we want sorted names instead, all we have to do is:

```
Comparator c = new NameComparator();
SortedList l = new SortedList(c);
l.add(aName);
l.add(anotherName);
```

The nice thing about Strategy is that it allows client programmers to implement their own strategies without touching the SortedList class at all. For example, if we want a sorted list of WeddingGift objects, we would implement our own WeddingGiftComparator with a biggerThan method that compares prices. It's as if the context is an incomplete jigsaw to which anyone can add the last piece.

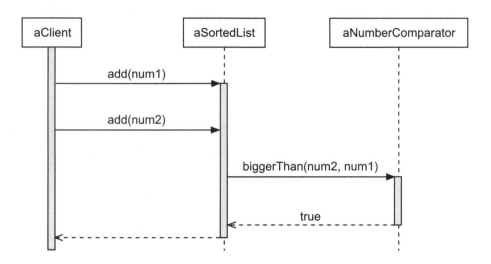

**Figure 11.23: SortedList sequence diagram**

Of course, the **insertion sort** described in our SortedList example is horribly slow. It would be much faster to jump to the middle of the list to begin with: if we hadn't gone far enough, we would then jump half way towards the end; if we had gone too far, we would jump half way towards the beginning; we would repeat this process until we found the correct location. This algorithm is called a **binary chop search**. It was omitted from our earlier discussion because it would just have got in the way.

## 11.3.10 Flyweight

Use sharing to support large numbers of fine-grained objects efficiently. [Gamma *et al.* 95]

**Flyweight** is a simple pattern that allows client programmers to think that they're using a factory method to create their own object, when 'their' object is actually being shared by multiple clients. Normally, this is done to save memory and improve performance, by avoiding the creation of many equivalent objects.

For example, if we wrote an application that dealt with people's first names, we would discover that many people had the same first name. Why should we create hundreds of instances of the name 'Sam' when we could create just one object, with multiple references to it? The two alternatives are shown in Figure 11.24. What we need is a cache, or **pool**, of names that have already been created. Thus, rather than creating a name every time we needed one, we could look in the pool to see if one already existed; if it did, we could use it; if it didn't, we could create a new one, add it to the pool and then use it (see Figure 11.25).

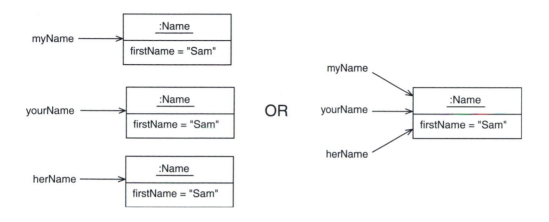

**Figure 11.24: To share or not to share**

Ideally, we would like the complexities of searching the pool and creating a new object to be hidden from client programmers: a Factory Method is ideal for this. Figure 11.26 shows a generic Flyweight alongside one that is specific to the name example.

Flyweights don't have to be 100% shared: if we make the clients store some of the state externally and then pass it back in as a parameter to every flyweight message, we have a hybrid. To take a trivial example, let's assume that we want to add a person's second initial to their first name. If we added the second initial to the flyweight itself, we would lose most of the sharing ('Sam J.' is far less common than 'Sam'). However, if we arrange for the clients themselves to manage the second initials, as long as the second initial is passed to the flyweight as a parameter to every message, the flyweight will still have all the information it needs. For example, in the following Java code fragment, we're performing some action if the first name or the second initial contains the letter 'j':

```java
public class Name {
    ...
    public boolean containsLetter(char letter, char secondInitial) {
        String namePlusSecondInitial = givenName +  secondInitial;
        return namePlusSecondInitial.containsIgnoringCase(letter);
    }...
}

Name n = aNameFactory.createName("Sam");
char secondInitial = 'J';
if (n.containsLetter('j', secondInitial)) { ...
```

State inside a Flyweight is referred to as **intrinsic**, while state managed externally, by the client, is **extrinsic**. The Flyweight pattern is particularly appropriate, and easiest to implement, when the flyweight's state is immutable (read-only), otherwise we tend to get

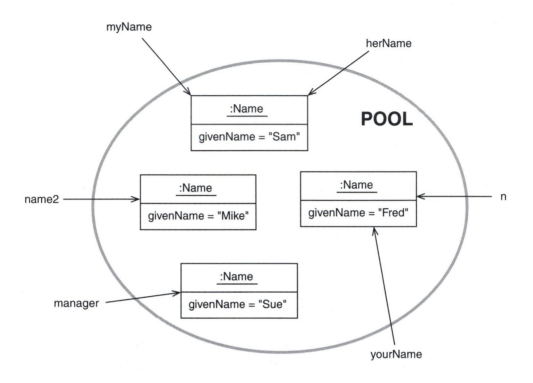

**Figure 11.25: Sharing objects in a pool**

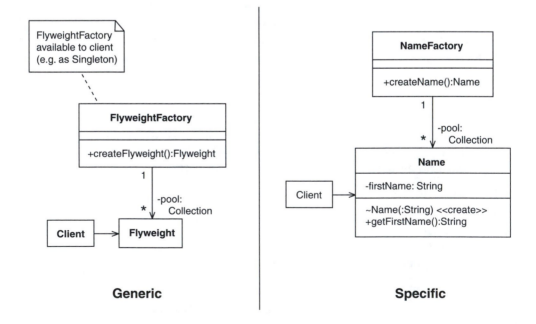

**Figure 11.26: Flyweight class diagrams**

more extrinsic state and less sharing. For example, consider changing the second character of the name 'Sam' to 'i'; would we really want to affect all other uses of the name?

## 11.3.11 Composite

Compose objects into tree structures to represent part–whole hierarchies. Composite lets clients treat individual objects and compositions of objects uniformly. [Gamma *et al.* 95]

A part–whole hierarchy is another name for a composition or an aggregation. Despite its name, **Composite** doesn't describe a composition in the strict UML sense; instead, it describes a design that we can use to *implement* an aggregation or a composition. Thus, Composite allows us to build a hierarchy of objects with an arbitrary number of levels. As an added bonus, Composite allows us to treat all levels of the hierarchy in the same way – this would allow us to, say, remove an entire section just as easily as we could remove a single piece.

Figure 11.27 shows one popular form of Composite. Here, we have an abstract class called Component that represents part of the hierarchical structure. Underneath that, we have the class Basic that represents the smallest possible component (one that can't contain any other components). Alongside Basic is the Composite class that represents a component that can contain other Components (hence the link back to Component). Because Composite can contain *any* type of Component – Composite or Basic – we can build any number of levels, rather than just two.

The use of aggregation with a * multiplicity may look a little odd at first, but there are three good reasons: firstly, a Basic component doesn't have to be inside a Composite at all (although it often is); secondly, although it would be a rare situation, the pattern itself doesn't prevent us from putting a Component inside more than one Composite at a time (if it did, the relationship might have been a UML composition); thirdly, the pattern doesn't specify that a Component should die when its Composite dies (although it often will) – shared death is another requirement for UML composition.

Because Composite has a link back up the hierarchy, it is often referred to as **recursive** (as in **recursive composition**). Recursive, in computing terms, means going around again and again. The end result is a bit like a Russian doll: the biggest doll has a smaller doll inside it, which has a smaller doll inside it, which has a smaller doll inside it, until, eventually, we get to the smallest, basic, doll. Unlike the Russian doll, however, each Composite can contain *any number of* components – this allows us to build broad hierarchies, with any number of children below each parent (three floors in a house, five rooms on each floor, four walls in each room).

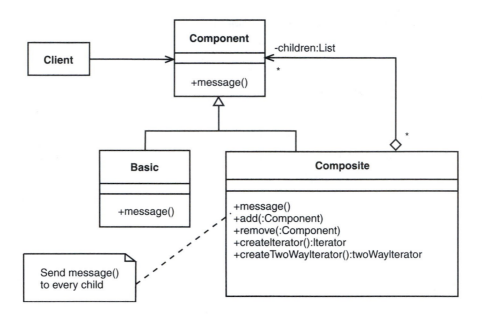

**Figure 11.27: Composite class diagram**

Figure 11.28 shows two hierarchies described by the generic Composite model. Here's how we might use Java to build hierarchy A:

```
Component small = new Component(), medium = new Component(),
   large = new Component();

Basic atom1 = new Atom(), atom2 = new Atom(),
   atom3 = new Atom(), atom4 = new Atom();

small.add(atom1);
small.add(atom2);

medium.add(small);
medium.add(atom3);

large.add(atom4);
large.add(medium);
```

The children in the Composite examples are ordered, left to right: generally, it's a good idea to preserve the order in which components are added, in case it's important to the client programmer. A createIterator method is provided which returns an instance of the Iterator pattern. For completeness, a createTwoWayIterator method is provided, to allow clients to iterate backwards.

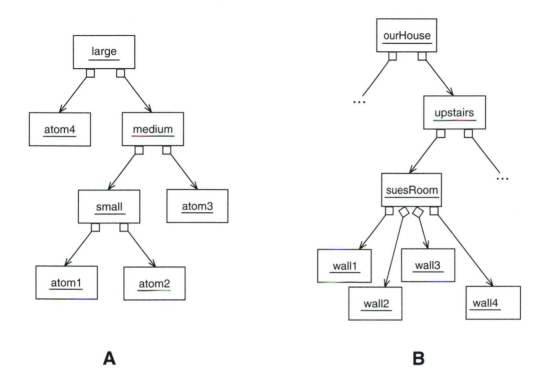

**A**                                        **B**

**Figure 11.28: Composite object diagrams**

Apart from dealing with the hierarchical structure, Composite also 'lets clients treat individual objects and compositions of objects uniformly'. In design terms, this means that any message at the Component level will also appear at the Basic and Composite levels, as is the case with message in Figure 11.27. A surprising (and pleasing) effect of the recursive nature of Composite, is that we can simply get message on Composite to pass the message on to its children. To see how this works, consider the house example in Figure 11.28B. If pink were our favorite color, we could paint every wall in the house pink. To do this, we would send the message paint("Pink") to ourHouse; ourHouse would send paint("Pink") to each floor in turn, up to and including upstairs; the floors would send paint("Pink") to the rooms; finally, paint("Pink") would be sent by the rooms to the walls; since the walls are basic objects, they would do the actual work. Ultimately, a single message sent by the client programmer results in every wall in the house turning pink. (To convince yourself of this, try drawing the messages on a sequence diagram.)

You may be wondering at this point what the difference is between collections and composites, especially since iterators have cropped up in our discussion. While it's true that collections and composites both contain objects, it turns out that most clients of collection classes are happy with four basic classes (and maybe sorted versions too):

- Bag: Unordered objects with duplicates (not available in Java).
- Set: Unordered objects without duplicates.
- List: Objects in a specified order.
- Map: A lookup table that needs a key to add or remove an object.

The common factor between these classes is that client programmers don't have to *build* the structure; they simply add and remove objects. (Okay, in the case of List, they do have to specify the position of each object but they don't have to create the object holders or arrange them side by side.) The Composite class, in contrast, forces the client programmer to build the structure piece by piece, explicitly combining small pieces into larger ones to produce some tree-like structure. In practice, we tend to use the Composite pattern if the client wants to or must handle the structure explicitly (because it could not have been determined beforehand) or if the client wants the convenience of a top-level message that gets sent to all children. (Can you think of a way of using Strategy to allow collection classes to send a top-level message to all children?)

Composite is sometimes used as part of the internal implementation of collection classes, to build an index, for example. Another area where you may encounter the Composite pattern is in user interfaces, since GUIs are usually treated as hierarchies of components.

## 11.3.12 Proxy

Provide a surrogate or placeholder for another object to control access to it. [Gamma *et al.* 95]

**Proxy** involves one object (the **proxy**) interposing itself between a client and another object (the **real subject**), as illustrated in the lower diagram in Figure 11.29. We might do this for any number of reasons, such as security control, lazy initialization or remote access. In the example illustrated, clients send message to the proxy which passes the message on to the real subject (which might involve checking security permissions, creating the real subject the first time around, or performing the network communication). Although not strictly necessary, it's a good idea to introduce an interface – Subject, for example – that lists the messages appearing on RealSubject and Proxy. For one thing, this makes sure that the interfaces of the proxy and the real subject are kept in step; secondly, it's reasonable from a modeling point of view, because the proxy and the real subject do the same thing.

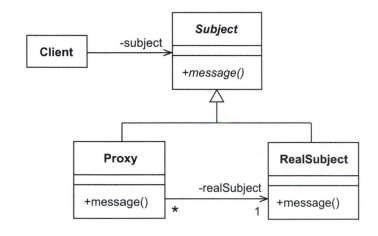

**Figure 11.29: Proxy class and object diagrams**

Probably the most common use of Proxy is in the area of **network programming**, which involves one piece of code invoking another piece of code that resides on a separate machine, with some kind of network between them. In the field of object technology, this mechanism has become a well-known part of frameworks such as CORBA, J2EE and .Net.

In object-oriented programs, the only way we can run a piece of code is to send a message to an object. But how do we send a message to an object that lives on a different machine? The answer is that we provide a local proxy that has the same interface as the remote object but whose methods perform the network communication for us. This way, the client is shielded from the complexities of the network communication.

Using a proxy to send a remote message is illustrated in Figure 11.30 (which combines elements of a deployment diagram and a communication diagram). Here, we have a remote system for looking up an employee's e-mail address by payroll number. The server machine has a process containing a ContactsImpl, called s, which waits for incoming client requests. The client machine has a process containing a ContactsClient, called c, and a ContactsProxy, called p, with the same interface as s. When c wants an e-mail address, it sends lookup to p, which does whatever it takes to pass the message on to s (create a communication channel, identify the type of message, pass on the parameters, and wait for the response). On the

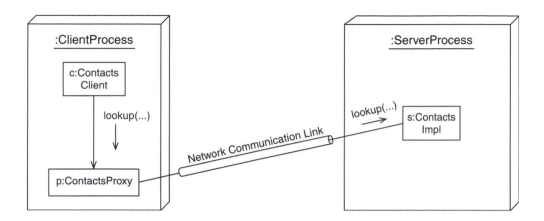

**Figure 11.30: Remote object implemented using Proxy**

server side, some complementary code (not shown) receives the incoming request and passes it on to s as a normal message. When s receives the message, it executes its lookup method, in exactly the same way as if the message had originated locally. When s has finished, the reply is returned to p. On receiving the reply, p completes its lookup method and returns the result to c.

The classes and interfaces involved in this proxy example are shown in Figure 11.31. In this figure, unlike most design-level class diagrams, the association between the ContactsClient and the ContactsImpl is not navigable. This is because, in the case of a remote object, the proxy doesn't have a physical pointer to the real subject: it has a reference to the communication channel, or to some kind of address for the subject (if it doesn't want to keep the communication channel open all the time).

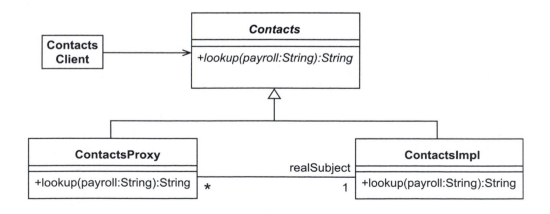

**Figure 11.31: Remote object class diagram**

# 11.4 USING PATTERNS

As you use patterns more and more, you will find that they become second nature for particular tasks, especially well-understood tasks such as creating objects (factories), remote objects (proxies) and complex life cycles (states). For other tasks, you have to watch out for areas where they might be useful. You will also find yourself using several patterns together to accomplish a single task (we saw an example of this when Factory Method was used as part of Iterator).

# 11.5 DISCOVERING, COMBINING AND ADAPTING PATTERNS

Although there is no definitive advice on how to do discover and combine patterns, it's a good idea to start by practicing with the patterns outlined in this chapter. Then, look for how patterns have been used in the code around you, in libraries and frameworks and in code written by your colleagues. Be sure to keep returning to [Gamma *et al.* 95] and the other resources mentioned in this chapter in order to expand your knowledge. There's a lot to absorb but the end result is better productivity, higher quality code and more peace of mind.

One thing that you will discover quickly is that patterns need to be adapted to each particular use. Here are some of the reasons for this:

- Language translation: The pattern you started with may not be implemented in your chosen programming language. All programming languages, even object-oriented ones, have differences. Some differences are large (such as how pure or hybrid the language is) and some are small (for example, the access protections available for messages), but the standard patterns will have to be modified to suit each language.
- Difference of opinion: For each design problem, there is more than one solution. Just because a pattern has been produced by an expert, or a group of experts, doesn't mean that it's perfect. Once you fully understand a pattern, feel free to change it, especially as you become more expert.
- Difference in style: Design and coding styles can come from many sources: experience, company coding guidelines, requirements of a library or framework, and so on. If a pattern doesn't fit the style that your project uses, adapt it. (Often, doing things the *same* way as those around you is more important than doing things in a *better* way – consider the benefits of reuse and easier maintenance.)
- Different problem: Each pattern is as general as possible – some of the class models presented here would never be used as they are. For example, in the Observer pattern, we had the Observer, Subject, ConcreteObserver and ConcreteSubject classes; we would not

expect to see any real application with classes called ConcreteObserver and ConcreteSubject. No pattern will fit your problem exactly.

- Composition, inheritance and multiple inheritance: Languages, and developers, differ in the way they use inheritance and composition. You may find yourself performing transformations from one representation to another, while trying to keep the overall effect of the pattern the same.
- Consequences: Every good pattern description includes consequences, areas where the author has identified particular benefits, shortcomings and trade-offs of using the pattern. (No pattern is perfect, after all.) As a result of this advice, you may decide that you prefer different trade-offs.
- Clarity: Sometimes, a full-blown pattern with all the extras can be more complex than you require. A little simplification can be beneficial (especially in a learning context).

All of these factors can be observed to some extent in the pattern descriptions given in this chapter. Language translation, at least, was necessary because the notation used here is UML and the programming language is Java, rather than the combination of OMT and C++/Smalltalk used in [Gamma *et al.* 95].

   Although the Observer pattern is undoubtedly a good idea, it has certain drawbacks in its simplest form – Figure 11.32 shows an adaption of Observer, reworked to deal with these shortcomings.

- Whenever there is a change in the state of the subject, update is called. An observer may read attributes that haven't changed and refresh itself unnecessarily.
  In the adapted pattern, the client specifies during registration which attribute the Observer is interested in, using the new parameter a (of course, the Observer can be registered for more than one attribute). The notify method also takes an a parameter: it only notifies Observer objects that have been registered for changes to a. Observers can observe some attributes and ignore others.
- The observer has to return to the subject to find out what the changes were, which involves more communication.
  In the adapted pattern, the update method takes the new value of the attribute as a parameter. Thus, the Observer doesn't have to return to the Subject to use a getter.
- The observer can observe only one subject.
  In the adapted pattern, the Subject is passed as a parameter to update. This allows the Observer to be registered with any number of subjects while still being able to identify them.

When using this modified form of Observer, the subject must notify observers when derived attributes change, not just stored attributes.

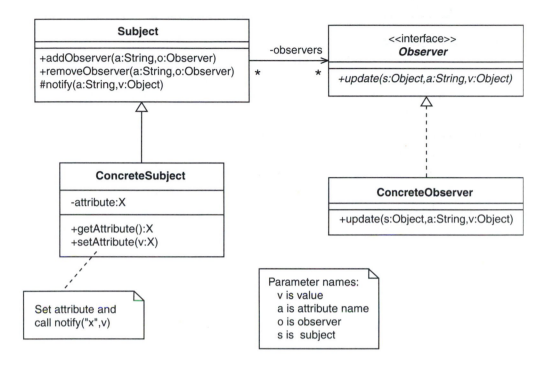

**Figure 11.32: Class diagram for an improved Observer pattern**

## Case Study

*Patterns in iCoot*

Let's see what impact the patterns described have on the iCoot system:

- Observer is used on the client side by the GUI interfaces (both desktop and mobile-device versions). These interfaces use a two-layer model consisting of GUILayer and ControlLayer – all upward communication uses Observer in its Java form, **event delegation**. In event delegation, all notifications take the form of **events** broadcast to **listeners**. Some events signal a change in attribute values and some, **pure events** such as 'logon succeeded', do not.
- Singleton is used on the server side where one **home** per entity manages the creation and finding of entities. Some homes also have general utility methods such as carModelHome.findEngineSizes().
- Multiton is not used. Despite the recent addition of multitons to the syntax of Java, it is still common to use public class constants of type int as an alternative, as in CarColor.MIDNIGHT_BLUE. (A class constant is a read-only (i.e. final) class field.)
- Iterator is used on the client and the server for all access to List objects.

**Case Study (cont'd)**

- Factory Method is used widely on the client and the server. For example, when the business layer needs to create an entity that contains data from the database, a factory method on the home is used: CustomerHome.getInstance().create("Fred Bloggs", "02723359853", 0).
- Abstract Factory is not used, although, in principle the homes might inherit from a common superclass.
- State is used to represent the state machine for a Reservation.
- Facade is used to encapsulate layers. The cleanest example is the ServerLayer objects which hide the complexity of the BusinessLayer from clients.
- Adapter is used in the Java-based clients to connect GUI components, which expect to send messages to event listeners, with controller objects, which have a generic interface.
- In the next increment, Strategy will be used in user interfaces to allow retrieved cars to be sorted according to attributes selected by the user.
- Template Method is used wherever possible in abstract classes to share logic between subclasses (to improve the quality of code, make maintenance easier and reduce the effort required).
- Flyweight is used on the server, where the business layer maintains a cache of entities populated with data from the database. Flyweight is used to avoid duplication of the data within the server process and to prevent different parts of the application working with different versions of the same data.
- Proxy is used in the Java-based clients. The ControlLayer uses proxies to access the facades in the ServerLayer (passing lightweight copies backwards and forwards).
- Composite is used in the GUI clients. It is part of the standard Swing facilities for constructing component trees.

# 11.6 SUMMARY

In this chapter, we looked at:

- How software developers use design patterns to avoid duplicating effort by applying the knowledge and experience of other developers to a particular problem. A pattern describes a particular way of doing something that has proved effective in real world projects.

- How patterns are used to record knowledge, to document solutions and to aid reuse.

- The pattern template proposed in [Gamma *et al.* 95].

- 14 of the most important patterns, to provide you with a good grounding and to whet your appetite.

- The practical implications of using patterns: how to discover and combine patterns and how to adapt them to your particular problem.

# FURTHER READING

The original Gang of Four book [Gamma *et al.* 95] is invaluable reference material despite the fact that the book is illustrated using OMT, C++ and Smalltalk. It contains a lot of extra discussion and advice.

Since the publication of the original book, many more books and research papers have been produced, and many more areas of interest have been explored. For further reading on pattern history and the state of the art, try the following Web sites: www.hillside.net and www.patterndigest.com.

For a comprehensive description of how to implement patterns in Java, see [Grand 02] and [Grand 99].

# 12

## Specifying the Interfaces of Classes

In this chapter, we consider the code specification process, traditionally the last development phase before implementation. Specification allows us to write down how our software should behave in a way that is less ambiguous and more precise than anything we've used so far.

# Learning Objectives

**Understand what a specification is and why we might want to produce one.**

•

**Understand the distinction between formal and informal specifications.**

**Write specifications in an object-oriented manner.**

•

**Understand the Design by Contract philosophy.**

•

**Use specifications and Design by Contract in Java.**

# Chapter Outline

# 12.1 INTRODUCTION

Although, in one sense, we've been specifying the behavior of our software at all the stages (from system use cases all the way through to the database schema), the discussion here relates to the interfaces of the system components, and classes in particular.

So why do we write a specification? Here are some good reasons:

- To remove the ambiguity remaining after earlier phases: Ambiguity means that artifacts can be read more than one way. Use cases are typically written in natural language, which is notoriously vague; analysis is not meant to dictate to the designer how the code should actually be implemented, so the analysis artifacts don't match the final code exactly; as for design, we may have specified exactly which classes are to be written and what their messages and fields should be but there may be no documentation of how the messages should work together or what constitutes a legal message parameter, a legal field value or other such detail.

- To improve our understanding of the implementation: The more we understand our design, the easier it will be to implement. Writing a specification requires us to think hard about our design, so we end up with a better understanding.

- To increase our confidence that the system will work: Often, in attempting to write down exactly how our software should behave, we discover that we've missed something out or assumed something that's impossible, or made some other human error. Thus, specification allows us to spot mistakes sooner than if we plough straight on into implementation.

- To help us debug our software: When our software misbehaves, we can check whether the implementation matches the specification. Thus, we have a starting point for identifying and removing faults.

- To help us test our software: A specification describes how our software must behave and a test verifies that our software behaves as described. Thus, tests can be used to check that our software fits the specification. Tests based on system use cases verify that we have produced a system that meets the system requirements. Specification-based testing is essential for libraries, patterns, frameworks and reusable objects, because none of these involve an actual system.

- To help us modify our software: If we decide to modify our system in some way – by adding functionality, for example – we can check that the modification does not break the specification. If the specification would be broken, the proposed modification is incompatible with the current system (or we have an error in the specification). Rather than just go ahead and break the specification, we should look at the proposed change more carefully.

- To allow us to pass the implementation task on to other developers: Although the other developers are still going to have to contact us to clarify detail, they should need to do so less often.
- To provide better documentation: Better documentation leads to easier maintenance, more reuse and less misuse.

# 12.2 WHAT IS A SPECIFICATION?

In general terms, a specification is a complete, unambiguous description of the required behavior of a piece of software. The piece of software in question could be an entire system, a subsystem, a layer, a class or a function. Although we would like our specification to be complete and unambiguous, that's not always practical or possible. However, even imperfect specifications have their uses (and they're better than nothing).

A specification describes one or more boundaries. For example, the boundary of a function library consists of the signatures (names, return types and parameter types) of its functions and of its global data values; the boundary of an object consists of its messages and its attributes; the boundary of a class (subtly different to the boundary of an object) consists of its class messages and class attributes. Although attributes logically sit on the boundary, we expect them to be accessed by object and class messages.

If we consider that each boundary has a client on one side and a supplier on the other, a specification describes:

- What information the client can pass over the boundary and when they're allowed to pass it; for example, the client may only be able to pass new address information to a customer object once a transaction has been started.
- What information the client can retrieve from the boundary and when they're allowed to retrieve it; for example, the client may only be able to retrieve a list of books for sale from a book server once it has logged on.
- When an event will be broadcast to registered clients and what information the clients will receive; for example, in a distributed chat system, every client will be notified of the name of each new client that joins the chat room.
- The legal states of the information managed by the boundary; for example, a collection object may state that it will never contain a negative number of objects.

Most of the time, a specification is concerned with the public boundary of a piece of software. However, we can equally well specify the nature of internal boundaries. As an example, consider a function library that provides sorting facilities for collection structures. Such a library might have a reusable `swap` function for swapping two values in a collection. It's unlikely that the `swap` function would be part of the public interface of the sorting library because it's an implementation detail; however, we could still specify its behavior – we could state, for example, that after the function has been called, the left-hand value will occupy the location previously occupied by the right-hand value, and vice versa.

There are two varieties of specification: a **formal specification** is scientific and rigorous; an **informal specification** is pragmatic and partial, but no less useful.

# 12.3 FORMAL SPECIFICATION

For the most part, software development is an imprecise activity. Historically, software has been developed more in the hope than in the certainty that it will do what it's supposed to do. This is because there is no science to back it up, unlike disciplines such as civil engineering or hardware engineering, which are backed by mechanics and Quantum theory. Most good software is a result of human ingenuity, experience, guess work, reuse and testing.

This is fine for noncritical applications such as word processors and consumer operating systems. We tolerate a word processor occasionally crashing in the middle of an edit (this is why we have features such as auto-save). We expect a consumer operating system to crash sometimes, leaving us with no alternative but to reboot (which is why system administrators run automated backups). We may lose time, we may get frustrated and angry, but no-one's life is endangered. The advantages of being able to use computers at all generally outweigh the disadvantages of those computers being imperfect: on the whole, we're more productive than if we had no computers at all.

However, some situations call for perfect, or near-perfect, reliability. **Safety-critical** systems are a good example – these include the software at the heart of nuclear power stations, air traffic control systems, fly-by-wire aircraft and hospital equipment. We can't afford to let such systems (or their operating systems) fail. In reality, we can't guarantee 100% reliability, because that would be too difficult or too expensive or would require knowledge of every possible abnormal condition. Instead, we settle for either a very long time between failures (for example, a control system in a nuclear power station may be acceptable if it makes a mistake, on average, less than once in a trillion years) or better reliability than a human (for example, a fly-by-wire plane may be acceptable if it makes one-tenth of the mistakes of a human pilot).

One way to improve reliability is to replicate hardware or software. For example, we could install three computers to control a fly-by-wire plane. Each computer would use different hardware, a different operating system and software developed by a different team. We could arrange these three computers in a voting system, where any command would be ignored by the plane unless it came simultaneously from at least two of the computers. Theory suggests that, using such techniques, we can make failure very unlikely. (We still can't be perfect, because two of the computers could fail in the same way at the same time, causing the plane to follow an incorrect command.) Further discussion of this kind of reliability assurance is beyond the scope of this book.

Another way to improve reliability involves trying to prove, in the mathematical sense, that the software is **correct** (that it does what it's supposed to do). This involves three steps:

1. Produce a **formal specification**, in a mathematical language, that describes how the software should behave.
2. Prove that the specification is feasible – i.e. that it has no logical contradictions or impossibilities.
3. Prove that the software conforms to the specification.

Examples of formal specification languages are **Vienna Development Method (VDM)** (originally from IBM Vienna), **Z** (originally from Oxford University) and **Object Constraint Language (OCL)** [OMG 03b], which is part of UML.

For example, if we want to write a formal specification for the behavior of a *squareRoot()* function, here are some things that we might want to say about it:

- The input value must be positive. (Assuming noncomplex numbers.)
- The square of the result will be equal to the input value. (This is a common trick when specifying a reversible function: applying the inverse function to the result must yield the input value.)
- The result will be positive. (Remember that $(2 \times 2 = 4)$ and also $(-2 \times -2 = 4)$, so 4 has two square roots; we choose to return the *positive* square root.)

Here's how we can specify the boundary conditions of *squareRoot()* in VDM:

*squareRoot*$(x : R)$ $y : R$

**pre** $x \geq 0$

**post** $(y^2 = x) \land (y \geq 0)$

where $R$ stands for **real numbers**, **pre** stands for **precondition** (something that must be true *before* the function can be invoked) and **post** stands for **postcondition** (something that will be true *after* the function has been invoked). Every logical expression in a specification is referred to as an **assertion** (so $y \geq 0$ asserts that $y$ will be greater than or equal to 0). Even if you do not know VDM, it's easy to see that the specification above reads as:

The *squareRoot()* function takes a real number $x$ as parameter and returns a real number $y$. For correct operation, the function requires that $x$ is greater than or equal to 0. If the precondition is met, the function guarantees that $y$ squared will be equal to $x$ and that $y$ will be greater than or equal to 0.

Thus, we can specify the exact behavior of *squareRoot*() without saying anything about its implementation.

Formal specification is a discipline that requires a great deal of training and skill. It is also a lengthy process. Sometimes, it's possible to use a computer to validate a specification (**automated theorem proving**). Under very limited conditions, we may even be able to verify that an implementation matches the specification. However, no computer could write the specification itself.

Even if you can rely on the mathematics of the formal specification and on your software implementation, you can't rely on the operating system, the hardware or the compiler. For this reason, safety-critical software is sometimes implemented in assembly language and then deployed on a cut-down operating system, so that we have a chance of proving that the end result is correct. (Even this doesn't stop cosmic rays firing through a chip and flipping a bit from 1 to 0, so we need external fail-safes too.) We also can't prove that the formal specification meets the system requirements, especially since the latter usually start out as natural language and change subtly over time.

Because formal specifications are so difficult and time-consuming to produce and to use, they're normally only employed for safety-critical systems and those that require advanced reliability techniques, such as voting systems. Although formal specifications are impractical for the software industry as a whole, we can still apply the underlying principles and get many of the benefits. Colloquially, the techniques described in the rest of this chapter are referred to as **informal specification**. With the help of formal specification theory, we can at least be clear about what an informal specification should contain.

# 12.4 INFORMAL SPECIFICATION

All programmers use informal specifications to a certain extent – adding a comment to a function for the benefit of other programmers is a simple example. A function comment will describe some or all of the information in the following list:

- when the client can call the function
- what parameters should be passed
- what the function does
- what kind of result is returned (type and value)
- what effect the function has on global data
- what action the function takes if there is a problem

Such information applies equally to subroutines, procedures and methods, since these are just variations on the basic idea of a function.

Usually, a function comment won't say anything about the internal implementation – just like any other form of specification, the comment only describes the conditions at the boundary. Occasionally a comment *will* say something about the implementation, but only when necessary and only in abstract terms. For example, it would be useful for a client programmer to be told the time/space trade-off of a particular sort function, such as This function executes at n-log-n speed and requires 2n internal locations for processing.

The following piece of C code (C looks a lot like Java) contains a comment that is used as an informal specification of the *squareRoot* function:

```
/*
   Returns the positive square root of x.
   Preconditions: x >= 0.
 */
float squareRoot(float x);
```

Anyone reading this comment knows that they will get back the positive square root of x as long as they provide a positive x.

The term precondition should be familiar to most programmers, or easy for them to work out. If you're concerned about maximum readability, you could use Requires that: instead of Preconditions: and Ensures that: instead of Postconditions:; or you could write the preconditions and postconditions in natural language. The informal specification above is incomplete, unlike the formal VDM version that we saw earlier: for example, we have said nothing about the square of the result being equal to the parameter. In the next section, we will see why this particular postcondition is not as straightforward in programming as it may seem.

A function signature (name, return type, parameter types) contains a lot of information in its own right so it could form part of the informal specification. For example, float squareRoot(float x) implies that the function takes a float value and returns a float value; the result will be the square root of the parameter. However, even an informal specification should not rely on implied information, hence the explicit comment. Since comments and signatures can be included in a number of UML artifacts, source code is not the only place where informal specifications can appear.

Another kind of informal specification that we've encountered in this book is the use case. Each use case describes some or all of the following information:

- when the use case can be used (preconditions)
- what the use case does (steps and postconditions)
- what effect the use case has on the system (steps and postconditions)
- what happens in abnormal cases

Thus, since use cases describe everything an external actor needs to know in order to use the system properly, they're similar to function comments. This should be no surprise since, by definition, a use case is supposed to describe a boundary – the system boundary in this case. For the purposes of this chapter, we're interested in the specification that takes place between subsystem design and implementation, so let's leave use cases for now.

Some programming languages, notably Eiffel, have a special syntax for recording informal specifications in source code, separate from comments.

# 12.5 DYNAMIC CHECKING

Authors of formal specifications use a mathematical notation that is separate from the software implementation. A formal specifier may be able to prove that the specification they produce has no logical errors. In limited circumstances, they may even be able to prove that a particular software implementation conforms to the specification. But, generally, formal specifiers rely on programmers using their knowledge and intuition to produce code that conforms to the specification.

The informal approach, in contrast, includes a pragmatic technique that we can call **dynamic checking**. A dynamic check is code embedded in our implementation that verifies that the software is behaving itself (i.e. that it's not breaking the specification). To see how a dynamic check might work, consider the square root function again. Below is a C implementation of this function (with the calculations omitted):

```
/*
   Returns the positive square root of x.
   Precondition: x >= 0.
*/
float squareRoot(float x) {
   if (x < 0) {
      fail("squareRoot", "Parameter x can't be negative");
   }
   ... /* Code to calculate y */
   return y;
}
```

Inside this function, we can see a piece of code that checks that the precondition x >= 0 has been met – if it hasn't, the program gives up. For convenience, a fail function has been provided that prints the function name and the error message and then stops the program (using the C library function exit). (Some languages provide a more elegant way of signaling failure using **exception handling**, but the facilities vary enormously.)

The client programmer is now protected from themselves: most of the time, the client calls squareRoot with a positive number and the function quietly succeeds; however, on the rare occasion that the client calls squareRoot with a negative number, it is told that the program can't continue until the problem is fixed.

You may be thinking that our squareRoot function is performing ordinary error-checking. It is certainly doing something that programmers frequently do, regardless of whether or not they understand the specification process. The interesting point, as far as we're concerned, is that this piece of error-checking code has only been put there in order to verify that the client programmer has not broken the specification – if they do break the specification, they have a fault in their code.

Dynamic checking only makes sense for informal specifications, not formal ones. There are many reasons for this, some of which are listed below:

- The aim of formal specification is to guarantee that the implementation doesn't violate the specification. With dynamic checking, in contrast, we accept that implementations tend to contain faults, so we look for violations at run time.
- Some formal requirements can't feasibly be checked. The fact that we can't check something is no reason to leave it out of a formal specification.
- Some formal requirements can't be expressed using **imperative** code. (An imperative programming language, by far the most common type, is one where the programmer has to tell the computer exactly what to do; with a **declarative** programming language, the programmer simply states what the outcome should be.) Again, such requirements should still be included in the formal specification.
- Some formal requirements can't be expressed accurately as imperative code. For example, in the squareRoot case, we would like to specify that the result returned by the function really is the square root. One way to do this is to specify that the square of the result is equal to the parameter, as in For result y, (y * y) == x. But imperative arithmetic is imprecise: squareRoot(4.0) probably returns 2.0, but squareRoot(3.79512) might return 1.94811, a number that is not *exactly* correct.

To deal with inaccuracy, how could we say that a result will be *close* to some value? Well, there's a whole branch of computing called **numerical methods** devoted to this kind of problem. To apply numerical methods, we would need to calculate a **maximum possible error** and use that in our specification.

In the squareRoot example, if we encapsulate the maximum possible error inside a function called squareRootError and have access to a pos function that returns the positive value of its parameter, we can specify For result y, pos((y * y) - x) <= squareRootError(). This specification can be added to the function comment and encoded as a check at the end:

```
/*
    Returns the positive square root of x.
    Preconditions: x >= 0.
    Postconditions: For result y,
```

```
            (y >= 0) and pos((y * y) - x) <= squareRootError()).
*/
float squareRoot(float x) {
   if (x < 0) {
      fail("squareRoot", "Parameter x can't be negative");
   }
   ... /* Code to calculate y */
   if (y < 0) {
      fail("squareRoot", "Calculation gave negative result");
   }
   if (pos((y * y) - x) > squareRootError()) {
      fail("squareRoot", "Calculation was inaccurate");
   }
   return y;
}
```

Now, rather than just protecting the client programmer from faults in their own code, we're guarding against faults in our code too.

If we aren't able to calculate a value for the maximum possible error (or if we decide that it is too much trouble), we should still add the specification to the comment as natural language:

```
   ...
   The square of the result is equal to x,
      subject to the accuracy of the current platform.
*/
```

# 12.6 OBJECT-ORIENTED SPECIFICATION

Formal specification languages such as VDM were originally designed to be used with structured software development. Some of these languages have since been extended to work with object-oriented languages. Others, such as OCL, have been designed specifically for object-oriented software development. The main difference between a structured notation and an object-oriented notation is that the latter uses any number of **class scopes** rather than a single **global scope**. (The term **scope** means name space, partition, subarea, or anything else that you can put a fence around.)

An object-oriented specification is simpler than a procedural specification, because all rules appear alongside their related concept (the class or object in question). An object-oriented specification language must allow us to assert:

- when a message can legally be sent to an object (**message preconditions**, expressed in terms of public attributes)

- the valid parameters for each message (**message preconditions**)
- the effect a message has on the receiving object (**message postconditions**, expressed in terms of public attributes)
- the valid replies from each message (**message postconditions**)
- the conditions that are always met by the object (**class invariants**, conditions that will always be true for instances of the class, expressed in terms of public attributes)

As well as objects, object attributes and object messages, we also have classes, class attributes and class messages; thus, the five categories above can also be applied to classes, although the notation usually makes it difficult to tell the difference.

As an example, consider a Container class with an add message. Let's assume that we want to assert the following:

- Precondition: An object reference passed to the add message must not be null.
- Precondition: An object passed to the add message must not already be in the Container.
- Postcondition: After the add message, the Container will have one more object than it had before.
- Postcondition: After the add message, the Container will contain the object that was passed in as a parameter.
- Invariant: The Container always contains a positive number of objects.

In the next two sections, we'll see how to express the Container assertions in OCL, a formal specification language, and in Eiffel, an imperative programming language that includes syntax for informal specifications.

## 12.6.1 Formal Specification in OCL

OCL is UML's formal specification language, so it fits well with object-oriented methodologies that use UML as their notation. For the Container example, we could use the following fragment of OCL (in which the contains method returns true if and only if the receiver contains o):

```
context Container::
   add(o:Object)
      pre: (o <> null) and not contains(o)
      post: contains(o) and (size = size@pre + 1)
context Container::
   inv: size >= 0
```

OCL allows us to connect assertions to a class using the context keyword, which means that we can also refer to global functions and global data in our specifications, for the sake of hybrid languages such as C++. Postconditions often need to refer to the value of an attribute *before* the method is executed – this allows us to talk about the effect that a method has on the receiver's attributes. In this case, size@pre refers to the value of size before add is executed. The OCL fragment above can be read as:

> When sending the add message to a Container, the parameter o must be non-null and o must not already be in the container. Once the method has completed, the container will contain o and the size of the container will be one more than it was before. The size of a Container is always greater than or equal to 0.

## 12.6.2 Informal Specification in Eiffel

Eiffel, a language developed by Bertrand Meyer in the mid-1980s [Meyer 90], was designed with informal, dynamically-checkable specifications in mind. Eiffel programmers can put assertions in the source code itself, but separate from the comments and the implementation code: the assertions are recognized by the Eiffel compiler as part of the syntax. Eiffel uses require instead of pre, ensure instead of post and old instead of @pre. For the Container example, we could use the following fragment of Eiffel:

```
class CONTAINER

    feature {ANY} -- Public stuff follows

        size: INTEGER

        add(o:OBJECT) is
            require
                (o != void) and not contains(o)
            do
                ...
            ensure
                contains(o) and (size = old size + 1)
            end

    invariant
        size >= 0

end
```

Eiffel's mixing of specification and implementation is convenient for the programmer. In addition, since the compiler understands the assertion syntax, the assertions can be verified (to make sure that they don't contain any syntax errors or semantic errors).

As we saw with the C version of the squareRoot function, programmers can write code to check assertions dynamically. With Eiffel, the compiler can easily identify the assertions because they are separated from the method bodies and it can generate checking code automatically because the compiler understands the assertion syntax.

As far as preconditions and postconditions are concerned, the effect of automatic checking is as if we had inserted if statements that check the require part at the start of the method and the ensure part at the end. But what about the invariants? Well, assertions in the invariant clause must always be true for objects of the class. However, in order to check that fact, we need to execute some code, and the only place that code can be executed in an imperative object-oriented language is inside methods. Therefore, invariants need to be checked whenever a method is run.

If the invariants are checked at the beginning of each method, we won't be able to tell if the object itself breaks the invariant; if they're checked at the end, we won't be able to tell whether the invariant was already broken when the method was called. Therefore, invariants must be checked at the start of the method (before the preconditions) and also at the end (after the postconditions). The reason for checking *before* preconditions and *after* postconditions is that preconditions and postconditions can modify attributes (even though they shouldn't). In effect, an invariant adds an extra precondition and an extra postcondition to every method.

You may be thinking at this point 'But if we always check that our own methods don't break the invariants, we can be certain that the invariants are safe when we enter a method'. However, other objects in the system might modify the attributes (by sending them messages), potentially violating our invariants. Since those other objects have no business checking our invariants, we must assume that invariants might have been broken when we start each method.

# 12.7 DESIGN BY CONTRACT

Whenever a piece of software is running, we have to accept that things can go wrong: there may be faults in the program; the user may provide incorrect data; external software that the program depends on may fail; there may be failures in the run-time system, the operating system or the hardware.

If we consider that every piece of software is an isolated process running on some platform (operating system plus hardware), we can partition the software universe into activity within the process and activity outside the process. To a large extent, we can control what happens inside the process using good design, good programming guidelines and good testing principles. We can't, however, control what happens outside the process (even if we access another process that was reliably implemented, the inter-process communication provided by our platform may fail; also, we might depart from our process to access hardware, such as a network or a file system – things that regularly fail). Before we can hope to write elegant, reliable and efficient software, we must have a clear understanding of the different categories of failure and who is responsible for coping with each category.

When we first learn to program, most of us assume that nothing will go wrong. Then we run one of our programs, an error occurs and the program falls over, so we learn that it's better to prevent errors from killing our programs – **error recovery** – or to make sure that our programs shut down with an explanatory message delivered to the operator – **elegant failure**. There are many possible failures, so there are many places where we might want to check for errors. To make things worse, best practice encourages us to implement software modules (functions, subsystems, classes) separately, making it difficult to identify who is responsible for detecting errors and who is responsible for handling them. This can result in large quantities of error-checking code, most of which is redundant.

**Figure 12.1: Sending a message to an object**

Let's look at the worst case in an object-oriented program: **design by fear**. For example, an object called aClient, inside its foo method, wants to send a message called bar to aSupplier, as shown in Figure 12.1. (Both objects are running in the same process.) Let's assume that the code for these two objects is written independently (even if the two classes were implemented by the same person, there may have been a significant gap between the implementations of each class, long enough for the implementor to have lost faith in the older class).

Let's assume that the implementor of Client is called Beryl and the implementor of Supplier is called Fred. In an ideal world, Beryl would simply write result = aSupplier.bar(anObject) and assume that result was valid. In that same ideal world, Fred would assume that bar was invoked correctly, perform the calculations and return the result. However, realizing that the world is imperfect, both programmers are likely to proceed more cautiously.

While writing the foo method, Beryl thinks to herself 'I'd better check that aSupplier is in an appropriate state to receive the bar message, before I send it', so she adds code to check the state of aSupplier. Having done that, she thinks 'I can't be sure that the parameter I'm about to pass is valid, so I'd better check that too.' Having coded two checks, she adds the code to send the message. For the returned result, Beryl thinks 'I can't be sure that the result I get back is valid', so she adds code to test the result. However, Beryl is being thorough. She decides that she can't trust aSupplier to be in a valid state after replying to the message – after all, the message may have had an undesired effect that wasn't predicted by its implementor. So, Beryl adds a fourth chunk of error-checking code to ensure that aSupplier is valid before proceeding.

Beryl's foo method would look like this in Java:

```java
void foo() {
    ...
    if (! ... check aSupplier ... ) {
        fail("Invalid state of a supplier");
    }
    if (! ... check anObject ... ) {
        fail("Invalid parameter for a supplier message");
    }

    int result = aSupplier.bar(anObject);

    if (! ... check result ... ) {
        fail("Invalid result from a supplier message");
    }
    if (! ... check aSupplier ... ) {
        fail("Invalid state of a supplier");
    }
    ...
}
```

In order to avoid nested if statements, the logic of the checks has been flipped using Java's 'not' operator, !. The fail function is a method on Client that prints the class name, the name of the failing method and the parameter passed in and then shuts down the process with System.exit(-1).

When Fred writes the bar method, he also does his best to write robust, fail-safe code. Before he performs any calculations, he checks that the current object is in a valid state to receive bar. Next, he checks that the parameter is valid – after all, it would be foolish to trust the client. Once he is sure that the receiver is ready and that valid data has been passed, Fred adds code to calculate the result. Before the return statement, Fred decides that it would be a good idea to check that the result is valid – because there may be faults in the calculations that he's written or in other code that he's called. Still not satisfied, Fred adds one more piece of checking code, to make sure that the calculations haven't corrupted the current object.

Fred's bar method would look like this:

```java
public int bar(Object anObject) {
    if (! ... check this object ...) {
        fail("Invalid state of this object");
    }
    if (! ... check anObject ...) {
```

```
      fail("Invalid parameter from a client");
   }

   int result = ...

   if (! ... check result ...) {
      fail("Invalid result for a client");
   }
   if (! ... check this object ...) {
      fail("Invalid state of this object");
   }
   return result;
}
```

The end result is a lot of code – perhaps more error-checking code than normal code: the state of aSupplier is checked twice before the calculation and twice after; anObject is checked twice; result is checked twice. Although you may not be quite as thorough (or paranoid) as Fred and Beryl, their code may still be uncomfortably familiar. This situation applies equally well to foo and bar written as stand-alone functions, procedures or subroutines.

Error-checking code can become even more verbose if we employ any of the common techniques listed below:

- Result codes: A result code is a number returned from a routine to indicate success or failure – for example, zero indicates success, a negative number indicates failure. Where used, result codes are typically applied to every kind of routine, regardless of whether it would normally return a result. This leads to many 'If result code is okay' checks.
- Global error variables: Here, rather than returning a success value, programmers set a global value instead (errno in the C function library is a good example). Functions return their values as normal, setting the error variable if there is a problem. However, this leads to multiple 'If the error variable is non-zero' checks. (An object-oriented equivalent of a global error variable would be a class attribute on a class called Error.)
- Exceptions: An exception is an error signaled by supplier code that causes the program to jump to **handler** code that is kept separate from the **normal path** code. Used well, exceptions can remove error-checking clutter from normal code. However, without a design rule that specifies who is responsible for handling what, exceptions make matters worse.

In the 1980s, Bertrand Meyer described how to combine the best features of formal methods and object-oriented programming in a pragmatic way, that makes it easy to produce code that is robust, elegant and efficient. Meyer called his technique **Design by Contract**.

Although Meyer described Design by Contract in the context of Eiffel, implemented using assertions and dynamic checking, we can use the same techniques in other languages – we've already seen some of them being used in C. (Don't be put off by the use of the word 'design' – the idea of a contract is relevant to all phases of software development.)

With Design by Contract, we're asked to imagine a binding contract between a client object and a supplier object, with obligations on both sides. The deal is that, as long as the client fulfills its obligations, the supplier will too (see Figure 12.2).

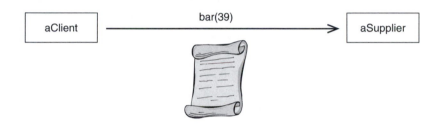

**Figure 12.2: A contract between client and supplier**

Using formal specification terminology, we can be precise about contractual obligations:

- The client must respect the supplier's invariants.
- The use of a supplier method is subject to its preconditions.
- The implementation of a supplier method must guarantee its postconditions.
- The implementation of a supplier method must guarantee the supplier's invariants.

While a method is doing its work, it is allowed to break the contract, as long as the contract is fulfilled when the work is finished. For example, if we have a Supplier invariant that $a + b = 4$ and both attributes have the value 2 when bar is called, it would be valid for bar to return with a set to 10 and b set to -6; however, since we can't set both values at the same time in most programming languages, $a + b$ will spend some time inside bar as 12 or -4.

A class can also have an internal contract, in the form of invariants for nonpublic attributes and preconditions and postconditions for nonpublic methods. An internal contract is for the benefit of implementors and maintainers; it is much less important than the external contract.

## 12.7.1 Contracts and Inheritance

Since object-oriented programming supports inheritance, we should consider the effect of inheritance on contracts. Because of polymorphism, we must guarantee that each subclass contract is the same or better, from the client's point of view, than that of its superclass (or superclasses, in the case of multiple inheritance). Without this rule, we could spring a nasty surprise on a programmer that was using a subclass object via a superclass variable: for example, if the contract for class Customer specifies that all customers have at least two bank accounts and we introduce a SimpleCustomer subclass with only one bank account, anyone accessing a SimpleCustomer object via a Customer variable might try to access a second, nonexistent, bank account.

As we move down the class hierarchy, class invariants are combined using 'and': we can only add to the invariants. For example, if class X has an invariant i1 and subclass Y adds an invariant i2, the total invariant on Y is i1 and i2. The implication is that we're providing extra guarantees about the attributes.

Preconditions and postconditions are only an issue if we redefine the associated method in a subclass. For preconditions, we must ensure that the redefined method accepts, at least, all of the messages that it accepted in the superclass: we can only **weaken** the preconditions. Therefore, any preconditions that we add to a redefined method are combined with those on the inherited method using 'or'. For example, if foo has a precondition pre1 and a subclass adds precondition pre2, the net effect is that the redefined method has the precondition pre1 or pre2.

For postconditions, we must ensure that each subclass guarantees at least as much as the superclass: we can only **strengthen** the postconditions. Therefore, postconditions are combined using 'and'. For example, if foo has a postcondition post1 and a subclass adds post2, the redefined method will have a combined postcondition of post1 and post2.

- If invariants are omitted, it means that 'nothing is guaranteed for this class'; if we add invariants to a subclass when there are none on the superclass, the net effect is the invariants that we added to the subclass.
- If preconditions are omitted, it means that 'this message applies in all cases'; if we add preconditions to a redefined method that previously had none, the new preconditions will have no effect (we can't weaken a method that already accepts everything).
- If postconditions are omitted, it means that 'this message doesn't guarantee anything'; if we add postconditions to a redefined method that had none, the net effect is the postconditions on the redefined method (anything that we add strengthens what was previously an empty guarantee).

With the help of Design by Contract ideas and formal specification terminology, Beryl, our paranoid programmer, can make her code much clearer:

```
void foo() {
    ...
    if ( ! ... check aSupplier's invariants ... ) {
```

```
      fail("Invariants broken for a supplier");
   }
   if (! ... check bar's preconditions ... ) {
      fail("Preconditions broken for a supplier message");
   }

   int result = aSupplier.bar(anObject);

   if (! ... check bar's postconditions ... ) {
      fail("Postconditions broken by a supplier method");
   }
   if (! ... check aSupplier's invariants ... ) {
      fail("Invariants broken by a supplier method");
   }
   ...
}
```

Similarly, Fred can change his code to look like this:

```
public int bar(Object anObject) {
   if (! ... check invariants ...) {
      fail("Invariants broken");
   }
   if (! ... check preconditions ...) {
      fail("Preconditions broken");
   }

   int result = ...

   if (! ... check postconditions ...) {
      fail("Postconditions broken");
   }
   if (! ... check invariants ...) {
      fail("Invariants broken");
   }
   return result;
}
```

## 12.7.2 Reducing Error-Checking Code

The main advantage of Design by Contract is the clear separation between the responsibilities of the client and the responsibilities of the supplier. Before the bar message is sent, the client is in control. Thus the client has responsibility for ensuring that the contract is not broken before the message is sent. While the method is executing, the supplier is in control. Thus the supplier must ensure that the contract is not broken by the time the method returns.

Let's apply this idea of responsibility to a more optimistic Fred and Beryl. This time Fred and Beryl trust each other: Fred writes the bar method assuming that Beryl won't break the contract; Beryl, for her part, uses the result of bar directly, confident that Fred won't break the contract either. Beryl's code can now look like this:

```
void foo() {
    ...
    if ( ! ... check aSupplier's invariants ... ) {
       fail("Invariants broken for a supplier");
    }
    if (! ... check bar's preconditions ... ) {
       fail("Preconditions broken for a supplier message");
    }
    int result = aSupplier.bar(anObject);
    ...
}
```

And Fred's code can look like this:

```
public int bar(Object anObject) {
   int result = ...
   if (! ... check postconditions ...) {
      fail("Postconditions broken");
   }
   if (! ... check invariants ...) {
      fail("Invariants broken");
   }
   return result;
}
```

This is excellent news: Design by Contract has shown us how to cut our checking code in half, by removing all redundancy. This results in faster development, better performance, fewer faults and easier maintenance.

Can we use Design by Contract to reduce checking code even further? Yes. There are many occasions when a piece of code that we write can't possibly break the contract. For example, consider the following implementation of Supplier:

```
// A supplier
// Invariant: x < 5
public class Supplier {

   private int fieldX;

   /*
      Constructor
   */
```

```
public X() {
    fieldX = 1;
}
/* Getter for x
    Preconditions: true (call this method any time)
    Postconditions: true (no side effects)
*/
public int getX() {
    return fieldX;
}
/* A method
    Preconditions: o != null
    Postconditions: For result r, r > x
*/
public int bar(Object o) {
    fieldX = o.toString().length() % 5;
    return fieldX + 1;
}
}
```

In this example, x refers to a UML-style attribute – the value of x is accessible to the outside world via the message getX. In order to emphasize the difference between the public attribute and the private implementation, the field has been given a different name, fieldX.

Because of the way it's been written, the Supplier code always respects invariants and postconditions:

- After the creation of a Supplier, x is less than 5 because fieldX is set to 1 by the constructor.
- After the execution of getX, x is less than 5 because getX has no side effects.
- After the execution of bar, x is less than 5 because fieldX is set to the remainder after dividing something by 5.
- After the execution of bar, the result is greater than x because bar returns fieldX + 1.

Since Supplier can't possibly break its half of the contract, no checking code is needed. (In principle, platform failures could break the contract, but it would not be feasible for us to add checking code for such situations.)

Now, consider the following implementation of foo, on Client:

```
void foo() {
    Supplier aSupplier = new Supplier();
    int result = aSupplier.bar(new Plate("Wedgwood"));
    ...
}
```

When the bar message is sent, we know that foo can't have violated aSupplier's invariants, because it hasn't touched the new object's attributes. Also, we know that foo can't have violated bar's preconditions, because it's passing in a non-null object. Thus, we don't need any checking code in foo either. The end result is a program with no checking code at all.

We've now seen that well-defined obligations, mutual trust and the nature of the code that we're writing can halve the amount of error-checking code, or even remove it altogether. What we haven't covered yet is how we should deal with the fact that our software exists in an imperfect world: client and supplier code can contain faults; if we jump out of our process to another process or another piece of hardware, nasty things can happen that are beyond our control. Faults within our process can be dealt with by **enforcing the contract**; problems outside our process can be dealt with by constructing **application firewalls**. We'll look at each of these techniques in turn.

## 12.7.3 Enforcing the Contract

Design by Contract relies on the assumption that as long as the client object meets its obligations, the supplier will meet its obligations too. But programmers are fallible; sometimes obligations won't be met, so we need dynamic checking to detect faults. But who is responsible for checking that contractual obligations have been met? And, what should we do if we detect a failure?

In the client and supplier example, the bar method should be responsible for checking postconditions and invariants before it returns, because only the bar method or one of its suppliers could have broken the contract between the start of the method and the end. Therefore, dynamic checking for the supplier half of the contract (postconditions and invariants) should appear at the end of the bar method.

The question of who should check the invariants and the preconditions before bar starts is more complicated. Client code is responsible for making sure that the client half of the contract is not broken. But, if we conclude that every client of bar has to have contract-checking code, the code will be duplicated all over the system.

Object-oriented theory states that responsibilities should be assigned to the relevant object. This suggests that checking the client side of the contract should be a service provided by the supplier (because the preconditions and invariants are associated with the supplier). Thus, in order to avoid duplicating the client's contract-checking code, we should place it at the start of bar. You can view this outcome in one of two ways: either bar is protecting the supplier from faults in the client or bar is providing a service for the client, to check that it has no faults. (In terms of Design by Contract, the second interpretation is preferable.)

Combining informal methods, Design by Contract, trust and dynamic checking, a Java implementation of the bar method looks like this:

```java
public int bar(Object anObject) {
   if (! ... check invariants ...) {
      fail("Invariants broken");
```

```
   }
   if (! ... check preconditions ...) {
      fail("Preconditions broken");
   }

   int result = ...

   if (! ... check postconditions ...) {
      fail("Postconditions broken");
   }
   if (! ... check invariants ...) {
      fail("Invariants broken");
   }

   return result;
}
```

With the implementation above, no contract-checking code is needed in the client.

## 12.7.4 Application Firewalls

As long as we stay within one process, we can rely on contracts to provide elegance, robustness and performance. When we jump out of our process, however, there is no contract enforcement to protect us. Therefore, we should be paranoid about everything we access beyond our process boundary, including, at least:

- other processes
- the operating system
- user interfaces
- file systems
- networks
- databases
- devices

We can construct an application firewall at the boundary to protect the code inside our process, for example, a user interface firewall would check the validity of user data before passing it on to business objects, while a database firewall would catch database errors. (These have nothing to do with Internet firewalls, which protect an intranet.)

Sometimes, we can prevent invalid data crossing an application firewall in the first place. For example, if a user must not try to log in until they've typed in a user name and a password, we can disable the Login button in our GUI until they have done so.

# 12.8 INFORMAL SPECIFICATION IN JAVA

If we're implementing our designs using a language such as Eiffel, best practice (using informal specifications and dynamic checking) is built into the language itself. When using other languages, we should apply similar principles, but we have to write the dynamic-checking code by hand. In this section, we'll see how to apply specification theory to Java, since Java is a common, pragmatic alternative to Eiffel.

## 12.8.1 Documenting a Contract using Comments

We should always, at the very least, document the contract of our classes using comments in the source code. This is because our code will end up being used, reused, or maintained by programmers who look at the source code rather than anything else. Any contract-related comments in the source code should also appear in the design and specification artifacts.

Every class should have a lengthy comment at the top – the **class comment** – that describes what the class is for and any invariants for its public attributes. Be aware that other programmers looking at the source code may not be familiar with formal jargon, so you might want to use phrases such as For all objects of this class, the following conditions apply:. The class comment can also contain examples of how the class should be used.

Every public message on the class should have a comment at the top – the **message comment** – that describes what the corresponding method is for and lists any preconditions and postconditions. For the sake of uninformed readers, you might prefer to use terms like requires and guarantees rather than preconditions and postconditions.

Always keep in mind, when implementing a method, that it's the caller's responsibility to make sure the invariants and preconditions are met before the method is called. In other words, your coding should be optimistic. The flip side of this, of course, is that you should make sure that your implementation doesn't violate the postconditions or the invariants.

## 12.8.2 Checking Conditions Dynamically

In principle, it's a good idea to add an invariant check and a precondition check to the start of every public method, and a postcondition check and an invariant check to the end. However, in the absence of special language mechanisms, such as those provided by Eiffel, you may prefer to be more selective.

It's a good idea to add checks to the start of any public method that you expect to be reused heavily (if the code is destined for a library, for example). Third parties will appreciate the extra help that your checking code provides, as they become familiar with your classes.

As for checks at the end of public methods, this is a matter of personal preference. If your method couldn't possibly break the supplier half of the contract, the checks would be redundant. If you think that your code *could* break the contract, perhaps you don't trust yourself: as your experience with implementing object-oriented code increases, your self-belief should grow, so such checks should also become redundant.

The only compelling reason to include end-of-method checks is if you believe that third-party code invoked by your method could break the invariants, by corrupting attributes: since most code is invoked in a client–server style, this should not happen often.

## 12.8.3 Signaling Contract Violations using RuntimeExceptions

Whatever choices we make about enforcing the contract, we need a clean, elegant way of signaling contract violations. Thus far, the issue has been side-stepped through the use of a fail message. But what code do we need inside the corresponding fail method in order to fail *elegantly*? One possibility is to quit the program: in Java we can do this with System.exit(-1). However, this technique discards most of the information about how we arrived at the failure point – we might be told which method was at the end, but not which method called that, or which method called that, and so on.

Instead of exiting explicitly, a Java method can **throw an exception**, a signal to the calling method that the current method can't proceed. Java has a particular type of exception, called a RuntimeException, that we can use in such cases. A RuntimeException should be used to signal that the method can't proceed because of a fault in its implementation or in the calling method. The calling method is not expected to **catch** the RuntimeException: instead, it should allow the run-time system to re-throw the exception to its own calling method, where it will be re-thrown to the method that called that, and so on; eventually, the exception will reach the skin of the process, the main method, having halted each method on its way out.

When a RuntimeException is thrown by main, the program will be stopped by the run-time system and the user (or tester, or administrator) will be shown a trace through the failing methods, along the lines of:

```
RuntimeException in bar() "Preconditions violated"
   main() called foo() on Client
   foo() called bar() on Supplier
```

This is exactly the kind of information we need to start debugging.

The Java style for signaling a broken contract is shown in the following example:

```
public class Supplier {
   ...
   // Precondition: o != null.
   public int bar(Object o) {
     if (o == null) {
        throw new RuntimeException("Preconditions violated");
     }
```

```
        ...
    }
    ...
}
```

(You can throw a subclass of RuntimeException, such as IllegalArgumentException, if you want to provide more detail to the user.)

When Java code is running inside a larger program, such as a servlet running inside a Web server or a business component running inside a GUI, we shouldn't allow RuntimeException objects (or any other kind of exception), to reach the main method, otherwise the whole program will shut down. Instead, generic code at the edge of the program can catch unhandled exceptions and report them to the administrator or the user, or both. For example, a Web server can append an error report to the system log file and then display an error message to the user, along the lines of Your request can't be completed because ..., plus some advice on what to do next.

## 12.8.4 External Systems

As we've seen, while running code within our own process, we can safely disable dynamic checking. Trust your own code; trust your colleagues' code; trust the code in patterns, libraries and frameworks. However, we still need to construct application firewalls to protect our code from the outside world. Application firewall code will never be switched off, even after testing. External systems can be categorized as clients or suppliers – we'll look at how to deal with each of these in turn.

### External Clients

Requests coming from external clients are destined for our business objects, so the contracts of our business objects must be respected. Thus, the application firewall should check the client half of the contract, on behalf of the business objects. However, the knowledge of the contract is best encapsulated in the business objects themselves (because that's where the knowledge should reside). We can resolve this apparent paradox by encapsulating the invariant and precondition checks in messages on the business objects.

For example, consider the following class:

```java
// Invariant: i1
public class Foo {

    public boolean invariantOK() {
        ... // Return true if i1 is okay
    }
    public boolean okForBar(s, f) {
        ... // Return true if s, f satisfy p1
    }
```

```java
// Precondition: p1
public void bar(String s, float f) {
    if (!invariantOK()) {
            throw new RuntimeException("Invariant violated");
        }
    if (!okForBar(s, f)) {
        throw new RuntimeException("Precondition violated");
    }
    ...
}
}
```

Code in an application firewall can extract the values for bar's parameters (from a user interface or a servlet, for example) and use the service messages on Foo to test whether invoking bar would be valid, as in:

```java
// Application firewall code
if (aFoo.invariantsOK() && (aFoo.okForBar(s, f)) {
    aFoo.bar(s, f);
}
else {
    ... // Signal error to client
}
```

As a variation on this idea, you could provide checking and non-checking versions of each ordinary Foo message, for example, bar and barWithChecks. This would move the application firewall code into Foo, as a service for clients. The downside of this approach is that you would be providing the checking versions of the messages even though they might never be used – they would only be used if the object ended up being invoked from an application firewall.

Another variation would be to put the checking versions of the messages into a separate class, called FooWithChecks perhaps. This approach is better than code in the application firewall itself but you would be providing an entire class that might never be used.

## External Suppliers

When we're jumping out of our process to access an external supplier, we must check the state of the external supplier and we must check any information that we get back. Again, the notion of an application firewall is useful here. But, what would we do if the application firewall detected an error? We will have been invoked originally by some client code and, if the application firewall detects an error, the client code must be told that there is a problem. A good way to do this, avoiding the messiness of result codes or error variables, is to throw an exception. However, unlike the 'broken contract' situation, we *don't* want client code to ignore this kind of exception – external problems are a predictable fact of life, even in fault-free code. Therefore, we must force the client to handle such cases.

To help with this, Java has a second kind of exception – represented by the Exception class – that the *compiler* will force client code to handle. In Java, Exception objects are called **checked exceptions** because the compiler requires checking code to be provided, while RuntimeException objects are called **unchecked exceptions** because no checking code needs to be (or should be) provided.

So, in order to signal a failure from an out-of-process supplier, we can do something like the following:

```
public class ExternalResourceUser {
   public void useResource()
      throws Exception // Checked exceptions must be listed
   {
      ... // Use the external resource
      ... // Detect a problem
         throw new Exception("External resource failure");
   }
}
```

As with RuntimeException, you can use subclasses of Exception, such as IOException, if you want to be more specific.

## 12.8.5 Enabling and Disabling Dynamic Checks

Dynamic checking has implications for the performance of your system: checking preconditions, postconditions and invariants in every method could easily make the code ten times slower than it would otherwise be. We aim to produce software that, when deployed, will never violate an assertion – if no assertion is ever violated, there's no need to do any checking. During development, on the other hand, we expect violations to happen often. What we need, in order to satisfy the different requirements of development and deployment, is a way to turn dynamic checking on and off.

Eiffel implementations vary in whether they use a run-time switch or a compile-time switch, but it is relatively simple to be selective about what we turn off and what we leave on. For example, we may turn postconditions off for the library code that we're using during development (because we expect the library to have been debugged already). With non-Eiffel languages, we have to work harder.

There are two ways to enable and disable dynamic checks. The first involves flipping a run-time switch (using a command-line parameter or an environment variable): if the switch is on, the run-time system will do the checks; if the switch is off, the run-time system will skip over the checks. The second method uses a compiler switch to build two versions of the system, one with checking code included and one without. In both cases, we can be more selective: for example, we might disable all postcondition checks or all the checks in library code.

In principle, Java implementations could use either a run-time or a compile-time switch but, in practice, the situation is a little more complicated. Java programmers can only use a compile-time switch by careful programming; a run-time switch (the assertion mechanism) is available, but it shouldn't be used to check all parts of the contract.

## Implementing a Compiler Switch

We can simulate a compiler switch using a well-documented trick. First, we introduce a class that stores the value of the switch as a **class constant** (a class field with a fixed value). This is how such a class might look (where final means 'constant'):

```
public class ContractSwitch {
    public static final DO_CHECKS = true;
        // It's okay to have a public field if it's final
}
```

Now, any dynamic checking code can be wrapped in an if statement that depends on the value of the switch, as in:

```
public class Supplier {
    ...
    // Precondition: o != null.
    public int bar(Object o) {
        if (ContractSwitch.DO_CHECKS) {
            if (o == null) {
                throw new RuntimeException("Preconditions violated");
            }
        }
        ...
    }
```

When the compiler gets to the if (ContractSwitch.DO_CHECKS) statement, it spots that the class constant is true, so it knows that the body of the if statement will always be executed: the precondition check is compiled and included in the current build. However, no code needs to be generated for the outer if statement because it would be redundant at run time. The net effect is that the current build includes the contract-checking code but not the code which checks the switch.

In order to build a version of the system with checks disabled, we find the definition of the ContractSwitch class, set DO_CHECKS to false and recompile our system. Now, when the compiler encounters the if (ContractSwitch.DO_CHECKS) statement, it will conclude that, since the constant is false, the outer if statement will always fail, so there is no point generating code for it or anything inside it. The net effect is a build of the system that contains no checking code and no switch-checking code.

This compiler-switch technique is part of the Java language specification, so we can expect it to work with every Java compiler. With a little thought, you should be able to work out how to make the technique more selective (by adding more class constants). Because Java compilers compile classes by package, we must add a ContractSwitch class to every package.

### Using the Assertion Mechanism

Java has an assertion mechanism that allows the programmer to insert statements such as assert o != null. A run-time switch can then be used to control whether assertions are on or off, i.e. whether assertion failure should cause the program to stop automatically. Although a run-time switch is used, it is possible for Java implementations, when the switch is off, to remove all the process size and performance overheads normally associated with assertions.

Traditionally, assertion mechanisms in programming languages have been used to enforce contracts and to insert fault-checking code at arbitrary points. According to the documentation for Java's assertion mechanism, it should not be used to enforce the client half of a contract. The reason given is that some checks are too important to allow them to be disabled (for reasons of safety). A better recommendation would have been to state that some checks, which reside in application firewalls, are mandatory and the assertion mechanism should not be used for those. Such a recommendation would have been compatible with everything else that we've seen in this chapter.

Despite the fact that the assertion mechanism has all the characteristics of a switchable mechanism for checking contracts, we have to accept that we shouldn't use it for this. Other programmers who have read the documentation won't expect it to be used in this way. Also, if assertions are on when a check fails at run time, the kind of exception that is thrown is an Error not a RuntimeException. An Error is an unrecoverable problem that programmers should not try to handle, such as a fault in the run-time system or running out of memory. As the assertion mechanism throws an Error, it doesn't fit in with the guideline that application faults should be signaled with RuntimeException objects.

This is a shame. Although automatic contract enforcement may be added to Java in the future, for now, we're stuck with the compiler-switch technique.

# 12.9 SUMMARY

In this chapter, we've looked at:

- Specifications, which are complete, unambiguous descriptions of the required behavior of our software. Formal specifications are scientific and rigorous and use specialized language; informal specifications are pragmatic and partial, and may be expressed in natural language or in the syntax of a language such as Eiffel.

- How specifications can be written in an object-oriented manner. An object-oriented specification allows us to assert the preconditions, postconditions and invariants for a class.

- Design by Contract, which combines formal methods and object-oriented programming in a way that makes it easy to produce robust, elegant and efficient code. A binding contract between a client object and a supplier object imposes obligations on both sides.

- How to use specifications and Design by Contract in Java, particularly by using comments and Exception objects. We also considered the Java assertion mechanism and discarded that as a potential solution.

# FURTHER READING

For a larger helping of OCL, see [Clark and Warmer 02] and the OCL specification itself [OMG 03b].

For a description of Design by Contract from the inventor himself, see [Meyer 97]. Bertrand Meyer also covers every aspect of object-oriented programming.

For a good discussion of what to do and what not to do in Java, including the proper use of exceptions, see [Bloch 01].

# REVIEW QUESTIONS

1. What is a 'class invariant'? Choose only one option.

   (a) A class whose source code is versioned and therefore cannot be changed.
   (b) A class whose objects have constant fields.
   (c) A condition that will always be true for an instance of the class.

2. What is meant by the term 'design by fear'? Choose only one option.

   (a) Design is scary.
   (b) You cannot know when to trust the code.
   (c) You design a system too quickly because of time pressures.

3. What is 'Design by Contract'? Choose only one option.

   (a) Designing code as if there were a contract between an object that sends a message and the object that receives it.

(b) Reinforcing the contract between every pair of objects by increasing the amount of error-checking.

(c) Protecting your software using a contract with a firewall.

(d) Designing a software system under contract.

# ANSWERS TO REVIEW QUESTIONS

1. A 'class invariant' is c. A condition that will always be true for an instance of the class.
2. The term 'design by fear' means that b. you cannot know when to trust the code.
3. 'Design by contract' means a. Designing code as if there were a contract between an object that sends a message and the object that receives it.

# 13

## Continuous Testing

In this chapter, we'll be covering all aspects of testing. As with other areas of software development, the discipline of engineering is often used as a guide.

# Learning Objectives

**Understand the many terms used in testing.**

**Consider a testing strategy.**

**Work through an example of test-driven development.**

# Chapter Outline

## 13.1 INTRODUCTION

Developing software is a complex business. No matter how hard we try, we won't be able to eliminate all **faults** (or bugs) simply by going through the phases of requirements, analysis, design, specification and implementation. However, through good practice, we can make sure that the most serious faults do not occur in the first place. In addition, we need a separate testing phase, with the goal of eliminating all remaining faults before release.

Nowadays, it is generally accepted that tacking a testing phase on to the end of the development is inefficient: we must also test our code, and other artifacts, as we go along. We should ensure that many different people are involved in testing: developers; peers (colleagues not directly involved in the current project); customers; project managers; testers (colleagues with primary responsibility for the testing phase). Essentially, there are three phases of testing activity: during development (by developers), during the testing phase (by an expert testing team) and after release, when all users and developers gather feedback and fix faults discovered while the software is live.

Since this book is aimed primarily at members of the development team, we will look at **test-driven development**, a form of continuous testing where developers test their code as they go along. The advantages of this approach are that:

- It improves the quality of the software (the more testers the better).
- It reduces the cost of the testing phase.
- It shows the programmers that they're making real progress (rather than just producing lines of code).
- It reduces the number of (embarrassing) faults that are linked to the programmer during the testing phase.
- It helps programmers to **refactor** (reorganize) their code, for style or performance reasons, without breaking anything that they've already written.

## 13.2 TESTING TERMINOLOGY

- A **test** checks that some aspect of our software is correct, such as 'Test whether we can log on', 'Test the purchasing subsystem' or 'Test that the memory footprint doesn't exceed 500 MB under maximum load'.
- An **error** is a mistake made by a programmer, based on a misunderstanding, for example. An error usually gives rise to one or more **faults**. (This is distinct from using 'error' to

mean an undesirable condition, expected or otherwise, that occurs while the system is running – see the definition of **failure**.)

- A **fault** is an incorrect piece of code: in the same way that a fault in a car's engine stops it running smoothly, a software fault stops the system from operating correctly. For example, a method written on the assumption that arrays are indexed from 1 has a fault if arrays are actually indexed from 0. The terms **fault** or **defect** are used in preference to **bug**, which is considered to be rather informal. **Faults of omission** occur when the developer has left something out (such as a customer requirement or code that should deal with a particular situation); **faults of commission** occur when there is a problem committing requirements to code, design or specification (such as stating that the area of a triangle is base times height or attempting to read from a file that has been closed).
- A **failure** is a system malfunction, usually caused by one or more faults, for example, 'Someone has hacked into the system because of the buffer overrun fault'.
- A **fix** is when a fault is repaired.
- **Verification** checks that the software is correct with respect to the requirements documentation (system use cases).
- **Validation** checks that the software is what the customer requires, i.e. that it performs the functions that the customer needs in a way that is acceptable to the customer and to the end users.
- A specification is a description of the interface of a piece of code, which lays out what can go in and what must come out. Therefore, **specification testing** is an umbrella term for **black-box testing** and **use case testing**.

## 13.2.1 Black-Box Testing

With black-box testing, whatever is being tested (the system, subsystem, class, or method) is treated as an impenetrable object (see Figure 13.1). The only access to the box is via its published interface – messages, parameters and so forth. Therefore, all the tester can do to assess the correctness of what the box does is to capture and analyze the replies (from messages); examine any external side effects (such as the creation of entries in a database); and check the time taken to answer requests or execute commands. Although each use of the interface may cause internal side effects (as the box changes from one state to another), the tester can only view the effect that these internal side effects have on the subsequent use of the interface: even if details of the internals of the box are available, they're ignored for the purposes of black-box testing.

Black-box testing arises from the philosophy of 'we don't care how the code achieves its ends, as long as it achieves them.' This fits well with the idea that the system requirements that are written down before the software is produced are the most important aspect of software

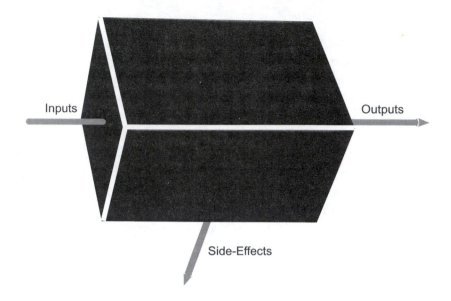

**Figure 13.1: Black-box testing**

development: beyond the requirements phase, the analysts, designers and implementors have free reign to fulfill the requirements in any way they see fit. Black-box testing insulates the tester from the internal complexity of the software.

A disadvantage of black-box testing is that, because the internal structure and lines of code are ignored, potential improvements may be missed – after all, it is possible for a piece of software to be correct and adequate without being good quality. Another disadvantage is that faults that are not caught by the tests themselves will remain undiscovered until much later.

Other terms for black-box testing include **behavioral testing**, emphasizing that the testing concentrates on how the box behaves, from an external point of view, rather than on how that behavior is achieved (which would require knowledge of the inside of the box), and **functional testing**.

## 13.2.2  White-Box Testing

In white-box testing, we're allowed to look inside the box, examining structure and detail right down to individual lines of code (see Figure 13.2).

The benefits of white-box testing include the fact that peers (other software developers) can propose improvements, such as refactoring, for better performance; easier maintenance; and more opportunities for reuse. Another benefit is the fact that deficiencies may be spotted early or spotted when they might otherwise be missed (because it is not possible

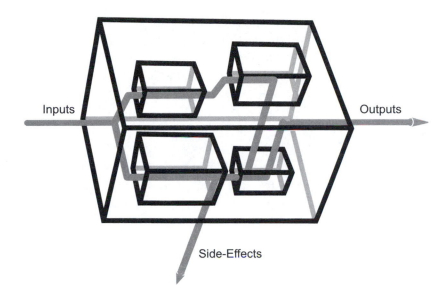

**Figure 13.2: White-box testing**

to test software exhaustively). Deficiencies spotted by white-box testing include classic programmer mistakes, such as traversing a collection of values more times than is necessary, and incomplete or incorrect interpretation of the requirements.

Since, during the course of development, the structure and content of code will change, white-box testing is best left until late in the development, usually during the testing phase. This is particularly true of development that is spiral, iterative and incremental, where we accept that analysis, design, coding and system requirements will need to be adjusted as we learn more about the problem and its solution.

Other terms for white-box testing include **structural testing**, reflecting the fact that the internal structure of the box is considered as well as its external behavior, and **glass-box testing**.

# 13.3 TYPES OF TEST

Most testing experts break the testing process up into a hierarchy of distinct levels:

- **Unit testing** is the lowest level of the hierarchy. A unit is a single, coherent piece of code (traditionally, a function or a procedure; in object-oriented software development, a class).
- **Integration testing** checks how independent pieces of code work together.

- **System testing** checks the operation of all the subsystems working together, along with any interaction they have with their environment. The most important form of system testing is **use case testing** because the system use cases describe completely what the system must be able to do. Having designed tests for each use case, we can go on to provide tests that check whether the use cases work in parallel.

## 13.3.1  Unit Testing

For each class, we design tests that check whether it works correctly, efficiently and elegantly. While designing unit tests, we aim to check that instances of the class have the correct message signatures (name, return type, parameter types and parameter names) and that they generate the correct replies from our test data. We also want to check that each object starts in a valid state and moves from one valid state to another, as it is used. (Recall that the state of an object is recorded in the values of its attributes.) For black-box testing, we can only verify the state using messages (getCustomerId, for example); if we do white-box testing, we can check the fields and we can look inside the methods for faults, poor style or poor quality. If the class makes use of class fields and class methods, we would have to check the class itself as well as its objects.

With unit testing we have a dilemma: how do we test the unit without testing its collaborators too? In object-oriented terms, we may decide that encapsulated objects are simply part of the unit and therefore take no special steps for black-box testing. (For white-box testing, we can simply ignore the collaborators.) However, if we wish to be pedantic, we can replace the collaborators with simulated, or **mock**, objects that provide the bare minimum behavior needed to test the original class. We may also need to use mock objects (or **stubs**, as they're sometimes called) as stand-ins for code that is not available yet (because it hasn't been implemented or because it requires some configuration, such as a database, that we don't want to be concerned with for the moment).

## 13.3.2  Integration Testing

In a finished system, every object collaborates with other objects, so integration testing is a necessary step after unit testing (especially since different classes are generally written by different developers). For example, we might want to test how well the objects in our business layer work together.

Integration testing usually takes place at one or more of the following levels:

- collaborating classes that form a logical unit
- layer
- package
- library

- framework
- system or subsystem

Subsystem testing is a form of integration testing where the collection of classes under test comprise a whole subsystem (as defined by the system designers).

## 13.3.3 Alpha Testing

With alpha testing, we accept that the system is a work in progress. The aim is to make sure that we're developing something that is likely to be correct and useful to the customer. For example, we may implement some core functionality within the framework of our system design and then make it available to colleagues and carefully-selected customers to try out. If the feedback is good, we know that we're on the right track (and we will gather useful information about improvements); if the feedback is particularly negative, we must go back to the drawing board, otherwise we will end up delivering a system that is, at best, useless or, at worst, something that the customer will refuse to pay for.

Alpha testing is often performed against a prototype, i.e. a version of the system that is produced quickly and cheaply. Thus, if the alpha testing fails, we have not wasted too much time or money. Once the alpha testing is complete, we should discard the prototype code in favor of the more elegant solution that we will produce during the full-scale development. Although it can be hard to throw code away, we must remind ourselves that the prototype was meant to be developed quickly, just for experimentation – it is highly unlikely, then, that the design or coding will be top quality. Although we throw the code away, we retain everything that we have learned about the problem and its solution up to that point (draft use cases and UML artifacts, for example).

## 13.3.4 Beta Testing

Beta testing occurs when an entire increment of the system is complete, after all phases of development and in-house testing. It involves asking people to try out the software in its real environment. We do this because we want to find the most obvious faults and fix them, before final release. No matter how good our development process is, there will usually be faults that have not been discovered by the developers or the special-purpose testing team. Normally, faults are missed because exhaustive testing is impossible (or at least infeasible), which means that testers must use their skill and judgment to anticipate the way that the software will be used. Beta testing is used to fill in the gaps between anticipated use and actual use.

Beta testing should be carried out by end users, not by any member of the testing team. Depending on the nature of the software, beta testers may be colleagues, real customers, or both. Since beta testing and producing feedback can be frustrating tasks, we normally need to offer some kind of incentive. For colleagues, we might try 'If you beta test my software, I'll beta test yours' or simply 'It's for the good of the company'; for real customers, we might offer a discount on the released version. For a system with only one eventual customer, we may have to persuade them that beta testing is a normal part of the process and doesn't imply poor quality – the beta version could then be tested by a few of the customer's employees before wider release within their organization.

## 13.3.5 Use Case Testing

With use case testing, we take each use case in turn and design tests that confirm that the system satisfies the use case. We may do this by considering a number of possible **scenarios** for each use case, each scenario being a legal sequence of events – hence the term **scenario testing**. (Although a use case may appear to be a single sequence of events, it will often describe alternative paths and repetitions – therefore, each scenario will be just one particular choice of path and repetitions.) Use case testing is a form of black-box system testing.

As well as the normal sequences of events, we can test the abnormal sequences that have been specified in the use case, i.e. how the system should behave when things don't go according to plan. For example, an attempt to rent a car will usually be successful but we may have decided to specify what should happen in the rare case that the customer owes us money from a previous transaction. In a multi-user system, it is also important to execute use case tests in parallel, to simulate what will happen after deployment.

Use case testing is particularly important in development driven by use cases, as described in this book. Since our development is incremental, based on the prioritizing of use cases, use case tests should be run incrementally.

## 13.3.6 Component Testing

A component, in general terms, is a logically separate piece of software, with a clean, well-defined interface. By analogy with hardware components, a software component is independent of the world around it and keeps its internals hidden. If we want to make use of a component, we're restricted to using its interface, we can't 'break it open' – this shields us from the internal complexity, while still allowing us to connect components to construct something bigger.

Any of the following can be considered as a component: an object (perhaps with other objects inside); any group of collaborating objects; a subsystem; an entire system. On that last point, thinking of a system as a component allows us to link systems together, perhaps at different locations. For example, the iCoot system, which runs inside an individual branch, delivers weekly reports to head office via a business-to-business-link – in this case, the systems are entirely separate, treating each other as components.

So, component testing is about running tests against whatever we have decided constitutes a component. As usual, we can choose whether we do black-box testing, white-box testing, or both.

## 13.3.7 Build Testing

A build test is used to ensure that our software can be built successfully. To build software means to collect together all the bits and pieces of the system, compile them, link them together and deploy them, along with any resources that they need (databases, files that are not actually source code). A build test is sometimes called a **smoke test**. While developing a new engine, a team of mechanical engineers will start up and rev the engine at frequent intervals; if the engine emits smoke, something is wrong (see Figure 13.3), so the engineers shut the engine down, diagnose the problem and fix it, before doing another smoke test to check the repair.

For anything less than a trivial system, we can use **build tools** to ensure that the construction of the system is automated, consistent and complete. For example, **Ant**, from the open source Apache project (ant.apache.org), takes as input XML files written by developers; these files describe how to construct all the pieces of the complete system. The XML files also contain information about the dependencies between individual pieces, so that the Ant tool can build them in the correct order: for example, we might specify that a particular set of source files must be compiled before they can be linked together into an executable.

Once the system has been built without failures (such as those caused by syntactical or semantic errors, reported by the compiler), the second stage of the build test is to start the system up and go through some critical scenarios – if these scenarios can be completed without any further failures (such as resources not being found or exceptions being thrown by the program), the test has succeeded. After a successful build test, we know that the code and resources we have implemented up to this point work together, so we won't have problems when we deploy the finished system. If the scenarios fail, we know that there are faults that must be dealt with before we continue with the development, since there is no point producing a finished system that won't build, deploy or perform its essential functions.

It is a good idea to perform a build test frequently, hence the term **nightly build**. This may seem to be over-enthusiastic, but it is beneficial for a large system with many pieces, especially since the pieces are usually developed by separate people, who may be at separate locations, unable to communicate on a daily basis. Regular build testing is also important because it avoids deferring problems until later, when they will generally have become larger (because of the tendency for the work of individuals to diverge over time). Even for a small system, perhaps with only one developer, regular builds still have the general advantages described above. It is natural for developers to build their own code several times

**Figure 13.3: An unsuccessful smoke test**

a day anyway – a successful build and a few scenario walk-throughs demonstrate that they're making progress.

For medium- to large-scale projects, there will usually be a dedicated **build team**, responsible for writing the build files, collecting pieces from developers and performing the build tests. This frees ordinary developers from a lot of administrative activity – indeed, as long as the pieces provided by a particular developer cause no problems, they can forget about the build test altogether. As soon as a build test fails, the build team must identify which developer is responsible for the failure and make sure that they help to fix the associated faults. (Of course, failures may also be caused by members of the build team, using invalid build files.) As an incentive to fix problems quickly, some kind of forfeit may be imposed by the development team. These may be humorous, low-impact forfeits, such as having to wear a hat marked 'Build Buster' until the problem is fixed, or they may be rather more serious, such as being on call twenty four hours a day, seven days a week to come in and fix any faults that you have caused.

# 13.3.8 Load Testing

While we're developing our system, however much we test as we go along, we're unlikely to be able to test its behavior under normal load. To use an analogy with engineering: when building a bridge, we may be able to test the strength of individual girders before we add them to the bridge, but we won't be able to test the whole bridge under a typical load of, say, a thousand lorries, two thousand cars and one thunderstorm. With software load testing, we take the finished system and apply the normal, expected load to it – for example, '100,000 users trying to examine the contents of their bank account simultaneously'. As well as normal (average) load, we may test the system under high load and maximum load, to check that it can cope under these extreme conditions.

Software load testing is, in many ways, easier than the load testing carried out by engineers: if a bridge were to fail, we would have a serious problem, so the engineer has to use techniques such as wind-tunnel tests and computer modeling to make sure that, even under extreme conditions, a collapse is impossible. Even then, the engineer allows the bridge to be opened knowing that their confidence is theoretical – how good can the application of scientific principles and modeling be, when we didn't actually test the real thing? With software, on the other hand, we can load-test the real code in deployment conditions, safe in the knowledge that, if anything goes wrong, we can fix the code before it goes live.

Another advantage of software load testing is that, if a failure does happen when the system is live, we can re-start the system (some would suggest that this is why software is less reliable than engineered products). In the case of a safety-critical system, such as a fly-by-wire airplane, this situation doesn't apply, so we may use different principles: if we can demonstrate that our fly-by-wire plane is more reliable than a similar plane under the control of a human being, we have a net gain.

## Soak Testing

Some faults in software only become evident when the software is used continuously for long periods. For example, a system that doesn't remove temporary files as it goes along will eventually run out of disk space, but only if it is allowed to run under load for an extended period of time. **Soak testing** means running our software continuously under high load, to make sure that it doesn't exhaust its own resources or exhibit any other cumulative problems.

## Stress Testing

Engineers often test a structure to breaking point, for two reasons: firstly, to find out what the breaking point actually is, regardless of the theoretical limits; secondly, to find out exactly what happens when the structure does fail, hopefully discovering that only part of it fails. Software **stress testing** is the process of overloading a system to the point where it can no longer cope. By doing this, we discover what the limits are and we can see how it behaves beyond the breaking point. When performing stress testing, we may deprive the system of the resources it needs, in order to see what happens: for example, we may deprive it of some of the computing power, memory or disk space that it needs to do its work.

Generally, with software, we aim to achieve **graceful failure**: the system tries to minimize the associated losses and stay running. For example, if we have put together a news Web site that typically handles a million simultaneous requests, an extraordinary news item may result in a hundred million attempts to access the system. In such cases, rather than the whole Web site falling over in a heap, it would be better if 10 million requests were handled as normal and the other 90 million users were informed that the Web site is too busy and they must try again later. With the help of live monitoring, we could be made aware of the problem, so that we could decide whether or not to increase the capacity of the site.

Another term for stress testing is **negative testing**. This is negative in the sense of 'pessimistic' because the software is taken beyond its operational envelope into areas for which it was not designed.

## 13.3.9 Installation Testing

Installation testing involves seeing how our software behaves in its operational environment. Since the majority of testing may be carried out in a specially built test environment (the test bed), we have not fully tested the software until we have checked it in the live environment too. This is especially true of software that is intended to be portable, designed to run in any number of environments (multiple operating systems or devices). Other terms for installation testing include **platform testing** and **environment testing**.

## 13.3.10 Acceptance Testing

Ultimately, the success of a piece of software depends on whether it satisfies the needs of its users. Even if the software has been commissioned by the management for the benefit of the organization, if it is not acceptable to the end users, they won't use it properly, defeating the original purpose. In the case of software manufactured for sale to third parties, the software will only sell, and continue to sell, if it is effective to those who use it. Naturally, we would prefer our software to be good rather than just adequate.

Acceptance testing allows end users to try the software before release, to see if they accept it. During acceptance testing, we may ask the users to perform particular tasks or we may ask them to try to do what they would normally have done by other means. While the tests are being carried out, we can monitor the users' effectiveness and then gather feedback. Monitoring may include videoing the users to gauge their visible and audible reactions, and recording their keystrokes and mouse movements (the general principle being 'less is more' – the less interaction required to get the job done, the better). Although monitoring and gathering feedback is user-focussed, parts of acceptance testing may take place at a higher level: discussing productivity with managers or asking a psychologist to interpret video recordings, for example.

Since full acceptance testing is carried out late in the day, during the testing phase, it can be expensive to modify the software to take account of negative results. Thus, we would normally defer the less critical modifications to a later increment. The principles of spiral and iterative development, with continuous customer involvement, help us to avoid any serious problems.

## 13.3.11 Regression Tests

Whenever software is modified, by adding, removing or editing source code, we need to be sure that the new version of the software is at least as good as the previous version. Making changes to code can introduce faults. It is not unusual for 'fixes' that are not intended to introduce new behavior to contain errors of their own.

Regression testing is the process of ensuring that modifications have *not* caused the code to regress, i.e. that the code has not ended up worse than before. Thus, we will usually have a suite of tests that we run against our software after every change – the new version of the software should pass these tests just as well as the old. (Ideally, as well as being just as correct, the new version should be just as effective, fast, secure, elegant, and so on.)

## 13.3.12 Documentation Tests

Documentation is an umbrella term that refers to manuals and training materials. Such documentation is crucial for the success of a system: if no-one can use the software or maintain it in the field, there was no point producing it in the first place. Documentation should be aimed specifically at both system administrators and end-users, even if that means that two sets have to be produced.

Documentation testing is the process of checking that documentation is correct and effective, with input from other authors, system administrators, end users and instructors.

## 13.3.13 Testing for Security

Security testing is the process of ensuring that the system is secure, but what does secure mean? As outlined in Chapter 8, security has the following aspects:

- privacy
- authentication
- irrefutability
- integrity
- safety

Our system must be protected against **hackers**, malicious third parties intent on mischief or criminal activity. Thus, we must test that it is impossible for invalid or unauthorized information, or software, to get in or out of the system. **Ethical hackers** are specialists in this area: with our permission, they will attempt to hack into our system on its test bed. Any weak points that the ethical hackers identify can then be fixed before release.

Most security testing will be performed as part of system testing, usually during the testing phase. This is because, although each piece of the system should be designed with security in mind, we should concentrate our testing efforts on making sure that hackers (and gremlins) can't get beyond the system boundary.

## 13.3.14 Metrics

A metric is a measurement that we take to assess the quality or effectiveness of our software. Typical metrics include:

- Code coverage: It is a widely held principle that code should only exist in a system if it is used, otherwise we have wasted time developing it and increased our maintenance costs and system size unnecessarily. In the context of code reuse, there is something of a conflict here: when we implement a class, we may be tempted to add extra public methods that we suspect will be useful in the future when the code is reused in other systems; however, any extra methods that we add aren't used by the current system. As a compromise, we would expect to tolerate low coverage within libraries and frameworks, while expecting high coverage for any code that is specific to the current system.
- KLOC: An old-fashioned metric, short for thousands (K) of lines of code. Often, KLOCs were used to measure the productivity of developers: the more lines of code a programmer produced, the more productive they were thought to be. However, a programmer who produces a lot of code quickly may be producing more than is necessary, while a methodical, accurate programmer may produce less code that is of better quality. The best object-oriented developers will try to avoid writing their own code, reusing code from libraries, frameworks and other applications, so the KLOC has become largely redundant. KLOCs are still sometimes used to indicate the relative size of an application or system: as in 'the XYZ system has 15 000 KLOCs'.
- Transaction time: A transaction, as the term is used here, is the handling of an incoming request – examples include business transactions such as 'buy a book' and database

transactions such as 'add a record to the CUSTOMER table'. We can measure the number of transactions handled per second or the average transaction time, as a way of gauging system performance.

- Depth of inheritance hierarchies: Some would say that an inheritance hierarchy with many levels is too deep. Others would say that there are no rules, it just depends on what you're doing. It's fair to say that most inheritance hierarchies, even complex ones, only stretch to half a dozen levels. Therefore, if we spot an inheritance hierarchy with 50 levels, it merits further investigation.

- Breadth of inheritance hierarchies: This measurement relates to the number of classes across a hierarchy. As with depth, this is a gray area. However, we might conclude that a hierarchy with only three levels but 50 classes at each level is in need of reorganization.

- Size of methods: A method that is more than, say, 50 lines, should probably be split into several smaller methods: each one would be easier to write and easier to maintain.

- Degree of coupling: Components with many links between them, passing many messages back and forth, are said to be **tightly coupled**. This is largely a maintenance issue, because changes to the interface of one component will have a large impact on the other components and vice versa. We should use a greater number of **loosely coupled** objects or, perhaps, write the system in a client–server style.

- Degree of cohesion: A **cohesive** object has a single, coherent, set of responsibilities. For example, an object that represents a pizza on a menu and an actual pizza that someone has ordered has **weak cohesion**: parts of the system would use the pizza exclusively as a description from the menu, while others would use it in relation to one particular customer. Another example of weak cohesion would be a collection that could be used as a set (unordered, without duplicates) or as a list (ordered, with duplicates). **Strong cohesion** encourages simplicity, ease of maintenance and reuse.

Most metrics are subjective, so they must be interpreted carefully by humans. Ultimately, the most important metric is 'Does the software achieve what was set out in the requirements?'

# 13.4 AUTOMATING TESTS

You may have realized by now that there is a lot of work involved in testing software thoroughly. You should also have realized that testing is essential, in order to ensure code quality, correctness and security. However, if it is too time-consuming, developers may be reluctant to do it, especially those who are not actually members of the testing team.

Therefore, the more we can automate the process of testing, the better. The ideal is for the tests to be implemented separately from the system software and to run at the touch of a button. Test automation software includes:

- Loading tools that simulate the load that the system can expect to be subjected to when it goes live. Tools can allow us to load servers in a client–server system by simulating multiple simultaneous client access; user interfaces by simulating the actions of a person; processes by simulating external access; and peers in a distributed system by simulating access by other peers.
- Testing frameworks that comprise reusable code and techniques. The frameworks take the drudgery out of running tests and allows the test developer to concentrate on writing the tests themselves.
- Performance monitoring tools that can monitor anything, from the virtual memory in use by an individual process to the network traffic between machines.
- Metrics-gathering tools that gather metrics from source code or running programs. For example, we could use such a tool to analyze source code, looking for common faults and examining code quality (in much the same way as a style checker in a word processor).
- Specification-exercising tools that take an informal specification of the interface of our software (written by test developers in some special-purpose, executable language) and attempt to test whether the underlying software conforms to the specification. For example, if we specify that a particular message always returns a value less than 10, the tool could verify that this is true for a number of randomly-generated parameters.
- Assertion checking tools that check the assertion code inserted by the developer. Assertion checking involves executing expressions at run-time to make sure that they do not fail (evaluate to false). Thus, assertions can be used to test the code every time it is run.

These tools (and others) are distinguished by the fact that, once they have been configured, the tester can start them up and then just sit back and wait for the results.

# 13.5 PREPARING FOR TESTING

From the point of view of a project manager, the major components of a testing strategy are:

- A test plan: A statement of how we're going to achieve the objectives of a system that is correct and meets the customers' needs. A draft test plan should be written before the development effort gets underway, addressing all phases of the development and all the artifacts produced. A test plan will cover large-scale issues such as testing philosophy and testing techniques, all the way down to tables of individual tests that specify the test name, description, procedure and expected results.
- A test bed: An environment that is similar to the live environment, constructed for the sake of testing. For example, if we're implementing a client–server system to work with clusters of Unix servers (containing the business logic), a database server running on

a mainframe, and multiple clients on arbitrary platforms, we could construct a test bed consisting of:

- ten client machines, using a variety of operating systems;
- three Unix servers;
- a mainframe;
- a TCP/IP-based LAN.

A test bed allows us to test the software safely before it is deployed in the live environment, which is much more sensitive.

- A test harness: A tool that helps us to run our tests or to develop them. A harness supports the testing process, so that our tests are not disorganized. (We could also say that a harness helps us to attach our tests to the code being tested.) For example, a harness may comprise a software framework that provides the code for running our tests and a tool for launching them: the tester only has to implement the tests.

- Test cases: Logical units each comprising a number of tests, designed to check one particular aspect of our software. For example, we might have a test case based on a logical piece of software – class, package, subsystem – or on a logical piece of the business – buying a book, viewing a bank statement, issuing a query.

- Test suites: Collections of related test cases. We can collect test suites into higher-level test suites. For example, we might collect the 'Buy a Share' and 'Sell a Share' test cases into the 'Trading' test suite; we might then combine the 'Trading', 'Banking' and 'Assets' test suites into the 'Money Management' test suite.

- Test procedures: Instructions (for people) on how to carry out each test. This will typically involve steps such as:

1. Set up the test.
2. Perform the test (comparing expected and actual results).
3. Report the test result.

Each of these will comprise smaller steps, such as 'Select File→New from the menu bar' and 'Enter a file name'.

- Test data: Data that we synthesize for the sake of running tests. Before our system is deployed, we do not have real world data available, so test data is our best guess as to the kind of information our system will eventually have to handle. Test data includes data in files; data in databases; and data passed into the system by typical users.

  Some form of test data is essential, because we can't test our software without it: for example, we can't test a component that is designed to retrieve data from a database unless there is something for it to retrieve. Normally, test data has to be hand-crafted by developers, based on intuition and experience, although we may be lucky enough to have it available from past projects, ideally collected from previous versions of the system in use by the real users.

# 13.6 TESTING STRATEGIES

You may think that software should be implemented and then tested, but this strategy is inadequate, for the following reasons:

- It takes no account of the other development artifacts, such as use cases and UML diagrams.
- It encourages developers to defer fault-finding to the testing phase, when faults will be more expensive to fix.
- It's unnatural: every programmer wants to try out pieces of code that they have written as soon as they can (it gives them a warm feeling of security and progress).

Therefore, what we need is a testing strategy that is continuous: everything we produce is tested, all of the time. Since we're dealing with different kinds of artifact, our strategy must also involve different kinds of testing (testing by hand, testing with sample code, automated testing, and so on). We do still need an explicit testing phase, because developers, no matter how brave and enthusiastic they are, won't try to break their own artifacts (their goal is always to ensure that 'it looks okay so far').

For non-code artifacts, testing involves manual checking by:

- The development team, since they're experts with an interest in success.
- Customers, because customers are domain experts who must be involved if we're to deliver a correct and useful system.
- Peers, colleagues who are developers but who are not directly involved in the current project (and who therefore will be less possessive about the artifacts).

For code artifacts, testing involves:

- The development team, so they can witness their own progress (and produce a better quality product).
- Peers, who take part in **code reviews**, helping to spot faults and opportunities for refactoring.
- The testing team, who seek to verify the correctness of the code and validate its effectiveness, for the good of all.

## 13.6.1 Testing During Development

During development, we should test all non-code artifacts manually. If we're using a tool that is tuned to a particular methodology, it may have traceability features that help us to check that dependent artifacts are consistent. However, there will still be a manual element: there is only so much a tool can do and we may have good reasons for disabling or relaxing automatic traceability (such as personal preference, experience, project guidelines or in-house adaptation of a particular methodology).

For the code itself, it is a good idea to encourage programmers to implement tests in parallel with their coding activity. A testing framework such as **JUnit** can help with this: before writing a piece of system code, the programmer writes some sample code that will test the new piece. Thus, when the new piece is complete, the programmer can verify immediately that they were successful. JUnit programmers perform unit testing, regression testing and, to a lesser extent, integration testing.

Programmers should also be encouraged to add dynamic assertion checks to their code. This will enable continuous testing of class invariants, method preconditions and method postconditions, as defined in the specification phase. Programmers may also add assertions within methods to check for other common faults, such as branches that should be impossible to reach.

**Peer reviews** should be organized on a regular basis, at the end of each development spiral, for example. All the artifacts under review are distributed to members of the development team and other peers and then a meeting is arranged to go through them in detail, looking for faults and inadequacies. The goal is to **certify** or **sign off** the artifacts before proceeding. How formal the peer review process is depends on: company policy; customer policy (for example, defense projects tend to be more stringent); project policy; the stage of the development we have reached (are we still feeling our way or is this a mature project?).

With customer reviews, we ask the customer to help us validate and verify the artifacts. Customers should not be involved in reviewing complex artifacts such as sequence diagrams or code. Peer reviews and customer reviews should not be combined, otherwise peers will be inhibited in their constructive criticism by the presence of customers and customers will have to sit through detailed technical discussions.

After the first increment, all increments should be subject to regular (nightly or weekly) build testing.

## 13.6.2 Testing During the Testing Phase

During the testing phase, the testing team takes over the verification and validation of the software before release. This will normally involve:

- Re-running the developers' tests.
- Subsystem testing (including layers), based on the design and specification phases.
- System testing, based mainly on the system use cases developed during the requirements phase.
- Acceptance testing, with end users and system administrators.
- Installation testing, on a variety of platforms if appropriate.

- Documentation testing, of manuals and training materials.
- Beta testing.
- Metrics gathering, both performance metrics and coding-style metrics.

Members of the test team should perform black-box testing and white-box testing.

### 13.6.3 Testing After Release

After release, the testing continues. Every time an end user or administrator starts up or interacts with part of the system, they test it again. There should be a reporting system in place, so that any failures that occur during live use of the system can be reported to the project team (via a support hot-line, e-mail, or a Web site, for example). The reporting system can also be used to provide feedback, such as suggestions for improvement or requests for new features.

Between increments, the project team should fix faults as they're identified. It is then a project management issue to decide whether fixes are released before the next increment. Normally, in order to reduce workload, a number of fixes will be combined into a single **fix pack** that customers can use to update their installation. Improvements, and new features, should be deferred until the next increment.

Any fix that is applied to the system between increments should be regression-tested.

## 13.7 WHAT TO TEST FOR

Since the real world is unpredictable, we can't hope to test everything that might happen to our software. Also, since the number of possible inputs and results grows exponentially with the size of the system, we don't have time to test all the inputs and outputs that we do know about. Therefore, our test cases must be based on experience and guess-work: we must use our experience of the kinds of things that typically go wrong and we must predict which tests will cover the most possibilities – for example, a test that follows ten paths through the system is more useful than a test that follows one path. Another way of thinking about test design is to consider that a test that finds no faults is a bad test: we would prefer our tests not to skirt around likely problems, because that would leave us with a false sense of security.

The kind of testing we do will vary according to the type of application we're dealing with (desktop application or server, for example) and the application domain (e-commerce system, embedded system, safety-critical system, and so on). Therefore, it is not possible to write down the kinds of tests that should be performed for every system. However, below are a few ideas to get you started (some of these ideas relate to black-box testing, some to white-box testing and some to both):

- Test that the code conforms to its specification: We have two main forms of specification: use cases and class-based specifications. These state what the result of correct inputs should be, so we can use them as a guide for designing test cases. We should also test any abnormal paths included in the specification (for example, the specification may state what should happen if an incorrect password is entered). It is not generally feasible to test for all situations where preconditions are violated, because the test space would be infinite. Instead, we should use application firewalls to make sure that preconditions are always respected.

- Test boundary conditions and mid-range conditions: Often, code is expected to deal with ranges. If, for example, a product id is four to ten characters long, we should test, at a minimum, that the code works for a product id of four characters, for ten characters and for somewhere in-between, say seven characters.

- Test for off-by-one faults: With an off-by-one fault, the developer has gone too far or not far enough. For example, when using a for loop to iterate ten times, in Java we might write for (i=1; i<10; i++) when what we actually meant was for (i=1; i<=10; i++). The first version of this loop iterates only nine times.

- Test special cases: Sometimes, developers are so concerned about what happens 99% of the time, they forget to deal with the other 1%. Special cases often need special test coding but exceptional cases are just as important as normal cases.

- Test for unusual situations: For example, when designing an HTML-based client, the developer may assume that the client will only issue one request at a time. But, what if they click a Submit button and then, because they don't receive the expected result, they click the Back button on the result page? The Web application on the server receives two identical requests from the same browser session, when only one was intended.

- Test for memory errors: When using a language such as C++, memory faults are common, because the language allows direct access to memory and because it is more difficult to program. There is also the classic **memory leak** fault, where memory is consumed by the application but never reclaimed. Even languages like Java that have an automatic garbage collector can suffer from high-level memory leaks, such as adding an object to a collection and forgetting to remove it when it's no longer needed.

- Test for code-copying errors: When a multi-branch statement (such as an if−then−else) has many similar branches, a programmer may copy a branch, paste it multiple times and then hand-edit each one; it's all too easy to forget to edit one of the branches.

- Check the use of operators and precedence: Programmers can confuse similar-looking operators, such as & and &&, or make incorrect assumptions about precedence, for example, + being evaluated before a subsequent *.

- Check correct use of equality and identity: As described in Chapter 2, equality and identity have subtle but important differences. For example, are two strings the *same* string or are they two strings with the *same characters*?

- Test that parameters are passed in the correct order: For example, with a method such as bar(int,int), it would be easy for the programmer to write bar(34,2) when they actually meant bar(2,34).
- Check for unintended infinite loops and infinite recursion: An infinite loop is one that never terminates; an infinite recursion is a method that calls itself with no exit condition.
- Test for unreachable code: A programmer can inadvertently implement a branch, in an if statement for example, that is impossible to get to: in this case, they have probably made a mistake in the conditional part of one of the if or else parts.
- Check that errors are reported: Programs occasionally encounter situations that can't be handled; in such cases, we need to make sure that an error message is printed to an error log, for further investigation.
- Test for calculation faults: It is common to make incorrect calculations based on separators. The analogy used is that of constructing a fence: if we're building a 16-meter fence, using 4-meter fence panels separated by fence posts, how many fence posts do we need? The correct answer is not $(16/4)$ but $(16/4 + 1)$, because we need an extra post at the end, as illustrated in Figure 13.4.

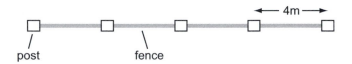

**Figure 13.4: Getting the right number of fence posts**

- Test application firewalls for robustness: Having fault-checking code within our system can be wasteful, especially in cases where there can be no fault. For example, if we have a method foo(int) that requires a parameter between 1 and 10, it is wasteful to check the parameter inside the method if we call the method using foo(2). A better approach is to add an application firewall – a layer of code around the application that ensures that invalid requests can't get in the first place. It's vital to test that our application firewalls protect the application, by trying to break through them.
- Test correct initialization: When a piece of software is initialized (for example, a system is started or an object is created), it should initialize itself to a sensible state. For example, when we start a server, it should be ready to receive requests from clients immediately after initialization: we should not have to start it and then issue several commands before it can be used.
- Test that variables are initialized: When we introduce a variable into our program, we should make sure that it is given a sensible value before it is used. Some programming

languages automatically initialize variables to a sensible default, such as 0 (for numbers) or null (for pointers). However: some languages do not do this and even if they do, the default value may not be what the programmer wanted.

- Test that an object complies with its state machine: A piece of software often has a specific set of legal states. For example, an object that represents a file may have the following legal states (recorded in the attributes): 'doesn't exist in the file system'; 'exists and is open for reading'; 'exists and is open for writing'; 'exists but is closed'. We would want to check that our file object can never enter an illegal state such as 'doesn't exist and is open for reading'. State models, as recorded in UML state machine diagrams, can help here.
- Test that code uses data structure theory: Much has been written about how to implement and use data structures (such as lists, trees, compositions, sets, collections, arrays). For example, if we wish to search for a value in an alphabetical list, it's wasteful to start at the beginning and go through the elements one after the other. Instead, we should look in the middle first: if the value we're seeking is bigger, we look half way towards the end; if the value we're looking for is smaller, we look half way towards the beginning, and so on. For a list with 32768 values, a straight linear search takes 16384 (that is, 32768/2) comparisons, on average, to discover whether the value is present; the **binary chop** search just described only requires 15 comparisons, on average. Familiarize yourself with data structure theory and test that your programmers have too. (If you're really keen, investigate complexity theory.)
- Test for previous faults: After release, every fault that is detected identifies a new test case (because you want to be sure the fault doesn't return after you've fixed it and because it may be an example of a common error). Try keeping a record of all the faults that you and your colleagues have ever discovered, as a guide to the kind of problems that are worth testing for.

What about the tests themselves? Should we test them too? If we did, we would have to test the tests of the tests, and the tests of the tests of the tests, and so on. Luckily, the code that is being tested tests the tests: whenever a test fails, we know that there is a fault in the code being tested *or* a fault in the test itself; during our investigations, we discover which has the fault (and fix it). Also, the tests themselves should be subject to peer review.

---

**Case Study**

*A test plan for iCoot*

A complete test plan for a system the size of iCoot would be a large document, certainly too large to reproduce here. Appendix B.7 contains an outline test plan, of the kind that might be produced early in the first increment.

# 13.8 TEST-DRIVEN DEVELOPMENT

In the mid-1990s, Kent Beck and Erich Gamma designed a framework for test-driven development in Smalltalk. Dubbed **SUnit**, the framework proved to be so popular that it now comes in many flavors: Java, C++, C#, VisualBasic, Eiffel, etc. The term **xUnit** is used to refer to all of these flavors, even though none of them is actually called xUnit (the Java variety is called **JUnit**, there is a C++ variety called **CPPUnit**, and so on). As the name suggests, the framework is designed for unit testing, where each unit is a class, or a combination of classes.

The xUnit family is a simple family: the designers knew that if it were complicated it would hardly ever be used. The idea is that we write testing code in parallel to the system code; the test code can be run easily (and therefore frequently) by developers. Within the test code, the programmer can write methods that test aspects of the application code – sample programs, if you like. Each method can create objects, check that they have been initialized properly, connect them together, send them messages and check the results, and so on.

The core of the framework is illustrated in Figure 13.5. This is an example of the Composite pattern, as described in Chapter 11. The composition allows us to build a hierarchy of tests, with TestSuite objects at the nodes and TestCase objects at the leaves.

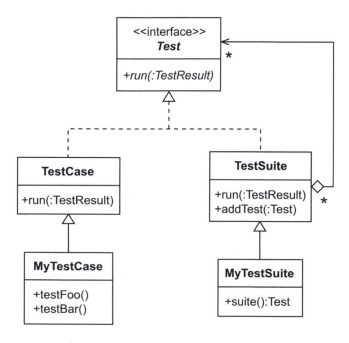

**Figure 13.5: A class diagram for xUnit**

Each test case comprises a number of test methods with the actual testing code inside. Each test suite is a logical grouping of tests, whatever we think makes a sensible hierarchy. For example, we might gather all the test cases for our business objects into one test suite and combine that into another test suite with a suite containing all of our server layer test cases, and so on, all the way up to the system itself.

Once we have implemented our composition, we can use the framework's tools to run the tests.

# 13.9 AN EXAMPLE OF TEST-DRIVEN DEVELOPMENT USING JUNIT

The best way to understand how test-driven development works is to go through an example. The following narrative starts part way through the development of the iCoot business code. For simplicity, this discussion only relates to the business code, rather than any layers above or below. You may think that this would make the narrative artificial. However, in keeping with best practice, the business code should be independent of higher layers anyway, so the steps described here are realistic. In addition, the persistence code would eventually be encapsulated by the business objects so, since we will only be testing the interfaces of the business objects, we will suffer no loss of realism in this respect either. (In the final system, the only major difference in the interface turns out to be that clients use factory methods to create business objects, rather than the actual constructors.)

Java is used as the language for code fragments. However, there is no complicated Java used here (anything unusual, with respect to other object-oriented languages, is only used where necessary and is clearly identified and explained). Since the code fragments are written in Java, the testing framework is, naturally, JUnit.

Let's start by looking at the objects that we're going to develop in the design-level class diagram shown in Figure 13.6:

- Store holds the address of this location and the cars that we have available for rent. (The Store class comes from the full Coot system rather than iCoot – it is introduced here because it helps with the discussion.)
- Address is a simple address class for recording the location of this particular branch.
- Car represents a particular instance of CarModel that we own. (For simplicity, we have omitted the CarModelDetails.)
- CarModel is the intangible complement to Car: it represents a particular model of car that we have available for rent.
- Category indicates the type of car (such as, sports, family, luxury).

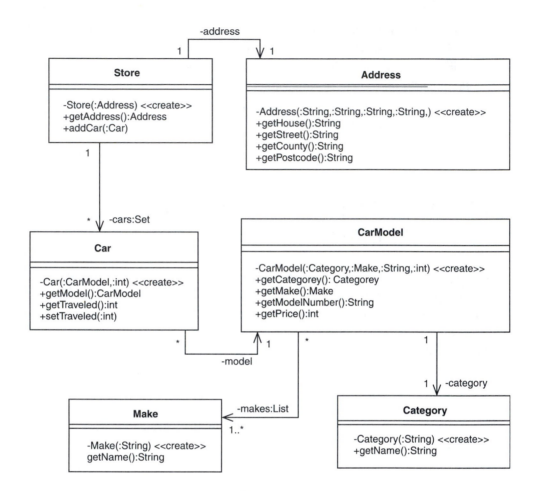

**Figure 13.6: Part of the design class diagram for Coot**

- Set is a Java collection class that allows us to hold on to any number of unique objects.
- Make represents a car manufacturer, identified by name.

Development is already well under way, with Address, CarModel, Category and Make already developed and tested. For each class, a test case has been written to confirm that it functions correctly: AddressTestCase, CarModelTestCase, CategoryTestCase and MakeTestCase, respectively. It is good practice to have one test case per class, designed specifically to exercise that class (because a class is a unit in its own right). Later, we can add test cases that exercise the classes in combination.

The classes have been placed in a package called com.nowherecars.business. The test cases have been placed in the same package as the business classes, so that the tests can use the constructors, which have package visibility.

The tests themselves must be public if we wish to use them with a JUnit test-runner, because the JUnit classes are not in the com.nowherecars.business package. The fact that the tests are visible to clients of the package is not necessarily a bad thing: after all, in the spirit of teamwork and openness, we would be happy for other members of the team to run our tests (especially since we won't release the code until all the tests have been passed). If we want the tests to be invisible to other clients when the code is deployed, we can simply omit the corresponding classes from the deployed version.

## 13.9.1 Testing the Car Class

Before reaching for our coding tools to start writing Car, we remember that the ultimate skill in test-driven development is to write the tests before the code. Thus, we decide to implement CarTestCase first. Writing a test case with JUnit is simple: the new class must inherit from the JUnit TestCase class and it must contain one or more methods that begin with test – the test runner automatically looks for such methods and executes them as part of the test case.

Remembering that each test method should test one thing and test it thoroughly, we decide that our first test will check the creation of a Car. So, our initial CarTestCase is as follows:

```
public class CarTestCase extends TestCase {
    public void testCreate() {
    }
}
```

Inside the testCreate method, we will create a Car, using the constructor which takes a CarModel and the distance traveled on the clock. The creation of the CarModel requires creation of a Category (with a name) and a List of Make objects (each with a name). For convenience, we will only add one Make to the CarModel – after all, we're not testing the CarModel implementation at this point. We will record each attribute as a local variable, both for clarity and in case we need to access the value later.

After writing the code for creating the objects, our testCreate method looks like this:

```
public void testCreate() {
    Category category = new Category("Saloon");
    Make make = new Make("Fort");
    List<Make> makes = new LinkedList<Make>();
    makes.add(make);
    String modelNumber = "Blur 1.6";
    int price = 30;
    CarModel carModel = new CarModel(category, modelNumber, makes, price);
    int traveled = 234243;
    Car car = new Car(carModel, 33445);
}
```

This code fragment uses a Java template class (List). The template type (<Make>) tells the Java compiler what kind of object will be in the collection, so that we can't add anything else.

Now that we've created a Car, we need to do the real work of the test: checking that it was created correctly. In order to do that, we will use the getters for the new Car to compare its attributes with the ones that we used during construction. Our test case has inherited a number of assertX methods from the TestCase class that we can use to make declarations about the expected state of the program – if any of these fail, the test runner will produce a failure report giving us details of where and when the failure happened.

The methods that we're interested in here are assertSame, which takes two objects as parameters and checks that they're identical, i.e. that they both refer to the same object; and assertEquals, which takes two object parameters and checks that they're equal, i.e. that they have similar attributes or that they're of equal value. For example,

- assertSame(aCar,aCar) will pass.
- assertSame(new Object(),new Object()) will fail.
- assertEqual(new Category("Sports"),new Category("Sports")) will pass.
- assertEqual(10,11) will fail.

For our business layer, when we create a Car, the CarModel that we pass in should be identical to the one returned by the getter. That is to say, our program will use the identity of internal objects to represent the identity of objects in the real world, rather than using attribute values. (An alternative approach would be to allow 'same attributes' to indicate 'same object', but this would lead to more copying of objects.) Thus, we need to use assertSame to check the correct setting of the CarModel. On the other hand, the distance traveled is a primitive value (a number of kilometers), so it should be tested using assertEqual. Therefore, we add two new lines to the end of testCreate:

```
...
assertSame(car.getModel(), carModel);
assertEquals(car.getTraveled(), traveled);
}
```

## 13.9.2 Implementing the Car Class

Having implemented the first test for the Car class, we turn our attention to the implementation of Car itself. Car needs: fields for the car model and the distance traveled; a package constructor that takes initial values for both fields; getters for each field; a setter for the distance traveled (we must be able to change the number of kilometers on the clock, so that we can update it when a customer returns the real car, but it wouldn't make sense to be able to change the model). Our Car class is shown below (package access is the default in Java, so the constructor needs no visibility specifier):

```
public class Car {

    private CarModel model;
    private int traveled;

    Car(CarModel m, int t) {
        model = m;
        traveled = t;
    }
    public CarModel getModel() {
        return model;
    }
    public int getTraveled() {
        return traveled;
    }
    public void setTraveled(int t) {
        traveled = t;
    }
}
```

Eager to try out our new test as soon as possible, we start up the JUnit test runner, select our test case and hit the Run button. To our surprise, the test runner indicates that there were failures (as shown in Figure 13.7) and the bar is filled with red. Looking closely at the information given by the test runner, we can see which kind of assertion failed (a numerical comparison between 234243 and 33445), and also where the failure happened.

Looking at the code for testCreate, we quickly discover that the fault is in the test code and not in the business code at all: during our coding of the test, we introduced a local variable called traveled, but we didn't use it when creating the car, so the assertEquals comparison failed. Once we have replaced the number 33445 with traveled, we recompile and re-run the test (which, conveniently, doesn't require a re-start of the test runner). This time, the bar fills up with green, the test runner's way of indicating that everything's fine (see Figure 13.8).

## 13.9.3 Refactoring Tests

We've now completed one test-driven development cycle: write a test, write the code, run the test, fix any problems and run the test again. To complete the testing of the Car class, we need to exercise the setTraveled method. As before, we decide to write the test first, adding the following testSetTraveled method to CarTestCase:

```
public void testSetTraveled() {
    Category category = new Category("Luxury");
    Make make = new Make("Plexus");
    List<Make> makes = new LinkedList<Make>();
    makes.add(make);
```

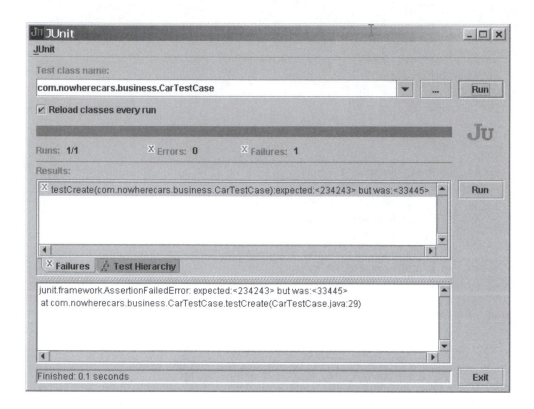

**Figure 13.7: An unsuccessful JUnit test run**

```
    String modelNumber = "Neo STS 3.0";
    int price = 109;
    CarModel carModel = new CarModel(category, makes, modelNumber, price);
    int traveled = 32432;
    Car car = new Car(carModel, traveled);
    int newDistance = 534;
    car.setTraveled(newDistance);
    assertEquals(car.getTraveled(), newDistance);
}
```

We run this test against the Car class and everything works fine, the test runner confirming that two tests have been run. However, we notice that testSetTraveled has a lot in common with testCreate – not surprising since they must both start by creating a Car. For our purposes, it would be quite reasonable for both test methods to use cars with similar attributes. Therefore, we decide to pull out the similar code and place it in a shared method. This process is called **refactoring**: reorganizing code to improve quality.

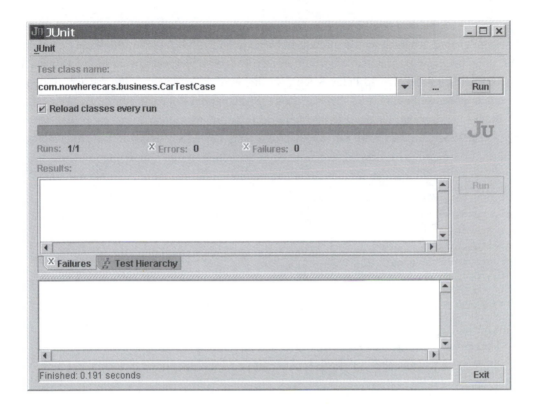

**Figure 13.8: A successful JUnit test run**

We could call the shared method explicitly at the start of each test, but the JUnit designers have already thought of that: if we add a method called setUp, it is called automatically before each test method is run. (If we define a tearDown method, it is also called automatically, after each test – we can use this to release any external resources used during the tests.)

So, what we need is a setUp method that looks like this:

```
protected void setUp() {
    category = new Category("Saloon");
    make = new Make("Fort");
    makes = new LinkedList<Make>();
    makes.add(make);
    modelNumber = "Blur 1.6";
    price = 30;
    carModel = new CarModel(category, makes, modelNumber, price);
    traveled = 234243;
    car = new Car(carModel, traveled);
}
```

Because of the way JUnit has been designed, the setUp method has protected rather than package visibility, which would allow it to be invoked by subclasses and by other classes in the same package. In practice, we would not expect test developers to do such a thing. Our shared fields will be created before each test; this may seem wasteful, but it's actually good practice, because it guarantees that our tests are independent of each other.

Before we proceed, we need to add field declarations for category, makes, modelNumber, price, carModel, traveled and car, so that they can be accessed inside any test method. Therefore, we add the following declarations to our class:

```
private Category category;
private List<Make> makes;
private String modelNumber;
private int price;
private CarModel carModel;
private int traveled;
private Car car;
```

Our testCreate and testSetTraveled methods can now be much simpler:

```
public void testCreate() {
   assertSame(car.getModel(), carModel);
   assertEquals(car.getTraveled(), traveled);
}
public void testSetTraveled() {
   int newDistance = 534;
   car.setTraveled(newDistance);
   assertEquals(car.getTraveled(), newDistance);
}
```

Having made the changes, we re-run our tests and everything still works: as well as checking our business code, the JUnit framework helps us to make sure that modifications to our tests are correct, a form of regression testing.

Having completed our implementation and testing of CarTestCase and Car, the finished classes look like this:

```
public class Car {

   private CarModel model;
   private int traveled;

   Car(CarModel m, int t) {
      model = m;
      traveled = t;
   }
   public CarModel getModel() {
      return model;
```

```
   }
   public int getTraveled() {
      return traveled;
   }
   public void setTraveled(int t) {
      traveled = t;
   }
}

public class CarTestCase extends TestCase {

   private Category category;
   private List<Make> makes;
   private String modelNumber;
   private int price;
   private CarModel carModel;
   private int traveled;
   private Car car;

   protected void setUp() {
      category = new Category("Saloon");
      make = new Make("Fort");
      makes = new LinkedList<Make>();
      makes.add(make);
      modelNumber = "Blur 1.6";
      price = 30;
      carModel = new CarModel(category, makes, modelNumber, price);
      traveled = 234243;
      car = new Car(carModel, traveled);
   }
   public void testCreate() {
      assertSame(car.getModel(), carModel);
      assertEquals(car.getTraveled(), traveled);
   }
   public void testSetTraveled() {
      int newDistance = 534;
      car.setTraveled(newDistance);
      assertEquals(car.getTraveled(), newDistance);
   }
}
```

## 13.9.4 Creating a Test Suite for Regression Testing

Our last task, according to the class diagram we saw earlier, is to implement and test the Store class. As usual, we start with the testing code, producing a StoreTestCase class. Here's how it looks after the implementation of testCreate:

```
public class StoreTestCase extends TestCase {

    private Address address;
    private Store store;
    private CarModel carModel;
    private Car car;

    protected void setUp() {
        address = new Address("9", "Ash Lane", "Greater Manchester", "SK4 3HJ");
        store = new Store(address);
        Category category = new Category("Vintage");
        Make make = new Make("Mostin");
        List<Make> makes = new LinkedList<Make>();
        makes.add(make);
        String modelNumber = "Wheely 1950";
        int price = 89;
        carModel = new CarModel(category, makes, modelNumber, price);
        int traveled = 435345;
        car = new Car(carModel, traveled);
    }
    public void testCreate() {
        assertSame(store.getAddress(), address);
    }
}
```

This time around, we've anticipated the need for a Store in multiple tests, so we've written a setUp method immediately. Our initial Store class looks like the following (notice how the task of adding a Car is delegated to the private Set):

```
public class Store {

    private Address address;
    private Set<Car> cars;

    Store(Address a) {
        address = a;
    }
    public Address getAddress() {
        return address;
    }
    public void addCar(Car c) {
        cars.add(c);
    }
}
```

When we run our first test, everything works fine. However, we have now built up a number of test cases – MakeTestCase, CategoryTestCase, CarModelTestCase, CarTestCase – each of which has to be run individually. This is inconvenient, especially since we should rerun all related tests whenever a piece of code changes. What we need is a test suite – a group of test cases and other test suites that can be run as one.

To build a test suite in JUnit, we add a class that inherits from TestSuite and give it a method called suite, which returns all the tests in the suite. Here's how ours looks:

```java
public class CootBusinessTestSuite extends TestSuite {
    public static Test suite() {
        TestSuite result = new TestSuite();
        result.addTestSuite(MakeTestCase.class);
        result.addTestSuite(CategoryTestCase.class);
        result.addTestSuite(CarModelTestCase.class);
        result.addTestSuite(CarTestCase.class);
        result.addTestSuite(AddressTestCase.class);
        result.addTestSuite(StoreTestCase.class);
        return result;
    }
}
```

The first thing to notice here is that suite returns an object of type Test, rather than TestSuite. However, you may recall from Figure 13.5, that TestSuite and TestCase both inherit from Test. By declaring that it returns a Test, the suite method allows us to return a TestCase instead, which means that we can build a hierarchy of test suites and test cases, while the test runner only has to worry about the single type called Test.

Another odd thing about the suite method is the way that we add our test cases to the suite: result.addTestSuite(MakeTestCase.class). This is a Java trick that allows the test runner to find all methods in the test case that start with test.

In order to run all the tests in a test suite, we use the same test runner as before, only now we point it at the CootBusinessTestSuite class instead of an individual test case such as CarTestCase. When we run our suite, we see the green bar again, indicating that our two new classes are okay, and also that every other part of the suite is okay. This is true regression testing: we have checked that adding new code hasn't broken anything that we already had.

## 13.9.5 Testing Across Methods

Next, we decide to test the addCar method, by providing a testAddCar method in the StoreTestCase:

```java
public void testAddCar() {
    store.addCar(car);
    assertTrue(store.containsCar(car));
}
```

The assertTrue assertion succeeds only if its parameter is true. Thus, the test will succeed if adding a Car to the Store results in the Store containing that Car – this may seem obvious, but even obvious tests need to be implemented.

While writing the assertTrue statement, we have discovered the need for a containsCar method on the Store class itself. Initially, we need this just to check that the addition was successful, but we decide to make it public, because it will probably be useful to other clients. The containsCar method wasn't included in the class diagram we saw earlier, because we didn't know that we needed it. This illustrates that there must be some flexibility between design and coding, which is generally considered to be a good thing. The addition we need to the Store class is:

```
public boolean containsCar(Car c) {
    return cars.contains(c);
}
```

Our new testAddCar method does more than just test addCar: it also tests containsCar. This is common for JUnit test methods.

This time, when we run the tests, we get a test failure with a message containing NullPointerException: a sure sign, to a Java programmer, that we've forgotten to create an object. This time the culprit turns out to be the Store constructor: we've remembered to initialize the address field from the parameter, but we've forgotten to create the Set field that's used to manage our Car objects. What we need to do is to add the following line to the constructor:

```
cars = new HashSet<Car>();
```

(Don't worry about HashSet, it's just one of Java's concrete implementations for the Set interface.)

Now JUnit has helped us spot the incomplete initialization of an object's innards, something that we might not otherwise spot until much later. Another win for test-driven development.

## 13.9.6 Completing the Store Class

There is one more method to add to Store before today's assignment is finished. This method, containsAlternativeCar will return true if and only if there is another Car in the Store that serves the same purpose as the Car given as a parameter: in car rental terms, this means any car that is the same model, regardless of the number of kilometers traveled.

First we add a test to StoreTestCase that will confirm that the new Store method works correctly:

```
public void testContainsAlternativeCar() {
    int traveled2 = 4435;
```

```
    store.addCar(car);
    Car car2 = new Car(carModel, traveled2);
    assertTrue(store.containsAlternativeCar(car2));
}
```

Finally, here's the method that we need to add to Store:

```
public boolean containsAlternativeCar(Car outer) {
    for (Car inner : cars) {
        if (inner.getModel() == outer.getModel()) {
            return true;
        }
    }
    return false;
}
```

The contents of this method may look strange if you're not familiar with Java. It uses a variety of the Java for loop, designed specially for Collection classes, to examine every Car in cars. Within the loop, the model of the inner Car is compared to the model of the outer Car (that was passed in as a parameter); if the models match, we return true. If we examine every Car in the Store without finding a match, we return false.

Happily, when we run our tests this time, the bar stays green, so we know the code is correct (the JUnit motto is 'Keep the bar green to keep the code clean').

The final versions of Store and StoreTestCase are shown below:

```
public class Store {

    private Address address;
    private Set<Car> cars;

    Store(Address a) {
        address = a;
        cars = new HashSet<Car>();
    }
    public Address getAddress() {
        return address;
    }
    public void addCar(Car c) {
        cars.add(c);
    }
    public boolean containsCar(Car c) {
        return cars.contains(c);
    }
    public boolean containsAlternativeCar(Car outer) {
        for (Car inner : cars) {
            if (inner.getModel() == outer.getModel()) {
```

```
                return true;
            }
        }
        return false;
    }
}


public class StoreTestCase extends TestCase {

    private Address address;
    private Store store;
    private CarModel carModel;
    private Car car;

    protected void setUp() {
        address = new Address("9", "Appletree Avenue", "SK5 9PT");
        store = new Store(address);
        Category category = new Category("Vintage");
        Make make = new Make("Mostin");
        List<Make> makes = new LinkedList<Make>();
        makes.add(make);
        String modelNumber = "Wheely 1950";
        int price = 89;
        carModel = new CarModel(category, make, modelNumber, price);
        int traveled = 435345;
        car = new Car(carModel, traveled);
    }
    public void testCreate() {
        assertSame(store.getAddress(), address);
    }
    public void testAddCar() {
        store.addCar(car);
        assertTrue(store.containsCar(car));
    }
    public void testContainsAlternativeCar() {
        int traveled2 = 4435;
        store.addCar(car);
        Car car2 = new Car(carModel, traveled2);
        assertTrue(store.containsAlternativeCar(car2));
    }
}
```

Our narrative ends at this point, having covered a real-world example of test-driven development (complete with faults and iterations, as they happened). The developers moved on to add homes, universal identifiers, persistence code and server code. Then, a simple client was added to test everything that had been developed. Throughout, test cases were created and composed into test suites, layer by layer, and the tests were run frequently.

# 13.10 SUMMARY

In this chapter we have looked at:

- The terminology used by testers to summarize complex concepts and tasks. Although there are a couple of dozen terms in common use, they're used consistently by the testing community, so it's worth knowing what they are.

- How to go about testing a large system. This involved discussions of test planning, continuous testing, testing of all artifacts (not just code), and how the different people should be involved.

- A worked example of test-driven development. Test-driven development is valuable, but it should never be considered a substitute for the aggressive attempts to break code by colleagues and customers, during the official testing phase.

# FURTHER READING

A long-standing text on all aspects of software testing is [Myers *et al.* 04], considered by many to be essential reading for those who wish to understand the theory of testing and how to apply it in the real world.

One of the inventors of test-driven development, Kent Beck, describes the philosophy and practice in [Beck 02]. The home page for JUnit is www.junit.org, containing the framework itself, plus technical documentation, articles and examples.

# Appendix A

## Ripple Summary

This appendix gives a complete overview of Ripple, the simplified methodology used in this book. Table A.1 summarizes the artifacts that you should produce, by phase. To produce these artifacts, proceed as follows (but remember to spiral, iterate and deliver incrementally):

1. **Project Genesis (with Customer)**

    (a) Get an idea of what the customer is looking for or tell them what they need.
    (b) Get requirements documentation from the customer, as a mission statement or a longer document; if neither of these exist, produce an informal requirements document with the customer.

2. **Assigning Responsibilities**

    (a) Decide on the development roles (e.g. planning, management, timekeeping, development, testing, system administration).
    (b) Decide who is going to be responsible for each role.

3. **Producing a Workbook**: Produce a paper or on-line workbook, to contain all project artifacts.

4. **Producing a Glossary**

    (a) Produce a glossary for recording the definitions of project terminology.
    (b) Update the glossary throughout development.

5. **Producing a Project Plan**

    (a) Do some initial planning for spirals, phases and increments, and produce a schedule.
    (b) Review and adjust the project plan at regular intervals throughout development.

6. **Producing a Test Plan**: Produce a test plan that addresses continuous testing, the testing phase, customer reviews, deployment and maintenance.

7. **Business Requirements (with Customer)**

    (a) Produce a business actor list (with descriptions).
    (b) Produce a business use case list (with descriptions).
    (c) (Optional) Brainstorm or illustrate business use cases with activity diagrams.

## Table A.1: Artifacts by phase

| Phase | | Artifacts | UML |
|---|---|---|---|
| Genesis | | Mission statement or informal requirements<br>Roles<br>Responsibilities<br>Project plan<br>Workbook<br>Glossary (update throughout)<br>Test plan | No<br>No<br>No<br>No<br>No<br>No<br>No |
| Requirements | Business | Actor list (with descriptions)<br>Use case list (with descriptions)<br>Use case details<br>Activity diagrams (optional)<br>Communication diagrams (optional) | No<br>No<br>No<br>Yes<br>Yes |
| | System | Actor list (with descriptions)<br>Use case list (with descriptions)<br>Use case details<br>Use case diagram<br>Use case survey<br>User interface sketches | No<br>No<br>No<br>Yes<br>No<br>No |
| Analysis | | Class diagram<br>Communication diagrams | Yes<br>Yes |
| Design | System | Deployment diagram<br>Layer diagram | Yes<br>No |
| | Subsystem | Class diagrams<br>Sequence diagrams<br>Database schema | Yes<br>Yes<br>No |
| Class Specification | | Comments | No |
| Implementation | | Source code | No |
| Testing | | Test reports | No |
| Deployment | | Shrink wrapped solution<br>Manuals<br>Training material | No<br>No<br>No |
| Maintenance | | Fault reports<br>Increment plans | No<br>No |

(d) (Optional) Brainstorm or illustrate business use cases with communication diagrams.

(e) Produce business use case details.

8. **System Requirements (with Customer)**

(a) Brainstorm system interaction using user interface sketches.

(b) Produce a system actor list (with descriptions).

(c) Produce a system use case list (with descriptions).

(d) Produce a system use case diagram.

(e) Produce a system use case survey.

(f) Produce system use case details.

(g) Produce supplementary requirements for the system.

(h) Produce system use case priorities.

9. **Analysis**

(a) Produce an analysis class diagram.

(b) Produce an attribute list (with descriptions).

(c) (Optional) Use state machines to model complex entity life cycles, recording results on state machine diagrams.

(d) Perform use case realization, documenting results using communication diagrams.

(e) Produce an operation list (with descriptions).

10. **System Design**

(a) Make technology choices.

(b) Look for reuse opportunities (libraries, patterns and frameworks).

(c) Produce layer diagrams.

(d) Write a layer interaction policy.

(e) Design the package structure and record it on package diagrams.

(f) Produce a deployment diagram.

(g) Write a security policy.

(h) Write a concurrency policy.

11. **Subsystem Design**

(a) Define business services.

(b) Look for more reuse opportunities (libraries, patterns and frameworks).

(c) Map analysis classes to business layer classes: class list (with descriptions), class diagram, field list (with descriptions).

(d) Produce a database schema.

(e) Design classes for other layers (e.g. server and protocol, servlets, control, persistence).

(f) Perform business service realization, recording results on sequence diagrams.

(g) Produce a message list (with descriptions).

(h) Finalize the user interface design.

12. **Class Specification**

(a) Produce an informal specification for each class.

(b) Record the informal specification in design and source code.

13. **Implementation**

(a) Write unit tests.

(b) Write implementation code.

14. **Testing**

(a) Get the test team to test the system.

(b) Fix faults.

15. **Deployment**

(a) Produce manuals and courseware.

(b) Install code artifacts on customer's system.

(c) Train customer.

16. **Maintenance**

(a) Fix faults.

(b) Incorporate customer feedback, ideas for improvement and market changes into new increments.

# Appendix B

## iCoot Case Study

# B.1 BUSINESS REQUIREMENTS

This section documents the business requirements modeling carried out during the requirements phase of the iCoot development, in terms of project mission statement and business use case model. The business use case model also applies to the full Coot system.

## B.1.1 Customer's Mission Statement

Below is the mission statement delivered by Nowhere Cars at the start of the Coot project:

> Since we automated the tracking of cars at our stores – using bar codes, counter-top terminals and laser readers – we have seen many benefits: the productivity of our rental assistants has increased 20%, cars rarely go missing and our customer base has grown strongly (according to our market research, this is at least partly due to the improved perception of professionalism and efficiency.
>
> The management feels that the Internet offers further exciting opportunities for increasing efficiency and reducing costs. For example, rather than printing catalogs of available cars, we could make the catalog available to every Internet surfer for browsing on-line. For privileged customers, we could provide extra services, such as reservations, at the click of a button. Our target saving in this area is a reduction of 15% in the cost of running each store.
>
> Within two years, using the full power of e-commerce, we aim to offer all of our services via a Web browser, with delivery and pick-up at the customer's home, thus achieving our ultimate goal of the virtual rental company, with minimal running costs relative to walk-in stores.

Working with the customer, this mission statement was expanded into business use cases.

## B.1.2 Actor List

- Assistant: An employee at one of our stores who helps a Customer to rent a Car and reserve a CarModel.
- Customer: A person who pays us money in return for one of our standard services.

- Member: A Customer whose identity and credit-worthiness have been validated and who, therefore, has access to special services (such as making a Reservation by phone or over the Internet).
- NonMember: A Customer whose identity and credit-worthiness have not been checked and who, therefore, must provide a deposit to make a Reservation and surrender a copy of their License to rent a Car.
- Auk: The existing system that handles Customer details, Reservations, Rentals and the Catalog of available CarModels.
- DebtDepartment: The department that deals with unpaid fees.
- LegalDepartment: The department that deals with accidents in which a rented Car has been involved.

## B.1.3 Use Case List

- B1:Customer Rents Car: Customer rents a Car that they have selected from those available.
- B2:Member Reserves CarModel: Member asks to be notified when a CarModel becomes available.
- B3:NonMember Reserves CarModel: NonMember pays a deposit to be notified when a CarModel becomes available
- B4:Customer Cancels Reservation: Customer cancels an unconcluded Reservation, by phone or in person.
- B5:Customer Returns Car: Customer returns a Car that they have rented.
- B6:Customer Told CarModel Is Available: Customer is contacted by an Assistant when a Car becomes available.
- B7:Car Reported Missing: Customer or Assistant discovers that a Car is missing.
- B8:Customer Renews Reservation: Customer renews a Reservation that has been outstanding for more than a week.
- B9:Customer Accesses Catalog: Customer browses the catalog, in-Store or at home.
- B10: Customer Fined for Uncollected Reservation: Customer fails to collect a Car that they have reserved.
- B11:Customer Collects Reserved Car: Customer collects a Car that they have reserved.
- B12:Customer Becomes a Member: Customer provides CreditCard details and proof of address to become a Member.
- B13:Customer Notified Car Is Overdue: Assistant contacts Customer to warn them that a Car they have rented is more than a week overdue.
- B14:Customer Loses Keys: Replacement keys are provided for a Customer who has lost them.
- B15:MembershipCard Is Renewed: Assistant contacts Member to renew membership when their CreditCard has expired.
- B16:Car Is Unreturnable: A Car is wrecked or breaks down.

## B.1.4 Use Case Communication Diagrams

Communication diagrams were not used widely during business requirements modeling (although they were used extensively during system requirements gathering). However, one diagram (see Figure B.1) was produced to illustrate the external and internal actors involved in B3:NonMember Reserves CarModel.

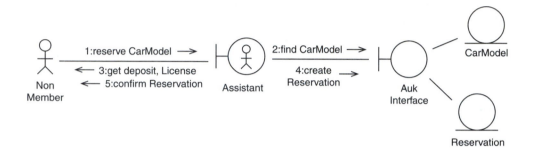

**Figure B.1: Communication diagram for B3:NonMember Reserves CarModel**

## B.1.5 Use Case Activity Diagrams

Activity diagrams were not used widely during the business requirements modeling. However, one diagram (see Figure B.2) was produced to illustrate the finer points of the B3:NonMember Reserves CarModel use case.

## B.1.6 Use Case Details

B1:Customer Rents Car.

1. Customer tells Assistant which CarModel they'd like to rent.
2. If Auk indicates no such Car is available, Customer is offered an alternative.
3. If there is a Car available, Assistant marks the Car as taken in Auk.
4. Assistant asks for Customer's License to confirm their identity.
5. For a Member, Assistant takes their number from their MembershipCard and checks that they have no outstanding fees and that they have not been barred.
6. For a NonMember, Assistant checks whether they're already in Auk; if they're not, Assistant scans a copy of their License into Auk, and records their name, phone number and license number.
7. If Customer's details are satisfactory and they have paid any outstanding fees, they're charged for the Rental.
8. If the payment fails, the Car is released in Auk.

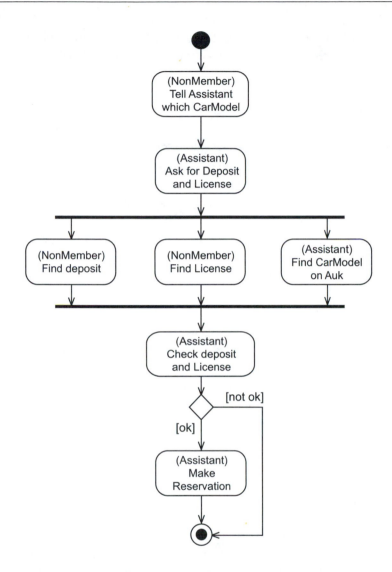

**Figure B.2: Activity diagram for B3:NonMember Reserves CarModel**

9. If the payment does not fail, the Customer is given the keys and directed to the display area.

B2:Member Reserves CarModel.
1. Member tells Assistant their membership number (over the phone or in person).
2. Member tells Assistant which CarModel to reserve.
3. If Member has not been barred, their CreditCard has not expired, and they have no outstanding fees, a Reservation is made on Auk.

4. If the Reservation is being made over the phone, Member can pay outstanding fees by confirming their CreditCard details, which must match those stored in Auk and must not have expired.

5. Member is told the reservation number.

### B3:NonMember Reserves CarModel.

1. NonMember tells Assistant which CarModel to reserve.
2. Assistant finds CarModel on Auk.
3. Assistant asks for a deposit for the Reservation.
4. Assistant asks for NonMember's License and phone number.
5. Assistant checks License visually.
6. If License looks valid, Assistant creates a new Reservation, recording the License number, phone number and a scan of the License in Auk.
7. Assistant gives NonMember a Reservationslip containing the unique reservation number.

### B4:Customer Cancels Reservation.

1. At any time, Customer can cancel a Reservation.
2. Member objects can do this over the phone or in person, by providing their membership number.
3. NonMembers must cancel in person: they present their License to an Assistant, who checks that it matches the scan in Auk, and refunds their deposit.
4. If a Car has already been moved to the reserved area, a matching Car is moved back to the display area.

### B5:Customer Returns Car.

1. When a Car is returned to the check-in area, Assistant scans bar code to confirm the return and checks that the tank is full.
2. Car is returned to the display area by an Assistant.
3. If Customer returns an overdue Car or a Car with a tank that is not full, Customer must pay the appropriate amount – Members can do this using their existing credit card details, if they have not expired.
4. If the Customer refuses to pay, their details are passed to the DebtDepartment.

### B6:Customer Told Car Model is Available.

1. When a Car is returned, Auk tells Assistant whether it matches any Reservation objects.
2. If so, Assistant moves Car to the reserved area.
3. On a first-come-first-served basis, Assistant will try to contact a matching Customer by phone.
4. If a Customer can't be reached within two days, their Reservation is canceled and the Car is moved out of the reserved area to the display area.

B7:Car Reported Missing.
1. If a Car that Auk indicates is in the display area can't be found when it is needed or during a stock check, Car is reported stolen to the police.
2. If a Car is reported missing by a Customer, it is reported stolen to the police, along with License details of the Customer (as the last known keeper of the vehicle).
3. In both cases, the date of loss is recorded on Auk.

B8:Customer Renews Reservation.
1. If a Reservation can't be satisfied within seven days, the Reservation must be renewed.
2. Assistant has two days to contact Customer by phone to see if they wish to renew the Reservation for a further seven days.
3. If the Customer doesn't wish to renew, the Reservation is canceled; Customer must return to the Store and present their License to retrieve their deposit.

B9:Customer Accesses Catalog.
1. Customers can come into the Store to browse a paper catalog.
2. For a fee, they can take a copy of the catalog home with them.
3. If they choose to join the mailing list, they will receive a free copy of the catalog by mail every six months.

B10: Customer Fined for Uncollected Reservation.
1. If a CarModel has become available for a particular Reservation and an Assistant told the Customer by phone that it's available, Customer has two days to collect.
2. If Customer fails to collect, the Reservation is concluded and an Assistant moves a matching Car from the reserved area back to the display area.
3. For NonMembers, their deposit is forfeited.
4. For Members, a fine is recorded on Auk and their details are passed to the DebtDepartment.

B11:Customer Collects Reserved Car.
1. Customer comes to the Store to collect a Car from the reserved area.
2. Customer presents License.
3. If the License matches the details on Auk, the Reservation is marked as concluded.
4. An Assistant gives the keys to the Customer and directs them to the reserved area.

B12:Customer Becomes Member.
1. In order to become a Member, Customer must offer their License, further proof of address, and a credit card.
2. Assistant checks License and proof of address.
3. Assistant checks CreditCard with CreditCardCompany.

4. If okay, Assistant records License number, address, phone number and CreditCard details in Auk.
5. Auk issues new MembershipCard with unique membership number.
6. If the CreditCard expires, no further member actions are permitted unless the member returns to the Store to show a new CreditCard.

B13:Customer Notified Car is Overdue.

1. Since a Rental is paid up-front, Customer is warned if they have forgotten to return a Car.
2. If Car is more than one week overdue, an Assistant will attempt to contact Customer by phone.
3. If Customer can't be contacted for two weeks, Car is reported missing (see B7).

B14:Customer Loses Keys.

1. If Customer notifies Assistant that they have lost keys, replacement keys are provided, by courier if necessary.
2. Cost of replacement is added to Customer's details in Auk.

B15:MembershipCard is Renewed.

1. Auk records that Member whose CreditCard has expired is not in good standing.
2. Auk informs Assistant that Member's Credit card has expired.
3. Assistant contacts Member by phone to tell them that they must renew their membership.
4. Member returns to Store with fresh CreditCard and details are entered into Auk.
5. Auk records that Member is in good standing.

B16:Car is Unreturnable.

1. If Customer tells Assistant that Car is wrecked or breaks down, Assistant arranges recovery.
2. If Car is wrecked, details are passed to LegalDepartment.

# B.2  SYSTEM REQUIREMENTS

This section documents the results of system modeling during the requirements phase of the iCoot development, in terms of user interface sketches and a system use case model.

## B.2.1  User Interface Sketches

The user interface sketches for iCoot, produced with the help of the customer, are shown in Figures B.3 through B.10.

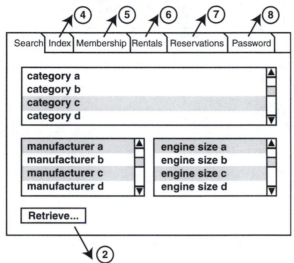

*Non-Members see only Search + Index pages;*
*Members needlogon and logoff mechanism too.*

**Figure B.3: User interface sketch 1 (creating a query)**

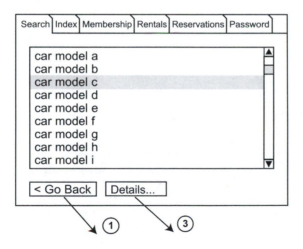

**Figure B.4: User interface sketch 2 (viewing results)**

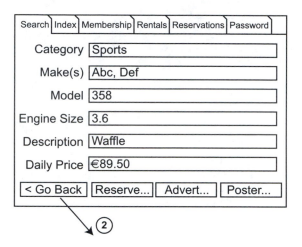

**Figure B.5: User interface sketch 3 (viewing car model details)**

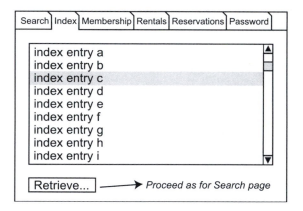

**Figure B.6: User interface sketch 4 (selecting an index heading)**

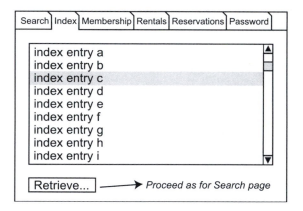

**Figure B.7: User interface sketch 5 (viewing membership details)**

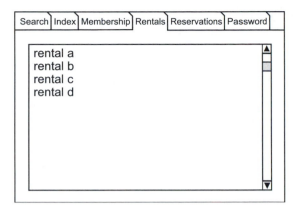

**Figure B.8: User interface sketch 6 (viewing rentals)**

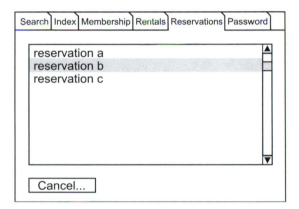

**Figure B.9: User interface sketch 7 (viewing reservations)**

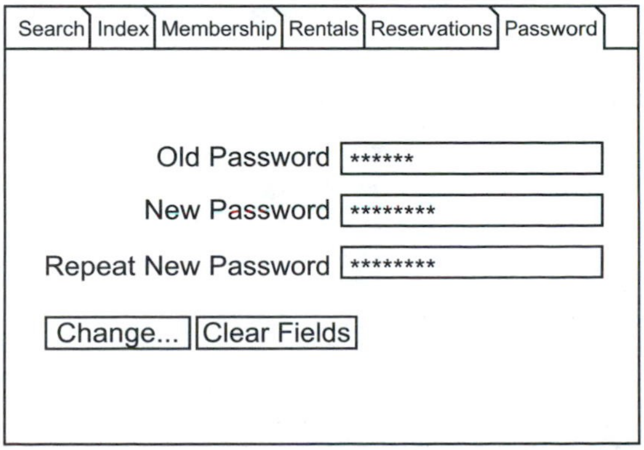

| Search | Index | Membership | Rentals | Reservations | Password |

Old Password    ******

New Password    ********

Repeat New Password    ********

Change... | Clear Fields

**Figure B.10: User interface sketch 8 (changing a password)**

## B.2.2 Actor List

- Customer: A person using a Web browser to access iCoot.
- Member: A Customer who has presented their name, address and CreditCard details at one of our Stores; each Member is given an Internet password to accompany their membership number. (Specializes Customer.)
- NonMember: A Customer who is not a Member. (Specializes Customer.)
- Assistant: An employee at a Store who contacts Members to tell them about the progress of their Reservations.

## B.2.3 Use Case List

- U1:Browse Index: A Customer browses the index of CarModels. (Specializes U13, includes U2.)
- U2:View Results: A Customer is shown the subset of CarModels that were retrieved. (Included by U1 and U4, extended by U3.)
- U3:View CarModel Details: A Customer is shown the details of a retrieved CarModel, such as description and advert. (Extends U2, extended by U7.)
- U4:Search: A Customer searches for CarModels by specifying Categories, Makes and engine sizes. (Specializes U13, includes U2.)
- U5:Log On: A Member logs on to iCoot using their membership number and current password. (Extended by U6, U8, U9, U10 and U12.)
- U6:View Member Details: A Member views some of the details stored by iCoot, such as name, address and CreditCard details. (Extends U5.)
- U7:Make Reservation: A Member reserves a CarModel when viewing its details. (Extends U3.)
- U8:View Rentals: A Member views a summary of the Cars they're currently renting. (Extends U5.)
- U9:Change Password: A Member changes the password that they use to log on. (Extends U5.)
- U10: View Reservations: A Member views summaries of their unconcluded Reservations, such as date, time and CarModel. (Extends U5, extended by U11.)
- U11:Cancel Reservation: A Member cancels an unconcluded Reservation. (Extends U10.)
- U12:Log Off: A Member logs off from iCoot. (Extends U5.)
- U13:Look for CarModels: A Customer retrieves a subset of CarModels from the catalog. (Abstract, generalized by U1 and U4.)

## B.2.4 Use Case Diagram

The use case diagram for iCoot is shown in Figure B.11.

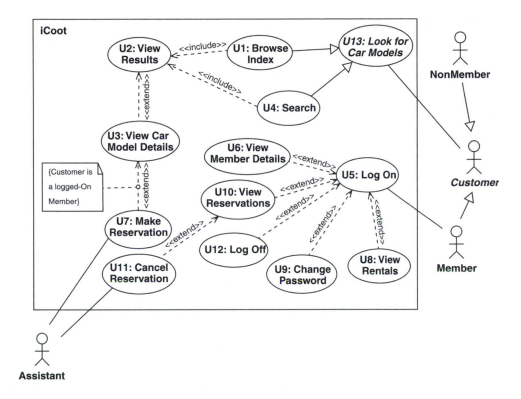

**Figure B.11: Use case diagram for iCoot**

# B.2.5 Use Case Survey

The use case survey for iCoot, describing how the use cases fit together, is:

Any Customer can look for CarModels in the catalog, by browsing the CarModel index (U1) or by searching (U4). In the latter case, the Customer specifies the Categories, Makes and engine sizes that they're interested in. Either way, after each retrieval, the Customer is shown the results as a collection of matching CarModels (U2), along with basic information such as CarModel name. The Customer can then choose to view extra information about particular CarModel objects such as a description and an advert (U3).

A Customer who has become a Member can log on (U5) and gain access to extra services. The extra services are: making a Reservation (U7), canceling a Reservation (U11), checking membership details (U6), viewing outstanding Reservations (U10), changing their log-on password (U9), viewing their outstanding Rentals (U8) and logging off (U12).

Assistants are involved in the life cycle of Reservations, moving Cars to and from the reserved area, for example.

Customers come in two varieties, Members and NonMembers.

Browsing the index and searching for CarModels are two different ways of looking for CarModels (U13). In order to view CarModel details, a Customer must be viewing the results of looking for models (via the browsing or searching route).

In order to reserve a CarModel, a Member must be viewing its details (NonMembers can't make reservations, even when they're viewing details).

In order to cancel a Reservation, a Member must be viewing their outstanding Reservations.

## B.2.6  Use Case Details

U1:Browse Index. (Specializes U13, includes U2.)

Preconditions: None.

1.  Customer selects an index heading.
2.  Customer elects to view CarModels for the selected index heading.
3.  Include U2.

Postconditions: None.

U2:View Results. (Included by U1 and U4, extended by U3.)

Preconditions: None.

1.  iCoot presents Customer with a summary of each retrieved CarModel, including model number and price.
2.  Extend with U3.

Postconditions: None.

U3:View CarModel Details. (Extends U2, extended by U7.)

Preconditions: None.

1.  Customer selects one of the matching CarModels.
2.  Customer requests details of the selected CarModel.
3.  iCoot displays details for the selected car model (makes, engine size, price, description, advert and poster).
4.  If Customer is a logged-on Member, extend with U7.

Postconditions: iCoot has displayed details of selected CarModels.

Non-Functional Requirements: r1. Adverts should be displayed using a streaming protocol rather than requiring a download.

U4:Search. (Specializes U13, includes U2.)

Preconditions: None.

1.  Customer selects required categories (if any).
2.  Customer selects required Makes (if any).

3. Customer selects required engine sizes (if any).

4. Customer initiates the search.

5. Include U2.

Postconditions: None.

Abnormal paths: a1. If Customer specifies no categories, makes or engine sizes, rather than retrieving the entire catalog, iCoot should not allow the search to be initiated.


U5:Log On. (Extended by U6, U8, U9, U10 and U12.)

Preconditions: Member has obtained a password from their local Store.

1. Member enters the membership number.

2. Member enters the password.

3. Since iCoot must enforce one logon for a Member, Member can choose to steal (invalidate and thus take over from) an existing session.

4. Member elects to log on.

5. Extend with U6, U8, U9, U10, U12.

Postconditions: Member is logged on.

Abnormal Paths: a1. If the membership number/password combination is incorrect, iCoot informs Member that one of the two is incorrect (for security, they're not told which one).

a2. If the membership number/password combination is correct, but Member is already logged on and they have not elected to steal, iCoot informs Member.


U6:View Member Details. (Extends U5.)

1. Member elects to view membership details.

2. Member is presented with membership details (name, address, status, amount owing, CreditCard details).

3. For security reasons, iCoot must display only the last four digits of the Member's CreditCard number.

4. iCoot informs Member that to correct details, they must contact their local Store.

Postconditions: Member has been presented with membership details.


U7:Make Reservation. (Extends U3.)

Preconditions: Customer is a Member who has logged on.

1. Member elects to reserve CarModel for the details on display.

2. iCoot asks Member for confirmation, issuing a warning that failure to collect a reserved CarModel will result in a fine.

3. Member confirms Reservation.

4. iCoot shows Member the Reservation number and indicates that Assistant will be in touch when a Car is available.

5. When an Assistant logs on to Coot, Assistant is given a list of Reservations that require action.

6. Assistant takes necessary action to progress Reservations (e.g. promoting to Collectable if a Car is available and moving the Car to the reserved area).

Postconditions: Any requested Reservations have been made.

Abnormal Paths: a1. If Member declines Reservation conditions, no Reservation is made.

U8:View Rentals. (Extends U5.)

Preconditions: None. Relationships: U5.

1. Member elects to view their Rentals.
2. iCoot presents Member with summary of each Car they currently have out for rent (including number plate and due date).

Postconditions: iCoot has presented Member with summaries of Cars currently rented.

U9:Change Password. (Extends U5.)

Preconditions: None.

1. Member elects to change password.
2. Member enters old password (which is obscured on screen).
3. Member enters new password (obscured).
4. Member enters new password again (for confirmation, also obscured).
5. Member initiates the change.
6. iCoot asks for confirmation (warning that new password must be memorable).
7. If Member confirms, password is changed.

Postconditions: Password has been changed.

Abnormal Paths: a1. If old password is incorrect or new passwords don't match, Member is informed (but not given details of the error, for security) and password is unchanged.

a2. If old passwords match but new password doesn't follow password rules (a mix of at least six letters and digits), Member is informed and password is unchanged.

U10: View Reservation objects. (Extends U5, extended by U11.)

Preconditions: None.

1. Member elects to view Reservations.
2. iCoot displays summaries of the Member's outstanding (unconcluded) Reservations (including number, state, timestamp and CarModel number).
3. Extend with U11.

Postconditions: Member has been presented with summary of outstanding Reservations.

U11:Cancel Reservation. (Extends U10.)

Preconditions: None.

1. Member selects a Reservation.
2. Member elects to cancel the Reservation.
3. iCoot asks for confirmation.

4. Member confirms that they wish to cancel the Reservation.

5. iCoot marks the Reservation as Concluded and updates Assistants' terminals accordingly.

Postconditions: Any canceled Reservations that were confirmed have been marked as Concluded.

Abnormal Paths: a1. If Member doesn't confirm a cancellation, iCoot takes no action.

U12:Log Off.

Preconditions: None.

1. Member elects to log off.

2. iCoot ends current session.

3. iCoot makes Member-only functions unavailable to Member.

Postconditions: Member is logged off.

Abnormal Paths: a1. For security reasons, a logged-on Member is logged off automatically if they do not interact with iCoot for ten minutes.

U13:Look for CarModels (Abstract, specialized by U1 and U4.)

Preconditions: None.

Postconditions: Customer has been presented with summaries of retrieved CarModels.

# B.2.7 Supplementary Requirements

s1. The client applet must run in Java PlugIn 1.2 (and later versions).

s2. iCoot must be able to cope with a catalog of 100,000 CarModels.

s3. iCoot must be able to serve 1,000,000 Customers simultaneously with no significant degradation in performance.

# B.2.8 Use Case Priorities

Below is the list of use case priorities for iCoot, with the scores that were used for the first increment.

- **Green**:
    - U1: Browse Index
    - U4: Search
    - U2: View Results
    - U3: View CarModel Details
    - U5: Log On
- **Amber**:
    - U12: Logoff.
    - U6: View Member Details
    - U7: Make a Reservation
    - U10: View Reservations

- **Red**:
  - U11: Cancel Reservation
  - U8: View Rentals
  - U9: Change Password

During the first increment, U6 was also completed. The other use cases were completed during the second increment.

# B.3 ANALYSIS

This section documents the results of the analysis phase of the iCoot development, in terms of analysis class model, a state machine for a Reservation and use case realization (communication diagrams). The Reservation state machine also applies to the full Coot system. The class model includes a few pieces from the full Coot schema, such as NonMember and dateLost.

## B.3.1 Class Diagram

The analysis class diagram for iCoot is shown in Figure B.12. Most of these classes also appear in the design class model (Section B.5), so their descriptions have been placed in the Glossary (Section B.8), to avoid repetition.

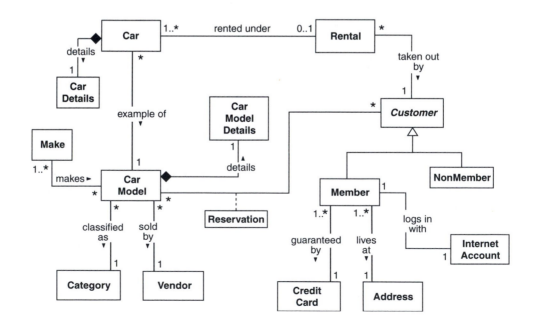

**Figure B.12: Analysis class diagram**

# B.3.2 Attributes

The class attributes for iCoot are shown in Figure B.13. These attributes also appear in the design class model as fields, where they're given types and descriptions – refer to the design documentation (Section B.5) for details.

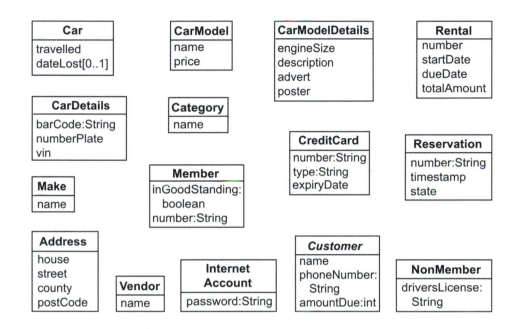

**Figure B.13: Analysis attributes**

# B.3.3 Operation List

- CarModel:
  - getSummary() – Fetch a summary of the receiver, including model number and price.
  - getDetails() – Fetch the receiver's details, including makes, engine size, price, description, advert and poster.
- CarModelHome:
  - findByIndexHeading(h:String) – Search for CarModel objects under index heading h.
  - findByQuery(categories,makes,sizes) – Search for CarModel objects with Category from categories, a Make in makes and engine size in sizes.
- LogonController:
  - logon(n:String,p:String,s:boolean) – Log on the Member with membership number n and password p, specifying whether or not to steal any existing session with s.

- changePassword(m:Member,o:String,n1:String,n2:String) – Change the password for m to n1, as long as n2 matches and the current password is o.
- logoff() – Log off the logged-on Member.
- Member:
  - getPassword():String – Fetch the receiver's password.
  - isLoggedOn():boolean – True if the receiver is logged on.
  - logon() – Log the receiver on.
  - logoff() – Log the receiver off.
  - getDetails() – Fetch the receiver's details, including name, address, status, amount owing and (concealed) credit card details
  - setPassword(p:String) – Set the receiver's password to p.
- MemberHome: findByMembershipNumber(n:String):Member – Find the Member with membership number m.
- MemberUI:
  - search(categories,makes,sizes) – Search for CarModel objects with a Category from categories, a Make in makes and engine size in sizes.
  - index(h:String) – Search for CarModel objects under index heading h.
  - logon(n:String,p:String,s:boolean) – Log on the Member with membership number n, password p, specifying whether or not to steal any existing session with s.
  - setMember(m:Member) – Set the logged-on Member to m.
  - showMemberDetails() – Show details for the logged-on Member.
  - showRentals() – Show Rental objects for the logged-on Member.
  - showReservations() – Show unconcluded Reservation objects for the logged-on Member.
  - changePassword(o:String,n1:String,n2:String) – Change the password for the logged on Member to n1, as long as n2 matches and the current password is o.
  - confirmChange() – Confirm that the password really should be changed.
  - reserve(c:CarModel) – Reserve c for the logged-on Member.
  - confirmReserve() – Confirm that the Reservation really should be made.
  - cancel(r:Reservation) – Cancel r.
  - confirmCancel() – Confirm that the Reservation really should be canceled.
  - showDetails(c:CarModel) – Show details for c.
  - logoff() – Log off the logged-on Member.
- NonMemberUI:
  - search(categories,makes,sizes) – Search for CarModel objects with a Category from categories with a Make in makes and engine size in sizes.
  - index(h:String) – Search for CarModel objects under index heading h.
- Rental: getSummary() – Fetch a summary of the receiver, including number plate and due date.
- RentalHome: findByMember(m:Member – Fetch the Rental objects for member m.

- Reservation:
  - getSummary() – Fetch a summary of the receiver, including number, timestamp, state and CarModel.
  - getNumber() – Fetch the receiver's number.
  - setState(s) – Set the receiver's state to s.
- ReservationHome:
  - findByMember(m:Member) – Fetch the reservations for m.
  - create(c:CarModel,m:Member) – Reserve c for m, with the current date and time.

## B.3.4  State Machine for a Reservation

Figure B.14 shows the state machine diagram for a Reservation, produced to model its complex life cycle. The accompanying state machine survey is:

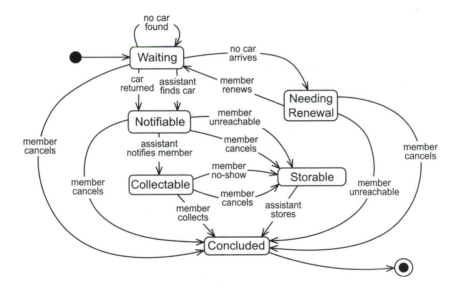

**Figure B.14: State machine diagram for a Reservation**

When a Member reserves a CarModel over the Internet, the Reservation is initially Waiting to be processed by an Assistant (this is so the Customer can make a Reservation without the intervention of an Assistant). The Reservation becomes Notifiable if, some time later, an Assistant finds a suitable unreserved Car in the display area of the car park, or if one is returned by a Customer. In this case, the Car is moved to the reserved area.

If no Car becomes available for a particular Reservation within a week, the Reservation becomes NeedingRenewal: the Member must be contacted, by phone or in person, so that they can cancel the Reservation, or ask for it to be renewed for another week. If the Member cancels or can't be contacted within five days, the Reservation is Concluded.

Once a Reservation is Notifiable, the Member must be notified by an Assistant, in person or by phone, within three days; if the Customer can be reached, the Reservation is Collectable otherwise it becomes Displayable (a Car that was moved to the reserved area must be returned to the display area).

Once a Reservation is Collectable, the Member must collect the Car within three days: if they do collect, the Reservation is Concluded; otherwise, the Reservation becomes Displayable.

Once a Displayable Reservation's Car has been put back in the display area, the Reservation is Concluded.

At any time, the Member may cancel the Reservation over the Internet, by phone or in person.

The system will keep Assistants informed as to the state of current (not yet concluded) reservations, so that they can take appropriate action.

## B.3.5 Use Case Realization

The communication diagrams for iCoot, verifying the analysis class model, are shown in Figures B.15 through B.26, one per system use case. Note the use of **guards** (arbitrary conditions in brackets), to specify conditional messages and * to specify iteration (iteration guards can be used to control iteration, but these would have made the diagrams more complex).

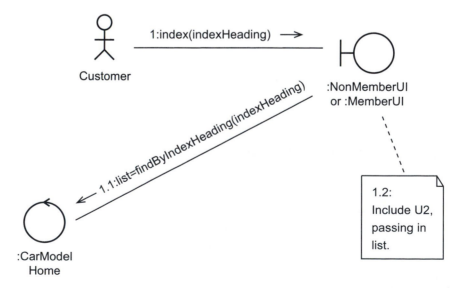

**Figure B.15: Communication diagram for U1:Browse Index**

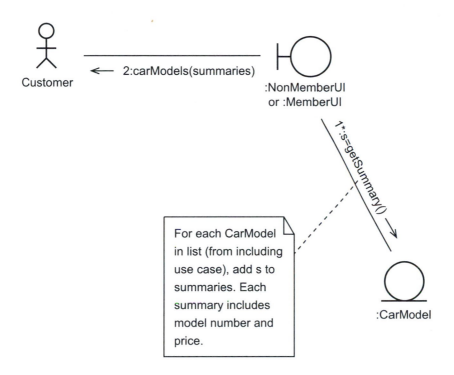

**Figure B.16: Communication diagram for U2:View Results**

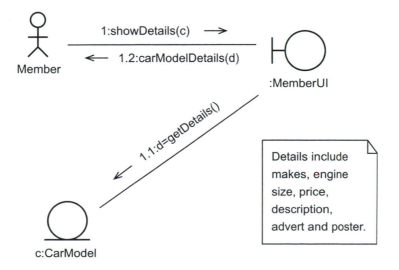

**Figure B.17: Communication diagram for U3:View CarModel Details**

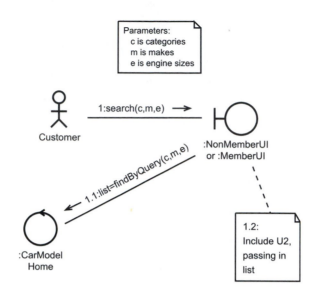

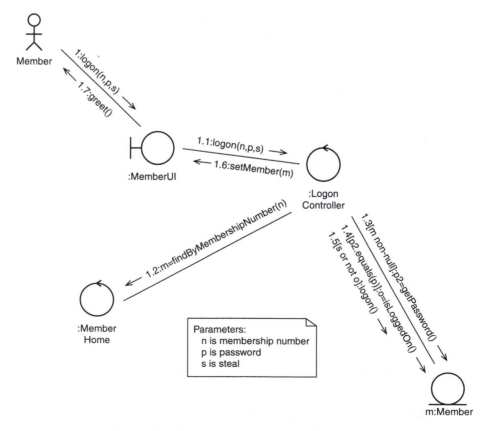

**Figure B.18: Communication diagram for U4:Search**

**Figure B.19: Communication diagram for U5:Log On**

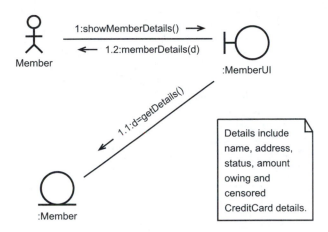

**Figure B.20: Communication diagram for U6:View Member Details**

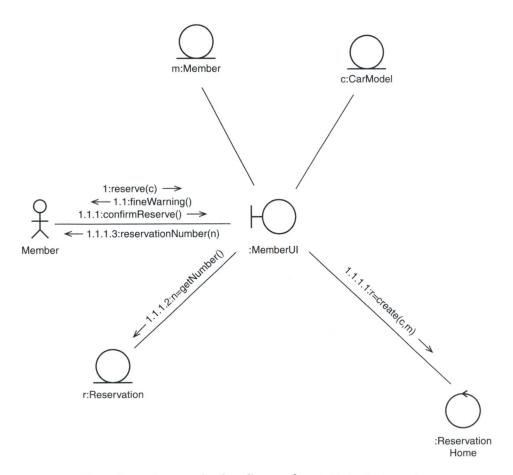

**Figure B.21: Communication diagram for U7:Make Reservation**

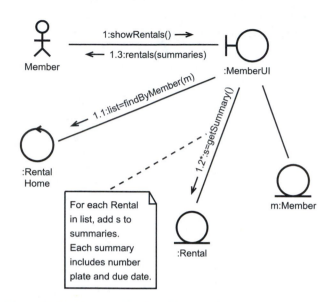

**Figure B.22: Communication diagram for U8:View Rentals**

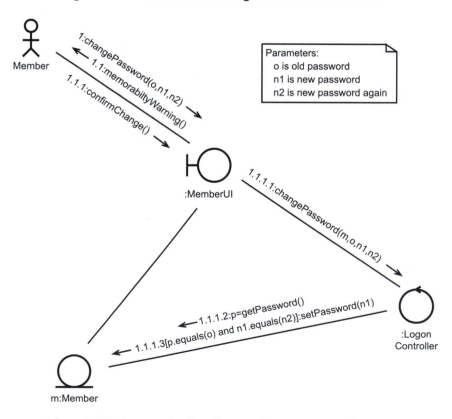

**Figure B.23: Communication diagram for U9:Change Password**

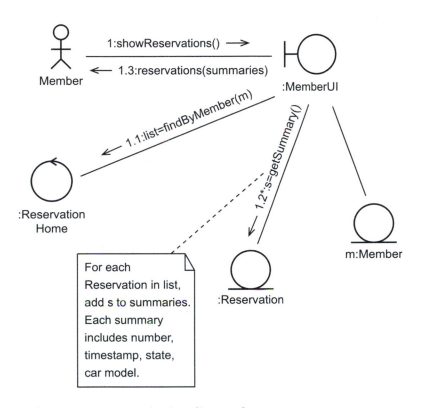

**Figure B.24: Communication diagram for U10: View Reservations**

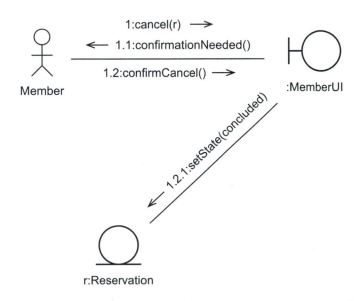

**Figure B.25: Communication diagram for U11: Cancel Reservation**

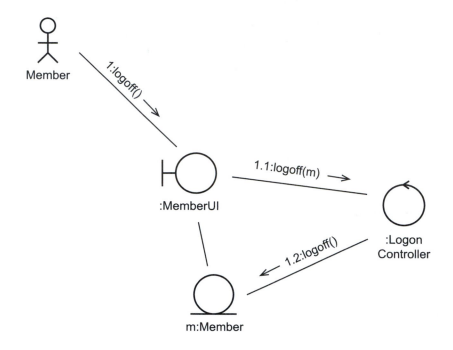

**Figure B.26: Communication diagram for U12:Log Off**

# B.4 SYSTEM DESIGN

This section documents the results of system design carried out during the design phase of the iCoot development, in terms of technology choices, layers, packages, deployment diagram, security policy and concurrency policy.

## B.4.1 Technology Choices

On the client side, the choice of technology is driven by convenience for the customer – we do not want customers to have to install any software in order to access our services. Also, we want them to be able to use any desktop machine, regardless of the operating system they have installed. The obvious choice for the client environment, therefore, is a web browser. Since the user interface must be interactive, in order to make a Reservation for example, we have to choose between technologies such as HTML/CGI, Java applets, ActiveX controls and Flash. Due to the need for portability (and client security), we can discount ActiveX controls. We would also prefer our customers to have almost-instant access to the user interface when browsing our site. This effectively discounts applets and Flash, both of which typically involve a delay while the interface is downloaded. Therefore, the initial user interface will be HTML/CGI.

Once on the server side, servlets are a good choice for processing CGI requests because they're portable, they're efficient and they have access to all the facilities of J2EE, which provides everything that the servlets might need (such as access to distributed transaction management). Traditional scripting raises issues with portability, expressive power and performance; .Net technologies raise issues with portability. Once servlets are being used as the entry point to our servers, the obvious choice for producing dynamic web pages is the JSP mechanism.

Initially, we will use an open-source (free) implementation of J2EE for development and deployment, being careful to avoid any proprietary lock-ins. The implementation must support the forwarding of requests to servlets and JSPs running in a separate process, so that the latter can be accessed directly by GUI clients. Should the open-source implementations prove inadequate, we can simply purchase a commercial product and redeploy our code.

Because of their portability, we can deploy our servlets on any combination of hardware and operating system, and then redeploy at a later date if necessary. Initially, each store will have the system software deployed on two budget Linux servers, providing fail-over and throughput without the expense of a higher-powered server or highly-available hardware.

For the business data, we will use an open-source database initially, switching to a commercial product later if necessary. A relational database will be used because of the maturity of the technology and because our application is business-oriented, with a large quantity of data but no great logical complexity. The database will also be deployed on a pair of Linux servers at each store.

For the future, we aim to provide a user interface that can be used on a mobile phone or PDA. We would prefer to avoid WAP on devices that can't manage the HTML/CGI interface because it tends to be clumsy and unpopular. Instead, we will use J2ME, allowing us to provide a rich interactive experience that scales automatically to the size of the screen. For those customers who wish to install J2SE on their client, either manually or by using their Web browser's plug-in mechanism, we will also provide a conventional graphical user interface as an applet. This applet will be deployed on touch-screen kiosks in each store to enhance the customer experience, when viewing adverts for example.

It is anticipated that the J2ME and J2SE interfaces will bypass the JSPs and servlets, for improved performance.

## B.4.2 Layer Diagram

iCoot layers are illustrated in Figure B.27.

Persistence is provided by the JDBCLayer, using the standard JDBC library to access a relational database. There is no separate persistence layer, because we expect a relational database to serve our needs for the lifetime of the system.

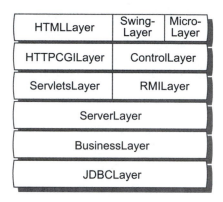

**Figure B.27: iCoot layer diagram**

The BusinessLayer contains implementations of the entity objects from the analysis class diagram, along with various supporting objects. These objects contain JDBC code for shipping data to and from the database.

The ServerLayer translates the objects and messages in the BusinessLayer into business services, in the form of messages on server objects. Objects in the ServerLayer are EJB session objects, which have two benefits: firstly, they give us access to J2EE transaction management; secondly, they allow us to provide direct access for GUI clients over RMI, bypassing the WebServer.

In order to keep the ServerLayer closed, all information returned by the business services takes the form of protocol objects, lightweight copies of the business objects.

The ServletsLayer is a control layer for HTML/CGI clients. Each servlet translates one or more objects in the ServerLayer into simple commands and questions that can be issued from the client. In response to each command or question, a servlet will perform whatever actions are necessary and then pass the next HTML page back to the client. So that page design and source code are separate, every reply page is built by a JSP that produces content dynamically based on the customer's interaction. The JSPs receive their dynamic data as protocol objects passed in by the servlets. The network communication for the HTMLLayer is provided by the standard HTTPCGILayer.

The RMILayer is a network layer allowing remote access from GUIs (Java applications and any device using J2ME). The objects in this layer are simply decorators for the EJB session objects in the ServerLayer: each server object is decorated with an RMI servant, while each RMI servant is accessed via an RMI proxy on the client. When communicating with the ControlLayer, the RMILayer uses the same protocol objects that the ServletsLayer uses when invoking JSPs.

The ControlLayer sits between the GUI objects and the RMI proxies. It serves to simplify interaction with the server objects and to hide the details of RMI. The RMILayer, ControlLayer, SwingLayer and MicroLayer are not documented fully because the graphical user interfaces are not part of the first increment of iCoot.

## B.4.3 Layer Interaction Policy

On the server, for the sake of simplicity, all layer communication will flow downwards. In other words messages will only be sent from one layer to the layer below. Events will be used on the client side for the benefit of the SwingLayer and the MicroLayer, so that application-specific knowledge can be pushed from the user interface components down to the ControlLayer. (The HTML/CGI front end does not need events because all information displayed to the user is calculated by the servlets and passed directly to JSPs for presentation.)

Layers will be closed, in order to make implementation and maintenance easier: each object will be able to access objects in the layer immediately below, but not beyond.

## B.4.4 Packages

The package diagram for Coot (including the graphical user interface/RMI packages not implemented in the first increment) is shown in Figure B.28.

## B.4.5 Deployment Diagram

The deployment diagram for iCoot is shown in Figure B.29.

The iCoot data tier comprises two database servers (which we have called DBServer). Having two such nodes improves throughput and reliability. Each DBServer hosts a DBMS process for managing access to data.

The cootschema.ddl artifact contains commands for creating database tables, in a format specific to the database being used. This is deployed to each DBMS process, using database-specific tools (no detail given here). Note that cootschema.ddl contains the schema for the full Coot system, since iCoot and Coot use the same data.

The middle tier, which communicates with the data tier, consists of two server machines (CootServer), again duplicated for the sake of reliability and throughput. Each CootServer hosts a CootBusinessServer (for handling business requests) and a WebServer (for handling static HTML content and forwarding business requests to the CootBusinessServer). Data access for the CootBusinessServer is provided by the DBMS. Because they're proprietary to the products that we select, the communication protocols between the WebServer

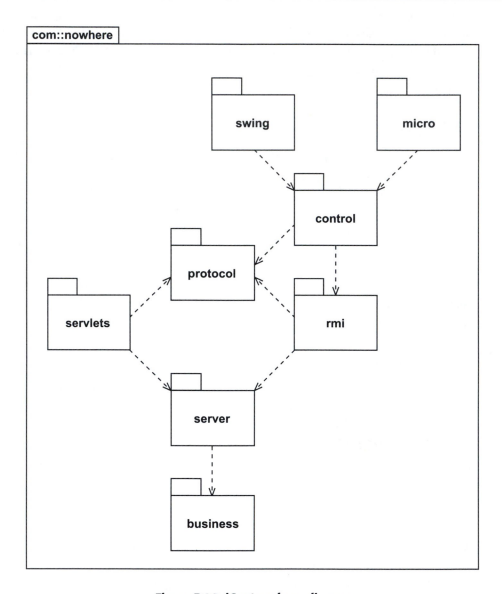

**Figure B.28: iCoot package diagram**

and the CootBusinessServer and between the CootBusinessServer and the DBMS are not specified.

Within each CootServer, the iCoot folder, containing static HTML pages, is deployed to the WebServer, while the icoot.ear archive is deployed to the CootBusinessServer. The icoot.ear archive contains servlets, JSPs, business objects and (eventually) RMI decorators, from the com::nowhere package.

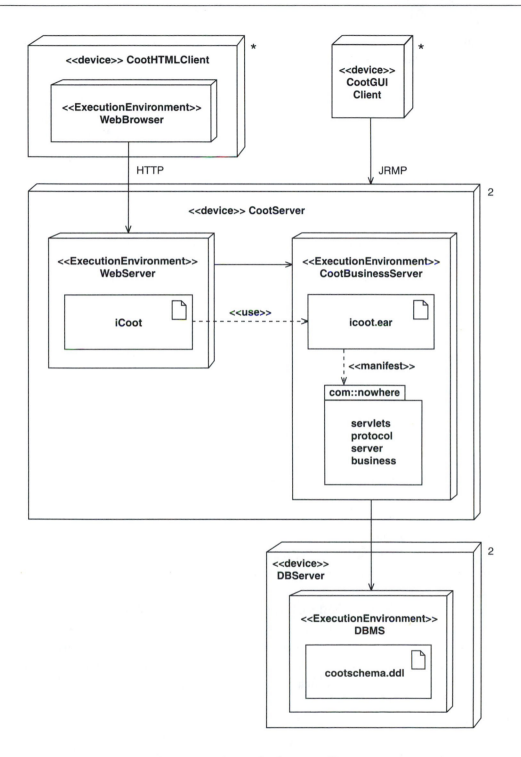

**Figure B.29: iCoot deployment diagram**

Each CootServer can be accessed simultaneously by any number of CootHTMLClients. Each CootHTMLClient hosts a WebBrowser, which accesses one of the WebServers using HTTP. No artifacts need to be deployed to the CootHTMLClients.

Eventually, we will also provide access from CootGUIClients. Each CootGUIClient will access one of the CootServers, using JRMP. Because the mechanism that allows such requests to get into the CootBusinessServer is the subject of a future increment, no details are given. Nor is any detail given for the CootGUIClient processes. The artifacts deployed to the CootGUIClients, if any, are not specified.

## B.4.6 Security Policy

Searching and browsing services will be available to all-comers, without logging in. In contrast, for Member-only services, each Member must first obtain a password in person from their local Store, then use it to log in to the Member's area from their chosen client. The membership numbers and passwords used to log in will be managed in a central directory, for ease of maintenance, using the standard Java integration mechanisms.

In order to keep Member activity private, all access to Member services from the client will be over SSL rather than plain TCP/IP. SSL will also be employed between servers for internal protection.

The servers will be deployed behind an Internet firewall so that external access can be tightly controlled.

## B.4.7 Concurrency Policy

Objects in the BusinessLayer will be managed using distributed transactions. At the start of each business request (i.e. each method on a ServerLayer object), a Java transaction will be created – this transaction will be associated with every database access made by business objects within that request. At the end of each request, the Java transaction will be committed, thus making updates available to other requests.

In order to minimize transaction conflict, all RMI servants, servlets and server objects will be stateless.

For GUI clients, access to local data (copies of protocol objects) will be single-threaded. For HTML clients, each JSP will have exclusive access to its protocol objects, so such access is also effectively single-threaded. For business data, low-level concurrency control is managed automatically by the EJB framework: every use of a business service is wrapped inside a transaction, which passes right through to the database management system.

To simplify concurrency control at the business level, two strategies will be employed: firstly, single log-on will be enforced for Members. Secondly, updates to the Catalog of available CarModels will be made off-line and switched with the live Catalog in the early hours of the morning. This will minimize the need to report errors such as 'Attempt to reserve a car model that has been withdrawn' to Customers and Assistants. (This will still occasionally happen, because client displays won't be updated explicitly when data changes on the server via concurrent paths; pushing all relevant changes to clients, although technically feasible, would be too inefficient.)

# B.5 SUBSYSTEM DESIGN

This section documents the results of subsystem design, carried out during the design phase of the iCoot development, in terms of business services, design class models (one per layer plus the protocol objects), database schema, user interface design and business service realization (sequence diagrams). In general, this documentation describes the subsystem artifacts required to support business service realization and the CootHTMLClient.

## B.5.1 Business Services

1. Read headings from the CarModel index.
2. Read CarModels for a given index heading.
3. Read all CarModel Categories.
4. Read all CarModel engine sizes.
5. Read all Makes of CarModel.
6. Read CarModels for a given set of Categories, engine sizes and Makes.
7. Read details for a given CarModel.
8. Reserve a CarModel.
9. Read details for a given Member.
10. Change a Member's password.
11. Read the Cars rented by a given Member.
12. Read the Reservations made by a given Member.
13. Cancel a Reservation.

## B.5.2 ServletsLayer Class Diagram

The class diagram for the ServletsLayer is shown in Figure B.30.

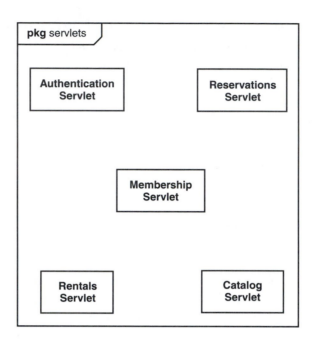

**Figure B.30: ServletsLayer classes**

## B.5.3 ServletsLayer Field List

All servlets are stateless and therefore do not have any fields. Any information about the state of a customer's interaction is recorded in the result pages themselves and in a state object stored in the browser's HTTP session. For logged-on members, the session identifier is also stored in the HTTP session. Objects in the server layer are located using their homes (implemented using the Singleton pattern).

## B.5.4 ServletsLayer Message List

Using the standard Java mechanism, each client request is passed to the selected servlet via a message called doGet(:HttpServletRequest,:HttpServletResponse). The questions and commands from the client are passed in as part of the HttpServletRequest. Below is a list of the questions and commands that can be passed in by the client, along with the JSPs that are invoked as a result.

AuthenticationServlet
- logon   From home page; takes a membership number, password and 'steal' parameter and, upon successful logon, returns the member page. (The steal parameter indicates whether the member would like to steal an existing session.)
- logoff   From member page; logs off the current Member.

CatalogServlet

- index    From member or non-member page; returns the index page containing index headings to choose from.
- browse    From index page; takes an index heading as parameter and returns the results page containing matching CarModels.
- search    From member or non-member page; returns the search page containing every Category, Make and engine size to choose from.
- query    From search page; takes Category ids, Make ids and engine sizes as parameters and returns the results page containing matching CarModels.
- details    From results page; takes a CarModel id as parameter and returns the details page containing details for that CarModel.

MembershipServlet

- membership    From member page; returns the membership page, containing details for the current Member.
- password    From member page; returns the password page.
- changePassword    From member page; takes an old password and a new password as parameters and returns the confirmChange page.
- confirmChange    From the confirmChange page; sets the new password for the current Member, if the old password given was correct.

RentalsServlet

- rentals    From member page; returns the rentals page, containing Rentals for the current Member.

ReservationsServlet

- reserve    From details page; takes a CarModel id as parameter and returns the confirmReserve page.
- confirmReserve    From confirmReserve page; reserves the CarModel already identified and returns the confirmation page.
- ok    From confirmation page; returns the details page.
- reservations    From member page; returns the reservations page, containing Reservations for the current Member.
- cancel    From the reservations page; takes the Reservation id as parameter and returns the confirmCancel page.
- confirmCancel    From confirmCancel page; cancels the previously selected Reservation and returns the reservations page.

## B.5.5 ServerLayer Class Diagram

The class diagram for the ServerLayer is shown in Figure B.31. Each class also has a home, implemented using the Singleton pattern (not shown).

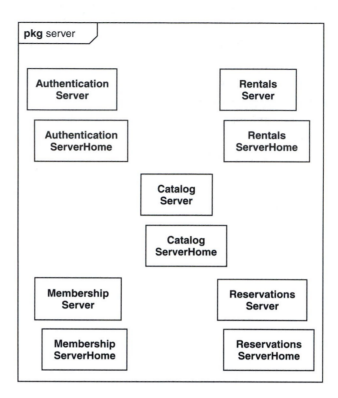

**Figure B.31: ServerLayer classes**

## B.5.6  ServerLayer Field List

The server objects are stateless, thus they have no fields. (All BusinessLayer classes are accessed via their respective homes.)

## B.5.7  ServerLayer Message List

For the server objects, the messages below correspond to the business services. (Homes have been omitted from this list because they simply create server objects, with no parameters.)

AuthenticationServer
- +logon(n:String,p:String,s:boolean):long   Log on the Member with membership number n and password p, specifying whether or not to steal any existing session with s.
- +logoff(i:int)   Log off the Member with session identifier i.

CatalogServer
- +readCategoryNames():String[]   Read the names of every Category.
- +readMakeNames():String[]   Read the names of all Makes.
- +readEngineSizes():int[]   Read the unique engine sizes of all CarModel details.
- +readIndexHeadings():String[]   Read the index headings, derived from all CarModel numbers and Make names.
- +readCarModels(h:String):PCarModel[]   Read all CarModels matching the index heading h.
- +readCarModelDetails(i:int):PCarModelDetails   Read details for the CarModel with identifier i.
- +readCarModels(q:PCatalogQuery):PCarModel[]   Read all CarModels that match the query q.

MembershipServer
- +readMember(i:int):PMember   Read the Member with session identifier i.
- +changePassword(i:int,o:String,n:String)   Change the password for the Member with session identifier i, using old password o and new password n.

RentalsServer
- +readRentals(i:int):PRental[]   Read all Rentals for the Member with session identifier i.

ReservationsServer
- +readReservations(i:int):PReservation[]   Read all Reservations for the Member with session identifier i.
- +createReservation(i:int,c:int)   Create a Reservation for the Member with session identifier i and the CarModel with identifier c.
- +cancelReservation(i:int,r:int)   Cancel the Reservation with identifier r, for the Member with session identifier i, as long as the Reservation matches the Member.

# B.5.8 BusinessLayer Class Diagram

The class diagram for the BusinessLayer is shown in Figure B.32. Most of these classes also appear in the analysis class model (Section B.3), so their descriptions have been placed in the Glossary (Section B.8), to avoid repetition.

Each entity class has a home, apart from Customer (because it's abstract). ReservationState-Home is an Abstract Factory for creating instances of its subclasses.

The Store class, used for illustration in Chapter 13, has not been included in this appendix since it plays no part in business service realization.

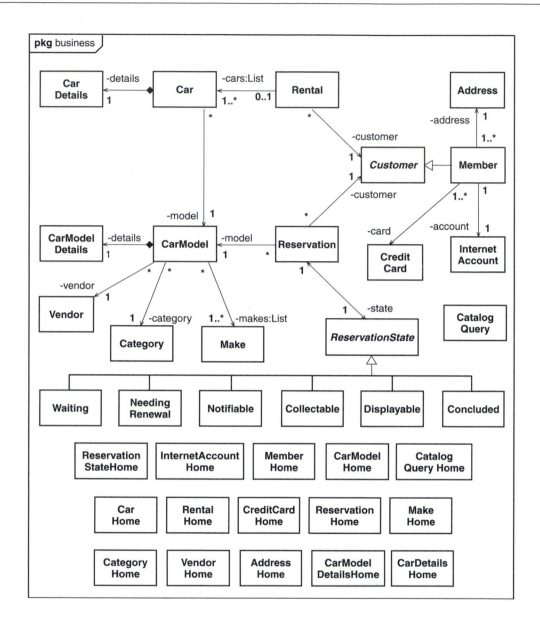

**Figure B.32: BusinessLayer classes**

## B.5.9 BusinessLayer Field List

The list below shows fields for stored attributes only; fields that store links are shown in Figure B.32. With the exception of the state objects, every object has an -id:int that stores the universal identifier but which has been omitted from the list. Classes with no fields other than links have been omitted.

Address
- -house:String   House number and/or name (unique within the postal code).
- -street:String   Street in which the house stands.
- -county:String   County where the street is.
- -postCode:String   Postal code for the sorting office and region.

Car
- -traveled:int   The distance, in kilometers, that the Car has traveled (taken from the odometer).
- -dateLost:Date   Date the Car was reported missing, null if not lost.

CarDetails
- -barCode:String   The bar code, attached inside the Car's windscreen.
- -numberPlate:String   The Car's license number as it appears on the plate.
- -vin:String   The Car's unique Vehicle Identification Number, on a plate riveted to the body.

CarModel
- -name:String   The Make's unique name for the CarModel.
- -price:int   The daily cost of hiring the Car, in cents.

CarModelDetails
- -engineSize:int   The capacity of the engine, in cubic centimeters.
- -description:String   A single-sentence description of the CarModel.
- -advert:String   The file name of a streaming advert for the CarModel.
- -poster:String   The file name of a poster for the CarModel.

CatalogQuery
- -makeIds:List<Integer>   Universal identifiers for relevant Makes (using identifiers avoids retrieving Makes when building the database query).
- -carModelIds:List<Integer>   Universal identifiers for relevant CarModels (using identifiers avoids retrieving CarModels).
- -engineSizes:List<Integer>   Engine sizes, in cubic centimeters.

Category
- -name:String   The name of the Category.

Collectable
- -dateNotified:Date   Date the Customer was notified that the car is ready for collection.

Concluded
- -reason:String   Why the Reservation is concluded: "Successfully rented", "Canceled by customer", "Wasn't renewed" or "Wasn't collected".

CreditCard
- -type:String   Type of Card (e.g. "Annex").
- -number:String   Number on the Card.
- -expiryDate:Date   Date Card expires.

Customer
- -name:String   The Customer's name.
- -phone:String   The Customer's phone number.
- -amountDue:int   Fees due, in cents, for the Customer (for example, for overdue Rentals).

Displayable
- -reason:String   Why the Car must be put back in the display area, either "Customer uncontactable" or "Failed to collect".

InternetAccount
- -password:String   Password for the associated Member; must be a mix of at least six letters and digits.
- -sessionId:long   Session identifier for the associated Member: 0 if not logged on; securely random, unique, non-zero number if logged on.

Make
- -name:String   The name of the manufacturer.

Member
- -number:String   The Member's unique number.
- -inGoodStanding:boolean   Whether or not the Member has any outstanding issues, such as disputed late fees.

NeedingRenewal
- -dateRenewalNeeded:Date   Date by which the Reservation must be renewed to avoid becoming automatically concluded.

Notifiable
- -datePutAside:Date   Date the Car was moved to the reserved area.

Rental

- -number:String    The unique number for the Rental.
- -startDate:Date    The date the Rental was taken out.
- -dueDate:Date    The date the Rental is due to end.
- -totalAmount:int    The amount paid for the Rental, in cents.

Reservation

- -number:String    The unique number for the Reservation.
- -timestamp:Timestamp    The date and time that the Reservation was made.

Vendor

- -name:String    Name of the Vendor.

Waiting

- -lastRenewedDate:Date    Date the Reservation was last renewed (initially the same as the date it was created).

## BusinessLayer Message List

Most of the public messages on the BusinessLayer classes are simply accessors for attributes, derived attributes or links, so no detail is given for these.

For the ReservationState hierarchy, and the Reservation class itself, every class has one message for each event shown in Figure B.14 and one getter for each state attribute. Details of these messages have been omitted, for brevity. In addition, the Reservation class has test messages to enable clients to discover which state the receiver is in, e.g. isConcluded and isWaiting.

For the homes, details resulting from the Singleton pattern are not given. To support the homes, every class created by a home has a package constructor that takes all attributes and links as parameters; no further detail is given for these constructors.

Apart from ReservationStateHome and CatalogQueryHome, every home has the following messages (where X is a stand-in for the corresponding BusinessLayer class):

- +findByPrimaryKey(id:int):X    Returns the instance of X with universal identifier id.
- +create(...):X    Takes every attribute and link as parameters and returns a new instance of X.

ReservationStateHome has one creation message for each subclass, taking all subclass attributes as parameters.
CatalogQueryHome has a create message that takes three List<Integer> parameters: makeIds, categoryIds and engineSizes.

All other home messages used in business service realization are listed below.

CarModelHome

- +findByIndexHeading(h:String):List<CarModel>   Returns all CarModels that have h as a model number or Make name, sorted by model name.
- +findByQuery(q:CatalogQuery):List<CarModel>   Returns all CarModels that have a Make, a Category and an engine size that appear in q, sorted by model name.

CarModelDetailsHome

- +findByCarModelId(id:int):CarModelDetails   Returns the instance that matches the CarModel with universal identifier id.
- +findEngineSizes():List<Integer>   Returns all engine sizes, in ascending order.

CategoryHome

- +findCategoryNames():List<String>   Returns all Category names, in alphabetical order.

MakeHome

- +findMakeNames():List<String[]>   Returns all Make names, in alphabetical order.

MemberHome

- +findByMembershipNumber(n:String):Member   Returns the Member with membership number n.
- +findBySessionId(id:long):Member   Returns the Member with session identifier id.

RentalHome

- +findByMember(m:Member):List<Rental>   Returns all Rentals for m, sorted by start date.

ReservationHome

- +findUnconcludedByMember(m:Member):List<Rental>   Returns all the unconcluded Reservations for m, sorted by creation date.

## B.5.10 Protocol Objects Class Diagram

The class diagram for the protocol objects, used for communication between the server layer and the servlets layer, is shown in Figure B.33.

### Protocol Objects Field List

The list below shows fields for stored attributes only; fields that store links are shown in Figure B.33. The meaning of these fields is the same as those for the BusinessLayer classes, with the exception that cardNumber only includes the last four real digits. The message variable on PServerException stores an explanation for the exception.

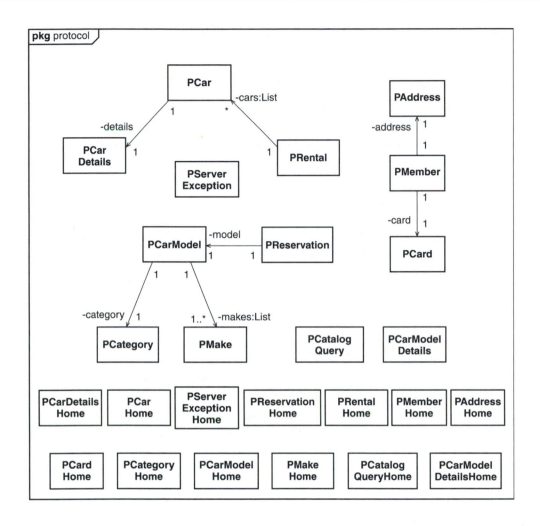

**Figure B.33: Protocol classes**

- PAddress  -house:String, -street:String, -county:String, -postCode:String
- PCar  -traveled:int, -numberPlate:String
- PCarModel  -id:int, -name:String, -price:int
- PCarModelDetails  -engineSize:int, -description:String, -advert:String, -poster:String
- PCatalogQuery  -makeIds:int[], -carModelIds:int[], -engineSizes:int[]
- PCategory  -name:String
- PCreditCard  -type:String, -number:String
- PMake  -name:String
- PMember  -name:String, -phone:String, -amountDue:int, -inGoodStanding:boolean
- PRental  -startDate:Date, -dueDate:Date

- PReservation     -id:int, -number:String, -timestamp:Timestamp
- PServerException     -message:String

### Protocol Objects Message List

Nearly all the messages on the protocol classes are accessors for attributes or links. In addition, each protocol class has a toString message that returns a human-readable summary of the receiver: these messages are used to display objects in user interfaces.

Each home has a single create message with a parameter to initialize each attribute and link. Beyond this, all messages on homes are derived from the Singleton pattern. To support the homes, each protocol class has a package constructor that takes every attribute and link as parameters. No further detail is given for these constructors.

In addition to its basic creation message, PCatalogQueryHome has a createCatalogQuery message that takes three int[] parameters (makeIds, categoryIds and engineSizes) and returns a new CatalogQuery.

Since none of the protocol classes or homes have any special messages, no detailed list is given here.

## B.5.11  Database Schema

The database schema is shown in Figure B.34. In this diagram, the names of primary key columns are shown in bold and the names of foreign key columns are shown in italics. The meaning of the attribute columns is the same as those for the fields in the BusinessLayer classes. Of all the columns, only DATELOST in the CAR table is nullable.

## B.5.12  User Interface Design

The user interface design is not given here since it is similar to the user interface sketches shown in Section B.3.

## B.5.13  Business Service Realization

Figures B.35 through B.46 show one sequence diagram, documenting business service realization, per system use case. Several diagrams use frames to show loops. The loop operator has a pseudocode guard controlling the number of iterations. Frames have also been used to enclose lifelines that refer to included use cases, using the ref operator – in this case, the name of the included use appears in the center of the frame, alongside a list of the parameters that are passed in.

For the sake of simplicity, each interaction between a customer's browser and a servlet has been shown as a message sent from the actor directly to the servlet. In reality, this is implemented by passing a command and its parameters into the servlet's doGet message.

**ADDRESS** (**ID**:INTEGER,HOUSE:VARCHAR(99),STREET:VARCHAR(99),COUNTY:VARCHAR(99),
POSTCODE:VARCHAR(99))

**CAR** (**ID**:INTEGER,TRAVELLED:INTEGER,DATELOST:DATE,*CARDETAILSID*:INTEGER)

**CARD** (**ID**:INTEGER,TYPE:VARCHAR(99),NUMBER:VARCHAR(99))

**CARDETAILS** (**ID**:INTEGER,BARCODE:VARCHAR(99),NUMBERPLATE:VARCHAR(99),VIN:VARCHAR(99))

**CARMODEL** (**ID**:INTEGER,NAME:VARCHAR(99),PRICE:INTEGER,*CARMODELDETAILSID*:INTEGER,
*CATEGORYID*:INTEGER,VENDORID:INTEGER)

**CARMODELDETAILS** (**ID**:INTEGER,ENGINESIZE:VARCHAR(99),DESCRIPTION:VARCHAR(256),
ADVERT:VARCHAR(99),POSTER:VARCHAR(99))

**CATEGORY** (**ID**:INTEGER,NAME:VARCHAR(99))

**COLLECTABLERESERVATION** (*RESERVATIONID*:INTEGER,DATENOTIFIED:DATE)

**CONCLUDEDRESERVATION** (*RESERVATIONID*:INTEGER,REASON:VARCHAR(99))

**CUSTOMER** (**ID**:INTEGER,NAME:VARCHAR(99),PHONE:VARCHAR(99),AMOUNTDUE:INTEGER)

**DISPLAYABLERESERVATION** (*RESERVATIONID*:INTEGER,REASON:VARCHAR(99))

**INTERNETACCOUNT** (**ID**:INTEGER,PASSWORD:VARCHAR(99),SESSIONID:INTEGER)

**MAKE** (**ID**:INTEGER,NAME:VARCHAR(99))

**MAKECARMODEL** (*CARMODELID*:INTEGER,*MAKEID*:INTEGER)

**MEMBER** (**ID**:INTEGER,NUMBER:VARCHAR(99),INGOODSTANDING:BOOLEAN,*CARDID*:INTEGER,
*ADDRESSID*:INTEGER)

**NEEDINGRENEWALRESERVATION** (*RESERVATIONID*:INTEGER,DATERENEWALNEEDED:DATE)

**NONMEMBER** (**ID**:INTEGER,DRIVERSLICENSE:VARCHAR(99))

**NOTIFIABLERESERVATION** (*RESERVATIONID*:INTEGER,*DATEPUTASIDE*:DATE)

**RENTAL** (**ID**:INTEGER,NUMBER:VARCHAR(99),STARTDATE:DATE,DUEDATE:DATE,TOTALAMOUNT:INTEGER)

**RENTALCAR** (*RENTALID*:INTEGER,*CARID*:INTEGER)

**RESERVATION** (**ID**:INTEGER,NUMBER:VARCHAR(99),TIMESTAMP:TIMESTAMP,*CUSTOMERID*:INTEGER,
*CARMODELID*:INTEGER)

**VENDOR** (**ID**:INTEGER,NAME:VARCHAR(99))

**WAITINGRESERVATION** (*RESERVATIONID*:INTEGER,LASTRENEWEDDDATE:DATE)

**Figure B.34: Database schema**

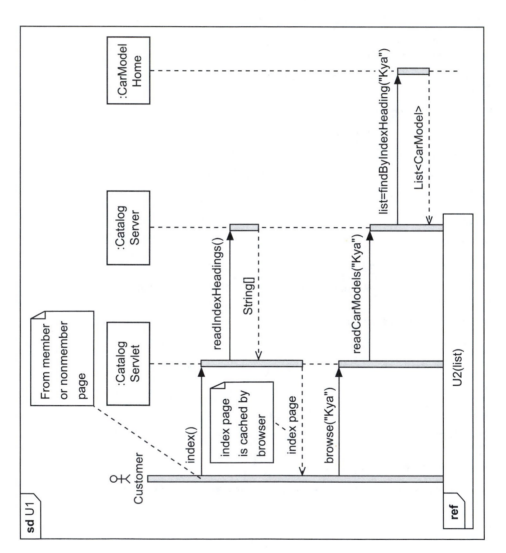

**Figure B.35: Sequence diagram for U1:Browse Index**

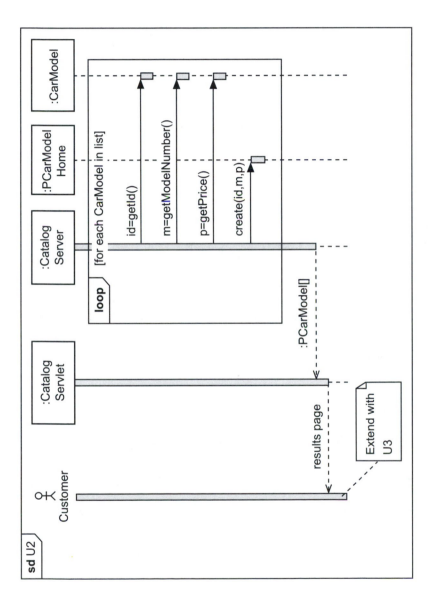

**Figure B.36: Sequence diagram for U2:View Results**

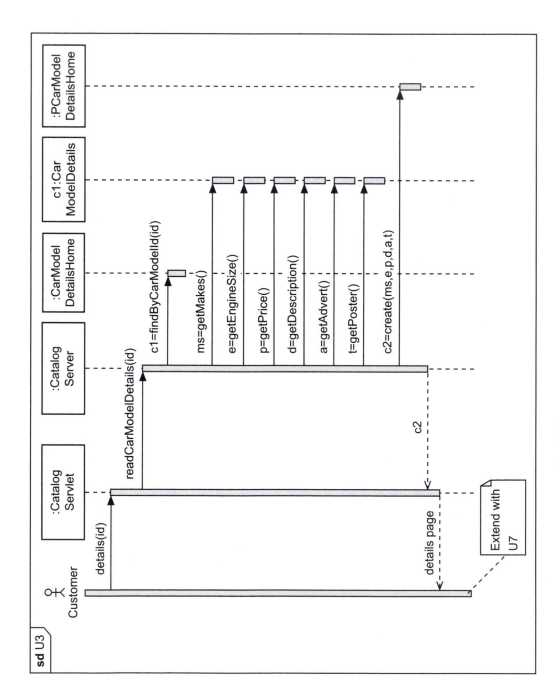

**Figure B.37: Sequence Diagram for U3:View CarModel Details**

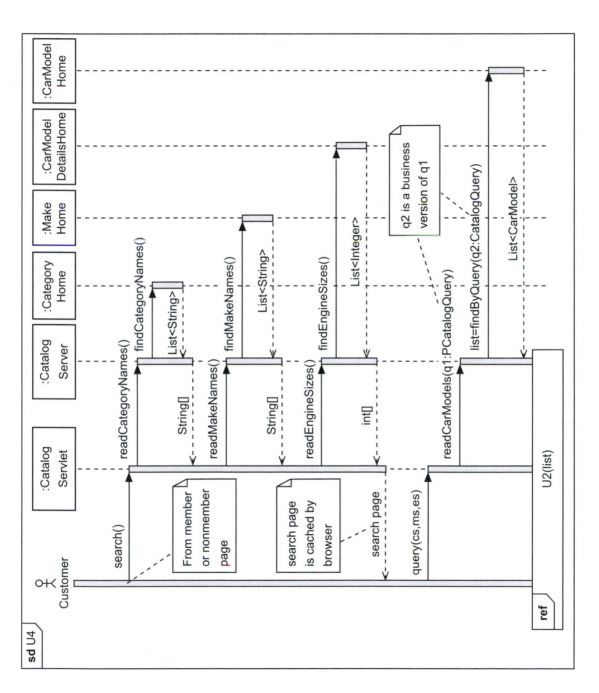

**Figure B.38: Sequence diagram for U4:Search**

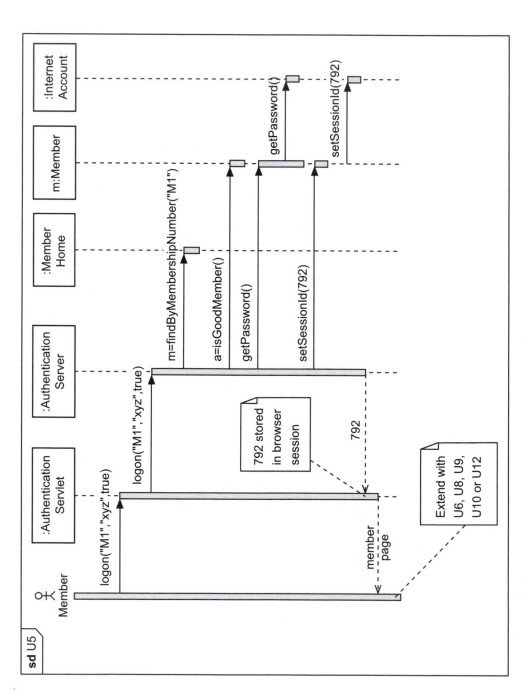

**Figure B.39: Sequence diagram for U5:Log On**

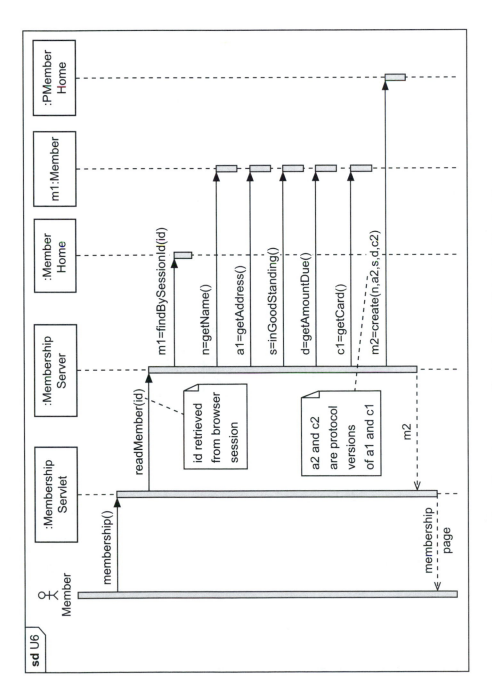

**Figure B.40: Sequence diagram for U6:View Member Details**

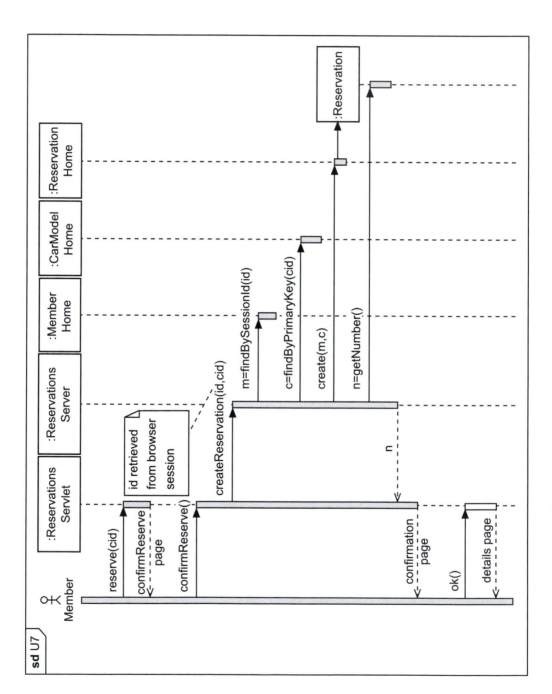

**Figure B.41: Sequence diagram for U7:Make Reservation**

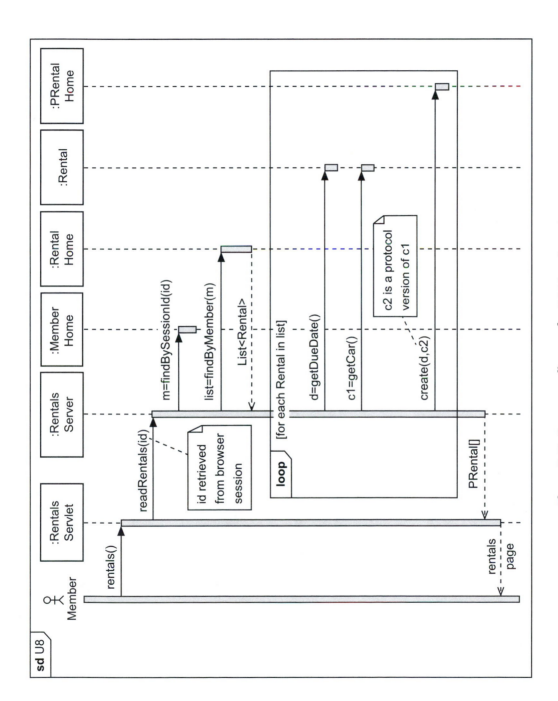

**Figure B.42: Sequence diagram for U8:View Rentals**

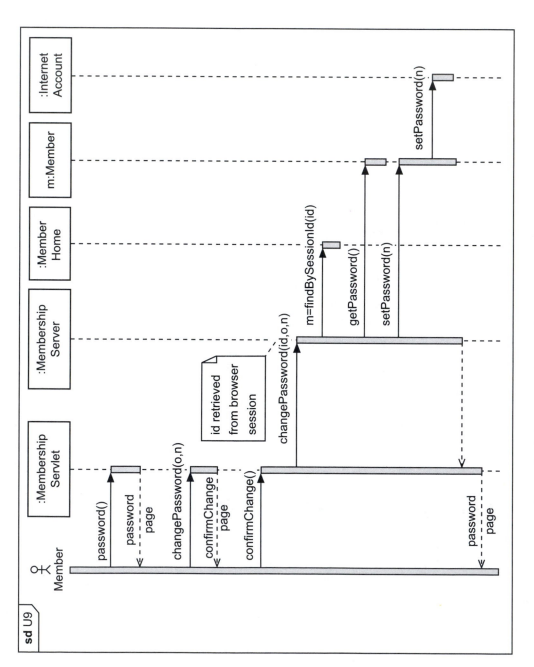

**Figure B.43: Sequence diagram for U9:Change Password**

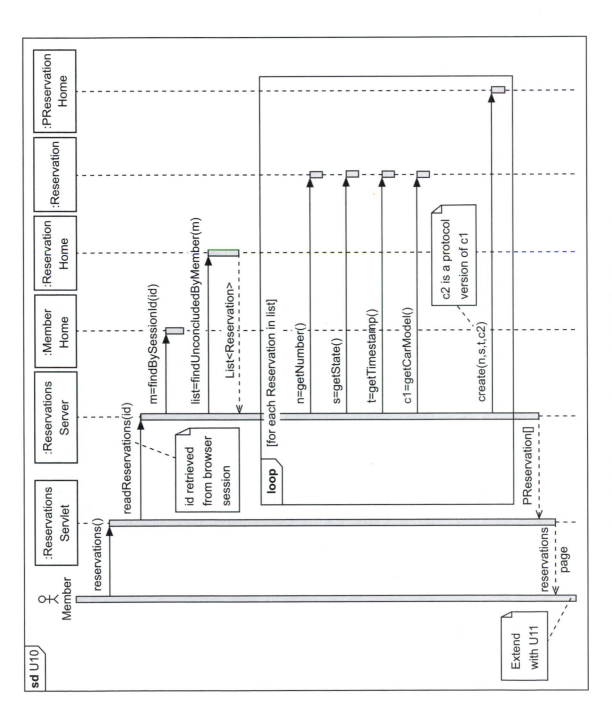

**Figure B.44: Sequence diagram for U10: View Reservations**

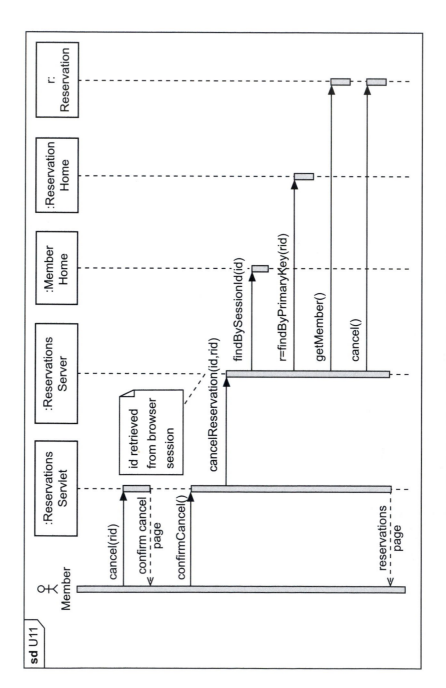

**Figure B.45: Sequence diagram for U11:Cancel Reservation**

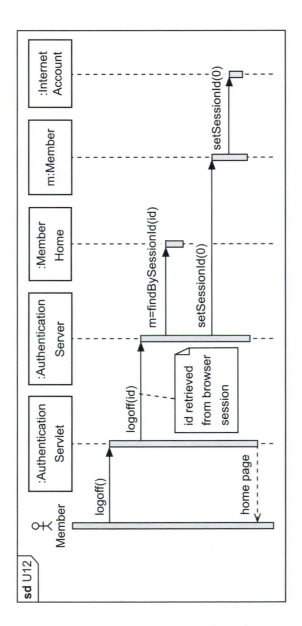

**Figure B.46: Sequence diagram for U12:Log Off**

# B.6 CLASS SPECIFICATION

This section documents the results of the specification phase of the iCoot development. Since there are many classes in iCoot, specifications are only included for one ServerLayer class and one BusinessLayer class, as examples. Each specification is given as comments in the source code.

## B.6.1 Server Class Specification

```
ReservationsServer Class Specification

Invariants: NONE
    // No invariants, because this is a stateless object

Methods:
    /*
     * Create a reservation for the member with session identifier i
     * and the car model with identifier c
     *
     * Preconditions:
     *     i != 0
     *     For mem = MemberHome.getInstance().findBySessionId(i),
     *         mem != null
     *         mem.isingoodStanding()
     *         mem.getAmountDue() == 0
     *     c != 0
     *     CarModelHome.getInstance().findByPrimaryKey(i) != null
     *
     * Postconditions:
     *     A new Reservation has been created for Member with session
     *     identifier i and CarModel with identifier c
     *
     * Exceptions:
     *     PServerException (checked) thrown if the server has a problem
     *     IllegalArgumentException (unchecked) thrown if parameters are
     *         invalid
     */
    public void createReservation(int i, int c)
       throws PServerException;

    /*
     * Read all reservations for the member with session identifier i
     *
     * Preconditions:
     *     i != 0
```

```
 *      MemberHome.getInstance().findBySessionId(i) != null
 *
 * Postconditions:
 *      result != null
 *      result contains all unconcluded reservations for Member
 *          with session identifier i
 *      result is a new array, exclusive to the client
 *
 * Exceptions:
 *      PServerException (checked) thrown if the server has a problem
 *      IllegalArgumentException (unchecked) thrown if parameters are
 *          invalid
 */
public PReservation[] readReservations(int i)
    throws PServerException;


/*
 * Cancel the reservation with identifier r for the member
 * with session identifier i
 *
 * Preconditions:
 *      i != 0
 *      For mem = MemberHome.getInstance().findBySessionId(i)
 *          mem != null
 *      r != 0
 *      For res = ReservationHome.getInstance().findByPrimaryKey(r)
 *          res != null
 *          res.getMember() == mem
 *
 * Postconditions:
 *      For res = ReservationHome.getInstance().findByPrimaryKey(r)
 *          res.isConcluded()
 *          res.getReason().equals("Canceled by customer");
 *
 * Exceptions:
 *      PServerException (checked) thrown if the server has a problem
 *      IllegalArgumentException (unchecked) thrown if parameters are
 *          invalid
 */
public void cancelReservation(int i, int r)
    throws PServerException;
```

## B.6.2 Business Logic Class Specification

```
Member Class Specification
```

```
Invariants:
    /*
     * Values named in invariants, preconditions and postconditions
     * are attributes, with a getter and an optional setter. Each
     * invariant is an extra precondition for the corresponding setter
     * and an extra postcondition for the corresponding getter.
     */
    id is fixed after creation
    id != 0
    number != null
    number.size() != 0
    internetAccount != null
    address != null

Methods:
    /*
     * Fetch the receiver's id
     *
     * Preconditions: NONE
     * Postconditions:
     *     result == id
     * Exceptions: NONE
     */
    public int getId();

    /*
     * Fetch the receiver's number
     *
     * Preconditions: NONE
     * Postconditions:
     *     result == number
     * Exceptions: NONE
     */
    public String getNumber();

    /*
     * Set the receiver's number to n
     *
     * Preconditions: NONE
     * Postconditions:
     *     number == n
     * Exceptions: NONE
     */
    public void setNumber(String n);
```

```
/*
 * Fetch the receiver's internetAccount
 *
 * Preconditions: NONE
 * Postconditions:
 *     result == internetAccount
 * Exceptions: NONE
 */
public InternetAccount getInternetAccount();

/*
 * Set the receiver's internetAccount to ia
 *
 * Preconditions: NONE
 * Postconditions:
 *     internetAccount == ia
 * Exceptions: NONE
 */
public void setInternetAccount(InternetAccount ia);

/*
 * Fetch the receiver's address
 *
 * Preconditions: NONE
 * Postconditions:
 *     result == address
 * Exceptions: NONE
 */
public String getAddress();

/*
 * Set the receiver's address to a
 *
 * Preconditions: NONE
 * Postconditions:
 *     address == a
 * Exceptions: NONE
 */
public void setAddress(Address a);

/*
 * Fetch the session identifier of the receiver's internetAccount
 *
 * Preconditions: NONE
 * Postconditions:
```

```
 *      result == internetAccount.getSessionId()
 * Exceptions: NONE
 */
public int getSessionId();

/*
 * Set the session identifier of the receiver's
 *     internetAccount to i
 *
 * Preconditions: NONE
 * Postconditions:
 *     internetAddress.getSessionId() == i
 * Exceptions: NONE
 */
public void setSessionId(int i);
```

# B.7 OUTLINE TEST PLAN

## B.7.1 Introduction

The testing of iCoot will be continuous, with the involvement of developers, peers, customers, the build team and the testing team.

- Developers will test their artifacts as they produce them.
- Customers will be involved in the verification of high-level artifacts, acceptance testing and beta testing.
- Peers will review the artifacts produced by developers.
- The build team will be responsible for build testing after the first increment.
- The testing team will be responsible for coordinating the testing process, including the production and maintenance of this plan, the testing phase itself and system testing in particular.

This test plan gives an overview of the testing that will be carried out, followed by details of the testing tasks for each phase of development. It doesn't address the implementation of a prototype for iCoot. The development of a prototype will be under the supervision of project managers, conducted using rapid, informal methods.

## B.7.2 The Impact of Spirals and Increments

Within each spiral of development, testing will be carried out by the developers. Each artifact will be subject to peer review, with the proviso that formal peer reviews won't be necessary for the first spiral. For every spiral after the second, formal peer reviews will concentrate on changes that have been made to the artifacts, to avoid duplicated effort. Similarly, customer reviews should concentrate on changes that have been made since the most recent review.

After each complete set of spirals, the testing team will take over to manage the testing phase before the release of the next increment.

After the first increment, regression testing will ensure that iCoot is at least as functional as it was after the previous increment.

## B.7.3  Testing of Non-Code Artifacts

Use cases and UML diagrams will be produced by the development team with input from customers. In the early spirals, members of the development team will review each other's work and changes will be made immediately.

During the last spiral before release of an increment, formal peer reviews will be held with colleagues who have relevant expertise but who are not directly involved with the project. These reviews will be used to certify the artifacts from use cases all the way through to class-based specifications.

Developers, peers and project managers will be responsible for ensuring that artifacts remain consistent over time.

## B.7.4  Code Reviews

After the final coding phase within each increment, formal code reviews will be held with peers who are not involved in the project itself. During these reviews, manual white-box testing and metric tools will be used to identify any refactoring that is needed.

## B.7.5  Test-Driven Development

During implementation of the design, programmers will perform continuous testing of their work with the help of JUnit. These programmer-developed tests will comprise unit tests at the class level and integration tests for all classes that the developer owns. Each developer will fix faults in their own code before making the code public.

At the end of each spiral, the developers will work together to perform integration testing and subsystem testing at a fairly informal level, again using JUnit, the aim being to eliminate as many faults as possible before the formal testing phase. The development team will fix any faults that they discover at this point, before the next spiral or the testing phase, as appropriate.

## B.7.6  Assertions

As detailed later in this test plan, programmers will be expected to add assertions to their code which will be enabled during development. During the testing phase, assertions will be initially enabled to make it easier to identify faults. Once all the tests are successful, they will be run again with assertions disabled, to check that none of the assertions have side effects. It will also allow performance with and without assertions to be compared. For release, assertions will be disabled but retained in the code so that they can be reactivated to help diagnose failures. So that the live system is not compromised by the disabling of assertions, further steps will be taken to protect iCoot.

In order to protect the servers from accidental or malicious attack when assertions are disabled, an application firewall will be implemented within the server layer. This firewall will largely enforce the server layer's preconditions in such a way that the checks can't be disabled. In order to reduce the amount of incorrect information that reaches the server layer, another application firewall will sit beneath the user interfaces (in the control layer) to reject invalid requests from the user. This client firewall will be based largely on the preconditions of the control layer, but again implemented in such a way that the checks can't be disabled. In addition, the Web server will be placed in a de-militarized zone, sandwiched between two conventional Internet firewalls to frustrate typical Internet attacks.

There will be two styles of client firewall. For HTML-based clients, the firewall will be implemented within the servlets and standard Web techniques for preventing invalid requests will be used (omitting invalid selections from Web pages and checking input data using JavaScript, for example). For GUI-based clients, the firewall will be implemented in the control layer and invalid requests will be prevented by using standard GUI techniques (such as disabling buttons that shouldn't be used and replacing text entry with drop-down lists and spin buttons).

## B.7.7  Testing Phase

Once the spirals for each increment have been completed, the code will be handed over to the testing team. Before formal testing begins, the testing team will re-run the unit and integration tests that have been produced by the development team, to verify that there are no known faults. The testing team will use the class and subsystem specifications to help them produce subsystem test cases, with accompanying test procedures. The system test cases will be based on the system use cases. Each test case will comprise a number of individual tests, each with test name, test description, test procedure and expected results.

The testing team will address the following requirements:

- Load testing, at average and maximum loads.
- Soak testing, to verify that there is no corruption or exhaustion of resources over time.

- Stress testing, to confirm that iCoot fails elegantly.
- Security testing.

Test automation will be used, wherever possible, to reduce the cost of testing.

In parallel, the testing team will organize acceptance testing, with the help of in-house volunteers and carefully selected customer personnel.

Installation testing will then be performed using a testbed that comprises a significant subset of the target platforms. Finally before release, beta testing will be performed at selected customer sites. All known faults will be fixed by the development team prior to release, wherever feasible.

Performance metrics (for example, average transaction time) and style metrics (for example, method size) will be gathered. Any unacceptable performance must be fixed prior to release. Style issues will be recorded for input to the next increment.

## B.7.8 Documentation Testing

After the first spiral, the documentation team will start to produce manuals and training materials. These will be subject to peer review. After several spirals, during the explicit testing phase that takes place before the release of each increment, the documentation will again be tested. This testing will comprise peer review, acceptance testing and beta testing.

## B.7.9 Build Testing

Programmers will use a source code management tool to ensure that all code is kept in a central location. They will be required to check out any code that they intend to work on, in order to avoid duplicated or overlapping effort. The project managers will be responsible for deciding who works on what. The build team will be responsible for managing the code repository. In order to cope with developer absences, the code management tool will be configured to allow checked-out artifacts to be checked back in, under controlled conditions.

After the first increment has been released, all further development will be subject to nightly build tests, run by the build team. This will involve building the entire system and running a significant subset of the system tests.

## B.7.10 Test Documentation and Logging

All test cases will be documented and kept in a test repository under the control of the testing team. As tests are carried out, test results will be recorded and added to the repository.

In order to encourage developers to test their own code before the testing phase, they won't have to record test failures in the test repository. Since the developers' test cases will be written in Java (using JUnit), they will be stored in the code repository; therefore, there will be no need to add such test cases to the test repository.

During the testing phase, test failures will be added to the repository. The testing team will collaborate with project managers to ensure that fixes are allocated to members of the development team and completed.

It will be the responsibility of project managers to ensure that adequate JUnit test cases are developed and run frequently. For reporting purposes, the development team must sign off the integration testing that takes place at the end of each spiral, by adding a corresponding entry to the test repository.

## B.7.11 Testing Activities by Phase

Set out below are the testing activities that will take place within each phase of development. The requirement for formal peer reviews will be relaxed for the first spiral. Peers will be selected on the basis of expertise.

- **Requirements phase** The business use cases, user interface sketches, the use case diagram, system use cases, use case priorities, supplementary requirements and activity diagrams (where used) will be reviewed by developers, peers and customers.
- **Analysis phase** The analysis class diagram, state machine diagrams (where used) and communication diagrams will be reviewed by developers, peers and customers.
- **System design phase** The deployment diagram, technology choices, layer diagram, layer interaction policy, concurrency policy and security policy will be reviewed by developers and peers.
- **Subsystem design phase** The design class diagrams; database schema; user interface design (for HTML access to servlets and JSPs, applets, applications, and interfaces for mobile devices); and sequence diagrams will be reviewed by developers and peers.
- **Specification phase** For each class, preconditions, postconditions and class invariants will be specified. These assertions will be reviewed by the developers and peers. Subsystem specifications may be used where appropriate. These will be tested in a similar way to class specifications.
- **Implementation phase** The testing during this phase consists of three parts:
  - Adding assertions (as per the class specification) to methods. Other types of assertion, such as checking loop termination and avoidance of impossible conditions, are optional, but recommended.
  - Creating JUnit test cases and JUnit test suites. There will be at least one test case (which is likely to involve some integration testing) per class and one test suite per package.
  - Performing code reviews, by developers and peers.
- **Testing phase** The testing phase will be the responsibility of the testing team. The development of test cases and test procedures by the testing team will be reviewed by peers. Testing will comprise:
  - The JUnit tests, to ensure that all known faults have been fixed.

- Subsystem testing, based on any subsystem interfaces specified during the design and specification phases.
- System testing, based on use cases (functional testing and load testing at average load and maximum load).
- Stress testing, to confirm elegant failure (as defined during the design and specification phases).
- Security testing (aggressive attempts to break into iCoot without authorization).
- Acceptance testing, based largely on productivity metrics.
- Metrics, based on system performance and coding style.
- Documentation testing, with the help of end users and system administrators.
- Installation testing, using a significant subset of target environments.
- Beta testing, at selected customer sites.
- **Maintenance phase** The testing team will be responsible for managing the reporting and fixing of faults discovered after release, with the help of project managers and the development team. Between increments, fixes may be implemented, regression-tested and released at the discretion of the testing team and project managers. Regression testing will comprise:
  - The JUnit tests.
  - Subsystem testing.
  - System testing.
  - Installation testing.

Feedback from customers about possible improvements to iCoot will be passed on to the project managers, with a view to incorporation in the next increment.

# B.8 GLOSSARY

| Term | Definition |
|---|---|
| Address (Business object, system object, analysis object, design object) | Where a Member lives. |
| AddressHome (Design object) | Home for creating and finding Address objects. |
| Assistant (Business actor, system actor) | An employee at a store who helps Customers to rent Car objects and reserve CarModels. |
| Auk (Business actor) | The pre-existing system that handles Customer details, Reservations, Rentals and the Catalog of available CarModels. |
| AukInterface (Analysis object) | Boundary for accessing Auk. |

| | |
|---|---|
| AuthenticationServer (Design object) | Controls the logging on and logging off of Members to iCoot. |
| AuthenticationServerHome (Design object) | Home for creating an AuthenticationServer. |
| AuthenticationServlet (Design object) | Makes the AuthenticationServer accessible in an HTML page in a Web browser. |
| BusinessLayer (Design layer) | Contains objects that convert the PersistenceLayer into clean object-oriented application objects. |
| Car (Business object, system object, analysis object, design object) | Instance of a CarModel for rent kept by a Store. |
| CarDetails (Analysis object, design object) | Extra details of a Car, such as number plate and VIN. |
| CarDetailsHome (Design object) | Home for creating and finding CarDetails. |
| CarHome (Design object) | Home for creating and finding Cars. |
| CarModel (Business object, system object, analysis object, design object) | A model in our Catalog, available for reservation. |
| CarModelDetails (Analysis object, design object) | Extra details about a CarModel, such as advert and poster. |
| CarModelDetailsHome (Design object) | Home for creating and finding CarModelDetails. |
| CarModelHome (Analysis object, design object) | Home for finding and creating CarModels. |
| Catalog (Business object) | A document describing CarModels available for rent. |
| CatalogQuery (Design object) | A Member's specification of CarModels that they're interested in when searching the iCoot on-line Catalog; includes categories, makes or engine sizes. |
| CatalogQueryHome (Design object) | Home for creating CatalogQuery objects. |
| CatalogServer (Design object) | Controls access to CarModels that can be browsed or reserved (Members only) over iCoot. |
| CatalogServerHome (Design object) | Home for creating a CatalogServer. |
| CatalogServlet (Design object) | Makes the CatalogServer accessible in an HTML page in a Web browser. |
| Category (Analysis object, design object) | Classification of a Car that helps Customers find what they're looking for, e.g. "Sports" or "Luxury". |

| | |
|---|---|
| CategoryHome (Design object) | Home for creating and finding Category objects. |
| Collectable (Design object) | A ReservationState indicating that a Customer has been informed about a matched Reservation but has not yet collected it. |
| com::nowhere::business (Design package) | Package containing the BusinessLayer classes. |
| com::nowhere::control (Design package) | Package containing the ControlLayer classes. |
| com::nowhere::micro (Design package) | Package containing the MicroLayer classes. |
| com::nowhere::persistence (Design package) | Package containing the PersistenceLayer classes. |
| com::nowhere::protocol (Design package) | Package containing the protocol classes, used by the ServletsLayer, RMILayer and ControlLayer for communication with the ServerLayer. |
| com::nowhere::rmi (Design package) | Package containing the RMILayer classes. |
| com::nowhere::server (Design package) | Package containing the ServerLayer classes. |
| com::nowhere::servlets (Design package) | Package containing the ServletsLayer classes. |
| com::nowhere::swing (Design package) | Package containing the SwingLayer classes. |
| Concluded (Design object) | A ReservationState indicating that a Reservation is finished because it was collected, canceled or timed out. |
| CootBusinessServer (Design node) | A process hosting iCoot services on a CootServer. |
| CootGUIClient (Design node) | A Customer's machine hosting a J2SE or J2ME GUI for accessing iCoot over RMI. |
| CootHTMLClient (Design node) | A Customer's machine hosting a Web browser to access iCoot. |
| cootschema.ddl (Deployment artifact) | Script used to generate database tables for Coot. |
| CootServer (Design node) | A machine hosting a WebServer and CootBusinessServer. |
| CreditCard (Business object, system object, analysis object, design object) | Used for confirming the credit-worthiness of Members; must not have expired for a Member to be in good standing. |
| CreditCardCompany (Business actor) | Company that issues CreditCards and confirms validity. |

| | |
|---|---|
| CreditCardHome (Design object) | Home for creating and finding CreditCards. |
| Customer (Business actor, business object, system actor, system object, analysis object, design object) | A person who pays money in return for one of our standard services. |
| DBMS | A process hosting a relational database management system. |
| DBServer | A machine hosting a DBMS. |
| DebtDepartment (Business object) | The department that deals with unpaid fees. |
| Displayable (Design object) | A ReservationState indicating that a Reservation that was Collectable has timed out or been canceled; means that a Car is in the Reserved area that must be moved back to the display area. |
| EJB | An Enterprise JavaBean; an object within a standard Java framework that can handle transactions, network access and database access, behind an Internet firewall; these come in two varieties, session beans (for remote access to business services) and entity beans (for automatic mapping of data to and from a database). |
| HTMLLayer (Design layer) | The client-side code for accessing the ServletsLayer; provided by the standard HTML Web browser. |
| HTTPCGILayer (Design layer) | The standard network layer that sits between the HTMLLayer and the ServletsLayer. |
| icoot.ear (Deployment artifact) | Java enterprise archive containing the servlets, JSPs and EJBs used by CootHTMLClients and, eventually, CootGUIClients. |
| iCoot (Deployment artifact) | Folder containing static HTML for the iCoot site. |
| IllegalArgumentException | Standard Java Exception that indicates an attempt was made to send a message with invalid parameters. |
| InternetAccount (Design object) | Details required for a Member to log on to iCoot plus a record of their logged-on status. |
| InternetAccountHome (Design object) | Home for creating and finding InternetAccounts. |

| | |
|---|---|
| J2EE | Enterprise Edition of the Java 2 platform. |
| J2ME | Micro Edition of the Java 2 platform. |
| J2SE | Standard Edition of the Java 2 platform. |
| JDBC | A standard Java library that provides access to all relational databases in a uniform way. |
| JDBCLayer (Design layer) | Layer that accesses a relational database from Java (within the EJB framework). |
| JRMP | The communication protocol used by RMI. |
| JSP | Java Server Page; a dynamic web page containing Java code, to be executed by the server, alongside static HTML. |
| Keys (Business object) | For operating a Car; Customers have copies when they're renting; Store keeps copies for available Cars and reserve copies for all Cars; Store has serial number for reproduction by Make if all copies are lost or broken. |
| LegalDepartment (Business Actor) | The department that deals with accidents in which a rented Car has been involved. |
| License (Business object) | A document that must be presented in order to rent a Car or as proof of identity when a NonMember makes a Reservation. |
| LogonController (Analysis object) | iCoot controller that controls logging on and off by Members. |
| Make (Analysis object, design object) | Each Car has one or more Makes that manufactures it. |
| MakeHome (Design object) | Home for creating and finding Makes. |
| MemberHome (Analysis object, design object) | Home for finding and creating Members. |
| MembershipCard (Business object) | A laminated document issued by a store to a Member as proof of membership. |
| MembershipServer (Design object) | Controls access to a member's details, such as Address and CreditCard, over iCoot. |
| MembershipServerHome (Design object) | Home for creating a MembershipServer. |
| MembershipServlet (Design object) | Makes the MembershipServer accessible within an HTML page in a Web browser. |
| MemberUI (Analysis object) | iCoot boundary used by Members to access the system. |

| | |
|---|---|
| MicroLayer | Objects using the Java 2 Micro Edition to access the RMILayer from a pervasive device, such as a mobile phone or set-top box; reserved for future versions of iCoot. |
| NeedingRenewal (Design object) | A ReservationState indicating that the Reservation has not been matched for a week and must be renewed if it is not to expire. |
| NonMember (Business actor, business object, system actor, analysis object, design object) | A Customer whose identity and creditworthiness have not been checked and who, therefore, must provide a deposit to make a Reservation or surrender a copy of their License to rent a Car. |
| NonMemberUI (Analysis object) | iCoot boundary used by NonMembers to access the system. |
| Notifiable (Design object) | A ReservationState indicating that a Reservation has been matched to an available Car but the Member has not yet been notified. |
| PAddress (Design object) | Protocol version of Address. |
| PAddressHome (Design object) | Home for creating InternetAccounts. |
| PCar (Design object) | Protocol version of Car. |
| PCarHome (Design object) | Home for creating PCar objects. |
| PCarModel (Design object) | Protocol version of CarModel. |
| PCarModelDetails (Design object) | Protocol version of CarModelDetails. |
| PCarModelDetailsHome (Design object) | Home for creating PCarModelDetails. |
| PCarModelHome (Design object) | Home for creating PCarModels. |
| PCatalogQuery (Design object) | Protocol version of CatalogQuery. |
| PCatalogQueryHome (Design object) | Home for creating PCatalogQuery objects. |
| PCategory (Design object) | Protocol version of Category. |
| PCategoryHome (Design object) | Home for creating a PCategory. |
| PCreditCard (Design object) | Protocol version of CreditCard. |
| PCreditCardHome (Design object) | Home for creating PCreditCards. |
| PMake (Design object) | Protocol version of Make. |
| PMakeHome (Design object) | Home for creating PMakes. |
| PMember (Design object) | Protocol version of Member. |
| PMemberHome (Design object) | Home for creating PMembers. |
| PRental (Design object) | Protocol version of Rental. |
| PRentalHome (Design object) | Home for creating PRentals. |
| PReservation (Design object) | Protocol version of Reservation. |
| PReservationHome (Design object) | Home for creating PReservations. |

| | |
|---|---|
| PServerException (Design object) | An indication that one of the objects in the ServerLayer has been unable to complete a request because of, for example, a database problem. |
| PServerExceptionHome (Design object) | Home for creating PServerExceptions. |
| Rental (Business object, system object, analysis object, design object) | A contract between Nowhere Cars and a Customer to keep one or more Cars for an agreed period; subject to late fees if Car is not returned on time. |
| RentalHome (Analysis object, design object) | Home for finding and creating Rentals. |
| RentalServerHome (Design object) | Home for creating a RentalServer. |
| RentalsServer (Design object) | Controls access to a Member's Rentals over iCoot. |
| RentalsServlet (Design object) | Makes the RentalServer accessible within an HTML page in a Web browser. |
| Reservation (Business object, system object, analysis object, design object) | The reserving of a CarModel by a Customer. |
| ReservationHome (Analysis object) | Home for finding and creating Reservations. |
| ReservationServerHome (Design object) | Home for creating a ReservationServer. |
| ReservationsServer (Design object) | Controls access to Reservations for Members over iCoot. |
| ReservationsServlet (Design object) | Makes the ReservationServer accessible within an HTML page in a Web browser. |
| ReservationsSlip (Business object) | A slip detailing the membership number, car model, timestamp and number for a Reservation. |
| ReservationState (Analysis object, design object) | The state of a reservation, e.g. Waiting or Concluded. |
| ReservationStateHome (Design object) | Home for creating a ReservationState. |
| RMI | Standard Java mechanism for sending messages to an object over a network. |
| RMILayer (Design layer) | Converts the ServerLayer into simple objects that can be accessed by the SwingLayer or MicroLayer; reserved for future versions of iCoot. |
| ServerLayer | Contains objects to access iCoot over a network. |
| ServletsLayer (Design layer) | The server-side objects that provide access to iCoot from an HTML Web browser. |

| | |
|---|---|
| Store (Business actor, design object) | A Nowhere Cars site from which Cars can be rented, CarModels reserved and Catalogs browsed or obtained. |
| SwingLayer (Design layer) | Objects using the standard Java library for accessing the RMILayer from a Java GUI; reserved for future versions of iCoot. |
| Vendor (Analysis object, design object) | Company that supplies one or more Cars. |
| VendorHome (Design object) | Home for creating and finding Vendor objects. |
| VIN | Vehicle Identification Number; unique number issued by the licensing authority and appearing on a plate riveted to the Car's body. |
| Waiting (Design object) | A ReservationState indicating that the Reservation has been made over the Internet but has not yet been satisfied, canceled or expired. |
| WebBrowser (Design node) | A process providing HTML access to a CootHTMLClient. |
| WebServer (Design node) | A process providing server-side access to a CootBusinessServer from a Web browser. |

# Appendix C

## Summary of UML Notation Used

This appendix summarizes the UML notation used in this book, organized by diagram type:

- object diagram
- communication diagram (business level)
- activity diagram
- use case diagram
- class diagram (analysis level)
- communication diagram (analysis level)
- state machine diagram
- deployment diagram (network topology)
- package diagram
- deployment diagram (with processes, artifacts and manifestations)
- class diagram (design level)
- sequence diagram

The order corresponds to the order in which the diagrams were discussed in this book. It's worth looking at them in order because, in order to avoid repetition and clutter, some notation is highlighted in earlier diagrams but not in later ones. Of course, UML comments can appear in any diagram – in many cases, it's better to use comments than to resort to a complicated piece of UML notation, especially if that means looking at the specification.

Although UML makes no distinction between the two flavors of class diagram, at design level and analysis level, a distinction is made here because the first of each pair is simpler in style and therefore uses less of the available notation.

In order to avoid confusion with respect to the Java code fragments, the primitive types used for diagrams in this book are Java primitives, such as int and boolean, rather than UML primitives, such as Integer and Boolean. As a matter of style, arrays are generally avoided in favor of collection classes (such as List).

Some types of UML diagram were not needed during iCoot development and they are not covered here: component diagram, composite structure diagram, interaction overview diagram, and timing diagram. This appendix cannot comprehensively cover even the diagrams it does address. See [OMG 03a] and [Fowler 03] if you want to find out more.

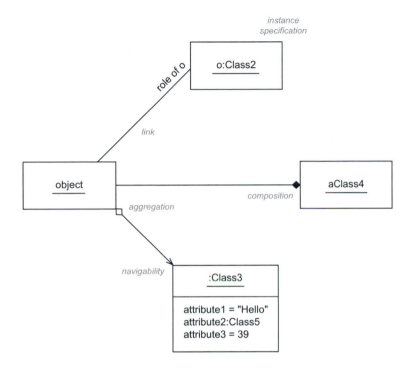

**Figure C.1: Object diagram**

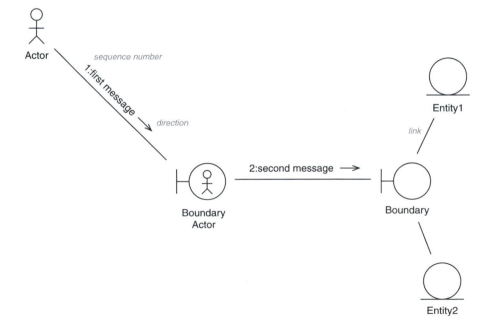

**Figure C.2: Communication diagram (business level)**

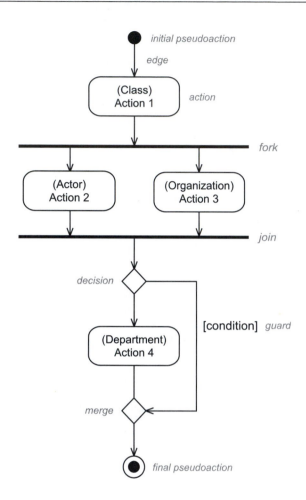

**Figure C.3: Activity diagram**

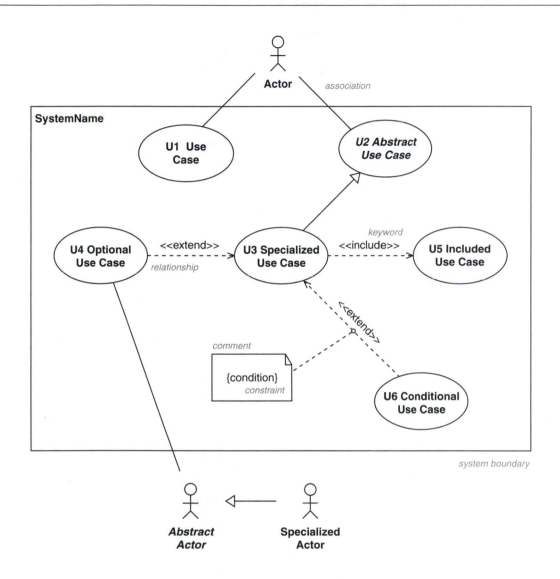

**Figure C.4: Use case diagram**

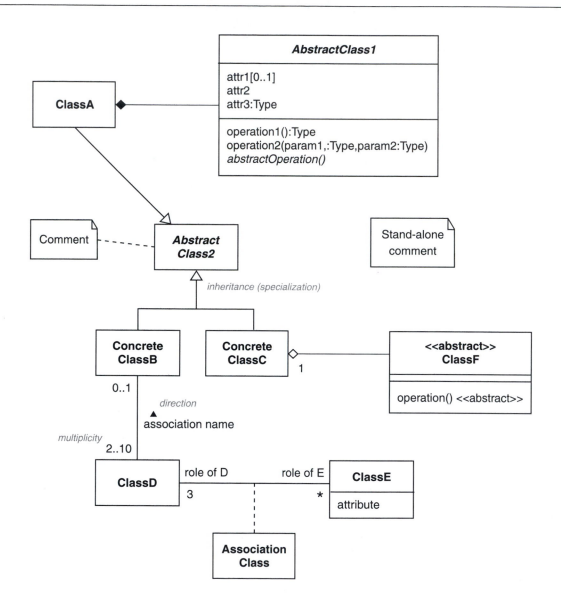

**Figure C.5: Class diagram (analysis level)**

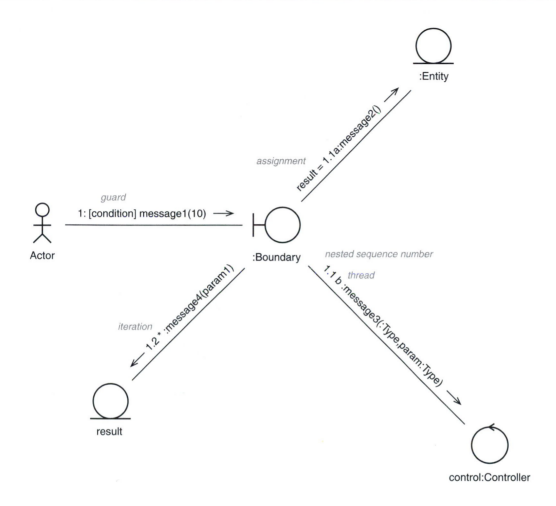

**Figure C.6: Communication diagram (analysis level)**

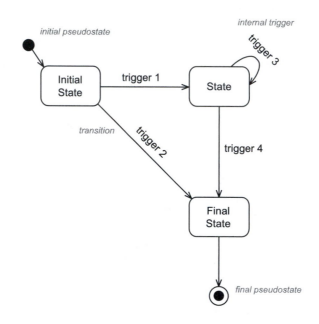

**Figure C.7: State machine diagram**

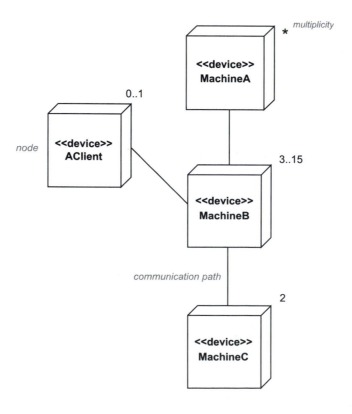

**Figure C.8: Deployment diagram (network topology)**

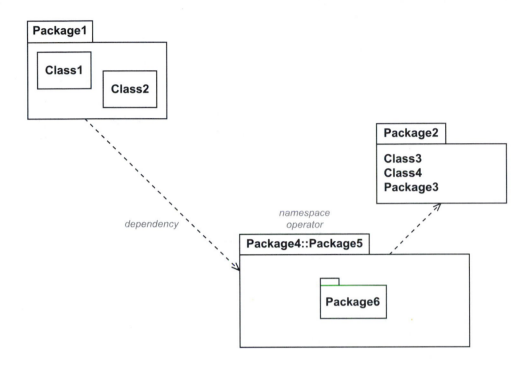

**Figure C.9: Package diagram**

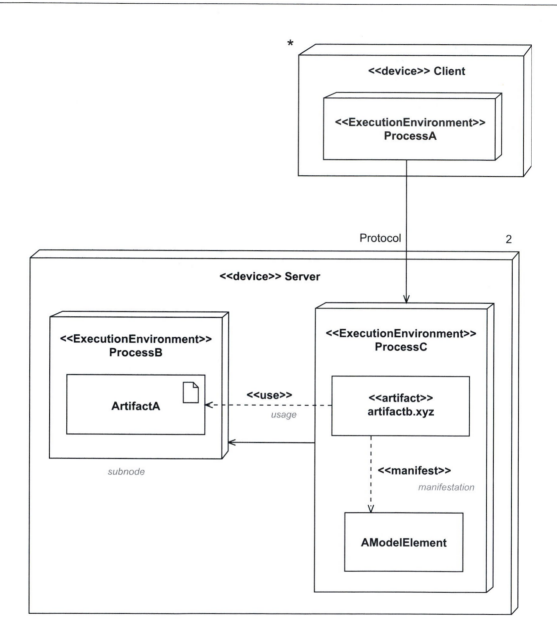

**Figure C.10: Deployment diagram (with processes, artifacts and manifestations)**

package frame

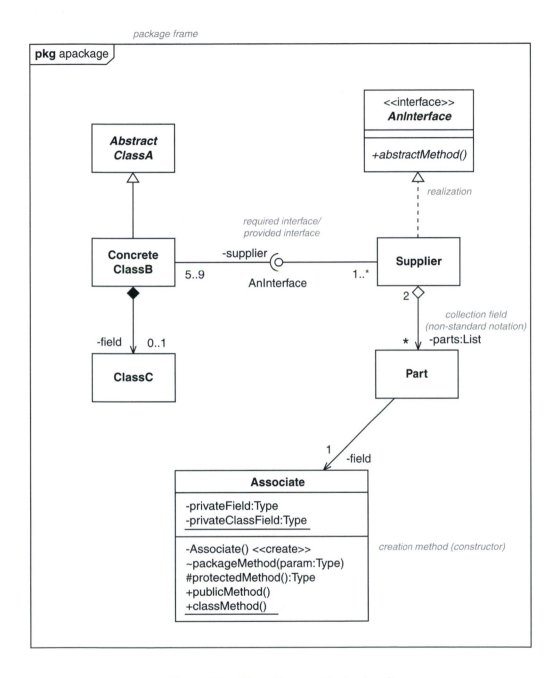

**Figure C.11: Class diagram (design level)**

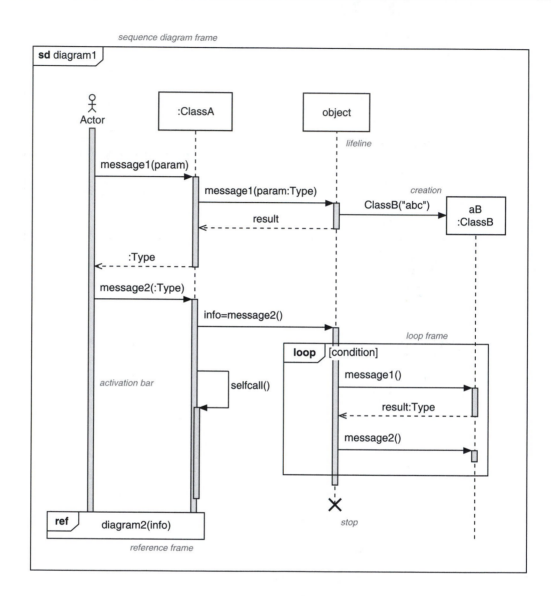

**Figure C.12: Sequence diagram**

# Bibliography

Alexander, C., Ishikawa, S., and Silverstein, M. (1977) *A Pattern Language: Towns, Buildings, Construction*, Oxford University Press, ISBN: 0-195-01919-9

Alur, D., Crupi, J., and Malks, D. (2003) *Core J2EE Patterns: Best Practices and Design Strategies*, Prentice Hall, ISBN: 0-131-42246-4

Ambler, S. (2003) *Agile Database Techniques*, John Wiley & Sons, ISBN: 0-471-20283-5

Beck, K. (1999) *Extreme Programming Explained: Embrace Change*, Addison-Wesley, ISBN: 0-201-61641-6

Beck, K. (2002) *Test Driven Development*, Addison-Wesley, ISBN: 0-321-14653-0

Bloch, J. (2001) *Effective Java Programming Language Guide*, Addison-Wesley, ISBN: 0-201-31005-8

Bodoff, S., Green, D., Haase, K., Jendrock, E., Pawlan, M., and Stearns, B. (2002) *The J2EE Tutorial*, Addison-Wesley, ISBN: 0-201-79168-4, available at http://java.sun.com

Bolton, F. (2001) *Pure Corba*, SAMS, ISBN: 0-672-31812-1

Booch, G. (1993) *Object-Oriented Analysis and Design with Applications*, Benjamin Cummings, ISBN: 0-805-35340-2

Bustard, D., Kawalek, P., and Norris, M. (2000) *Systems Modeling for Business Process Improvement*, Artech House, ISBN: 1-580-53050-8

Campione, M., Walrath, K., and Huml, A. (1998) *The Java Tutorial Continued: The Rest of the JDK*, 2nd Edition, Addison-Wesley, ISBN: 0-201-48558-3, available at http://java.sun.com

Campione, M., Walrath, K., and Huml, A. (2000) *The Java Tutorial: A Short Course on the Basics*, 3rd Edition, Addison-Wesley, ISBN: 0-201-70393-9, available at htttp://java.sun.com

Clark, A., and Warmer, J. B. (2002) *Object Modeling With the OCL: The Rationale Behind the Object Constraint Language*, Springer-Verlag, ISBN: 3-540-43169-1

Cockburn, A. (2000) *Writing Effective Use Cases*, Addison-Wesley, ISBN: 0-201-70225-8

Cockburn, A. (2001) *Agile Software Development: Software Through People*, Addison-Wesley, ISBN: 0-201-69969-9

Constantine, L., and Lockwood, L. (1999) *Software For Use: A Practical Guide to the Models and Methods of Usage-Centered Design*, Addison-Wesley, ISBN: 0-201-92478-1

Fowler, M. (1996) *Analysis Patterns: Reusable Object Models*, Addison-Wesley, ISBN: 0-201-89542-0

Fowler, M. (2003) *UML Distilled: A Brief Guide to the Unified Modeling Language*, 3rd Edition, Addison-Wesley, ISBN: 0-321-19368-7

Gamma, E., Helm, R., Johnson, R., and Vlissides, J. (1995) *Design Patterns: Elements of Reusable Object-Oriented Software*, Addison-Wesley, ISBN: 0-201-63361-2

Grand, M. (1999) *Patterns in Java, Volume 2*, John Wiley & Sons, ISBN: 0-471-25841-5

Grand, M. (2002) *Patterns in Java: Catalogue of Reusable Design Patterns Illustrated with UML, Volume 1*, 2nd Edition, John Wiley & Sons, ISBN: 0-471-22729-3

Jacobson, I., Booch, G., and Rumbaugh, J. (1999) *The Unified Software Development Process*, Addison-Wesley, ISBN: 0-201-57169-2

Jacobson, I., Christerson, M., Jonsson, P., and Övergaard, G. (1992) *Object-Oriented Software Engineering: A Use Case Driven Approach*, Addison-Wesley, ISBN: 0-201-54435-0

Joy, W., Steele, G., Gosling, J., Bracha, G. (2000) *Java Language Specification*, 2nd Edition, Addison-Wesley, ISBN: 0-201-31008-2, available at http://java.sun.com

Kay, A. (1972) 'A Personal Computer for Children of All Ages', *Proceedings ACM National Conference*, August , Boston

Larman, C. (2001) *Applying UML and Patterns*, Prentice Hall, ISBN: 0-130-92569-1

Lea, D. (1999) *Concurrent Programming in Java: Design Principles and Patterns*, 2nd Edition, Addison-Wesley, ISBN: 0-201-31009-0

Martin, J., and Odell, J. (1998) *Object-oriented Methods: A Foundation – UML Edition*, Prentice Hall, ISBN: 0-139-05597-5

McConnell, S. (1998) *Software Project Survival Guide*, Microsoft Press, ISBN: 1-57231-621-7

Meyer, B. (1990) *Eiffel: The Language*, Prentice Hall, ISBN: 0-13-247925-7

Meyer, B. (1997) *Object-Oriented Software Construction*, 2nd Edition, Prentice Hall, ISBN: 0-13-629155-4

Myers, G., Sandler, C., Thomas, T., and Badgett, T. (2004) *The Art of Software Testing*, 2nd Edition, John Wiley & Sons, ISBN: 0-471-46912-2

Object Management Group (2003a) *UML 2.0 Superstructure Specification*, ptc/03-08-02, available at www.omg.org

Object Management Group (2003b) *UML 2.0 OCL Specification*, ptc/03-10-14, available at www.omg.org

Object Management Group (2004) *Common Object Request Broker Architecture: Core Specification*, Version 3.0.3, OMG, formal/04-03-12, available at www.omg.org

Raggett, D., Lam, J., Alexander, I., and Kmiec, M. (1997) *Raggett on HTML 4*, 2nd Edition, Addison-Wesley, ISBN: 0-201-17805-2

Robinson, M., and Finkelstein, E. (2004) *Jakarta Struts for Dummies*, John Wiley & Sons, ISBN: 0-764-55957-5

Rumbaugh, J., Blaha, M., Premerlani, W., Eddy, F., and Lorensen, W. (1991) *Object-Oriented Modelling and Design*, Prentice Hall, ISBN: 0-13-630054-5

Singh, S. (2000) *The Code Book: The Science of Secrecy from Ancient Egypt to Quantum Cryptography*, Anchor Books/Doubleday, ISBN: 0-385-49532-3

Taylor, D. (1997) *Object Technology: A Manager's Guide*, 2nd Edition, Addison-Wesley, ISBN: 0-201-30994-7

Weaver, P., Lambrou, N., and Walkley, M. (2002) *Practical SSADM 4: A Complete Tutorial Guide*, Prentice Hall, ISBN: 0-273-65575-2

Wirfs-Brock, R., and McKean, A. (2002) *Object Design: Roles, Responsibilities and Collaborations*, Addison-Wesley, ISBN: 0-201-37943-0

World Wide Web Consortium (1999) *HTML 4.01 Specification*, REC-html40, available at www.w3c.org

World Wide Web Consortium (2003) *SOAP Version 1.2 Part 1: Messaging Framework*, REC-soap12-part1-20030624, available at www.w3c.org

Yergeau, F., Bray, T., Paoli, J., Sperberg-McQueen, C. M., and Maler, E. (1999) *Extensible Markup Language (XML) 1.0*, 3rd Edition, W3C, REC-xml-20040204, available at www.w3c.org

# Index